JOURNAL FOR THE STUDY OF THE OLD TESTAMENT
SUPPLEMENT SERIES
337

Sheffield Academic Press
A Continuum imprint

Amos in Song and
Book Culture

Joyce Rilett Wood

Journal for the Study of the Old Testament
Supplement Series 337

Hear the voice of the Bard!
Who Present, Past & Future sees
Whose ears have heard,
The Holy Word,
That walk'd among the ancient trees.

William Blake, *Songs of Experience,*
Plate 30: Introduction

Copyright © 2002 Sheffield Academic Press
A Continuum imprint

Published by Sheffield Academic Press Ltd
The Tower Building, 11 York Road, London SE1 7NX
370 Lexington Avenue, New York, NY 10017-6550

www.SheffieldAcademicPress.com
www.continuumbooks.com

British Library Cataloguing-in-Publication Data

A catalogue record for this book is available from the British Library

Typeset by Sheffield Academic Press
Printed on acid-free paper in Great Britain by MPG, Bodmin, Cornwall

ISBN 1-84127-244-2

CONTENTS

ACKNOWLEDGMENTS

To David Harry Wood
in loving memory

This book is based on my dissertation (Toronto School of Theology, 1993) but it has been rewritten, edited and updated to reflect current scholarship and my present understanding of the subject.

Sheffield Academic Press has made this volume take shape according to my hopes, and I am appreciative of the co-operative spirit and labour of the editorial staff.

The doctoral version of the book was read by Paul E. Dion, William H. Irwin, Brian Peckham, Gerald T. Sheppard and Robert R. Wilson, and I am thankful for their helpful evaluations. I am also indebted to classicist John H. Corbett for reading the comparative sections and even more for his ongoing support and encouragement.

It is no more than the truth to say that without Brian Peckham this book would not exist. His own critical theories on the composition and editing of prophetic texts are the foundation for the book's idea that biblical prophecy originated in the performing arts. To him I owe an enormous debt. He taught me the importance of asking better questions of the text, and he constantly challenges my thinking. My interest in the field has been sustained by his activity of thought, wisdom and insight.

Caven Library at the University of Toronto is a glorious place to read and think, and I am grateful to Kathleen Gibson, Lizabeth Kanhai and Chris Tucker who have tirelessly worked to create a superb research library.

My students at the Atlantic School of Theology, Halifax, Nova Scotia, eagerly performed the poetry of Amos in St. Columba Chapel at a symposium banquet, and the production was made possible by musician Christopher Allworth, director Nancie Erhard, and actors Mary Burey, Howard Crooks, and Art Fisher. My thanks are also extended to the 'Madison Avenue Pub' in Toronto for providing the right setting for countless symposia.

David Harry Wood encouraged me to do biblical studies with the words, 'What else are you going to do with your time?' As the result of his own studies in the thought of Paul Tillich and Alfred North Whitehead, he saw the study of the Bible as an adventure in ideas: 'Its purpose is not to close our minds but to open them. It does not offer facts and answers but visions of what might be and what ought to be. Its greatest value to us is its power to set us free from the socially inculcated values of our own time'. My husband's life and work have made a significant difference in my own. This book is dedicated to him, in joyful memory.

Toronto, Ontario
August, 2000

ABBREVIATIONS

AB	Anchor Bible
ANET	James B. Pritchard (ed.), *Ancient Near Eastern Texts Relating to the Old Testament* (Princeton: Princeton University Press, 3rd edn, 1969 [1950])
ANQ	*Andover Newton Quarterly*
AOAT	Alter Orient und Altes Testament
ATD	Das Alte Testament Deutsch
BA	*Biblical Archaeologist*
BARev	*Biblical Archaeology Review*
BASOR	*Bulletin of the American Schools of Oriental Research*
BBB	Bonner biblische Beiträge
BDB	Francis Brown, S.R. Driver and Charles A. Briggs, *A Hebrew and English Lexicon of the Old Testament* (Oxford: Clarendon Press, 1907)
BETL	Bibliotheca ephemeridum theologicarum lovaniensium
Bib	*Biblica*
BibInt	*Biblical Interpretation: A Journal of Contemporary Approaches*
BibOr	Biblica et orientalia
BKAT	Biblischer Kommentar: Altes Testament
BN	*Biblische Notizen*
BZ	*Biblische Zeitschrift*
BZAW	Beihefte zur *ZAW*
CBQ	*Catholic Biblical Quarterly*
ClQ	*Classical Quarterly*
CRBS	*Currents in Research: Biblical Studies*
CurTM	*Currents in Theology and Mission*
ExpTim	*Expository Times*
GKC	*Gesenius' Hebrew Grammar* (ed. E. Kautzsch, revised and trans. A.E. Cowley; Oxford: Clarendon Press, 1910)
HAR	*Hebrew Annual Review*
HBT	*Horizons in Biblical Theology*
HSM	Harvard Semitic Monographs
HTR	*Harvard Theological Review*
HUCA	*Hebrew Union College Annual*
IB	*Interpreter's Bible*
ICC	International Critical Commentary
IDB	George Arthur Buttrick (ed.), *The Interpreter's Dictionary of*

	the Bible (4 vols.; Nashville: Abingdon Press, 1962)
IDBSup	*The Interpreter's Dictionary of the Bible*, Supplementary Volume (Nashville, Tenn: Abingdon, 1976)
IEJ	*Israel Exploration Journal*
Int	*Interpretation*
JANESCU	*Journal of the Ancient Near Eastern Society of Columbia University*
JAOS	*Journal of the American Oriental Society*
JBL	*Journal of Biblical Literature*
JCS	*Journal of Cuneiform Studies*
JETS	*Journal of the Evangelical Theological Society*
JHS	*Journal of Hellenic Studies*
JNES	*Journal of Near Eastern Studies*
JSOT	*Journal for the Study of the Old Testament*
JSOTSup	*Journal for the Study of the Old Testament*, Supplement Series
JSS	*Journal of Semitic Studies*
KAT	Kommentar zum Alten Testament
LCL	Loeb Classical Library
NICOT	New International Commentary on the Old Testament
NJPSV	New Jewish Publication Society Version
NRT	*La nouvelle revue théologique*
OBO	Orbis biblicus et orientalis
OTA	*Old Testament Abstracts*
OTG	Old Testament Guides
OTL	Old Testament Library
OTS	*Oudtestamentische Studiën*
RB	*Revue biblique*
ResQ	*Restoration Quarterly*
RSR	*Recherches de science religieuse*
RSV	Revised Standard Version
SBLDS	SBL Dissertation Series
SBT	Studies in Biblical Theology
ScrB	*Scripture Bulletin*
SEÅ	*Svensk exegetisk årsbok*
SJT	*Scottish Journal of Theology*
SOTSMS	Society for Old Testament Study Monograph Series
SR	*Studies in Religion/Sciences religieuses*
ST	*Studia theologica*
UF	*Ugarit-Forschungen*
VT	*Vetus Testamentum*
VTSup	*Vetus Testamentum*, Supplements
ZAH	*Zeitschrift für Althebraistik*
ZAW	*Zeitschrift für die alttestamentliche Wissenschaft*
*	An asterisk in a Biblical reference marks passages that include Amos' text and that of his editor.

Prophets with books named after them have traditionally been called 'the writing prophets'. Early critical scholars described Amos as 'the oldest prophetic author', considered the prophets as poets and writers, and essentially distinguished Amos's poetry from passages which were intrusive and incompatible with the historical circumstances or theological concerns of the prophet's age.[1] The present study will verify this older scholarly theory by using literary analysis to distinguish two editions of Amos. It will show that later expansions are not random glosses but are part of a connected secondary text that totally revises and updates the poetry of Amos. Each edition is a complete literary composition by a different author. The two editions are related to each other by text and commentary, and each edition is distinguished by its unique structure and organization as well as by its different form, content, sources, language and style.[2]

In recent decades scholars have drawn attention to the existence of large blocks of composition in the book,[3] have shown that 'large rhetorical

1. Bernhard Duhm, *Die Zwölf Propheten* (Tübingen: J.C.B. Mohr, 1910), pp. xxiii-xxiv; *idem*, 'Amos und seine Schrift', in Heinrich Weinel (ed.), *Israels Propheten* (Tübingen: J.C.B. Mohr, 2nd edn, 1922), pp. 89-98; William Rainey Harper, *A Critical and Exegetical Commentary on Amos and Hosea* (ICC, 18; Edinburgh: T. & T. Clark, 1905), pp. cvi, cxxv-cxxvi, cxxix, cxxx-cxxxiv; Hermann Gunkel's introduction in Hans Schmidt, *Die Schriften des Alten Testaments.* II/Part 2. *Die grossen Propheten* (Göttingen: Vandenhoeck and Ruprecht, 1923), pp. xxxiv-lxx; Samuel Rolles Driver, *The Books of Joel and Amos with Introduction and Notes* (Cambridge: Cambridge University Press, 1898), pp. 115-24; *idem*, An Introduction to the Literature of the Old Testament (Edinburgh: T. & T. Clark, 9th edn, 1913), pp. 313-18.

2. The theory that the prophets wrote continuous and complete literary texts which were subsequently revised by later authors originated with Brian Peckham, *History and Prophecy: The Development of Late Judean Literary Traditions* (Anchor Bible Reference Library; Garden City, NY: Doubleday, 1993).

3. Three large compositions (chs. 1–2; 4.6-12; chs. 7–9) are singled out by Hartmut Gese, *International Organization for the Study of the Old Testament Congress* (10th: 1980: Vienna) *Library of Congress* (Congress volume: Vienna, 1980 edited by

units'[4] are thematically and structurally linked to one another,[5] and have included Amos himself in the compositional activity.[6] The first edition of the book is a cycle of seven poems composed by Amos, and while each poem stands out as a separate entity, they are all interrelated and have references back and forth that weave the group into a coherent and consistent narrative sequence. Each poem makes a completely fresh start, but the compositional procedure is to link and unify the seven poems by the

---

J.A. Emerton; London: E.J. Brill, 1981) ('*Komposition bei Amos*', VTSup 32 [1981], pp. 74-95) as having the same paired sequences with the last step reaching the climax and goal of the whole. Large intentional groupings of seven have been isolated by James Limburg, 'Sevenfold Structures in the Book of Amos', *JBL* 106 (1987), pp. 217-22. Four blocks of composition (chs. 1–2; chs. 3–4; 5.1–9.6; 9.7–15) are identified by Klaus Koch, *Amos: Untersucht mit den Methoden einer strukturalen Formgeschichte* (3 vols.; AOAT, 30; [The book is in 3 volumes] Neukirchen–Vluyn: Neukirchener Verlag, 1976). It is Koch's thesis that the basic structure of the book is the work of a late Judaean 'composer' who wrote down Amos's prophecy for the first time by assembling a wealth of prophetic materials into a unified text and composing new material as well (*Amos*, II, pp. 96, 105, 125). However, he contradicts his idea of a single late Judaean composition by proposing that the first written undertaking might have been carried out by the prophet himself (*Amos* II, pp. 95, 125). For a discussion of the internal coherence of the book and a precise ordering of its literary units, see Claude Coulot, 'Propositions pour une structuration du livre d'Amos au niveau rédactionnel', *RSR* 51 (1977), pp. 169-86.

4.   John H. Hayes, *Amos the Eighth Century Prophet: His Times and his Preaching* (Nashville: Abingdon Press, 1988), p. 39; Francis I. Andersen and David Noel Freedman, *Amos: A New Translation with Introduction and Commentary* (Anchor Bible; Garden City, NY: Doubleday, 1989), pp. 8, 200-206, 764-65, 785.

5.   Careful attention to the thematic and structural elements that unify sections into a literary work is the significant contribution of Shalom M. Paul, *Amos: A Commentary on the Book of Amos* (Hermeneia; Minneapolis: Fortress Press, 1991), pp. 5, 13-15, 47, 55, 113, 143, 182 see; J. Rilett Wood, review of *Amos: A Commentary on the Book of Amos* by Shalom Paul, in *Toronto Journal of Theology* 9 (1993), pp. 253-54.

6.   There is no reason to deny that Amos 'wrote his own words', as Hayes observes, but he thinks that they were 'more likely…written down by someone in the audience' (*Amos*, p. 39). It is curious that Hayes recognizes the lack of proof for the existence of a circle of disciples but not the lack of evidence for someone transcribing the words of Amos. Andersen and Freedman argue that 'the prophet's spoken words' have been 'preserved' in 'the form of a literary composition, which has more structure than a mere anthology of Amos' oracles but less symmetry than a completely fresh literary work' (*Amos*, p. 10). They vacillate between identifying Amos himself or an immediate disciple as the master hand who unified the text and created its literary or artistic scheme (Amos, pp. 5, 11, 25).

same themes or content, or to tie the poems together by a number of recurrent images and expressions. The structure of the cycle tends to be discontinuous, but the same themes and imagery are prominent throughout.

The new trend in Amos studies is to argue that the book comes mostly from Amos himself,[7] but the theory can be sustained only by arguing that hopeful prophecies of remnant and restoration are indeed consistent with those of judgment and doom,[8] or by supposing that the inconsistencies and contradictions in the book reflect different stages in Amos' career.[9] The literary problems of the book are not explained on literary grounds but are related to presumed historical contexts or hypothetical reconstructions of the life and times of Amos. Although present-day scholars are inclined to argue that the rightful author of the book is Amos, they do not really show it by literary analysis. Their ideas of authorship exhibit the same theoretical conflict that has always existed in the scholarship—between a freshly composed literary work on the one hand, and a mere collection or anthology of Amos's oracles on the other hand. So in the end even those who think of Amos as the author of the book are compelled to understand the book as we now have it in terms of some redactional process or editorial development.[10]

---

7. Hayes, *Amos*, p. 39; Andersen and Freedman, *Amos*, pp. 11, 76, 141-44, 148, 196; Paul, *Amos*, pp. 100-102, 221; Max E. Polley, *Amos and the Davidic Empire: A Socio-Historical Approach* (New York: Oxford University Press, 1989), pp. 3, 49, 70-71, 107-11, 122-24, 147, 174-75; Stanley N. Rosenbaum, *Amos of Israel: A New Interpretation* (Macon, GA: Mercer University Press, 1990), pp. 83-95.

8. Hayes, *Amos*, pp. 165-68, 220-28; Paul, *Amos*, pp. 288-95; Polley, *Amos and the Davidic Empire*, pp. 69-71, 147.

9. Andersen and Freedman, *Amos*, pp. 5, 25, 43-45, 65-73, 76-80, 84-88, 144, 195-98, 446, 863, 889, 893-94, 924; Polley, *Amos and the Davidic Empire*, pp. 160, 174-75. The idea that the book reflects successive phases in Amos's thought was first proposed by Robert Gordis, 'The Composition and Structure of Amos', *HTR* 33 (1940), pp. 239-51. See also John D.W. Watts (*Vision and Prophecy in Amos* [Leiden: Brill, 1958]), who argues that Amos' first three visions (7.1-3; chs. 4–6; chs. 7–9) correspond to what he said at Bethel (1–2; 3–6) and the last two visions (8.1-2; 9.1-4) to what he later said in Judah (8.3–9.15). The present order of the book is explained by identifying two independent collections of Amos's oracles, a book of words (Amos 1–6) and a book of visions (Amos 7–9), that were placed together by the prophet's editors: John D.W. Watts, *Studying the Book of Amos* (Nashville: Broadman, 1965).

10. At times Andersen and Freedman envisage Amos himself or an editor who was close to the prophet as unifying the text or arranging and integrating the oracles (*Amos*, pp. 5, 9, 74, 76, 141-44, 148, 196). At other times they contemplate the book not simply as the work of a redactor who collected and assembled original prophetic

Redaction-critical studies give emphasis to the different levels of meaning in the book of Amos, and rightly characterize the prophetic tradition as developing over time to meet the needs of changing historical situations.[11] However, redaction-historical methodology has not established objective criteria for assigning material in the book so precisely to different historical strata.[12] It proceeds by accommodating units of text to precon-

material but as the product of significant editorial labour, including expansion, modification, incorporation of headings, closings, liturgical formulas, and especially the creative rewriting or composition of new material at the hands of later editors and scribes (*Amos*, pp. 17, 100, 141, 147-48, 198, 487). Paul identifies Amos 3.1b as an editorial gloss, agrees that Amos 3.7 resembles Deuteronomistic language and might be editorial, and considers Amos 6.2 as a possible later insertion (*Amos*, pp. 100, 112-13, 203-204). Paul, like Andersen and Freedman, suggests that Amos was his own editor by taking responsiblity for the final form of his own work (*Amos*, p. 221).

11. Hans Walter Wolff, Dodekapropheton 2, ET Joel und Amos (BKAT, 14.2; Neukirchen–Vluyn: Neukirchener Verlag, 1975 [1969]) *Joel and Amos* (trans. W. Janzen, S.D. McBride, Jr and Charles A. Muenchow; ed. S.D. McBride, Jr; Hermeneia; Philadelphia: Fortress Press, 2nd edn, 1977), pp. 90, 94, 107-18; James L. Mays, *Amos: A Commentary* (OTL; Philadelphia: Westminster Press, 1969), pp. 12-14; Ina Willi-Plein, *Vorformen der Schriftexegese innerhalb des Alten Testaments: Untersuchungen zum literarischen Werden der auf Amos, Hosea und Micha zurückgehenden Bücher im hebräischen Zwölfprophetenbuch* (BZAW, 123; Berlin: Walter de Gruyter, 1971), pp. 15-69; Hans F. Fuhs, 'Amos 1,1: Erwägungen zur Tradition und Redaktion des Amosbuches', in H.-J. Fabry (ed.), *Bausteine biblischer Theologie* (BBB, 50; Bonn: Peter Hanstein, 1977), pp. 271-89; Robert Coote, *Amos among the Prophets: Composition and Theology* (Philadelphia: Fortress Press, 1981), pp. 11-19, 46-109, 110-20; J. Alberto Soggin, *The Prophet Amos: A Translation and Commentary* (trans. John Bowden; London: SCM Press, 1987), pp. 12, 16-18; Hartmut N. Rösel, 'Kleine Studien zur Entwicklung des Amosbuches', *VT* 43 (1993), pp. 88-101; Jörg Jeremias, *Der Prophet Amos* (ATD, 24.2; Göttingen: Vandenhoeck & Ruprecht, 1995); ET *The Book of Amos* (trans. D.W. Stott; OTL; Louisville: Westminster/John Knox Press, 1998), pp. xix-xxii; D. Rottzoll, *Studien zur Redaktion und Komposition des Amosbuches* (BZAW, 243; Berlin: Walter de Gruyter, 1996), pp. 285-90.

12. John Bright, 'A New View of Amos', Int 25 (1971), pp. 355-58; W. Eugene March, 'Redaction Criticism and the Formation of Prophetic Books', in Paul J. Achtemeier (ed.), Society of Biblical Literature 1977 *Seminar Papers* (Missoula, MT: Scholars Press, 1977), pp. 87-101 (91-92); Roy F. Melugin, 'The Formation of Amos: An Analysis of Exegetical Method', in Paul J. Achtemeier (ed.), *Society of Biblical Literature 1978 Seminar Papers*, I (Missoula, MT: Scholars Press, 1978), pp. 369-91 (373-74); Jennifer Dines, 'Reading the Book of Amos', *ScrB* 16 (1986), pp. 26-32. The need for criteria can be illustrated by the fact that the same passages are assigned by commentators to different historical periods. For instance, Wolff dates the hymnic sections (4.13; 5.8-9; 9.5-6) to the time of Josiah in the late seventh century, but Willi-

ceived reconstructions of the history[13] rather than first setting up the literature and then letting the literary evidence itself determine the historical realities.

Scholars have argued for three, four, six and twelve levels of composition or editorial levels,[14] but the idea of one editor seems to resolve the literary problems of the book. The second edition is written by an exilic author who preserved Amos's prophetic text but thoroughly rewrote it and converted it into a book with ten parts.[15] The theory of a running commentary on Amos's poetry allows readers to see that the whole book has a system or order and enables them to find the continuity and connection among all the ten parts. Scholarly debate is divided on the question of whether the book of Amos comes mostly from the prophet himself or is the product of several redactional levels.[16] The present study answers this question by arguing on the one hand that the entire artistic structure of

Plein assigns them to the post-exilic age; Willi-Plein disagrees with Wolff's idea of a Bethel exposition of the Josianic age, arguing instead that 4.6-12 belongs to the eighth-century collection of Amos's words (*Vorformen der Schriftexegese*, pp. 59, 61); Wolff thinks that 1.1b combines a supplement from Amos's prophetic school and a Deuteronomistic addition, but Fuhs assigns 1.1b to a post-exilic redactor.

13. A good example is Wolff's argument that the fourth redactional level was occasioned by Josiah's destruction of the temple in Bethel. Josiah is nowhere mentioned in the book of Amos, but even if Wolff were right that passages in the book refer directly to Josiah's reform, it would not prove that they date from his reign. At work here is the naive view that writing has to be contemporaneous with the events it reports.

14. Six levels of redaction are proposed by Wolff, four by Willi-Plein, and twelve by Rottzoll. Coote and Jeremias simplify matters by identifying a three-stage process.

15. Scholars argue for a highly structured unity of the book. Andersen and Freedman (*Amos*, pp. 23- 72) structure the book into four parts. A twofold structure is identified by Adrian van der Wal, 'The Structure of Amos', *JSOT* 26 (1983), pp. 107-13. A threefold structure is presented by Douglas K. Stuart, *Hosea–Jonah* (Waco, TX: Word Books, 1987), p. 287; by Gary V. Smith, *Amos: A Commentary* (Grand Rapids, Zondervan, 1989), pp. 7-9, and by David A. Hubbard, *Joel and Amos: An Introduction and Commentary* (Leicester: Inter-Varsity Press, 1989), pp. 118-19.

16. The two scholarly positions are summarized and critiqued by Roy F. Melugin, 'Amos in Recent Research', *CRBS* 6 (1998), pp. 65-101. For further summaries and bibliography, see Adrian van der Wal, *Amos: A Classified Bibliography* (Amsterdam: Free University Press, 3rd edn, 1986); Gerhard F. Hasel, *Understanding the Book of Amos: Basic Issues in Current Interpretations* (Grand Rapids, MI: Baker Book House, 1991), pp. 121-66; Henry O. Thompson, *The Book of Amos: An Annotated Bibliography* (American Theological Library Association Bibliographies, 42; Lanham, MD: Scarecrow Press, 1997).

Amos's prophetic text was updated so it can be read synchronically as a unified whole. On the other hand, I attempt to reconstruct the editorial process, arguing that the book can be read diachronically as two distinct levels of meaning coming from two different historical eras.

My book confirms what scholars have always maintained, namely, that prophecy is both oral and written,[17] but it represents a reformulation of the relationship between the spoken and the written word. It sets up a new paradigm for understanding the origins of the prophetic tradition. The early prophets were not, as is commonly assumed, itinerant preachers,[18] but performing poets who engaged their audiences in the spiritual and theological issues of the day through a combination of words, music and song.

The scholarly consensus is that Amos and the other prophets delivered oracles at different times in their preaching ministries, that these were memorized and passed on until they were finally collected and written down, either by the prophet himself shortly before his death or by his editor at a very early stage, or by a series of tradents and editors at later stages in the history. The theory is sustained by ancient and present-day examples of oral learning or by some rules of oral tradition, but resists verification in the prophetic books themselves. There is no evidence for the idea that Amos composed orally, or that his prophecy was transmitted orally or was subject to a period of oral development.[19] It is widely believed that prophetic schools of disciples were responsible for the transmission of the prophet's oral speeches, but there is no evidence for their existence in the book of Amos, and 'almost total silence about them

17. The idea that the prophets were both speakers and writers is outlined in an article in the first edition of the encyclopedia *Religion in Geschichte und Gegenwart* (Tübingen: J.C.B. Mohr, 1927–32) by Hermann Gunkel, 'The Israelite Prophecy from the Time of Amos', reprinted in J. Pelikan (ed.), *Twentieth Century Theology in the Making*. I. *Themes of Biblical Theology* (trans. R.A. Wilson; New York: Harper & Row, 1969), pp. 48-75. It is Gunkel's theory that the prophetic books are collections of originally separate oracles or sayings from oral tradition. This theory became the basis of all subsequent work on the prophets, but Gunkel also talked about 'the prophets as writers' (pp. 62-63).

18. The paradigm of prophet as preacher is presented, for example, in Joseph Blenkinsopp, *A History of Prophecy in Israel* (Philadelphia: Westminster Press, 1983), pp. 94, 101-102, 122-23, 143, 145; James Limburg, *Hosea–Micah* (Interpretation: A Bible Commentary for Teaching and Preaching; Atlanta: John Knox Press, 1988), pp. 31-34, 45-46, 71-72, 80, 93, 103, 116-17, 169-77.

19. See also Peckham, *History and Prophecy*, pp. 21-22.

and their activities' in the other prophetic books.[20]

The evidence for oral performance in the book of Amos is not a sign that prophecy circulated orally before it was written down.[21] On the contrary, the book preserves evidence of a written text and evidence that it was written to be performed.[22] Prophecy originated in the performing arts, and corroboration for the idea comes generally from ancient poetry which, as early as Sumerian times, was recited before an audience,[23] and specifically from the contemporary poetry of Greek performing artists who sang, chanted and recited their written lyrics and elegies during the seventh and sixth centuries BCE.[24] The poetic texts of the early prophets and Greek

20. Ronald E. Clements, *A Century of Old Testament Study* (Guildford and London: Lutterworth Press, 1976), p. 68.

21. The idea that the biblical prophets extemporaneously composed in oral performance, and that their oral compositions were subsequently written down through dictation, or by someone who took notes during the oral rendition, is found in the recent work of Susan Niditch, *Oral World and Written Word: Ancient Israelite Literature* (Library of Ancient Israel; Louisville, KY: Westminster John Knox Press, 1996), pp. 5, 9-10, 117-19. There is, however, no reason to multiply writers or invent recorders for whom there is no evidence. Niditch argues that Isa. 1.4-29 contains formula patterns, conventionalized patterns of content and recurring themes which are typical of orally composed works (p. 118): see her essay, 'The Composition of Isaiah 1', Bib 61 (1989), pp. 509-29. But, as Niditch herself acknowledges, repetition is not just 'typical of orally composed works', it 'also characterizes works composed in writing' (*Oral World*, p. 11).

22. Niditch agrees that there was an oral performance and a written version. She argues: 'If there were…written versions of oral performances in the Hebrew Bible, the poetry of the classical prophets seems a likely possibility' (*Oral World*, p. 120). However, what she envisages as 'a move from oral performance to written text' is the standard theory that independent oracles such as Isa. 1 and Amos 5 were written down and preserved by a later collector (pp. 118-19).

23. Bendt Alster, 'Interaction of Oral and Written Poetry in Early Mesopotamian Literature', in Marianna E. Vogelzang and Herman L.J. Vanstiphout (eds.), *Mesopotamian Epic Literature: Oral or Aural?* (Lewiston, NY: Edwin Mellen Press, 1992), pp. 23-69.

24. Written texts of Greek poetry existed already by the seventh century BCE and until the late fifth century were mainly known through performance: George A. Kennedy (ed.), *The Cambridge History of Classical Literature*. I. Classical Criticism (Cambridge: Cambridge University Press, 1989), pp. 87-89; J.P. Barron and P.E. Easterling, 'Elegy and Iambus', and Charles Segal, 'Archaic Choral Poetry', in P.E. Easterling and B.M.W. Knox (eds.), *The Cambridge History of Classical Literature*. I/Part 1. *Early Greek Poetry* (Cambridge: Cambridge University Press, 1989), p. 76, 79, 124.

poets were the actual scripts of live performances.[25] Although their poetry became known through performance, the performed texts 'rested on a firm substructure of carefully mediated written texts'. Only the existence of written texts can account for the 'astounding sophistication, refinement and variety' and also the 'transmission and preservation' of the poetry from one generation to the next.[26] This book will develop the idea of prophecy as performance by using early Greek poetry as an analogy, and by showing that the prophetic tradition falls, like Greek tradition, into the familiar genres of lyric and elegy, poetic drama and oratory.

The present study does not invent a new methodology. It uses historical-critical methods, but modifies the procedures of literary, form and redaction criticism to fit the literary evidence of the book of Amos. Literary criticism is not the study of fragmentary texts but is redefined as the study of complete literary works. Form criticism is not just the identification of smaller literary units but is explained more broadly to include the form of whole literary works. Redaction criticism is not simply the study of how older literary materials were edited to produce the book as we presently have it but involves a thoroughgoing analysis of the final literary edition as the work of an author who took on the task of completely rewriting an earlier literary text.

The first chapter, in accordance with literary-critical methodology, attempts to discover the original writing of Amos and establishes that he wrote a continuous poetic text. It examines the recurring themes, motifs and language of the text and relates particular units of poetry to their immediate and larger context. It shows how repetition is used to emphasize key ideas. It demonstrates the consistency of thought, or the threads of continuity between one unit of the text and another and the developing argument of a whole composition. It considers the various compositional

25. Brian Peckham (*History and Prophecy*) has reconstructed the performance texts of the early prophets by distinguishing their poetry from its editorial rewriting. His book contains no comparative data, but his comprehensive analysis of the primary evidence provides all the major clues for understanding prophecy as performance: cf. Philip R. Davies, 'The Audiences of Prophetic Scrolls: Some Suggestions', in Stephen Breck Reid (ed.), *Prophets and Paradigms: Essays in Honor of Gene M. Tucker* (JSOTSup, 29; Sheffield: Sheffield Academic Press, 1996), pp. 48-62 (53-54 n. 9).

26. John Herington, *Poetry into Drama: Early Tragedy and the Greek Poetic Tradition* (Sather Classical Lectures, 49; Berkeley: University of California Press, 1985), pp. 41-42. Herington's working hypothesis is that even the Homeric epics 'must have been embodied in a text from the beginning'; see also Henry Theodore Wade-Gery, *The Poet of the Iliad* (Cambridge: Cambridge University Press, 1952), esp. p. 39.

techniques and rhetorical devices that tie together the multiple literary units or give literary symmetry to the work as a whole.

The second chapter, following literary-critical exegesis, shows that the genius of two literary artists, or two stages of literary composition, are present in the book of Amos. It looks for intrusive verses or breaks in the continuity of thought, and observes thematic inconsistencies and contradictions. It decides whether different linguistic usages mark simply variations in language or style or actual changes in viewpoint or perspective. It shows how repetition is used to change Amos's prophetic text and to subordinate it to a new system of interpretation. It takes up the redactional-critical concern for whole meanings by uncovering the continuity of argument or consistency in perspective of all the subtexts or footnote commentary in the book.

The third chapter addresses the question of form at the level of whole literary texts. Gunkel included books themselves in form-critical analysis, but fell short of including the books of the prophets because he thought they were not literary works at all but simply the repositories of independent literary genres.[27] An analysis of both the structure of the original text and its linguistic evidence supports the form-critical view that prophets were speakers and that oral communication was an essential feature of their work. Questions of structure demand a paradigm shift with respect to the origins and development of the prophetic tradition: Amos's prophecy has its origins, not in discrete preaching speeches, but in the oral performance of a whole written text.[28] The chapter discusses the structure that binds and separates the seven poems and details the larger structure of the book that sets out both text and commentary into ten parts. It considers the

27. On Hermann Gunkel, see Klaus Koch, *The Growth of the Biblical Tradition: The Form–Critical Method* (trans. S.M. Cupitt; New York: Charles Scribner's Sons, 1969), pp. 25, 28.

28. Form-critical analysis has identified as many as 33 independent oracles or sayings in the book of Amos: see Sigmund Mowinckel, *Prophecy and Tradition: The Prophetic Books in the Light of the Study of the Growth and History of the Tradition* (Oslo: Jacob Dybwad, 1946), pp. 48-51. An alternative proposal is that Amos delivered a single great speech: see Julian Morgenstern, *Amos Studies: Parts I, II and III*, I (Cincinnati: Hebrew Union College Press, 1941). Morgenstern does not attempt to reconstruct the original written text of Amos but rather 'the original sequence of thoughts' in his spoken address. Since Morgenstern thinks that the book contains 'abundant and unmistakable evidence of textual disarrangement and disorganization', his study is a 'rearrangement' of the materials in the book and not a literary analysis of its different parts (pp. 7, 11-13).

linguistic evidence for dramatic composition and shows how a dramatic plot is converted into history writing. In accordance with the form-critical goal of establishing the various sociological settings of different literary types,[29] the chapter relates the overall genre of Amos's prophetic text to its original historical setting which in turn is illuminated by the broader cultural context of the Mediterranean world.

The fourth chapter deals with the source-critical side of literary criticism. It does not presuppose that actual sources were incorporated into Amos's text, but examines the written sources or literature that inspired and informed his composition. It shows that Amos did not compose his work in a vacuum but relied on previously written prophecy and history, and that these indigenous literary traditions were readily available to or known by the prophet and his audience alike. It assumes that Amos wrote for a literate society[30] and for an audience living in a vibrant creative age in which biblical writing flourished through its contact, either direct or indirect, with literary works from other parts of the ancient world. It relates Greek epic, lyric and elegy to the poetry of Amos, arguing that his day of Yahweh has its appropriate cultural background in the contemporary literary traditions of the Mediterranean world.

The fifth chapter is tradition history in the sense that it traces the development of the prophetic tradition. It deals with the written transmission of Amos's prophecy and the significant influence it had on all the prophets who came after him. It shows that they knew Amos's text, were inspired or intrigued by his message, and composed their own texts with respect to his work by either developing his ideas or criticizing his worldview. It then turns to the two biographies of Amos, one found in the history of the Deuteronomist, the other presented by the author of the book of Amos, and argues that tradition has preserved quite distinct biographies of the prophet. The chapter meets a basic goal of redaction criticism by under-

---

29. Robert R. Wilson, *Prophecy and Society in Ancient Israel* (Philadelphia: Fortress Press, 1980); Herbert B. Huffmon, 'The Social Role of Amos' Message', in H.B. Huffmon, F.A. Spina and A.R.W. Green (eds.), *The Quest for the Kingdom of God: Studies in Honor of George E. Mendenhall* (Winona Lake, IN: Eisenbrauns, 1983), pp. 109-16.

30. Alan R. Millard, 'An Assessment of the Evidence for Writing in Ancient Israel', in *Biblical Archaeology Today: Proceedings of the International Congress on Biblical Archaeology, Jerusalem*, April 1984 (Jerusalem: Israel Exploration Society, 1985), pp. 301-12 (307-308); Brian Peckham, 'Literacy and the Creation of the Biblical World', Scripta Mediterranea 12–13 (1991–92), pp. 1-36.

taking a historical analysis of the written sources used by the author of the book in composing the final literary edition of the prophet's message. It demonstrates that sources do not give immediate access to historical events. It shows that the reviser of Amos is indebted to the exilic historian or Deuteronomist, but that the tradition has preserved two different theologies of history.

The following study of the book of Amos is carried out in the light of current biblical methodology and builds on the cumulative insights of scholars, both past and present. Literary analysis precedes historical analysis by establishing the relationship between Amos's prophetic text and its commentary. Once the literary evidence is set up, it becomes possible to ask historical questions about it and to determine the function of two distinct literary works within the history of Israelite literature.

Chapter 1

THE WRITTEN PROPHECY

Recovery of the original prophecy of Amos has always intrigued scholars, and is considered a legitimate exercise, but it is not believed that much certainty can be achieved.[1] I shall argue that the older theory of a written prophecy is sound and that earlier scholars, in distinguishing Amos from editorial rewriting, had essentially discovered the text of the prophet. The question of the present form of the book will be temporarily set aside. It becomes possible to see that Amos's prophetic text is thoroughly rewritten once we grasp its flow from beginning to end. The study starts with Amos: it shows how he composed his seven poems, how every poem develops the thought of the previous one, how the poems are linked in a continuous narrative, and how each poem contributes to the meaning of a complete composition.

Poem 1 (1.1a, 3-5, 6-8, 13-15; 2.1-3, 6-8, 13-16)

The title, 'The words of Amos who was among the shepherds of Tekoa' (1.1a), is followed by divine words which are delivered by Amos as messenger. The text is a mixture of God's speech and prophetic speech, and the title anticipates Amos's words, which begin in 3.3-6.[2] Poem 1 situates Israel within the nations to the north, south and east: God proclaims war against Syria (1.3-5), the Philistine cities (1.6-8), the Ammonites (1.13-15), the Moabites (2.1-3) and finally against Israel (2.6-8, 13-16). Common to each unit is the messenger formula כה אמר יהוה 'Thus says Yahweh' followed by the numerical idiom על־שלשה פשעי...ועל־ארבעה 'for three

---

1. Andersen and Freedman, *Amos*, pp. 10-11.
2. Cf. Andersen and Freedman (*Amos*, pp. 184-85), who argue that the prophecy of Amos 'consists of oracles of Yahweh, not sayings of the prophet', in accordance with 'the Word of Yahweh' at the beginning of other prophetic books (Hos. 1.1; Joel 1.1; Mic. 1.1; Zeph. 1.1; Mal. 1.1; Hag. 1.1; Zech. 1.1).

transgressions of X and for four'. The phrase לֹא אֲשִׁיבֶבּוּ 'I shall not cause
it to turn back' is reiterated five times. One crime is cited for each foreign
nation, and the crime leads directly into Yahweh's punishment. What
rounds off the divine edict against each nation is אָמַר יהוה 'says Yahweh'
(cf. נְאֻם־יהוה 2.16).

Each indictment details a war crime. Damascus is accused of beating
Gilead with iron sledges, Gaza of deporting a captured people to Edom,
Ammon of disembowelling pregnant women in Gilead and Moab of dese-
crating the corpse of the Edomite king (1.3b, 6b, 13b; 2.1b). Each charge
makes clear that Yahweh's judgment is war expressed in terms of a fire
devouring nations and cities: 'I will send a fire upon X, and it shall
consume the strongholds of X'.[3] A significant development in the argument occurs precisely where there is a departure from the expected, 'I will
send a fire', to the irregularity, 'I will kindle a fire' (1.14a). Yahweh's
punishment is executed 'on the day of battle' amidst the cries of war and
the trumpet blast (1.14; 2.2b). The exact meaning of לֹא אֲשִׁיבֶנּוּ is now
disclosed. The suffix-pronoun refers to 'the day of battle' (1.14b) and
לֹא אֲשִׁיבֶנּוּ points to its irreversibility.[4]

The series of war proclamations against the nations reaches its destination in Yahweh's judgment against Israel. At first the divine address
follows the established pattern but suddenly goes off in a direction
different from the other nations. Unexpectedly it moves from the international stage to the domestic, from heinous war crimes to oppressive acts
within Israel's own borders. The disturbing and shocking message is that
the nation's socio-economic offences are comparable to violent acts perpetrated by foreign nations against Israel and other peoples.

'For three transgressions and for four' implies a multiplicity of crimes.

---

3. Duane L. Christensen, *Transformations of the War Oracle in Old Testament
Prophecy: Studies in the Oracles against the Nations* (Missoula, MT: Scholars Press,
1975); R.M. Good, 'The Just War in Ancient Israel', *JBL* 104 (1985), pp. 385-400; H.
Neil Richardson, 'Amos 2:13-16: Its Structure and Function in the Book', in Paul J.
Achtemeier (ed.), *Society of Biblical Literature 1978 Seminar Papers* (Missoula MT:
Scholars Press, 1978), pp. 361-68.
4. The suffix 'it' is translated as God's punishment/his word of judgment/his
anger: William L. Holladay, 'I will not revoke the punishment', *The Root sûbh in the
Old Testament, with Particular Reference to its Usages in Covenantal Contexts*
(Leiden: E.J. Brill, 1958), p. 102; Rolf P. Knierim, '"I Will not Cause it to Return" in
Amos 1 and 2', in George W. Coats and Burke O. Long (eds.), *Canon and Authority:
Essays in Old Testament Religion and Theology* (Philadelphia: Fortress Press, 1977),
pp. 163-75. These translations are not specific referents to be found in the text itself.

The numerical idiom does not correlate one crime with each foreign nation but anticipates Israel's four crimes (2.6-8).[5] One crime leads into another, and except for the third, each crime has two parts. The first is that 'they sold the righteous for silver and the needy for a pair of sandals' (2.6b).[6] The second crime expands on the idea of the poor used for unjust profit. The image of sandals foreshadows the poor who were trampled while others were thrust aside (2.7a).

The path or road (דרך) of the afflicted anticipates the third crime detailing the conduct of a father and son who profaned Yahweh's name by going to a young woman (2.7b).[7] 'To go/walk' (הלך) is a *double entendre*, suggesting a journey to the temple where sexual relations occur. Both הלך and the desecration of Yahweh's holy name prepare for the fourth crime which recalls acts of exploitation in the house of God. Beside the altar people reclined on garments they had seized in pledge for unpaid debts, financing their drink by imposing penalties on defaulting debtors.[8] The

5.   Scholars argue that only the fourth and most serious crime is mentioned; e.g. Menahem Haran, 'The Graded Numerical Sequence and the Phenomenon of "Automatism" in Biblical Poetry', in International Organization for the Study of the Old Testament Congress (7th: 1971: Uppsala, Sweden) *VT*Sup 22 (1972), pp. 238-67. Scholars homogenize the text and stress its unity, noting that 3 + 4 = seven. The number seven corresponds with seven nations, and seven crimes match seven consequences resulting from divine judgment: Hayes, *Amos*, pp. 107-08, 119; Andersen and Freedman, *Amos*, p. 339.

6.   Many argue that 2.6b conveys the idea of debt slavery: e.g. Bernhard Lang, 'Sklaven und Unfreie im Buch Amos (II 6, VIII 6)', *VT* 31 (1981), pp. 482-88. He supposes that 2.6b refers to the sale of debtors abroad and cites 1.6 as evidence. But since the context is war, there is every reason to assume that 2.6 refers to deportation or resettlement of whole peoples as the result of defeat.

7.   If scholars are correct that the topic is sexual impropriety (e.g. Wilhelm Rudolph, *Joel–Amos–Obadja–Jonah* [KAT 11.3.2; Gütersloh: Gerd Mohn, 1971], pp. 142-43; Wolff, *Amos*, p. 167; Andersen and Freedman, *Amos*, p. 318), then 2.7 is the only text where הלך אל is used instead of בוא אל (Gen. 16.2; 30.3-4; 38.8; Deut. 22.13; 2 Sam. 16.21-22) to refer to sexual intercourse. Some say נערה is a cult prostitute: e.g. Mitchel Dahood, 'To Pawn One's Cloak', *Bib* 42 (1961), pp. 359-66; James M. Ward, *Amos, Hosea* (Knox Preaching Guides; Atlanta: John Knox Press, 1981), pp. 135-37. That father and son go to a hostess (נערה) at a banquet (מרזח 6.7) is the view of Hans M. Barstad, *The Religious Polemics of Amos: Studies in the Preaching of Amos* 2,7b-8; 4,1-13; 5,1-27; 6,4-7; 8,14 (Leiden: E.J. Brill, 1984), pp. 17-36, 126-42.

8.   The creditor is to return a garment before sundown to a poor person whose possessions were handed over to another in security (Exod. 22.25-26; Deut. 24.12-13).

fourth crime overlaps or illustrates the first crime. People were sold for money, wine was acquired from fines, and the sandals and cloak were the commodities bartered. The context establishes that the poor were not sold into slavery but forced into destitution by the seizure of their money and pledges.[9]

The sentence against Israel drops the image of fire, but a graphic picture is presented of devastating defeat in battle (2.13-16). Yahweh overwhelms and immobilizes the army: the swift one cannot flee, the strong one cannot assert his might and the experienced warrior cannot save himself (2.13-14). The idea is repeated with reference to three definite military types: the archer cannot stand, the infantryman cannot run away, and the horseman or charioteer cannot save his life (2.15).[10] The noun 'flight' is rounded off by the verb 'to flee': the swift seek safety in flight but in vain, while the most valiant warriors flee away naked with nothing to protect them (2.14a, 2.16b). No one can escape. All are destined for destruction.

Yahweh's proclamations are not short sayings collected by an editor but rather a continuous literary section in a larger composition.[11] Amos uses the same ideas and imagery to connect one report about a nation to another. Similar phraseology and catchwords weave the units into a coherent whole and drive home its unwavering message of disaster and doom. The defeat of each foreign nation results in the death or deportation of rulers and citizens (1.5b, 8b, 15b; 2.3). The threat against Aram, 'I will cut off the inhabitants from X and him that holds the scepter from X', is repeated against Philistia (1.5b, 8a). The catchword 'exile' is Aram's punishment but Philistia's crime (וגלו 1.5b; על־הגלותם 1.6b). 'Gilead' is cited twice as the territory against which Aram has committed atrocities (1.3b, 13b). Ammon and Moab are united by key phrases: בתרועה 'with shouting' (1.14; 2.2) and שריו 'his princes' /שריה 'its princes'(1.15; 2.3). The wordpairs מלכם 'their king' and שופט 'the judge' link Moab and Ammon, indicating that death and exile come to the nations' rulers (1.15; 2.3).

The proclamation against Israel is tied to the denunciations against

---

9.　Barstad (*Religious Polemics of Amos*, p. 14, n. 14) argues that the topic is socio-economic abuse, not slavery. Selling is used 'figuratively': Harper, Amos, p. 49; Driver, Joel and Amos, p. 148.

10.　The symmetrical arrangement of 2.13-16 into corresponding parts (2.13-14, 15-16) conflicts with six military types: Gerhard Pfeifer, 'Denkformenanalyse als exegetische Methode, erläutert an Amos 1.2–2.16', *ZAW* 88 (1976), pp. 56-71.

11.　So also John Barton, *Amos's Oracles against the Nations: A Study of Amos 1.3–2.5* (SOTSMS, 6; Cambridge: Cambridge University Press, 1980), p. 3.

foreign nations. 'Flight shall vanish from the swift' complements 'the remnant of the Philistines shall perish' (ואבד 2.14a; אבדו 1.8): The impossibility of escape for the swiftest of Israelite warriors is compared to the escape of the last Philistine survivors whose destiny is annihilation. The word יום links the fate of Israel and the nations: Yahweh causes Israel to fall 'on that day' or specifically on the day of war and on the day of the raging storm-wind when he destroys the nations (2.16b; 1.14b). Amos binds the beginning and end of Poem 1 with harvest imagery: threshing by which grain is crushed metaphorically depicts the cruelties of war while a heavily laden cart crushed beneath the weight of sheaves of grain metaphorically expresses the overpowering force of Yahweh's action against Israel (1.3b; 2.13).[12]

Amos creates a series of similarly structured proclamations of war which are designed to lead up to the climactic announcement of doom against Israel. A surprising reversal is produced by means of a chain of war proclamations which directs our expectations one way but gives a conclusion opposite to what is expected. The startling shift in focus away from the nations signals that Israel's crimes and crushing defeat in war are the actual subject matter of the first poem.

Poem 2 (3.1a-2, 3-6, 9-11)

Amos's second poem develops the argument against Israel. It begins with an introductory summary which repeats that Israel will be punished and acts as a resumptive passage by singling out Israel from all the other nations (3.1a, 2). The children of Israel are summoned to hear Yahweh's word against them (3.1a; cf. 4.1; 5.1), and the exhortation returns to the second person plural address (3.1a; 2.13). Yahweh's indictment consists of two contrasting statements, the second of which is the consequence of the first: 'I have known you…; therefore, I am going to punish you' (3.2).

Amos illuminates his paradoxical proposition with rhetorical questions (3.2, 3-6). The maxim that two things must agree if they go together is

---

12. Scholars link עוק (2 hiphil, 'to press down', 'to split open') with the earthquake announced in 1.1 (Soggin, *The Prophet Amos*, p. 49, 51; Wolff, *Amos*, pp. 171-73). But there is nothing in the context to suggest that the earth shakes and splits open. The pressing down of Israel by the enemy is compared to a cart breaking apart beneath the weight of its load (Hayes, *Amos*, pp. 118-19). Just as a waggon becomes bogged down in the mud (2.13), so the soldier becomes immobile and unable to escape (2.14).

illustrated with concrete examples from the natural world.[13] Every event in nature has a cause-and-effect relationship: the lion does not roar without capturing his prey nor does the bird fall to the ground without being ensnared. What follows is a sudden shift from the world of nature to the socio-political world. Harmless argument is replaced by ominous questions which bring the point of the paradox to a close: 'Does a trumpet blow in a city if people are not afraid (3.6a)?' Then the climactic question, 'Does evil strike a city if Yahweh has not done it?', explains how God will punish Israel (3.2b, 6b). Analogical reasoning is a persuasive technique that elicits the desired negative response and compels Amos's listeners to agree that Yahweh is behind disaster in a city. And once caught in the logic of the rhetoric they become convinced of the truth of the paradox (3.2).

The astonishing reversals from Israel's election to the nation's punishment (3.1-2), from innocuous images of nature to threatening images of war in a city and Yahweh's involvement in it (3.3-5, 6), associate the second poem with the first, in which expectations about war are turned upside down. The argument flows from one section to another. Amos singles out a city which he identifies as Samaria, and the social crimes of the capital city bring about its demise (3.6, 9-11).

Poems 1 and 2 illuminate each other. The sound of the trumpet means that enemy cities will be defeated in battle (2.2). This positive image turns into its opposite when the trumpet blast signifies Samaria's destruction in war (3.6). It is ironically inappropriate for those who alone have been 'known' by Yahweh not 'to know how to do right' (יׇדׇע 3.2, 10). A magnificent scene is depicted in which Ashdod (3.9a = 1.8a) is summoned to witness violence and injustice in Samaria and Yahweh's proclamation of doom against the city (3.9b-11).[14] The word אַרְמֹנוֹת 'strongholds/fortresses' repeatedly refers to the fortifications of Ashdod and Samaria, linking the destiny of the two cities. Yahweh plunders the fortresses of Samaria just as he sends a fire to devour foreign fortresses (1.4–2.2).

---

13. Gerhard Pfeifer, 'Unausweichliche Konsequenzen: Denkformenanalyse von Amos III 3-8', *VT* 33 (1983), pp. 341-46; 'Die Denkform des propheten Amos (III 9-11)', *VT* 34 (1984), pp. 476-81.

14. Paul (*Amos*, pp. 116-17) explains the *MT* אַשְׁדּוֹד (3.9). LXX's reading אַשּׁוּר gives scholars a text in which Amos mentions Assyria in his prophecies. However, Paul recognizes Amos's penchant for paronomasia by showing that שֹׁד (3.10b) is a pun upon אַשְׁדּוֹד who is invited to witness Samaria's crimes. Ashdod fits the context and points back to Ashdod in 1.8a.

The first poem introduces all the images and ideas which are developed throughout the composition. The second poem, like the first, includes the crimes and the threat of war. The familiar phrases נאם־יהוה and כה אמר אדני יהוה are used in the middle of the indictment against Samaria and at the beginning of the punishment to emphasize that Yahweh pronounces Samaria's guilt and promises to destroy the city along with the enemy cities (3.10-11).

Poem 3 (4.1-3, 4-5)

The third poem begins with the same summons to 'hear this word' (הזה שמעו הדבר 4.1; 3.1). Amos develops his argument against the city of Samaria by counting its women among those who commit acts of extortion and who make their husbands the instruments of exploitation by urging them to drink (העשקות 4.1; עשוקים 3.9b). That the women are implicated in the oppression of the poor is evident from the charge that wine is drunk in the temple by those who imposed fines on the destitute (2.8). The women of Samaria are called 'the cows of Bashan' (4.1), their husbands are the bulls who give themselves horns (6.13), and the husbands are called אדון rather than איש or בעל (4.1). In light of the recent inscriptional evidence depicting Yahweh as a bull and his Asherah as a cow, perhaps Amos mockingly portrays the women of Samaria as goddesses and their husbands as gods (1 Kgs 12.28).[15]

The indictment against the women of Samaria and their husbands is followed by Yahweh's word or oath of judgment against them (4.1-3). The women speaking to 'their lords' (אדניהם 4.1b) leads into and balances what 'the Lord Yahweh' (אדני יהוה 4.2aA) says to the human lords and their ladies: 'the days are coming against you...even the last of you' (עליכם ... ואחריתכן 4.2).[16] The reference to the days ahead is a return to

---

15. On the representations at Kuntillet 'Ajrud and their interpretations see Othmar Keel and Christoph Uehlinger, *Gods, Goddesses, and Images of God in Ancient Israel* (trans. Thomas H. Trapp; Minneapolis: Fortress Press, 1998), pp. 210-48; Paul F. Jacobs, '"Cows of Bashan"—A Note on the Interpretation of Amos 4.1', *JBL* 104 (1985), pp. 109-10.

16. Andersen and Freedman (*Amos*, p. 421) emend the pronominal suffix of אדניהם from masculine to feminine. However, through a weakening in a description of gender, masculine suffixes are often used to refer to feminine substantives (GKC no.135 o, p. 440). The gender of the pronominal suffix is fixed by the noun's gender. So the masculine noun אדון and its masculine plural suffix אדניהם agree and also the feminine noun אחרית and its feminine plural suffix אחריתכן.

'the day of battle' (1.14b) and the fall of Israel 'on that day' (2.16). War imagery reappears with the flight, capture and deportation of the women and husbands (4.2-3). God causes the fall of Samaria and uses hooks to fasten and drag away its citizens (3.6; 4.2). The judgment scene portrays women fugitives going out through the breaches in the walls of the ruined city, and they are metaphorically compared to a herd of cows stampeding headlong through a hole in a fence (4.3). Each woman exits straight ahead, one before the other (4.3a). And the image of women being driven towards Harmon recalls the exile of Syrians to Kir (4.3b; 1.5b).[17]

The sequel summons בני ישׂראל 'the children of Israel' to worship at Bethel and Gilgal, but another reversal occurs with the report that people come to these northern shrines to commit more and more crimes (4.4-5). The noun פשׁע is repeated, and the verb פשׁע links the crimes at Bethel and Gilgal with those of Israel, especially those committed at every altar or in the house of God (1.3, 6, 13; 2.1, 6-8). The phrase בית אלהיהם 'house of their God' anticipates, by way of a pun with בית־אל 'Bethel'/'house of God', the shrine where oppressive acts were perpetrated (2.8; 4.4).

Amos returns to the rhetorical argument in Poem 3 by disclosing that coming to the temple and sinning are two things that do not belong together. 'Bring your sacrifices' imitates the command of the women of Samaria: 'Bring so we may drink!' (הביאה...והביאו 4.1b, 4b). Offerings and tithes are to be carried to the temples, but the instruction leads to improper worship. The people 'love' to offer thanksgiving sacrifices and freewill offerings in their shrines at Bethel and Gilgal, but they muddle this ritual activity with the practice of acquiring offerings from others they have exploited (4.1, 5).

Poem 4 (5.1-2, 4-5, 6-7)

Poem 4 begins with the familiar summons, 'Hear this word', but now Amos addresses the 'house of Israel', the dynasty or kingdom of Israel (5.1; 4.1; 3.1). The word is identified as the prophet's lament over the fall of Israel, its collapse made all the more poignant by the image of a young woman left fallen and forsaken on her land (5.2).[18] The dirge does not

---

17. The locative ending ה 'towards' is added to both Harmon (ההרמונה for הרמון) and Kir (קירה for קיר).

18. The term בתולה, usually translated 'a virgin', refers to a young adolescent female who was potentially fertile but had not yet given birth: see Peggy Day, 'From the Child is Born the Woman: The Story of Jephthah's Daughter', in Peggy Day (ed.),

predict Israel's demise but assumes it has already occurred. Perfects נפלה and נטשה stress that the disaster is a past event.[19] Poem 4 marks a significant development in thought, moving from the prediction of war and deportation to the report of Israel's downfall (4.2-3; 5.1-2). The divine oath of impending deportation is linked with Amos's subsequent song of grief: 'He [Yahweh] will take you away' is already played out and past (נשא 4.2b), as is evident from the dirge which Amos 'takes up' over Israel (נשא 5.1-2).

The sequel to the elegiac verses resumes God's address to the house of Israel and his discussion of Bethel and Gilgal. The injunction 'come to Bethel, to Gilgal and transgress' is prohibited by the charge 'seek me and live' (4.4; 5.4b). In the spirit of his rhetorical questions, Amos argues that 'seeking Yahweh' and 'seeking Bethel' are opposites that clearly do not go together. Seeking Yahweh means life but seeking Bethel means death in the fire that engulfs the city (5.6). Amos moves back to the time before disaster has taken place, anticipating the exile of Gilgal and the doom of Bethel as consequences of multiplying crimes at these shrines (5.4-5; 4.4-5).

The fourth poem gradually fills in details omitted from the previous poems. Amos tells us for the first time that the fire which God sends to devour the foreign cities is also the fire which breaks out in the house of Joseph and devours Bethel (אכל 1.3–2.1-3; 5.6). The threat of disaster applies no less to the South than it does to the North. Amos warns not only against frequenting the sanctuaries of Gilgal and Bethel but also against crossing over into Beersheba at the extreme south of Judah (5.5a).[20]

Hopelessness and doom are the prevailing mood of the fourth poem. Negative statements mark the opening and conclusion: the woman Israel 'will rise no more' (לא־תוסיף קום 5.2a), 'there is no one raising her up' (אין מקימה 5.2b), and 'no one extinguishes' the fire in Bethel (אין מכבה 5.6b). The grim fate of Gilgal and Bethel is summed up in two word plays:

Gender and Difference in Ancient Israel (Minneapolis: Fortress Press, 1989), pp. 58-74; for a discussion of the word, see John J. Schmitt, 'The Virgin of Israel: Referent and Use of the Phrase in Amos and Jeremiah', *CBQ* 53 (1991), pp. 365-87.

19. Most scholars call the perfects 'prophetic perfects': *the future is depicted as if it has already happened*. See GKC no.106 n, pp. 312-13; Soggin, *The Prophet Amos*, p. 82; Paul, *Amos*, p. 159; Andersen and Freedman, *Amos*, pp. 473-74.

20. No marker identifies Beersheba as editorial: it is the centre of the structure Bethel–Gilgal–Beersheba–Gilgal–Bethel. See N.J. Tromp, 'Amos V 1-17: Towards a Stylistic and Rhetorical Analysis', *OTS* 23 (1984), pp. 56-84.

הגלגל גלה יגלה 'Gilgal will surely go into Golah' and ובת אל יהיה לאון
'house of El shall become a house of idols' (5.5b).[21] 'House of Israel' is
offset by 'house of Joseph', and an inclusion identifies 'house of Israel' as
the Northern Kingdom (5.1, 6). The 'you' addressed at the poem's beginning and end refers to those who perverted justice in the dynasty of Israel.

Poem 5 (5.10-12, 18-20, 21-24)

The fifth poem resumes the topic of righteousness that closes the previous
poem. People show aversion towards the reprover at the city gate, the one
who speaks honestly at the place where justice is administered.[22] The
introductory לבן יען 'therefore, since' links one verse with the other (5.10-
11). It marks the logical conclusion by recounting the reproof and citing
the punishment for ignoring or dismissing the reprover's words. The יען
clause establishes that the rebuker speaks out against those who crushed
the poor (5.10-11aA). But the conjunction לבן points forward to the
punishment that is the consequence of subverting justice: Those haters of
the reprover will not live in houses they have built or drink wine from
vineyards they have planted (5.11aBb).

What links the penalty for oppression with the crimes is the subordinate
conjunction כי ('because' 5.12aA). The oppressors are talked about and
then directly addressed for mistreating the poor (5.10, 11-12). It is knowledge of their innumerable crimes and sins that provides the motivation for
the punishment. The charge of extortion is levelled against the wrongdoers
(5.11aA, 12bA). The theme of perverted justice at the city gate opens and
closes the poetic unit, and the third person plural formally indicates its
beginning and end (שנאו 'they hate' 5.10 ; הטו 'they turn aside' 5.12).
What begins as a vague description of the gate receives clarity and
precision: the claims of justice for the righteous poor are overlooked at the
public court; the oppressors hate the reprover because he chided them for
turning aside the needy; they also despised anyone else who spoke in
defence of the innocent (5.10, 12).

Poem 5 expands on the theme of unjust oppression that has been
discussed in previous poems. That Israel trampled upon the poor or weak
is repeated (בושסכם 5.11aA = השאפים 2.7aA; דל 5.11aA = רלים 2.7aA;
4.1aB). Drinking wine is once again associated with the exploitation of the

---

21. For other translations of these puns, see Paul, *Amos*, pp. 163-64.
22. Cf. Lawrence A. Sinclair, 'The Courtroom Motif in the Book of Amos', *JBL* 85
(1966), pp. 351-53.

poor, and the penalty for those who procure wine from unfair fines is no more wine from the vineyards (5.11b; 2.8b; 4.1b). There is recurrence of the terminology of פֶּשַׁע (1.3–2.8; 4.4a): פִּשְׁעֵיכֶם 'your transgressions' is combined with חַטֹּאתֵיכֶם 'your sins' (5.12aA). The word pairs צַדִּיק וְאֶבְיוֹן reappear (2.6b; 5.12b): extortion of the righteous and needy involves the unjust seizure of money and pledges (2.6b, 8) and two equally punishable crimes, the seizure of grain and the acceptance of bribes (לְקַח 5.11aA; לֹקְחֵי 5.12bB). The oppressors thrust aside the innocent poor when they come up for justice at the city gate (יַטּוּ 2.7; הַטּוּ 5.12bB).

Characteristically the description of the crimes and sins is followed by the punishment that is now announced as the 'day of Yahweh' (יוֹם יהוה 5.18-20). This motif stands out as a real progression in the plot. Divine judgment is introduced by Amos's cry of grief for those who earnestly desire the day of Yahweh (הוֹי 5.18a).[23] The rhetorical question, 'What is this day of Yahweh to you?', is posed for the purpose of asserting that the day 'is darkness and not light' (5.18). The question elicits a contrast between the expected day of light and the unanticipated day of darkness. Key words are repeated: 'Is not the day of Yahweh darkness and not light?'. And this image of the coming day is stressed: 'and gloom with no brightness in it'. The inevitable day of Yahweh and its unavoidable disastrous consequences are illustrated by the story of a man who flees from a lion only to have a bear pounce upon him or who seeks refuge in his own house only to have a snake bite him when he leans against a wall (5.19). Running away from danger or arriving home safely does not deflect fate or the unalterable course of events.

So the meaning of the 'day of Yahweh' is understood in light of its description in previous and subsequent poems.[24] It is a day of war characterized by flight and defeat, the arrival of punishment and deportation of Israel's citizens. It spells danger and destruction and inescapable doom for Israel and Samaria (1.14b; 2.14-16; 4.2). God's day will arrive on the feast days (5.18-20, 21-24). He will punish those who hate the

---

23. R.J. Clifford, 'The Use of Hôy in the Prophets', *CBQ* 28 (1966), pp. 458-64; E. Gerstenberger, 'The Woe-Oracles of the Prophets', *JBL* 81 (1962), pp. 249-63.

24. Since יוֹם יהוה only appears in Amos 5.18-20, it has been interpreted by its 'more unequivocal' or 'broader' meaning in later prophetic texts: see Gerhard von Rad, 'The Origin of the Concept of the Day of Yahweh', *JSS* 4 (1959), pp. 97-108. But the meaning of יוֹם יהוה in Amos should not simply be determined by its later meaning. The idea develops and changes over the course of time: Yair Hoffman, 'The Day of the Lord as a Concept and a Term in the Prophetic Literature', *ZAW* 93 (1981), pp. 37-50.

reprover (שׂנאתי 'they hate' 5.10), and the objects of his hatred (expressed in the first person, שׂנאתי 'I hate' 5.21) are the feasts whose essential elements are sacrifice and song. Various offerings are added to the list already detailed in Poem 3 (4.4-5). The sacrifices are for Yahweh, the songs are sung in praise of him and not in honour of other gods, but the feasts are celebrated without righteousness (5.24; 2.6-8; 4.1, 4).

Poem 6 (6.1-3, 4-7, 12-13)

Poem 6 marks a transition in Amos's thought. Taking up his allusion to 'the whole family' (3.1bA), Amos directs his mourning-cry to the smug and self-confident leaders in both Zion and Samaria (הוי 6.1aA = 5.18a).[25] Zion is not mentioned in passing but is given a prominent position at the beginning of Amos's exclamation of grief. The paired cities of Zion and Samaria are balanced by the report 'the house of Israel comes to them', that is, to the great ones of Judah, the first of the nations.[26]

The verb ובאו leads forward to other verbs of motion which introduce

---

25. Scholars have always been baffled by the reference to 'Zion' because of the widespread consensus of Amos as a prophet to the North. LXX translates 6.1, Οὐαὶ τοῖς ἐξουθενοῦσι Σιὼν 'woe to them who despise Zion', as an address to Samaria. Some emend or delete the reference to Zion. So ציון is replaced by חרצה to agree with Tirzah (2 Kgs 15.16). Or בציון 'in Zion' is replaced by בעיר 'in a city' or by בבצרן 'in strength' or is treated as a Deuteronomistic supplement (Wolff, Amos, pp. 269-70; Soggin, The Prophet Amos, p. 102). A few argue that Amos is talking about Zion and Samaria: e.g. J.J.M. Roberts, 'Amos 6.1-7', in James T. Butler, Edgar W. Conrad and Ben C. Ollenburger (eds.), Understanding the Word: Essays in Honor of Bernhard W. Anderson (JSOTSup, 37; Sheffield: JSOT Press, 1985), pp. 155-66. But all the evidence in Amos of a larger Israel which includes Judah is often ascribed to later editorial work: see Ronald E. Clements, 'Amos and the Politics of Israel', in Daniele Garrone and Felice Israel (eds.), Storia e Tradizioni di Israele: Scritti in onore di J. Alberto Soggin (Brescia: Paideia, 1991), pp. 49-64.

26. The translation of 6.1bB has always posed a problem. LXX attaches some words to the preceding sentence and some to the following, translating as though a dative reinforces the subject: καὶ εἰσῆλθον αὐτοί. οἶκος τοῦ Ἰσραὴλ διάβητε πάντες καὶ ἴδετε 'and they have come in themselves, O house of Israel, pass by all of you and see'. Some scholars emend 6.1bB or delete it: see William L. Holladay, 'Amos VI 1Bβ: A Suggested Solution', VT 22 (1972), pp. 107-10. Andersen and Freedman (Amos, pp. 544, 560) translate בית ישׂראל as locative: 'they have come for themselves to the house of Israel'. I agree with Wolff that 'the house of Israel' is the subject of the sentence: but the 'house of Israel' does not come to the nations (Wolff, *Amos*, p. 271) but to Judah's prominent leaders.

the summons: 'Cross over to Calneh...go to Hamath...go down to Gath' (6.2). Zion and Samaria (6.1a) are balanced by foreign cities in Syria and Philistia. Two questions follow the list of cities: 'Are they [i.e. the foreign cities] better than these kingdoms [i.e. the kingdoms of Judah and Israel]? Or is their territory larger than your territory?' (6.2b).[27] The answer to the questions is no. Foreign cities are not fairer nor is their territory larger than 'these kingdoms'. The implication is that foreign cities have fallen or are reduced in size, and allusion to their defeat anticipates the report about the 'ruin of Joseph' (6.6b). The reference to הממלכות האלה 'these kingdoms' points backwards and confirms that the two kingdoms mentioned at the beginning of the poem are Judah and Israel, identified respectively as 'the first of the nations' and 'the house of Israel' (6.1).

Amos describes the activities of wealthy Judaeans who are addressed and explains how they have avoided the evil day by indulging in opulent banquets, sprawling upon ivory couches, eating the best meat, drinking wine, and singing songs while failing to mourn over Joseph's ruin or showing the slightest distress at Israel's downfall (6.3, 4-6). This picture of elegant luxury and callous unconcern leads to the punishment which refers to sprawling festivity and repeats the motif of being first. The play on words, 'pre-eminent men of the first of the nations' (ראשית הגוים, 6.1bA) 'finest of ointments' (ראשית שמנים, 6.6aB), 'at the head of the exiles' (בראש גלים, 6.7a), ironically portrays Judah as the first nation whose citizens will go first into exile.

Poem 6 addresses the complacent in Zion and Samaria. Though the house of Israel is mentioned and its furniture of ivory (6.1, 4), we become aware that the lesson is not for Samaria and its leading citizens but for the wealthy ruling classes of Zion. The noun שבת ('seat/throne/chair') leads into a description of beds and couches (6.3-4a); it anticipates the reference to David and alludes to his throne (6.5b).[28] Since Amos speaks about the

---

27. Those who argue that 'they' refers to Israel and Judah and 'these kingdoms' to Calneh, Hamath and Gath emend the MT by supplying an explicit or implicit אתם and inverting the position of the pronominal suffixes: 'Are you better than these kingdoms? Or is your territory greater than their territory?' (Coote, *Amos among the Prophets*, p. 14; Roberts, 'Amos 6.1-7', p. 154). But the more difficult MT reading fits Amos's fluctuation between second and third persons.

28. Scholars, influenced by LXX's omission of David, assume that Israel is the audience and כדויד is an addition: Wolff, Amos, pp. 272-73 n. j; Mays, Amos, p. 113 n. a.

ruin of Joseph or the North as an event that has already happened (6.6b),[29] his prophecy can be directed only to the South. Amos does not speak directly about Judah's exile, but by means of balanced pairs (Zion and Samaria, 'first of the nations' and 'house of Israel,' the 'foreign cities' and 'these kingdoms') and an artistically contrived pun, he identifies the leaders of Judah as the ones who head the column of captives (6.7a).

Poem 6 develops themes that have already been introduced. Unrestrained feasting and singing to the melody of the lute complements the scene of a religious feast or festival (6.4-6; 5.21-24). Rich Judaeans reclining on couches and drinking from bowls mirror wealthy Israelites lying on garments and consuming wine in the house of God (6.4-6; 2.8). The worshippers congregate to prepare offerings to Yahweh and listen to musical entertainment (5.21-23; 6.5). Male worshippers represented as bulls match female worshippers who are called cows (6.12b; 4.1). Lambs and calves are partially burned as a community sacrifice and partially eaten by devotees (5.22; 6.4b), but God takes no delight in feasts whose participants ignore righteousness and lack concern for the unfortunate (5.21-22, 24; 6.6b, 12).

Amos ends Poem 6 with a double rhetorical question, with an observation on the behaviour of those who are rebuked and with an elaboration on their misguided worship (6.12-13). As in the poem's opening (6.2), Amos poses questions that elicit the answer 'No', and then there is a sudden shift to direct address. The questions depict what is unnatural and absurd: it is obvious that horses do not run on rock, nor is rock plowed with oxen (6.12).[30] Yet Judah's nobles have done what is preposterous and unreasonable by perverting justice and turning the order of things upside down. The poem ends with a festive mood: 'you who rejoiced in a non-

---

29. Scholars explain away the fact that Joseph's ruin refers to a past event: Wolff (*Amos*, pp. 274, 277) interprets Amos 6.6b as a late supplement; Bruce Vawter (*Amos, Hosea, Micah, with an Introduction to Classical Prophecy* [Old Testament Message, 7; Wilmington, DE: Michael Glazier, 1981], p. 61) argues that Joseph's ruin refers to the people of the north and their present spiritual disintegration. Hayes (*Amos*, p. 187) thinks the phrase refers to 'internal civil strife'; and Andersen and Freedman (*Amos*, pp. 553, 565) talk about 'the imminent breakdown' of the North.

30. This traditional Jewish translation ('Is rock plowed with oxen?') is often rejected: בבקרים is redivided to בבקר ים 'Does one plow the sea with oxen?' (RSV; Wolff, *Amos*, p. 284; Mays, *Amos*, p. 120; Soggin, *The Prophet Amos*, p. 109; Andersen and Freedman, *Amos*, p. 574). But ellipsis is an acceptable solution: 'rock' is implied in the second question but not written. See also Hayes, *Amos*, pp. 181, 191.

word' (6.13).[31] At their feasts the leaders of Zion and Samaria have uttered gibberish: 'Is it not by our own strength that we have acquired horns?' The question fits images of oxen and calves and points to some cultic rite (6.4b, 12).

Gath is not listed among the Philistine cities in Poem 1, but the reason for Gath's absence is explained by the allusion to its defeat in Poem 6 (6.2). Yahweh's promise, 'the remnant of the Philistines shall perish', suggests that Gath is no more and that the Philistine remnant is Gaza, Ashdod, Ashkelon and Ekron (1.8b).[32] Poem 1 talks about the Ammonites enlarging their territory (למען הרחיב את־גבולם 1.13bB), and Poem 6 poses the question to which a negative answer is expected: 'Is their territory greater than your territory?' (אם־רב גבולם מגבלכם 6.2b). Observing that foreign cities no larger than the territory of Israel and Judah have disappeared, Amos compels us to agree that the survival of these two kingdoms would be absurd.

The recurrent theme of the shrines links the sixth poem with earlier poems. The allusion to the house of Israel coming to Judah is compatible with the description of a feast in Zion (6.1, 4-6). A journey to the Jerusalem temple is implied and is consistent with imagery about coming to the shrines to worship (ובאו 6.1b; ...והביאו באו 4.4-5; תבאו 5.5). Judah's cult is associated with indifference towards the ruin of Joseph. The failure of Judah's aristocrats to show concern for the fall of the Northern Kingdom is the antithesis of Amos's lament over the fall of Israel (5.1-2).

Amos connects the crimes of the house of Israel with those of Judah's dynasty by quoting his own text. So his accusation against Israel, 'you who turned justice to wormwood, who cast down righteousness to the earth', is joined to his attack on Judah, 'but you have turned justice to poison and the fruit of righteousness into wormwood' (5.7; 6.12). Israel and Judah are linked in their crimes, and the deportation of Samaria's upper classes is matched by the approaching exile of Zion's leaders (4.3; 6.7).

---

31. The MT is retained in LXX: ἐπ' οὐδενὶ λόγῳ 'over no word'.

32. It has long been recognized that the omission of Gath from 1.6-8 presupposes its destruction: e.g. K. Marti, *Das Dodekapropheton erklärt* (Kurzer Hard-Commentar zum Alten Testament, 13; Tübingen: J.C.B. Mohr [Paul Siebeck], 1904), p. 160; Wilhelm Nowack, *Die kleinen Propheten Übersetzt und erklärt* (Göttingen: Vandenhoeck & Ruprecht, 3rd edn, 1922), p. 123; H.E.W. Fosbroke and S. Lovett, 'The Book of Amos: Introduction and Exegesis', *IB*, VI (Nashville: Abingdon Press, 1956), pp. 761-853 (780-81).

The rhetorical argument in Poem 6 matches the one offered in the second poem (6.12-13; 3.3-6). Questions are lined up in pairs, there is consistent use of animal imagery, and Amos makes his point by observing the laws of nature. So a lion's roar belongs with his seizure of prey or a bird's fall with a hunter's snare (3.3-5). Conversely, examples are given of ludicrous events that violate the laws of nature: horses and oxen have nothing to do with rocky crags (6.12a). A series of observations with which we must agree lead us from nature to socio-political issues.

So we are forced to agree that Yahweh causes war in a city and that justice and righteousness have nothing to do with poison and wormwood (3.6b; 6.12b). The elite are responsible for the perversion of justice which precipitates Yahweh's war in the city (6.12; 3.6b). The phrase לֹא דבר השׂמחים 'those who rejoice in no-word' (6.13a) suggests an outcome opposite to what is expected from the exhortation שׁמע הדבר הזה 'hear this word' (3.1; 4.1; 5.1). Instead of obeying God's word the people prefer to revel in nonsensical talk.[33] This idea of the people preferring nonsense to the prophetic word provides the transition to the visions, which are now directed exclusively to the prophet, as if they were for his own personal instruction.[34]

Poem 7 (7.1-3, 4-6, 7-9; 8.1-3a, 4-6, 9-10)

Amos's visions open Poem 7 and mark a new phase in the thought of the prophet. The futility of the prophetic word means that God now informs only his prophet about what is going to happen. The visions contain the same basic elements: the opening clause כה הראני אדני יהוה 'Thus the Lord Yahweh showed me' (cf. 7.7a) is followed by the demonstrative particle והנה 'look' which introduces what Amos saw, and each vision is accompanied by an interpretation in the form of a dialogue with God. The first two visions of locusts (7.1-3) and fire (7.4-6) are paired, and the last two visions of everyday objects correspond to each other (7.7-9; 8.1-3a).

In the first vision someone 'was forming' (יוצר) locusts to destroy the last growth of vegetation provided by the late spring rains (7.1-3). This

33. Translations of לֹא דבר as 'no-thing', 'a non-entity' and 'a thing of naught' make it impossible for scholars to see that Amos uses דבר in an ironic way to convey a meaning opposite to what is intended by its earlier usage: Cf. Driver, *Joel and Amos*, p. 198; Soggin, *The Prophet Amos*, p. 110; Coote, *Amos among the Prophets*, p. 86.

34. See also Samuel Amsler, 'La parole visionnaire des prophètes', *VT* 31 (1981), pp. 359-63.

vision of a locust plague prompts Amos to plead on behalf of Jacob for Yahweh's forgiveness. Amos rests his appeal on the rhetorical question, מִי יָקוּם יַעֲקֹב כִּי קָטֹן הוּא 'How can Jacob stand, for he is so small?'. Yahweh accepts Amos's role as intercessor and changes his mind: לֹא תִהְיֶה 'It shall not be'.[35]

The second vision makes explicit what is only implied in the first, namely, that God causes destruction (7.4-6). So the participle קֹרֵא refers to his calling for a judgment by fire that dries up the subterranean depths and depletes the water sources of the land. The image of locusts devouring the green plants of the earth corresponds to a fire devouring the deep and the land (7.1, 4). The second vision replaces the appeal to forgive with the urgent command that Yahweh desist. Once again Amos urges Yahweh to repent on grounds of Jacob's small size. The success of Amos's intervention is indicated by the same report that Yahweh repented, and his words, 'that too shall not be', link the second vision to the first.

The last two visions are constructed differently from the first pair: they do not begin with a punitive divine deed but focus on a familiar object Yahweh has shown Amos. In lieu of Amos's question and a divine response, God asks a question to which Amos replies, and then God announces imminent disaster. So the third vision depicts Yahweh standing beside a wall, holding a plumb line in his hand (7.7-9), asking Amos what he sees, and he replies, 'a plumb line'.[36] What follows is God's decree expressed in the first person, 'I am about to set a plumb line in the midst of

35. Yahweh's plan is revoked and is cited with feminine forms: זֹאת 'this'; תִהְיֶה 'it shall be'; הִיא 'that'. The feminine is used in impersonal verbs, and the third person singular is used impersonally in the feminine and masculine: GKC no.144B-C, p. 459.

36. No ancient version reads אֲנָךְ as 'plumb line': in LXX God holds an adamant. 'Plumb line', originating in medieval Jewish exegesis, is retained by many scholars on literary and contextual grounds: RSV; Mays, *Amos*, pp. 131-32; Wolff, *Amos*, pp. 293, 300-301; Soggin, *The Prophet Amos*, pp. 114-16; Coote, Amos among the Prophets, pp. 192-93; H.G.M. Williamson, 'The Prophet and the Plumbline: A Redactional-Critical Study of Amos 7', *OTS* 26 (1990), pp. 101-21; Dalene Heyns, 'Space and Time in Amos 7: Reconsidering the Third Vision', *Old Testament Essays* 10 (1997), pp. 27-38. The widespread view is that אֲנָךְ is based on the Akkadian *annaku* 'tin' used for weapons (7.9): B. Landsberger, 'Tin and Lead: The Adventure of Two Vocables', *JNES* 24 (1965), pp. 185-96; Gilbert Brunet, 'La vision de l'étain: réinterpretation d'Amos VII 7-9', *VT* 16 (1966), pp. 387-95; Hayes, Amos, pp. 204-205; Martin-Achard, The End of the People of God: A Commentary on the Book of Amos, p. 55. On tin's unsuitability for weapons see: Susan Niditch, The Symbolic Vision in Biblical Tradition (Chico, CA: Scholars Press, 1983), p. 22, n. d.

my people Israel'. The image of God as a builder who uses a cord and lead weight to test the wall, its uprightness and stability, is overturned by the preview of the destruction of the high places of Isaac and the sanctuaries of Israel.[37] The divine building of a wall with a plumb bob anticipates God's decision to destroy the house of Jeroboam: אֲנָךְ suggests the double image of a plumb line for construction and for demolition.

In the fourth vision Yahweh asks Amos what he sees, and Amos replies 'a basket of summer fruit'. Then Yahweh proclaims 'The end has come upon my people Israel' (8.1-3a). As the consequence of divine judgment, the songs of the temple or palace will be turned into mourning cries. A wordplay is created out of the key words, קָיִץ 'summer fruit' and קֵץ 'end'. Just as the positive image of the plumb line is transformed into its opposite with the utterance of the divine word,[38] so the positive image of summer fruit is revoked by God's announcement of the end.

The vision of the אֲנָךְ does not culminate in a wordplay in the way that 'summer fruit' is converted into 'end'. However, since the emphasis is first on the vision (7.1-2a, 4) and then on the proclamation (7.8a-9; 8.2b-3a), it is fitting that a wordplay on the divine word קָם follows the visionary image of אֲנָךְ. The shift of meaning in the image of the plumb line leads to an expected shift in the image of the summer basket. But instead there is variation with the unanticipated change in the meaning of קָיִץ. What the third vision has in common with the fourth is that it contains an assonantal wordplay. The play on words between יֶחֱרָבוּ 'shall be laid waste' and

---

37. The analogy is a plumb bob which tests the perpendicularity of a structure and a wrecking ball which destroys existing walls. As later texts (2 Kgs 21.13; Isa. 34.11; and Lam. 2.8) suggest, the plumb line functioned as a standard for either erecting or wrecking walls. The part of the wall which passes the test is built up, and the part which does not pass the test is pulled down. Scholars argue that tin in Yahweh's hand is an image of his military might against his people: see Christoph Uehlinger, 'Der Herr auf der Zinnmauer: Zur dritten Amos-Vision (Am 7.7-8)', *BN* 48 (1989), pp. 89-104; Jörg Jeremias, 'Das unzugängliche Heiligtum', in Rüdiger Bartelmus, Thomas Krüger and Helmut Utzschneider (eds.), *Konsequente Traditionsgeschichte: Festschrift für Klaus Baltzer zum 65. Geburtstag* (OBO, 126; Göttingen: Vandenhoeck & Ruprecht, 1993), pp. 155-67. But the image of Yahweh setting a plumb line in the midst of his people is equally a sign of his unlimited destructive power: Harper, *Amos*, pp. 165-66; Wolff, *Amos*, p. 301; Francis Landy, 'Vision and Poetic Speech in Amos', *HAR 11* (1987), pp. 223-46 (228-31).

38. Klaus Baltzer, 'Bild und Wort: Erwägungen zu der Vision des Amos in Am 7.7-9', in Walter Gross, Hubert Irsigler and Theodor Seidl (eds.), Texte, Methode und Grammatik: Wolfgang Richter zum 65. Geburtstag (St Ottilien: EOS, 1991), pp. 11-16.

בחרב 'with the sword' relates the devastation of the high places to God's judgment with the sword (7.9). And this wordplay anticipates the climactic pun that transforms the summer fruit into a word of destruction.

The rhetorical series reaches its climax in the fourth vision, and it ends with words and images that complete the thought of the first vision. The formula 'Thus the Lord Yahweh showed me' is matched by 'says the Lord Yahweh' (7.1a; 8.3). The first and last visions use agricultural imagery, the first referring to the new growth of herbage and the last referring to the harvest bounty. The visions trace the progression of the calendar year from לקש to קץ or from the season of the late spring crop to the last season of the fruit-gathering in late summer or early autumn (7.1; 8.1-2).[39] Between the visions of the late spring crop and of the autumn harvest is the vision of the cosmic fire which denotes an excessively hot dry spell in summer (7.4). The general reference to the king anticipates the naming of Jeroboam and the reference to palace wailings (7.9b). Visions 1 and 4 make a complete whole: Yahweh's respite of Jacob is cancelled by his proclamation of death on all his people (7.3; 8.3a).

Amos's rhetorical question, 'How can Jacob stand? He is so small!', must be understood in the context of passages where concern is expressed about expanding borders and the size of foreign territories compared with that of Israel and Judah (7.2, 5; 1.13b; 6.2). The crime of Ammon was the murder of defenceless women for the sake of extending its frontier into Gilead. Yahweh puts an end to Ammon's conquests and destroys the nation. If Ammon's increased size does not protect it from defeat, then the small kingdoms of Israel and Judah will not escape punishment. Using the visions of the locusts and fire, Amos emphasizes that Jacob is too small to regain his upright position when faced with God's superior might.[40]

The clue that Jacob cannot be Israel comes from associating the question, 'How can Jacob stand?' (יקום) with the image of the fallen woman Israel, unable to rise and without anyone to raise her up (לא־תוסיף קום...

---

39. The term לקש is a hapax legomenon. It appears in 'The Gezer Calendar' after the first season of sowing and stands for the months of late sowing or late spring growth. The Gezer agricultural year ends with קץ and denotes the harvest of summer fruit: see *ANET*, p. 320.

40. Scholars recognize that קטן 'small' has other dimensions: Jacob is helpless, dependent, fragile, insignificant and vulnerable. But these meanings should be determined by the immediate or wider context of Amos and not by the usage of קטן in other texts (Gen. 20.7, 15, 42; 1 Sam. 9.21; 1 Kgs 3.7): see Walter Brueggemann, 'Amos's Intercessory Formula', *VT* 19 (1969), pp. 386-99.

אֵין מְקִימָה 7.2, 5; 5.2). Locusts and fire topple Jacob, but the unexpected reprieve enables Jacob to stand. Jacob can be identified once the lament and visions are situated within a whole narrative. There is a move from Israel's death to Jacob's vulnerability, and the transition is prepared for by linking Zion with Samaria and the crimes of the house of Israel with the first nation who does not grieve for Joseph. The pairs suggest that the first nation is Judah, Joseph is Israel, Joseph anticipates Jacob, and Jacob stands for Judah.[41]

The expression קֹרֵא לָרִב בָּאֵשׁ 'calling for a dispute by fire' recalls the city gate where the people scoff at the one who makes the right decisions (7.4; 5.10-12).[42] Images of fire and the law court are combined. Fire is God's instrument in carrying out the judicial process. The second vision, of 'the devouring fire', develops the point of Poems 1 and 4. On the day when Yahweh sends a fire it rages against walls of foreign palaces and fortresses (1.3–2.16). It breaks out against the house of Joseph and destroys Bethel (5.6b). It spreads with unabated intensity against Jacob or Judah, and the searing flames reach down into the depths of the sea and engulf the whole earth (7.4). The picture of fire destroying the walls of buildings suggests that the visions of the fire and the wall are intended to overlap each other (1.7a, 14a; 7.4-6, 7-9). That fire involves war is indicated from the references to the assault on walls and fortifications (1.4b, 7, 14; 2.2a),[43] from the allusion to fallen Israel and the corresponding image of Judah's powerlessness to rise (5.2, 6; 7.4-5).

References in the vision of the plumb line can be explained when they are related to other poems. Israel's sanctuaries are called 'the house of God' (7.9; 2.8b) and known as Bethel and Gilgal (4.4-5; 5.4-5, 6b). The explanation for their destruction is introduced and developed (2.6-8; 4.1, 4-5; 5.21-24). 'The sanctuaries of Israel' and 'the high places of Isaac' are paired in the same way that Zion is complemented by Samaria (6.1a), or the first of the nations by the house of Israel (6.1b), or Joseph by Jacob (6.6b; 7.2, 5). Isaac stands for Judah and is anticipated by Beersheba (5.5b) and the allusion to Jerusalem in Israel's journey to the first nation

41. However, Jacob is understood as the name for either the Northern Kingdom (Mays, *Amos*, p. 129) or the larger Israel embracing Judah (Andersen and Freedman, *Amos*, p. 631).

42. James Limburg, 'Amos 7.4: A Judgment with Fire?', *CBQ* 35 (1973), pp. 346-49.

43. Patrick D. Miller, Jr, 'Fire in the Mythology of Canaan and Israel', *CBQ* 27 (1965), pp. 256-61.

(6.1b). The reason for the desolation of Judah's shrines is tied to the destruction of Israel's sanctuaries: in conducting their worship the ruling classes of both nations have perverted justice (6.12-13).

The whole story moves towards 'the house of Jeroboam' as indicated by the names of foreign rulers, Hazael and Benhadad, the royal house of Damascus (1.3-4), the exile of Samaria's upper classes (4.1-3), 'the house of Israel' or the northern monarchy (5.1), and the references to 'David' and 'the king' (6.5; 7.1). The naming and rejection of Syrian kings antici-pate the naming and rejection of King Jeroboam and his dynasty (1.4; 7.9). David, the first king of Jerusalem, anticipates Jeroboam, the first king of Samaria.

Vision 4 ends solemnly with wails being heard on the day of Yahweh (8.1-3a). Viewed together with 'the king' and 'Jeroboam', היכל identifies the palace as the location where singing turns into mourning (7.1, 9; 8.3a). But the wider context of Amos's text indicates that feasts take place in God's house, either the temple or some shrine (2.8; 4.4-5; 5.4-5, 21-24; 6.1, 4-6). Within the last poem היכל has the *double entendre* of temple and palace, embracing high places and sanctuaries, kingship and dynasty (7.1, 9).

The fourth vision derives its full meaning from the preceding poems. The verb קום 'to rise'/'to stand' recalls Israel's lament which is matched by Judah's dirge (7.2, 4; 8.3a; 5.1-2). The dirge over the death of the woman Israel develops into community songs of lamentation over the des-truction of the whole people Israel (5.1-2; 8.1-3a). The vision of harvest completes the thought of Poem 1; a full cart ready to topple over from the weight of grain is used metaphorically to describe Yahweh's crushing force in toppling Israel. Harvest imagery signifies war, and the combined imagery comes together to convey a sudden and complete end to the people Israel (2.13; 7.4-5, 7-9; 8.1-3a).

The wordplay on קיץ 'summer fruit' and קץ 'end' marks the climax of the last poem: Amos sees the end of his people Israel (8.1-3a).[44] This pun forms an inclusion with yet another sound-play on the words תקוע 'Tekoa' and תקע 'blow a trumpet', which vividly sums up the whole point of Amos's poetry. Metaphorically, Amos from Tekoa is the trumpet which heralds the doom of the nation (1.1a, 3.6).

Amos's visions correspond with his speeches against the nations.[45] With

---

44. Al Wolters, 'Wordplay and Dialect in Amos 8.1-2', *JETS* 31 (1988), pp. 407-10.

45. Jörg Jeremias, 'Völkersprüche und Visionsberichte im Amosbuch', in Volkmar

respect to formal similarities, the four visions and four proclamations against the nations are structured in sequential pairs. The introductory formula to each vision כה הראני יהוה is balanced by אמר אדני יהוה in the same way that the messenger formula כה אמר יהוה and the concluding phrase אמר יהוה frame the oracles against the nations. The phrase נאם־יהוה marks both the conclusion of Yahweh's speech against Israel and his announcement of doom on all his people (2.16; 8.3a).[46] It is a formal clue that the visions and proclamations must be understood in light of one another. The recurring words of Yahweh, 'I will not take it back' (1.3a, 6a, 13a; 2.1a, 6a), are matched by his promise, 'I will never again pass by it' (7.8b; 8.2b). Both statements are expressed in the negative with a third person masculine suffix, and the emphasis is on the irrevocability of God's word.

The two rhetorical series point in a predictable direction but suddenly reverse to the unpredictable ending that defeats all expectations. The repetitive pattern of the oracles leads us to expect judgment on the nations, but it is suddenly reversed onto the nation Israel. The repeated pattern of the visions leads us to expect intercession and repentance, but Yahweh finally announces Judah's demise.[47] The oracles and visions mention kingship, dynasty, worship, war and the day of Yahweh, and these common themes unite the beginning and end of the composition.

As the composition winds down to a close, we are returned to the familiar injunction, 'Hear this', and to a summation of the nation's offences (8.4-6; 5.11-12; 2.6b-7a). The people confess to the crime, 'we buy the needy for silver and the poor for a pair of sandals' (8.6). The situation of the first poem is now made explicit. Dishonest merchants are condemned for buying and selling the poor (מכר 2.6; קנה 8.6), and these crimes are detailed as extortion and fraud.[48] A small measure is used to fix the price

Fritz, Karl- Friedrich Pohlmann and Hans-Christoph Schmitt (eds.), *Prophet und Prophetenbuch: Festschrift für Otto Kaiser zum 65. Geburtstag* (Berlin: Walter de Gruyter, 1989), pp. 82-97.

46. The notation is redundant, according to some scholars: Niditch, *Symbolic Vision*, pp. 34-36; Landy, 'Vision and Poetic Speech in Amos', p. 231; Wolff, *Amos*, p. 317.

47. On intercession in Amos and the prophets, see Edmond Jacob, 'Prophètes et Intercesseurs', in M. Carrez, J. Doré and P. Grelot (eds.), *De la Tôrah au Messie: études d'exégèse et d'herméneutique bibliques offertes à Henri Cazelles pour ses 25 années d'enseignement à l'Institut Catholique de Paris*, October 1979 (Paris: Desclée, 1981), pp. 205-17.

48. See also Hartmut Gese, 'Amos 8.4-8: Der kosmische Frevel händlischer

of the wheat the merchants sell to the poor but a heavy weight determines the amount of silver to be paid by the purchaser (8.5). Economic exploitation of the poor has already been touched on, but the last poem reports precisely how the wealthy get rich at the expense of others.[49]

Using the rhetorical technique of direct citation (4.1; 6.13), Amos quotes the cunning merchants: 'When will the new moon be over and the sabbath so that we may offer wheat for sale?' (עבר 8.5). The festival of the new moon occurs on the first day of the lunar month and is filled with 'songs of the temple' and cultic celebration (8.3a; 2.8; 4.1; 4.4-5; 5.21-24; 6.4-6).[50] Yahweh swears twice, 'I will never again pass by him' (עבר לו 8.2b; 7.8b). Just as the new moon passes through its equinox, God is expected to pass by his people or be present at their feasts. The merchants eagerly wait for the sabbath and festival days to be over, believing that they will gain greater prosperity through wheeling and dealing. The irony is that festival time has ended and is the tragic reversal of all expectations: God will no longer appear but has fated his people to a day of adversity and lamentation (8.1-3a, 9-10).

The punishment of Judah's crimes occurs 'on that day' (ביום ההוא 8.9; 2.16). Imagery of light and darkness (אור...חשך 5.18-20) is joined with God's promise of darkening the bright light of the noonday sun into night. The day of Yahweh coincides with the end of religious festivals, and his day, contrary to all expectations, is marked not by festive rejoicing but by songs of mourning for the dead (8.10a). The lament is linked with Vision 4, and חגיכם 'your festivals' and שיריכם 'your songs' refer to the immediate context (שירות היכל 'songs of the temple' 8.3a) and also to the distant context (חגיכם 5.21; שריך 5.23; כל־שיר 6.5). A dirge over the death of the woman Israel anticipates the lament over the fall of Judah (קינה 5.1; 8.10). The bitterness of the day is comparable to 'the mourning for an only child', and Amos's prophecy ends on this tragic note (8.10b).

Amos wrote seven separate but related poems. Each poem is complete

---

Habiger', in Fritz, Pohlmann and Schmitt (eds.), *Prophet und Prophetenbuch* pp. 59-72.

49. Amos addresses economic injustices and trade infractions, connecting them to practices at worship centres: Edward F. Campbell, 'Archaeological Reflections on Amos's Targets', in Michael D. Coogan, J. Cheryl Exum and Lawrence E. Stager (eds.), *Scripture and Other Artifacts: Essays on the Bible and Archaeology in Honor of Philip J. King* (Louisville, KY: Westminster/John Knox Press, 1994), pp. 32-52.

50. Timo Veijola, 'Die Propheten und das Alter des Sabbatgebots', in Fritz, Pohlmann and Schmitt (eds.), *Prophet und Prophetenbuch*, pp. 246-64.

in itself, but each poem is crucial to the totality. The integrity of each poem is its impetus towards a climactic or surprise ending, but each is part of the whole and contributes to an ongoing narrative. The poems are different, but individual topics flow into a great theme uniting all we have heard or read. The linking issue is the day of Yahweh and the fall of the nation, and all the poems express it, directly or indirectly. The subsequent chapters build on this preliminary evidence of a whole composition and demonstrate it from a variety of perspectives.

Chapter 2

Writing and Editing in Amos

The editor of Amos has the task of transmitting the written prophecy. Thus the received text is preserved intact, updated and made useful and relevant to a different historical era. The best argument that Amos is a written text is the evidence of an anonymous person who saw that the seven poems belonged together as a unity but changed the structure to give the text new meaning and application. Amos's composition is not relegated to the past but is made relevant to the present by reworking and transforming its content. The editorial version shows how written tradition is developed and reflects the growth in understanding of Amos's prophecy over the course of time. The reviser, by handing on the whole composition, explains what it originally meant. Conversely, new ideas and argumentation are incorporated into Amos's prophecy in order to explain what his text means to a later age. Since people are naturally inclined to have different views about what a text might mean, it is reasonable to suppose that the book partially represents and partially refutes contemporary thinking about the work of the prophet.

The reviser is not simply an editor but an author who totally rewrites the original text by integrating it into a new system of interpretation. The author of the book converts Amos's seven poems into ten parts, adding to each part a commentary which separates one poem from another.

The seventh poem is divided into two parts, and two final parts summarize the distinctive viewpoint of the book. The revision destroys the original connection between the poems but reconnects them with a commentary that develops an independent or contradictory line of argument. In each part the reviser comments on the preceding Amos text to which it is attached and develops the argument of the book.

The editorial version is not a separate composition but a running commentary on Amos's poetry. The reviser reorganizes the poems by continually combining and interweaving them with commentary. The argument of the commentary is inserted piecemeal and is distributed over the prophet's seven poems. The way in which the text and the commentary are combined makes it look as though the book is a collection of independent prophetic words interspersed with random additions from one or more editors. Editorial comments are added to correct some statement of Amos; however, they are not isolated additions but pointers to the interpretative commentary at the end of each part. Every addition has a context and contributes to the development of the book's argument. By relating the various sections of the running commentary we discover that the reviser is continually building up a consistent secondary argument that stands in tension with or opposition to the original version.

Understanding the additions as simply the work of an editor does not do justice to the literary contribution of the reviser. The fact that whole sections of interpretation are added to produce a cumulative argument can only mean that the editor is an author. The various parts consist of a fairly even distribution of text and commentary. Part 1 (chs. 1–2) contains substantially more Amos text, but this is offset by Parts 9 and 10 (9.1-6; 9.7-15) in which the reviser brings the argument of the book to a resounding conclusion.

The author of the book develops written tradition by means of the editorial process of literal or deictic repetition, quotation, and cross-referencing.[1] Deictic repetition consists in the use of adverbial or pronominal elements that loosely attach commentary to the preceding Amos text. With this type of repetition the additions are easily detected and stand out from the surrounding context. Another way in which commentary is inserted is through the literal repetition of a few words or whole phrases from the preceding and following Amos text. With this type of repetition the additions are so carefully blended into the original context that it becomes difficult to distinguish text from commentary. Nonetheless the insertions are marked by using the prophet's words in a different or opposite order and employing quotations in a different or contradictory sense. The third type of repetition is cross-referencing which links and relates all the comments and interpretations of the revision. Cross-references signal additions and enable readers to follow the developing argument of the secondary text.

---

1. For a discussion of the signs of editing in historical and prophetic books, see Brian Peckham, 'Writing and Editing', in Astrid B. Beck, Andrew H. Bartelt, Paul R. Raabe and Chris A. Franke (eds.), *Fortunate the Eyes that See: Essays in Honor of David Noel Freedman in Celebration of his Seventieth Birthday* (Grand Rapids, MI: William B. Eerdmans, 1995), pp. 364-83.

These three types of repetition make possible a total rewriting and re-vamping of the original text. Repetition is the means by which the reviser gives coherence and unity to the book. Despite the different viewpoints expressed by the two authors, repetition smoothes out the whole text into a single continuous or unified message. Repetition draws attention away from the primary to the secondary argument and makes the revision the principal thought of the book.

What follows is an analysis of the ten parts of the book. The reader will see how the secondary passages are fitted into the original, how quotations change the initial argument, how cross-referencing anticipates and advances the secondary argument, and how this continual interplay of quotation and cross-referencing creates a whole subtext.

Part 1 (1.1–2.16)

The reviser expands on the original title (1.1a) by writing a duplicate relative clause (1.1b) and a motto (1.2). Three more nations are added (1.9-10, 11-12; 2.4-5), and a historical summary is inserted (2.9-12). These additions introduce new themes or content and alter the structure and meaning of the original prophecy.

The original heading, identifying Amos as a shepherd of Tekoa (1.1a), is expanded by repeating אשר. The editorial clause אשר חזה ('which he saw…') imitates the original one אשר היה ('who was…'), but identifies 'the words of Amos's as the subject, indicating that he saw his own words. The editorial clause alludes to Amos's visions, but חזה replaces the prophet's ראה (7.1a, 4a, 7a; 8.1a). The new title makes Amos's words a part of his visions, and anticipates his being called חזה 'seer' by the book (7.12a).

The prophecy of Amos is undated, but its relative dating in the seventh century is decided by the contents of his poetry. The editorial title, however, provides a precise dating for the prophet, in the reigns of Uzziah, king of Judah, and Jeroboam, king of Israel, and the exact date of his prophecy, 'two years before the earthquake' (1.1b).[2] Thus scholars, in regarding the book's title as historically sound, situate Amos in the eighth century and during the reign of Jeroboam II. However, the title cannot be

---

2. Earthquake evidence dating to the eighth century is consistent with Amos 1.1b and summarized by William G. Dever, 'A Case-Study in Biblical Archaeology: The Earthquake of ca. 760 BCE', *Eretz Israel* 23 (1992), pp. 27-35.

considered a decisive argument for faithful historical dating but provides 'a built-in interpretive key' for the book.[3]

So the book's superscription anticipates its story about Amos's journey to Bethel to denounce King Jeroboam (7.10-17). Amos's seeing the words concerning Israel (1.1b) is a proleptic marker to the book's interpretation of his visions (7.1–9.4). Amos reported what God showed him about the destiny of Judah (7.1-3, 4-6, 7-9; 8.1-3a). By contrast the reviser's title presents Amos as a prophet to both kingdoms and anticipates the book's shift in focus from Judah to Israel, emphasizing that he predicted the actual fall of the North. From the outset the book specifies that Amos spoke God's word against Israel and relegates his speech against the nations and Judah to a subordinate position. The editorial heading distinguishes between Israel and Judah, in contrast to Amos himself, who referred to Israel and Jacob, or included both North and South in the phrases 'the children of Israel' (3.1a) and 'my people Israel' (8.2b). The distinction of the two kingdoms anticipates the book's diatribe against Judah (2.4-5) to match Amos's diatribe against Israel (2.6-8). This pairing of Israel and Judah occurs throughout the book (2.4-5, 6-8; 3.12-13; 6.8, 14; 7.9, 10-12, 16; 9.8, 11).

The motto, 'Yahweh roars from Zion/he utters his voice from Jerusalem' (1.2), is not a random saying or hymnic addition[4] but summarizes the perspective of the new version. The reviser links the motto to the heading (1.1b) by ויאמר and interprets Amos as speaking his words at the urging of Yahweh who dwelt in Zion and Jerusalem. The idea of the prophet as God's spokesman is a *leitmotif* of the book and reaches its climax in the confrontation at Bethel (7.10-17).

Specifically, the motto depicts Yahweh as a roaring lion (ישאג) who utters his voice (יתן קולו). The metaphor anticipates and reinterprets the lion motif in Amos's riddle by using its language (3.3-6): 'Does the lion roar? (הישאג אריה). Does the young lion raise his voice?' (היתן כפיר קולו).

3.   The assumption that titles of prophetic books are claims of actual history has preordained the results of scholarly inquiry: see Ehud ben Zvi, 'Studying Prophetic Texts against their Original Backgrounds: Pre-Ordained Scripts and Alternative Horizons of Research', in Reid (ed.), *Prophets and Paradigms*, pp. 125-35.

4.   Cf. C. van Leeuwen, 'Amos 1.2, épigraphe du livre entier ou introduction aux oracles des chapitres 1–2?', in M. Boertien and Aleida G. van Daalen (eds.), *Verkenningen in een Stroomgebied: Proeven van oudtestamentisch Onderzoek (Festschrift M.A. Beck)* (Amsterdam: Theologisch Instituut van de Universiteit van Amsterdam, 1974), pp. 93-101.

Yahweh's roaring alludes to prophecy, and prophetic inspiration is taken up as a sign of prophecy (3.7-8).

The motto introduces the arguments of the book: it introduces shepherds and their pastures (נאות הרעים 1.2), in line with Amos who calls himself a shepherd (נקד 1.1a); it anticipates that Yahweh took him from following the flock (7.15a); its reference to Zion and Jerusalem prepares for the diatribe against Judah and Jerusalem (2.4-5) as well as Amos's prophecy concerning Zion (6.1-7) and its interpretation (6.8-14). That God's voice produces dire consequences in nature is a prolepsis of hymnic passages in the book (4.13; 5.8-9; 9.5-6) which celebrate his sovereignty over the universe: the report that his voice causes the pastures to mourn and Carmel to wither anticipates the developing commentary (4.7-8; 8.7-8; 11-14).

The shorter pronouncements against Tyre (1.9-10), Edom (1.11-12) and Judah (2.4-5) are the book's insertions.[5] They reiterate Amos's formulae but deviate in structure from his judgments. So the crime is expanded by combining the infinitive with one (1.9) or more finite verbal clauses (1.11; 2.4); the announcement of Yahweh's punishment is shortened to the general formula of a divine fire consuming the enemy, and the final phrase, 'says Yahweh', is omitted. These structural differences mark a significant change in emphasis from the punishment to the crime.[6]

The definite structural deviations and new subject matter of the Tyre–Edom–Judah indictments change the meaning of the original proclamations. The commentator, in describing Tyre's first offence, imitates Amos's charge against the Philistines by partially quoting and mixing up the order of his words (על־הגלותם גלות שלמה להסגיר לאדום 'because they exiled an entire people, to deliver [them] up to Edom' 1.6b = על־הסגירם גלות שלמה לאדום 'because they delivered up an entire people to Edom' 1.9b). But the book links Tyre's crime of deportation with a second crime of violating 'the covenant of brotherhood' or treaty pact between nations.

The breach of brotherhood is also the indictment against Edom (1.11b), but the reviser replaces Amos's imagery of deportation with his language

---

5. Arguments in favour of the insertion of these three proclamations are stronger than those for the original unity of 1.3–2.16. See summary of the arguments in James Nogalski, *Literary Precursors to the Book of the Twelve* (BZAW, 217; Berlin: Walter de Gruyter, 1993), pp. 89-97.

6. Deviation in form and content implies different authors and theological views: see Werner H. Schmidt, 'Die deuteronomistische Redaktion des Amosbuches: Zu den theologischen Unterschieden zwischen dem Prophetenwort und seinem Sammler', *ZAW* 77 (1965), pp. 168-93.

of combat. Citing a weapon Amos never mentioned, the commentator accuses Edom of pursuing his brother with the sword. The reviser reproduces a list of Edom's four crimes to mirror Amos's list of Israel's four crimes (2.6-8). The commentator also adopts Amos's procedure of balancing one crime against the other. So Edom's pursuit of his brother in order to kill him leads into the second crime that Edom 'destroyed' (שחת) his mercy (רחמיו).[7] Just as Tyre failed to remember a pact between brothers, Edom too destroyed his own compassion by disregarding the obligations expected of a treaty partner.[8] Anticipating Amos's reference to the lion and his prey (3.4), the reviser employs the verb 'to tear apart' (טרף) to describe Edom's third crime of venting his anger continuously (ויטרף לעד אפו lit. 'and he tore his anger perpetually'). This accusation is balanced by the fourth charge which expresses the relentless fury of Edom (lit. 'and he retained his rage forever').

The reviser's list of multiple crimes contrasts with Amos's citation of one crime for each nation. For Amos the numerical sequence, 'for three and four', suggested an unlimited number of transgressions,[9] but the book interprets it as a definite number of offences.[10] Thus the commentator literally accepts 'for three transgressions and for four' by listing four crimes of Edom and three crimes of Judah.

Judah's first and second crimes are thematically linked. Judah is accused of rejecting the תורה of Yahweh and deserting his statutes. Employing שמר as the verbal link between 1.11b and 2.4b, the reviser contrasts Edom who kept his wrath burning with Judah who did not keep Yahweh's statutes. The commentator partially constructs Judah's third crime from

---

7.   M.L. Barré, 'Amos 1.11 Reconsidered', *CBQ* 47 (1985), pp. 420-27.

8.   The traditional reading 'his compassion' fits other abstract terms (אפו 'his anger'; עברתו 'his wrath') which explain what happens when a nation shows no mercy for another (1.11b). Cf. Michael Fishbane, 'The Treaty Background of Amos 1, 11 and Related Matters', *JBL* 89 (1970), pp. 313-18; 'Additional Remarks on RHMYW Amos 1,11', *JBL* 91 (1972), pp. 391-93; Robert B. Coote, 'Amos 1:11: RHMYW', *JBL* 90 (1971), pp. 206-208. Cf. Paul Noble, 'Israel among the Nations', *HBT* 15 (1993), pp. 56-82.

9.   It has been argued that a numerical sequence in which the second number is one unit higher than the first number refers to an indefinite total (GKC, no.134 r, p. 437). But the ascending order might mean countless transgressions, as in the modern idioms 'for lots and lots', 'for more and more': cf. Soggin's non-literal translation, 'because of the innumerable crimes of X' (*The Prophet Amos*, pp. 32-46).

10.   W.M.W. Roth, 'The Numerical Sequence x/x+1 in the Old Testament', *VT* 12 (1962), pp. 300-11 (301-304).

the language used by Amos to describe Israel's third crime. The reviser comments on Amos's report of a man and his father going to the same maiden by adding the interpretation that the people of Judah imitated their fathers by going after (הלך אחר) or following lies.

The reviser integrates two different thought-patterns into a continuous argument that flows from one proclamation to another. The commentator uses Amos's language to blend distinct versions into a single unified text. In smoothing out and homogenizing the text, the reviser copies Amos's procedure of linking units contiguous to one another by means of similar catchwords or phrases.[11] Thus the words Amos used to describe Philistia's crime (גלות שלמה להסגיר '...a whole band of exiles to deliver up', 1.6b) are repeated in the charge against Tyre (על־הסגירם גלות שלמה 'because they delivered up a whole band of exiles', 1.9b); אב 'father' and הלך 'to go/walk' are repeated to link Judah and Israel; and אחיו/אחים 'brothers'/ 'his brother' are repeated to connect the commentary on Tyre and Edom.

Just as Amos did not give a precise verbal linkage between Ammon and Philistia, so the reviser provides no exact word or phrase to tie Edom and Ammon together. Nonetheless, the book unites Edom and Ammon by imitating Amos's penchant for wordplays. The consonants of the hiphil infinitive 'construct' הרחיב (1.13b) are reversed to create בחרב 'with the sword' (1.11b), a similar sound but different meaning: the play on הרחיב and בחרב (1.11, 13) suggests that Ammon's border was enlarged by use of the sword.

The reviser replaces the original shift from the nations' crimes to Israel's domestic crimes by a movement in thought from international customary law governing human relations to divine law dictating the conduct of Judah. The commentator, by inserting Judah before Israel, makes Judah the climax of the prophet's diatribe against the nations and interprets Israel's oppressive acts as their rejection of the law of Yahweh. Amos argued that miscarriages of justice profane God's name, but the book argues that disrespect for his name means that Israel and Judah have rejected the law.

---

11. The coherent and systematic ordering of Amos 1–2 is used as evidence for the basic unity and originality of the whole text: Shalom M. Paul, 'Amos 1.3–2.3: A Concatenous Literary Pattern', *JBL* 90 (1971), 397-403; *idem*, 'A Literary Reinvestigation of the Authenticity of the Oracles against the Nations of Amos', in Carrez, Doré and Grelot (eds.), *De la Tôrah au Messie*, pp. 189-204; Andrew E. Steinmann, 'The Order of Amos's Oracles against the Nations', *JBL* 3 (1992), pp. 683-89.

The first person pronoun is a deictic that attaches 2.9-12 loosely to Amos's text (2.6-8). The book contrasts Israel's evil deeds and God's good acts and develops the point with God's direct address to Israel. The historical summary (2.9-11) fragments the recurrent pattern of crimes and punishment. It separates Israel's crimes (2.6-8) from Israel's defeat in battle (2.13-16) and sends the thought off on a tangent. The intrusive retrospect recalls Yahweh's saving acts, the Exodus, the guidance through the wilderness, the possession of the land, and the sending of the Nazirites and the prophets. Then the commentator returns to what Amos said before the insertion (2.8). A grievous crime for Amos was the practice of drinking in the temple the wine of those who are fined (2.8b). The commentator partially repeats the words of Amos but gives them new application by accusing the people of making the Nazirites drink wine (2.8b = 2.12a).

The insertion at 2.9-12 alters the shape of the original indictment against Israel (2.6-8) and submerges the thought of Amos. The crimes are arranged in an order of increasing importance so that they culminate with the spurning of the prophets (2.12b).[12] To emphasize the crime of rejecting the prophets (2.11), the reviser places it just before the punishment (2.13-16). Amos cited exploitation of the innocent poor as the reason for divine judgment, but the book specifies disregard of Yahweh's word. The proliferation of the crimes and Yahweh's saving acts have the dual purpose of compounding the guilt of 'the children of Israel' and affirming the inherent goodness of Yahweh.

Part 2 (3.1-15)

The commentary is interwoven with Amos's second poem to produce Part 2 (3.1-15). So the reviser adds the perfect editorial comment, 'against the whole family which I brought up out of the land of Egypt' (3.1b), to Amos's introductory statement (3.1a). The book repeats the language of Amos, namely the preposition עַל 'against' (3.1aB) and the noun מִשְׁפָּחָה 'family' (3.2a), and cross-references its own text by reiterating the reference to the Exodus (3.1b = 2.10).

Editorial techniques of quotation and cross-referencing are employed to create a duplicate statement that provides a different context and meaning for Amos's words. The book makes explicit what is implicit in Amos: that בְּנֵי יִשְׂרָאֵל (lit. 'sons of Israel') is the family of Jacob's twelve sons whom

12. So also Coote, *Amos among the Prophets*, p. 70; Andersen and Freedman, *Amos*, p. 331.

Yahweh brought out of Egypt. For Amos the phrase כל משפחות ('all the families') referred to all nations of the earth (3.2a), but for the reviser כל־המשפח ('the whole family' 3.1b) alludes to all the clans of the North and South. Amos made Israel's special status among the nations (3.2a) the reason for Yahweh's punishment (3.2b). The reviser expands on the idea of Israel's election by appealing to Yahweh's guidance from Egypt, but establishes the Exodus as the ground for punishment. The addition at 3.1b has the same function as the historical summary at 2.9-12. By detailing Yahweh's saving acts the book intensifies the guilt of Israel and Judah.

In 3.7-8[13] the book's topic of prophecy intrudes upon Amos's continuous text. It interrupts Amos's sequence of thought, which moves from disaster in a city (3.6b) to evidence against Samaria (3.9-10) and to a word of doom against the nation's capital city (3.11). The reviser quotes Amos in order editorially to link and correct his prophecy.[14] Amos's last three words in 3.6 (ויהוה לא עשׂה 'Yahweh has not done it') are repeated in 3.7 (כי לא יעשׂה...יהוה דבר 'surely Yahweh does not a thing'). His image of a roaring lion is given a new context, and the words are cited in reverse order. (הישׁאג אריה 3.4a = אריה שׁאג 3.8a). His term חרד ('to tremble/be startled' 3.6b) is replaced by ירא ('to fear/be afraid' 3.8a). But the quotations are used in a different or opposite sense in order to change the meaning of Amos's imagery. So Yahweh who does evil in a city (3.6b) is replaced by Yahweh who does not act without disclosing his secret to a prophet (3.7b).[15] The lion's roar (3.8a) is substituted for the trumpet blast (3.6) as the source of the people's fear. The roar of Amos's lion (3.4) is extended to God's speech (3.8b): the lion is no longer a simple beast of prey but Yahweh himself, and his roar is a sign of prophecy (3.8b).

Imitating the prophet's style of raising questions, the reviser proceeds

---

13. Scholars recognize that Amos 3.7 disrupts its context, but they think it is a random addition and not part of a connected commentary that revises Amos's prophecy: A. Graeme Auld, *Amos* (OTG; Sheffield: JSOT Press, 1986), pp. 30-32. Usually they identify 3.8 as the original conclusion of 3.3-6 (Wolff, *Amos*, p. 182; Mays, *Amos*, p. 62; Rudolph, Joel–*Amos*, p. 154).

14. Bernard Renaud ('Genèse et Théologie d'Amos 3, 3-8,' in A. Caquot and M. Delcor (eds.), *Mélanges bibliques et orientaux en l'honneur de M. Henri Cazelles* [AOAT, 212; Neukirchen–Vluyn: Neukirchener Verlag, 1981], pp. 353-72) observes that a second author knows perfectly the prophet's procedures of composition.

15. For the wider biblical context of Amos 3.7 (e.g. Dan. 2.2), see A. Graeme Auld, 'Amos and Apocalyptic: Vision, Prophecy, Revelation', in Garrone and Israel (eds.), *Storia e Tradizioni di Israele*, pp. 1-13.

from what is obvious (3.8a) to what is difficult to accept (3.8b). After gaining momentum by the reader's negative reaction to seven questions (3.3-6), the reviser asserts: 'The lion has roared; who will not be afraid? Yahweh...has spoken; who will not prophesy?' The sheer weight of the questions evokes the response, 'No one!' By adding more questions, the commentator skilfully establishes the authenticity and credibility of Amos's word as the climactic question of the series. Thus Amos's line of argument is subsumed under a theory of divine and prophetic speech. Amos asserted that Yahweh is the cause of disaster in a city and the agent of Samaria's destruction (3.6b). However, the reviser contends that the prophet has the authority to speak the divine word (3.7-8). By using the recurrent formulae, 'thus says Yahweh' (3.11) and 'says Yahweh' (2.16; 3.10), Amos identified himself as messenger of God, but the book describes Amos as a prophet who is compelled to pass on the word God has spoken to him (3.8b).

The reviser duplicates Amos's prophecy of Samaria's destruction (3.11) to add an interpretative commentary (3.12) which draws on his language: 'the children of Israel', 'the lion's roar', 'Thus says the Lord Yahweh' (3.1a, 4, 11). The nouns מטה/ערש 'couch' or 'bed' (3.12) are employed in anticipation of Amos's usage of these words to describe the luxury of upper classes (6.4), and the term דמשק (3.12b) is a pun on דמשק 'Damascus' (1.3a).[16] The book confirms Amos's prophecy about Samaria (3.11) and stresses the thoroughness of its devastation: the people of Samaria survive only as 'scraps' after the catastrophe. They are like pieces of a mutilated animal left by the lion, or like fragments of furniture that are salvaged from the ruined city.

Peculiar to the revision, however, is the idea of rescue, used in both its hiphil and niphal forms (נצל/הציל 3.12), to give new meaning to Amos's picture of total defeat. The reviser agrees with Amos that the Northern

---

16. The reading of ובדמשק as two words ובד משק 'and a part from a leg' (בד 'a part', שק 'a leg') fits a context in which the legs of an animal and pieces of its ear are mentioned: see Isaac Rabinowitz, 'The Crux at Amos III 12', *VT* 11 (1961), pp. 228-231. Making equally good sense is the elliptical rendering, 'and (those who dwell) in Damascus (by the corner of) a bed', but it presupposes that the MT changed the consonant ש to שׂ and added faulty vowels. If the difficult MT reading ובדמשק is retained, the term may refer to a cushion or covering on a couch: Carl Friedrich Keil, *Biblical Commentary on the Old Testament*. I. The Twelve Minor Prophets (trans. James Martin; Grand Rapids, MI: William B. Eerdmans, 1954), p. 264; Harper, *Amos*, pp. 81-82.

Kingdom of Samaria has been destroyed.[17] But the book, by couching the theme of destruction in the language of rescue, offers a glimmer of hope. Picking up on Amos's pastoral allusion (1.1a), the reviser uses a pastoral simile, both to explain the catastrophe (3.11) and to introduce the idea of survival. Just as the shepherd rescues a few scraps from the mouth of the lion, so will 'the children of Israel' who dwell in Samaria be rescued (3.12). The lion does not totally devour its victim nor does Yahweh bring total destruction.

The book's idea that a few persons might survive is developed in the following verses (3.13-15). So it repeats Amos's words, 'on the day I punish the crimes of Israel' (ביום 3.14a = ביום־ההוא 'on that day', 2.16; פקד 2× in 3.14 = 3.2b; פשעי־ישראל 3.14a = פשעי ישראל 2.6), but then limits the punishment to the altars of Bethel (3.14b) and to the few in Israel who inhabit separate winter and summer houses,[18] the houses of ivory and the 'great' houses (3.15).[19] The book introduces the topic of the Bethel altars in anticipation of Amos's discussion about worship at Bethel (4.4-5).

The commentary at 3.13-15 is constructed out of Amos's words, but it develops a different line of argumentation. Amos commanded 'the children of Israel' to listen to the word of Yahweh (3.1a). The reviser repeats the summons, שמעו 'Hear' (3.13a = 3.1a), but gives it a different context. Amos called on Ashdod to witness (ראה) the violence and oppression within Samaria (3.9), but the reviser alters the appeal by summoning both Ashdod and Egypt to listen (שמעו) and testify (והעידו) against 'the house of Jacob' (3.13a). The reviser stresses that Amos spoke the word of Yahweh: נאם־אדני יהוה 'says the Lord Yahweh' (3.13b) is a conflation of Amos's words (3.10b, 11a),[20] but the book's naming of Yahweh as אלהי הצבאות 'the God of hosts' (3.13) introduces the idea of divine sovereignty (4.13; 5.8-9, 25-27; 9.5-6).[21]

---

17. Gerhard Pfeifer, '"Rettung" ' als Beweis der Vernichtung (Amos 3,12)', *ZAW* 100 (1988 Supplement), pp. 269-77.

18. Cf. Jer. 36.22; Shalom M. Paul, 'Amos III 15—Winter and Summer Mansions', *VT* 28 (1978), pp. 358-60.

19. The reviser's source seems to be Isa. 5.9 where 'many houses' (בתים רבים) refers to large and splendid houses of the wealthy. Cf. George S. Glanzman, 'Two Notes: Am 3,15 and Os 11, 8-9', *CBQ* 23 (1961), pp. 227-29.

20. Paul R. Noble, 'The Function of *n'm Yhwh* in Amos', *ZAW* 108 (1996), pp. 623-26.

21. Stephen Dempster, 'The Lord is His Name: A Study of the Distribution of the Names and Titles of God in the Book of Amos', *RB* 98 (1991), pp. 170-89.

The reviser ends Part 2 (3.13-15), as Amos ended his first poem (2.13-16), with a vision of destruction and ruin. While the verb אבד is used by Amos to describe Israel's warriors perishing in war (2.14), the reviser repeats אבד to portray the ruin of Israel's luxurious houses (3.15). The book's reference to pieces of furniture (3.12b) anticipates the demolition of houses, and its association of ivory with houses (3.15) is proleptic of Amos's beds of ivory (6.4).

Inclusion is a compositional technique used to edit the work of Amos and to divert attention from his argument. In marking off 3.8 as the conclusion of the unit beginning in 3.1, the reviser repeats Amos's declaration that Yahweh has spoken but adds that God's words necessitate prophetic speech. The creation of a new literary unit in 3.1-8 severs the original connection between 3.3-6 and its sequel in 3.9-11. Another inclusion is fashioned so that Part 2 begins in 3.1 and ends in 3.15. So the reviser repeats Amos's key words, שמעו 'hear', פקד (אפקד 'I will punish' 3.2b = פקדי 'my punishing' and ופקדתי 'and I will punish', 3.14), but quotations are used in a contrary sense. They change the idea of Yahweh's indiscriminate punishment of the children of Israel for their iniquities (3.2) by restricting punishment to worshippers at the altars of Bethel and to those prosperous ruling classes who occupied the impressive winter and summer residences in Samaria. The inclusion is also formed by repeating words that simply blend the revision into the original without altering its meaning. So the commentator reapplies Amos's language of trapping birds to a different context (התפל צפור על־פח הארץ 'Does a bird fall in a trap on the ground?', 3.5a; ונגדעו קרנות המזבח ונפלו לארץ 'and the horns of the altar shall be cut off and fall to the ground', 3.14b).

The end of Part 2 makes explicit what is only implicit at its beginning. The allusion to the whole family which Yahweh brought out of Egypt (3.1b) anticipates the reviser's cross-reference to 'the house of Jacob' (3.13a). According to the book, Yahweh has spoken against all the clans (3.1b) and they are identified separately as 'the children of Israel who dwell in Samaria' (3.12) and 'the house of Jacob' (3.13a). This pairing anticipates or cross-references the later association of 'Jacob' (6.8) with 'the house of Israel' (6.14) and the association of 'the house of Jacob' (9.8b) with 'the house of Israel' (9.9a).

The consequence of using inclusion as an editorial device is that the internal insertion (3.7-8) and the concluding addition (3.13-15) seem to relate harmoniously to the words of Amos (3.1-6).[22] The inclusion created by repetition allows the commentator to assimilate two different interpretations and at the same time give heightened emphasis and priority to the ideas of the book. Repetition by inclusion helps to smooth out the text and make it flow as a single unified argument.

Cross-referencing also homogenizes the text and harmonizes the two different interpretations or relates separate comments and interpretation by prolepsis and resumption. Proleptic references reinterpret the original version and anticipate the ongoing commentary of the book. So the reviser's preemptive phrase, 'Yahweh roars from Zion' (1.2), corrects Amos's lion imagery (3.4) by identifying Yahweh as the lion who roars and Israel as his prey. According to the book, Yahweh says: 'I brought you out of the land of Egypt', and his words are duplicated in 3.1b. The Exodus theme is cross-referenced (2.10 = 3.1b) in anticipation of the book's story about Egypt who is summoned to observe Samaria's guilt (3.9a). The anticipatory insertion on the prophets (2.11-12) determines that the reader will understand Yahweh's disclosure of his word to the prophets (3.7-8) as the goal or climax of Amos's rhetorical series. The verb נבא 'to prophesy' (3.8b) cross-references what the commentator said earlier (2.12) and changes Amos's question from what Yahweh has done (3.6b) to what he has spoken (3.8b). So Yahweh's specific charge to the prophets, לא תנבאו 'You shall not prophesy' (2.12b) prepares us for Amos's response (3.8b). The book has Amos answer the prohibition: יהוה דבר מי לא ינבא 'Yahweh...has spoken; who can but prophesy?' Faced with being silenced, Amos appeals to God's speech as the driving force that obliges him to prophesy.

Part 3 (4.1-13)

The reviser produces Part 3 by adding the narrative of Yahweh's past deeds (4.6-13) to Amos's third poem (4.1-5). The disasters brought by Yahweh are enumerated in 4.6-11: famine (4.6), drought (4.7-8), crop blight and locusts (4.9), pestilence and war (4.10), overthrow or defeat (4.11). The calamities are catalogued in first person style, and second person plural direct address is sustained throughout. Each disaster begins with the announcement of what Yahweh did, each concludes with the refrain ולא־שבתם עדי 'but you did not return to me', and each contrast-

---

22. See Yehoshua Gitay, 'A Study of Amos's Art of Speech: A Rhetorical Analysis of Amos 3.1-15', *CBQ* 42 (1980), pp. 293-309.

statement, 'I... but you', ends with נאם־יהוה 'says Yahweh'.

The introductory לכן 'therefore' (4.12a) follows on from 4.6-11 because it draws the formal and logical conclusion from the content of these verses. The summary at 4.12 points backwards to the series of disasters described in 4.6-11. It contains deictic elements, כה 'thus' and זאת 'this', and these deictics point to the preceding context (4.6-11) without repeating it.[23] The imperfect אעשה expresses ongoing or repeated action of divine judgment in the past.[24] Thus the repetitive speech, כה אעשה־לך ישׂראל לכן 'therefore thus I regularly did to you, O Israel' and final kap אעשה־ל עקב כי־זאת 'because this I kept doing to you', stresses that God makes himself responsible for past disasters against Israel, and cites them as the motivation for his summons that Israel must prepare to confront him for resisting all previous opportunities to repent (4.12).[25] The introductory deictic phrase כי הנה 'for look' (4.13a) formally links 4.13 to 4.12: 4.13 fits its context by bringing the point of 4.12 to its logical conclusion. The past deeds of Yahweh are validated by the affirmation of his absolute authority over the universe and his unceasing activity as Creator (4.13): the reviser reiterates that Yahweh, the God of hosts, is the name (4.13; 3.13b) to which the deeds are ascribed (4.12b).

The editorial at 4.6-13 is loosely fitted to 4.1-5 by the deictic particle, וגם־אני (4.6a), which generally refers to the whole preceding context. The first person pronoun אני 'I' (4.6a) points back to the previous Amos text with its continuous reference to the name Yahweh (4.2a, 3b, 5b). The book emphasizes the deictic pronoun by quoting Amos's formula נאם אדני יהוה 'says the Lord Yahweh' (4.3b; 5.5b) at the end of each calamity (4.6b, 8b, 9b, 10b, 11b). In contrast to Part 2, no effort is made to integrate the

---

23. Deictic elements include demonstrative and personal pronouns, subjects with pronominal suffixes, proper names, vocatives and phrases such as 'on that day'. For a detailed discussion of deictic markers, see Michael Fishbane, *Biblical Interpretation in Ancient Israel* (Oxford: Clarendon Press, 1985), pp. 44-55, 80, 447-58, 512.

24. The first clause in 4.12 begins with a conjunction and the verb is first. In this type of clause the imperfect expresses ongoing action in the past. The second clause begins with a conjunction and the object is first. In this type of clause the imperfect expresses repeated or distributive action in the past: see Brian Peckham, 'Tense and Mood in Biblical Hebrew', *ZAH* 10 (1997), pp. 139-68 (145). Andersen and Freedman recognize that the deictics point backwards to what Yahweh has done (*Amos*, p. 450). Most scholars think that 'thus/'this' and the imperfect אעשה refer to future divine judgment (e.g. Mays, *Amos*, p. 78; Hayes, *Amos*, p. 148).

25. Cf. G.W. Ramsey, 'Amos 4, 12: A New Perspective', *JBL* 89 (1970), pp. 187-91; Ronald Youngblood, לקראת in Amos 4.12', *JBL* 90 (1971), p. 98.

editorial insertion of Part 3 (4.6-13) into Amos's poetry by repeating its language and changing its meaning. Apart from the recurrence of נאם יהוה and the number 3, there are no precise verbal connections between 4.1-5 and 4.6-13. However, the topics raised in the book (4.6-13) point back- wards to the preceding Amos text (4.1-5):[26] the lack of 'bread' (4.6aB) is linked with leavened sacrifice (4.5a), the report about cities (4.6a, 7-8) is related to the discussion about the cities of Samaria, Bethel and Gilgal (4.1, 4), and the phrase בכל מקומתיכם 'in all your places' (4.6aB) is an allusion to the shrines at Bethel and Gilgal where offerings are made (4.4- 5). Further, Yahweh's punishment is the over-arching theme of 4.1-13.

Despite these connective links, 4.6-13 stands out as conspicuously dis- tinct from 4.1-5. This passage does not seem to fit into the preceding con- text because it points backwards and also forwards to Amos's prophecy. So the book (4.6-13) marks an abrupt shift in focus from Yahweh's imminent punishment (4.1-5) to his past punitive acts. The explanation for the sudden transition is that the revision reflects a major turning point in Amos's composition. The book's story of past punishments (4.6-13) anticipates the movement in thought from threat of war and deportation (4.1-3) to the report about Israel's actual demise (5.1-2). The oath 'he [Yahweh] shall take you away…'(4.2) is replaced by his first-person speech (4.6-13). This emphasis on God as speaker is proleptic of his first- person address.[27] 'Hear this word which I am taking up over you…'. (5.1).[28]

The revision at 4.6-13 interrupts the prophecy of judgment (4.1-5) and its fulfilment (5.1-2) to offer hope beyond destruction. It interprets the fall of Israel (5.1-2) as the occasion for repentance, but the people did not return to Yahweh. The point is illustrated with typical events that lay in the past: Yahweh tells the people that disasters were heaped upon them because of their constant reluctance to be converted to him. And this rehearsal of misfortunes contains the warning that future disasters can only

---

26. Scholars have interpreted 4.4-13 or the entire chapter as a unifed speech with a covenant form: Walter Brueggemann, 'Amos IV 4-13 and Israel's Covenant Worship', *VT* 15 (1965), pp. 1-15; Marjorie O'Rourke Boyle, 'The Covenant Lawsuit of the Prophet Amos: III 1–IV 13', *VT* 21 (1971), pp. 338-62.

27. The editorial וגם אנכי (4.7a) is an imitation of Amos's use of אנכי (5.1a). Also אנכי (2.9) links the editorial (2.9-12) with the Amos text (2.6-8).

28. In the original text Amos is proclaiming Yahweh's word (5.1-2; see also LXX). However, the first-person divine address (4.6-13) is the clue that Yahweh, from the book's perspective, is the singer of the song of grief (5.1-2).

be averted by turning back to Yahweh. Past punishments are thus the grounds for the urgent appeal (4.12b) to return to God and be rescued from total destruction.

The book (4.6-13) interprets Amos's day of Yahweh. The reviser imitates Amos by repeating שׁוּב five times (1.3a, 6a, 13a; 2.1a, 6a [=_4.6b], 8b, 9b, 10b, 11b). In Amos 1–2 שׁוּב expresses the irreversibility of 'the day of battle' (1.14) and points to global disaster. Specifically, שׁוּב refers to the day in which Yahweh brings total defeat to Israel (2.13-16). However, the book makes שׁוּב refer to God's unrelenting efforts to bring Israel back to him.

Thus the reviser, by combining the idea of conversion with the topic of the remnant, preempts and changes Amos's day of Yahweh (5.18-20). For the prophet the day was marked by total defeat, darkness and gloom (5.18, 20) and by a fire that engulfs and consumes (5.6a, 7.4). The book both acknowledges and softens this picture of destruction. On the one hand, it depicts the fall of Israel as a terrible day in which all cities suffered famine (4.6a), a day in which ironically no bread was left to offer a leavened sacrifice (4.6a; 4.5a), a day in which locusts ruined the land (4.9 = 7.1),[29] a day in which young warriors were killed and the stench of death filled the war camp (4.10). On the other hand, the book mitigates the disaster by reporting that drought occurred in one city but not in another, that only part of the population[30] was overthrown and that a remnant was rescued out of the fire (4.7b, 11).

The book does not explicitly refer to 'the day of Yahweh', but the key words שׁוּב and עֵיפָה 'darkness' (4.13a = חֹשֶׁךְ 5.18b, 20a) point backwards and forwards to 'the day', suggesting that the reviser read Amos's entire prophetic text. The addition (4.6-13) begins the reviser's interpretative paraphrase of Amos's day of Yahweh. So the book describes God as one who makes the dawn darkness (4.13) in preparation for Amos's day of Yahweh as darkness and not light (5.18b, 20a).[31] The day for Amos was an

29. Shemaryahu Talmon, 'Prophetic Rhetoric and Agricultural Metaphora', in Garrone and Israel (eds.), *Storia e Tradizioni di Israele*, pp. 267-79 (271-72).

30. Since ב has the partitive value of מן, the overthrow refers to part of the population (4.11a).

31. Contrast the usual view of 4.13 as a hymn that was added to the book but not written for the present context: Theodor H. Gaster, 'An Ancient Hymn in the Prophecies of Amos', *Journal of the Manchester Egyptian and Oriental Society 19* (1935), pp. 23-26; John D.W. Watts, 'An Old Hymn Preserved in the Book of Amos', *JNES* 16 (1956), pp. 33-40; James L. Crenshaw, 'The Influence of the Wise upon

unexpected catastrophic event, but the book downplays destruction by fitting the day into the normal scheme of Yahweh's creative activity (4.13).

The commentator imitates Amos's rhetorical series (3.1-6) by composing a series (4.6-12) whose point is clear only when the sequence is heard or read to the end. The book also copies Amos's movement from the realm of nature to the political or military sphere. But the revision replaces the analogies drawn from nature (3.3-5) with a catalogue of natural catastrophes caused by Yahweh (4.7-10a). The accumulation of divine calamities bears witness to the fact that God has used his sovereign power over nature to intervene and cause Israel's defeat. Amos used the verb עשׂה to convey the fact that Yahweh was behind the defeat of a city (3.6b). Likewise the duplicate report of what Yahweh 'has done' to Israel (4.12) alludes to war and destruction in 'all the cities' (4.6a). The repetition of structural and thematic elements from an earlier original context is the means by which the reviser makes the second edition seem like a continuous reading.

The revision at 4.6-13 is related not only to 3.1-6 but also to its own text in 3.7-8. In accordance with every deed of God being preceded by his communication to the prophets (3.7-8), the reviser presents Amos as assuming the prophetic task of warning the people and insisting on their conversion to Yahweh (4.6-12). The report that Yahweh told human beings what he thought (4.13), presumably before he acted, is related to the declaration that Yahweh does not do anything without first telling a prophet (3.7), who is then bound to proclaim in advance what Yahweh will do (4.6-12).

Cross-references (e.g. 3.7 = 4.13a) show that the addition (4.6-13) continues the argument of the commentator. The remnant idea introduced in 3.12-15 is developed in 4.6-13. The survivors of the overthrow of Israel are likened to a fire-brand plucked out of the burning (4.11a). An elaborate simile links 4.11 and 3.12. The hophal participle מֻצָּל (4.11a) is a cross-reference to the hiphil יַצִּיל and the niphal יִנָּצְלוּ (3.12): those rescued from the destruction somehow resemble parts of a mutilated animal (3.12a), scraps of furniture (3.12b) and a piece of burning wood (4.11a).

That deliverance and destruction represent two sides of God's activity is shown by relating his punitive deeds (4.6-12) to his saving action (2.9-11). Both narratives begin with the first-person report of the divine acts followed by the indictment (2.12; 4.6b, 8b, 9b, 10b, 11b). The contrast-

Amos: The 'Doxologies of Amos' and Job 5.9-16; 9.5-10', *ZAW* 79 (1967), pp. 42-52 (49).

statement, 'I destroyed…but you made the Nazirites drink wine…' (2.9-12), is balanced by a series of five contrast-statements, 'I gave…but you did not return to me' (4.6-12).[32] The deictic pronouns וגם־אנכי/ואנכי (2.9a; 4.6a) loosely attach the two narratives in 2.9-11 and 4.6-12 to Amos's text.

Yahweh's history of destruction is more than a 'parody upon "salvation history"'.[33] The book argues that Yahweh has punished his own to lead them back to himself (4.6-11). Confirmation of his intervention on behalf of Israel comes from the history of his saving acts (2.9-11). So the pre-emptive salvation history (2.9-11) establishes in advance how the history of destruction (4.6-11) is to be understood, namely, that God has been at work in past crises to bring about Israel's deliverance.

Part Four (5.1-9)

Two passages are added to Amos's fourth vision (5.1-2, 4-7) to produce Part 4 of the book (5.1-9). The first editorial passage (5.3) is a duplication of the original divine word (5.4) and is constructed out of its language. The reviser splits up Amos's messenger formula, 'for thus says Yahweh to the house of Israel' (5.4a), so that it marks the beginning and end of the insertion (5.3). The introductory כי links the comment in 5.3 with Amos's dirge in 5.1-2: the conjunction כי, the repetition of original language, and the enclosure of the lament by God's speech (5.1, 3) make it seem that all the verses of 5.1-3 belong together, despite their contrasting points of view.

The reviser (5.3) comments on Amos's dirge by confirming Israel's overwhelming defeat but emphasizing survival in the midst of destruction. Providing a brief statistical count of military might, the book reports that most of the warriors who marched out to war did not return. Yet despite the great numbers of fallen men, the book notes that defeat did not bring about the death of all the troops and the end of the nation: 'The city that used to march out a thousand…shall have but ten left to the house of Israel.' The book softens the original picture of the fall of Israel (5.2) by referring to specific casualties of war in individual cities (5.3). In this way the book continues its preoccupation with the fate of Israel's cities (4.6-8). The verb שאר (5.3) is used twice in the hiphil to stress that at least a tenth

---

32. See Joseph Blenkinsopp, 'The Prophetic Reproach', *JBL* 90 (1971), pp. 267-78 (267-70).

33. See Martin-Achard, 'End of the People of God', p. 36.

of the fighting force in a city is left after the catastrophe.[34] Similar to remnants of bone, furniture (3.12) and firewood (4.11), 5.3 reports that at least a few Israelites remained after the devastation. Just as יציל and נצל are used to stress rescue (3.12), so is תשאיר duplicated to stress survival in the midst of destruction (5.3).

The second passage (5.8-9)[35] of the book is a new ending to Amos's fourth poem. The commentator uses the qal participle הפך (5.8a) to provide a loose connection with the Amos text (5.7a), whose qal participle ההפכים refers to those in Israel who 'turned justice to wormwood'. But the book uses הפך and other participles to advance its own argument. So it interprets Amos's day in terms of primordial creation and ongoing divine creative activity.[36] As the one who 'made' (עשה) the constellations Pleiades and Orion,[37] God keeps turning on the lights of the heavens at night and turning them off in the morning (5.8aA). The book fits the day of Yahweh's destruction of Israel into the regular succession of night and daybreak, darkness and light, thereby creating a contrast between the one who 'keeps making (עשה) the dawn darkness' (4.13aA) and the one who

34. Andersen and Freedman (Amos, p. 477) argue that 5.3 refers either to the loss of 10 per cent and the survival of 90 per cent, or to the loss of 90 per cent and the survival of 10 per cent. Dealing with the logic of the word rather than the text itself, they miss its plain message that only a hundred survived out of a thousand and ten out of a hundred.

35. Scholars think that the so-called hymnic fragments (4.13; 5.8-9; 9.5-6) were secondarily inserted from some lost source and not written for the context in which they stand: e.g. Klaus Koch, 'Die Rolle der hymnischen Abschnitte in der Komposition des Amos-Buches', *ZAW* 86 (1974), pp. 504-37; James L. Crenshaw, *Hymnic Affirmation of Divine Justice: The Doxologies of Amos and Related Texts in the Old Testament* (ed. Howard C. Kee and Douglas A. Knight; SBLDS, 24; Missoula, MT: Scholars Press, 1975).

36. Understandably, if participles seem to be referring to primeval creation, scholars translate them in the past. If participles point to current creative acts, scholars translate them in the present. But criteria need to be established for the translation of participles. 'Participial...clauses also express time, aspect, and tense, and fill out the verbal system...The participle expresses relative time like *qatal* and continuous action like *yiqtol*. Their tense depends on word order and clause type, and is subject to the usual syntactic conditions': see Peckham, 'Tense and Mood in Biblical Hebrew', p. 142 n. 7.

37. In Greek mythology, the groups of stars bearing the names of the Pleiades and Orion were celebrated for their brilliance and for their regular risings and settings with the sun: Catherine B. Avery (ed.), *The New Century Classical Handbook* (New York: Appleton-Century-Crofts, 1962), pp. 793, 903.

'keeps turning (הָפַךְ) deep darkness into morning' (5.8aB).[38]

At this juncture the book abruptly shifts its focus from the present to the past by portraying Yahweh as the one who 'darkened (הֶחְשִׁיךְ) the day into night' (5.8). The noun יוֹם and the hiphil perfect הֶחְשִׁיךְ are direct links with Amos's day of Yahweh, which is 'darkness' (חֹשֶׁךְ) rather than light (5.18, 20a). The book interprets the day of Yahweh as an exceptional divine historical act resembling the great flood which Yahweh once summoned and poured out upon the surface of the earth (5.8b). By linking the day with the deluge of the remote past, the book treats Israel's defeat as only one small event in the overall scheme of divine activity that stretches back to primeval time (4.13aA).

The book ends its account of past and present creative acts by affirming the name of Yahweh (5.8b = 4.13b). And Part 4 ends by a return to its opening: Israel's defeat in war is associated with the fortified city and not the whole nation (5.3, 9).[39] Yahweh's recurring creative activity is the basis for interpreting the fall of Israel's cities (5.8-9): his sovereignty over the natural world is our assurance that he can change defeat into salvation.

Part 5 (5.10-27)

The reviser rewrites Amos's fifth poem (5.10-12, 18-20, 21-14) by inserting 5.13, 14-15, 16-17, 25-27. The first editorial passage (5.13) in Part 5 is connected to Amos's text (5.10-12) by the adverb לָכֵן 'therefore' and by the deictic particle בָּעֵת הַהִיא which refers in general to the preceding context and introduces the book's idea that the wise person is quiet 'at that time' (5.13). This terse comment disrupts the initial connection between the crimes and judgment on the day of Yahweh (5.10-12; 5.18-20). The book preempts Amos by calling the day 'an evil time' (כִּי עֵת רָעָה הִיא 5.13).

The reviser repeats the word 'evil' (רַע 5.14a) in order to establish 5.13 as part of the ongoing commentary. The injunction דִּרְשׁוּ־טוֹב וְאַל־רָע לְמַעַן תִּחְיוּ 'seek good and not evil in order that you may live' (5.14a), שִׂנְאוּ־רָע 'hate evil', וְהַצִּיגוּ בַשַּׁעַר מִשְׁפָּט 'establish justice in the gate' (5.15), show that the book is referring to the evil deeds that Amos observed at the gate (5.10-12). It imitates the directives in his previous poem,

38. See Susan Gillingham, ' "Who Makes the Morning Darkness": God and Creation in the Book of Amos', *SJT* 45 (1992), pp. 165-84.

39. So also Lawrence Zalcman, 'Astronomical Illusions in Amos', *JBL* 100 (1981), pp. 53-58.

'seek me [Yahweh] and live but do not seek Bethel' (5.4); 'seek Yahweh and live' (5.6).

The book (5.14-15) refers to Amos and uses his language to convey its ideas. By quoting Amos (5.4-6) the reviser blends in the addition (5.14-15) with an opposite viewpoint. The book splits the charge of illegal misdeeds (5.10-12) and divine punishment (5.18-20) to announce Yahweh's graciousness to the remnant of Joseph (5.15). The book preempts and contradicts Amos's report about the ruin of Joseph (שבר יוסף lit. 'the fracture of Joseph' 6.6b) by claiming survivors for the Northern Kingdom. Yahweh's compassion for Joseph (5.15) alters Yahweh's destruction of Joseph (5.6).[40] The glimpse of a remnant in 3.12, 4.11a and 5.3 is finally specified in 5.15. Amos announced the destruction of Israel with only an inkling that doom could have been prevented (5.4-6). But all the additions that develop the idea of survival make it appear that a remnant did repent by seeking Yahweh.

The introductory לכן 'therefore' (5.16aA) joins God's word in 5.16-17 to the book's previous statement (5.14-15), and 'God of hosts' interlocks the two passages (5.14b, 15b, 16aA). The book returns to Amos's lament over fallen Israel (5.16-17; 5.1-2)[41] and continues to interpret it with reference to each city and its environs (5.3; 4.6-8). The book envisages a catastrophe in which cries of anguish pervade the city and the countryside, in the wide squares of the city, in the narrow city streets, and even in the vineyards. There is total community involvement in wailing and weeping, from professional mourners who have experience in grieving to the farmers who are called to mourning.[42] By repeating the word 'all' (5.16 = 4.6a), the book stresses that mourning occurs both within and outside the city walls.

That survivors mourn (מספד 'wailing' 3×; אבל 'mourning'; הו 'woe' 2×; נהי 'lamentation') for those who have died develops the book's idea of

---

40. Cf. J. Lust ('Remarks on the Redaction of Amos V 4-6, 14-15', *OTS* 21 [1981], pp. 129-54 [145-46] who recognizes that the idea of 'the remnant of Joseph' (5.14) is a later response to the statement about the destruction of 'the house of Joseph' (5.6).

41. J. de Waard, 'The Chiastic Structure of Amos V 1-17', *VT* 27 (1977), pp. 170-77; Tromp, 'Amos V 1-17', pp. 56-84; Donald W. Wicke, 'Two Perspectives (Amos 5.1-17)', *Cur*TM 13 (1986), pp. 89-96.

42. The statement וקראו אכר אל־אבל should be translated 'and the farmers are called to mourning' (5.16bA; cf. RSV: 'they shall call the farmers to mourning'). The passive is expressed by the third person plural active; see GKC, nos.144 f, 144 g, p. 460.

the remnant (5.16). The exclamations הוֹ־הוֹ (5.16a) are proleptic references to Amos's cry of lament over the day of Yahweh (5.18). The reviser gives a different focus to this day by prefacing it with God's speech about the day of lamentation (5.16-17). Yahweh's day in Amos is changed from a day of doom to a day of mourning for the dead. Yahweh's word כִּי־אֶעֱבֹר בְּקִרְבֵּךְ 'I will pass through your midst' (5.17) anticipates and contradicts what he says in Amos's text: לֹא־אוֹסִיף עוֹד עֲבוֹר לוֹ 'I will never again pass by him' (= the people of Israel, 7.8bB, 8.2bB).

The revision in Part 5 ends with a passage (5.25-27) that is partly created out of Amos's poetry. The question 'Did you bring to me sacrifices and offerings for forty years in the wilderness, O house of Israel?' (5.25) reuses Amos's nouns הַזְּבָחִים and מִנְחָה 'your sacrifices' 4.4bA; מִנְחֹתֵיכֶם 'your cereal offerings' 5.22a). The vocative בֵּית יִשְׂרָאֵל 'O house of Israel' (5.25) is a deictic inserted by the reviser as an artificial link to Amos's text (5.1, 4). The verbs וּנְשָׂאתֶם 'you shall take away' 5.26 and הִגְלֵיתִי 'I will take into exile' 5.27 are retrieved from Amos's text: וְנָשָׂא 'and he shall take away' (4.2bA); גָּלֹה יִגְלֶה '[Gilgal] shall surely go into exile' (5.5). And the commentary at 5.25-27 continues the first-person divine address established by Amos (5.21-24).

The concluding verses (5.25-27) of Part 5 are also constructed out of the language of the book's own text. The allusion to forty years in the wilderness is a cross-reference to the first part of the book (2.10bA). The clause 'which you made (עֲשִׂיתֶם) for yourselves' 5.26b cross-references other instances of עָשָׂה (4.13a; 5.8a). Just as 2.9-11 traces the history of the people of Israel from the Exodus to the conquest, so 5.25-27 traces cultic practices from the early days of the wilderness (5.25) down to the time of the fall and exile of the nation Israel (5.27). The reviser combines quotation with cross-reference to change the original text and develop a different argument. The book, in contrast to Amos (4.2bA), depicts the Israelites as being deported along with their gods: 'You shall carry away (וּנְשָׂאתֶם) Sakkuth your king, and Kaiwan your images, your star-god, which you made for yourselves' (5.26-27). This scene determines that God's rhetorical question, 'Did you bring to me sacrifices and offerings those forty years in the wilderness?', is answered in the negative. Thus the book rejects Amos's view that sacrifices and offerings were made to Yahweh (4.4-5; 5.21-24). The book argues that Israel succumbed to idolatry as early as the wilderness days by offering sacrifices to images of foreign gods.

The book at 5.25-27 not only contradicts what Amos said but also continues its own argument. Now the reader discovers the reason for the book's interest in God's sovereign power over the universe (4.13; 5.8). It contrasts Yahweh who made (עשה) groups of stars known as the Pleiades and Orion (5.8a) with the Israelites who made (עשה) images of a star-god for themselves (5.26a).[43] The two passages make the point that when the Israelites worshipped astral images at the Bethel sanctuary (3.14), they rejected Yahweh as the creator of light and darkness (4.13a; 5.8a). While Amos talked about Bethel, Gilgal and Beersheba, the reviser is concerned with Bethel. Yahweh's speech is brought to a close at 5.27b with reference to him as 'God of hosts', a phrase which links 5.8 and 4.13. As sovereign over heavenly bodies, he deports people along with their astral deities.

Part 6 (6.1-14)

The adjustments the reviser makes to Amos's sixth poem are confined to the concluding verses. The book separates Amos's depiction of the disso-lute behaviour of Judah's upper classes (6.4-6) from its portrait of their irrationality and self-deception (6.12-13). So the commentary (6.8-11, 14) is added before and after Amos's rhetorical argument (6.12-13) to produce Part 6. The reviser makes the first addition (6.8) look like Amos's text by partly citing what the prophet said earlier. 'The Lord Yahweh has sworn by himself' (נשבע אדני יהוה בנפשו 6.8) is a quotation from the distant context where Amos reported that 'Lord Yahweh has sworn by his holi-ness' (נשבע אדני בקדשו 4.2aA). The phrase נאם־יהוה 'says Yahweh' marks a quotation and is accompanied by 'the God of hosts', a phrase which relates the insertion to other sections of the book (e.g. 3.13; 4.13; 5.27). The book also follows Amos in putting שנאתי 'I hate' into Yahweh's mouth (6.8a = 5.21).

What is striking about the first addition (6.8) is that the book confirms Judah as the target of Amos's diatribe. The commentator grasps the implied message of Amos and strengthens it by having God direct his animosity against Judah. That Jacob stands for Judah (6.8) anticipates Amos's use of Jacob to represent Judah (7.2, 5). The book imitates the brevity and allusiveness of the original text (6.1-7) but transforms the third-person report about Judah's future demise (6.7) into a first-person

---

43. E.A. Speiser, 'Note on Amos 5.26', *BASOR* 108 (1947), pp. 5-6; Charles D. Isbell, 'Another Look at Amos 5.26', *JBL* 97 (1978), pp. 97-99; Stanley Gevirtz, 'A New Look at an Old Crux: Amos 5, 26', *JBL* 87 (1968), pp. 267-76; Paul, Amos, pp. 197-98.

oath of divine judgment (6.8). Amos employed the verb סגר in the hiphil to describe the exile of a people (1.6b). The book reuses סגר in the hiphil when Yahweh swears he will deport the city of Zion (6.8).

The book provides a totally different context and meaning for the material it quotes from Amos. According to Amos, Yahweh promised that he would deport the women of Samaria and their husbands (4.2-3). In the book's application, however, Yahweh promises to deliver up the city of Zion (6.8b). For Amos שׂנא referred to Yahweh's 'hatred' of the feasts (5.21a). But the book reuses the term to talk about Yahweh's hatred of Judah's fortresses. It creates a parallel statement: 'I abhor (מתאב אנכי)[44] the pride of Jacob, and I hate (שׂנאתי) his strongholds' (6.8). Amos used the two verbs in parallelism to express the people's objection to the arbitrator of justice at the city gate (5.10), but the book reuses the verbs to express Yahweh's objection to Judah's misplaced confidence in its strong fortifications or in the survival of Jerusalem's majestic temple.

Taken generally גאון 'pride' (6.8a) seems to be a reference to the indulgent luxury and loftiness described by Amos. But just as עיר refers to a specific city, גאון suggests a specific object of the nation's pride. In the immediate context עיר points to the royal city of Zion (6.1aA). Likewise גאון seems to be an allusion to the Jerusalem temple because this is where Judah's pride is manifest (6.4-6) and where the house of Israel comes (6.1b). The allusion to Judah and Jerusalem in 6.8 is related to the book's perspective in which Yahweh promises to send a fire upon Judah and its strongholds in the city of Jerusalem (2.4-5). What is explicit in 2.4-5 is only implicit in 6.8 because Part 6 is written to match the style of Amos's poem.

The reference to the city (6.8) leads into the next addition (6.9-11), in which the book resumes the subject of war in individual cities: one city had only a hundred survivors out of a thousand and another ten out of a hundred (5.3). These statistics continue with the report that if ten men are left in one house they will die (6.9). What follows is a story about the removal of the remains from the house (6.10-11). The task devolves upon the dead man's uncle who burns off the flesh and carries the bones out of the house. A conversation takes place between the kinsman who is outside

---

44. The reviser substitutes the unusual האב (6.8) for Amos's תעב (5.10) but the verbs have the same meaning. It has been shown that words with an initial or final א have variants with ע: Stanley Gevirtz, '"Formative" 'ayin in Biblical Hebrew', *Eretz Israel* 16 (1982), pp. 57*-66*. Perhaps in Amos we have an instance of the same interchange in medial position.

the house and the man who is inside, and the dialogue alternates between the two. The kinsman asks, 'Is any one still with you?' The survivor inside replies, 'No one', and the kinsman answers back: 'keep silent, for there will be no mention of the name of Yahweh.'[45] The story concludes with the interjection כי־הנה 'for look'. The reason for the imposed silence is God's command which will smite the great house into fragments and the little house into splinters (6.11). In accord with the book's perspective, men dying in a house is a tale of both destruction and survival. Presumably the man cowering inside the house has somehow beaten the odds and lived.

While 6.8 recapitulates and interprets the content of Amos's prophecy to Zion (6.1-7), the subtext at 6.9-11 drifts away from the critical things Amos said about the leaders of Zion, their conduct and worship in the temple. To eliminate any thought that David might be implicated in the wrongdoing of Zion the book replaces Amos's reference to דויד (6.5b) with a story about the דוד or the nearest relative of the dead (6.10-11). The wordplay provides the connection between Amos's text and the book. The reference point of the story in 6.9-11 is not simply Amos's text but also other passages of the book. The command to be silent (6.10b) resumes the idea introduced by the reviser in 5.13. So the story in 6.9-11 illustrates why silence is the policy for an evil time: evil time is wartime when people die and are the target of God's judgment. The idea that Yahweh's command will smash (הכה) houses great and small (6.11) is a cross-reference to his promise to punish Israel by smashing (הכיתי) the winter house with the summer house and bringing its many houses to an end (3.14-15).

Another passage (6.14) is inserted at the end of Amos's rhetorical argument and marks the close of Part 6. The book changes the structure and shape of the original text (6.12-13) by surrounding it with a commentary that begins and ends with 'says Yahweh' and 'God of hosts' (6.8, 14). By sealing off 6.8-14 as a separate section, the book diverts attention away from Amos's cultic celebrations (6.4-7) with their mumbo-jumbo (6.12-13) to God's punishment of both Judah (6.8) and Israel (6.14). While Amos drew a picture of Judah's total defeat (6.7), the reviser moves away from complete doom to a remnant of Judah (6.9-11) and to the invasion of the Northern Kingdom, which is defeated but still demarcated by boundaries (6.14). What is new in the book is the idea of a nation used as

---

45. The preposition ל plus an infinitive (here להזכיר 6.10b) expresses a future impersonal future: GKC, no.114 h–k, pp. 348-49.

Yahweh's agent of punishment (6.14a). While Amos concentrated on oppressors in Judah (6.1-7, 12), the book focuses on the foreign nation or enemy who will oppress northern Israel from Hamath to the Brook of Arabah (6.14b).

Differences in viewpoint between the two versions are not immediately apparent because the book homogenizes the text. So the pairs created by Amos, namely Zion and Samaria (6.1), are balanced by allusions to Zion (6.8b) and Samaria (6.11); his pairs 'first of the nations' and 'house of Israel' are matched by Jacob (6.8aB) and 'house of Israel' (6.14); his comparison between the territory of foreign cities and that of Judah and Israel (6.2) is offset by the fall of Judah and by an enemy who overruns Israel (6.14).

Thus numerous cross-references are employed by the reviser to assimilate Amos's poem to its interpretation. The terms לֹא דָבָר, 'non-word' and קְרָנַיִם, 'horns' that Amos used to describe cultic practices (6.13) are turned into actual geographical localities because of their proximity to place names in the book (6.14b).[46] The original meaning of the terminology is that the people rejoice in nonsense and make themselves strong by sprouting horns. In the book, however, the people rejoice because they have captured two cities. The book's additions make Amos's sixth poem all the more allusive by redirecting attention away from Judah's leaders and their senseless rites to war against Israel and Judah, their defeat by an enemy chosen by Yahweh, and their survival as a remnant.

Part 7 (7.1-17)

The reviser distributes Amos's visions (7.1–8.3*) over Parts 7 and 8. As a result of the restructuring process, the visions are put into separate contexts and hence their meaning is changed. In the seventh part a biographi-

---

46. The impression that 6.13 refers to actual victories at Lo-Dabar and Qarnaim is created by the book: Lo-Dabar is a place name in Josh. 13.26; 2 Sam. 9.4; 17.27; Qarnaim is identified with Ashtarot in Gen. 14.5, and the book, by adding Hamath and Arabah (6.14b), creates a wordplay between Amos's terms (6.13) and place-names found in the Deuteronomistic history. Geographical references, Teman and Bozrah (1.12), Sodom and Gomorrah (4.11), Damascus (5.27), Hamath, Brook of the Arabah (6.14b) are consistent with the book's interest in expanding Amos's discussion about Samaria, Bethel and Gilgal to 'all your cities' (4.6). The nouns סֶלַע and בְּקָרִים (6.12) are a pun on place-names, Sela and the Valley of Beqa, and anticipate the account of the conquest in its southern and northern extents: see Alan Cooper, 'The Absurdity of Amos 6.12a', *JBL* 107 (1988), pp. 725-27.

cal narrative is inserted into the visions (7.10-17), and it interrupts the connection between the third and fourth visions. The book, by separating these paired visions, makes the intrusive story (7.10-17) resemble the third vision (7.7-9), and the book substitutes the biography of Amos (7.10-17) for the fourth vision as the new member of the pair. Thus the story about Amos at Bethel displaces the fourth vision as the new climactic point of the visions, and the visions become assimilated to the book's argument.

The story of Amos's encounter with Amaziah, the Bethel priest, begins abruptly (וישלח 'and he sent') and is coupled with a shift in person. Yet the reviser skilfully attaches the story composed in the third person to the first-person vision reports. Formal connection with the preceding Amos text is made by verbal links or catchwords: 'Jeroboam', 'sword', 'in the midst of', and 'sanctuary' occur at the end of the third vision (7.8b-9) and reappear at the beginning of the story (7.10-11, 13). Editorial work is also evident in the closing verses of the narrative (7.16-17), where the book brings us back to Amos's prophecy of judgment and repeats 'Israel' and 'Isaac' from it (7.8-9). The reviser creates a smooth transition to the fourth vision by ending the intrusive story in the same way as the third vision, with Yahweh's speech and his proclamation of punishment.

Our understanding of the story of Amos and Amaziah is limited if we treat it as an independent tradition[47] and isolate it from its present context. The narrative has been composed to fit the visions into which it is now inserted. The story is intended to stand out in its present context but contains language and themes that blend it into the visions. The book uses repetition to establish continuity between the Amaziah episode and the third vision, despite their incongruent viewpoints.[48] Yet words that are repeated from the third vision receive a new context and new interpretation and are subordinate to the argument of Amos's biography.

The biographical narrative is inserted at the end of the third vision just after Yahweh, in Amos's text, has announced the demise of the house of Jeroboam (7.9b). The book's reference to the death of Jeroboam by the

47. So also Clements, 'Amos and the Politics of Israel', p. 59. Cf. Gene M. Tucker, 'Prophetic Authenticity: A Form-Critical Study of Amos 7.10-17', Int 27 (1973), pp. 423-34 (425-26); Peter R. Ackroyd, 'A Judgment Narrative between Kings and Chronicles? An Approach to Amos 7.9-17', in George W. Coats and Burke O. Long (eds.), *Canon and Authority: Essays in Old Testament Religion and Theology* (Philadelphia: Fortress Press, 1977), pp. 71-87 (81-82).

48. Lyle Eslinger, 'The Education of Amos', *HAR* 11 (1987), pp. 35-57; Landy, 'Vision and Poetic Speech in Amos', pp. 223-46.

sword (7.11a) parallels Amos's statement that Yahweh will rise up against the house of Jeroboam with the sword (7.9b). Yet a significant difference exists between Amos's proclamation against Jeroboam in the third vision (7.9) and the book's restatement in the biography (7.11).[49] While Amos spoke about the fall of a dynasty founded by Jeroboam I, the book talks about the prophet's encounter with Jeroboam II. Amos's reference to the northern dynasty and its founder (7.9b) is prepared for and balanced by his reference to the foreign dynasty founded by Hazael and carried forward by Benhadad as son and successor (1.4). Amos's allusion to the origins of the northern dynasty is balanced by his reference to David (6.5), the founder of the dynasty in the South. The book takes advantage of this solitary reference to the fall of Israel's dynasty (7.9) to record that Amos went to Bethel and predicted the actual fall of Israel during the reign of two contemporary kings, Uzziah of Judah and Jeroboam II of Israel (1.1b).

At the beginning of his text Amos speaks as if his message is directed to the North, but as the text advances Israel lies in ruins and his prophecy is to the South. At first his visions move from the divine threat against Jacob or Judah to Yahweh's repentance but then proceed to the divine proclamation against both the southern and northern places of worship and finally to Yahweh's climactic statement of doom for the whole people. The book shifts the emphasis back to Israel by tracing Amos's prophecy against the North to his conflict with Bethel's king and priest.

The book develops a story that alters the details of the preceding visions in a variety of ways. So Yahweh's destruction in the midst of the whole people (7.8) is displaced by Amos's conspiratorial activity in the midst of the dynasty of Israel (7.10). Amaziah misquotes Amos's threat against the house of Jeroboam (7.9b) by singling out King Jeroboam as the target of the sword (7.11a). And Amos responds to Amaziah's false words by reapplying the divine judgment by the sword (7.9b) to the priest's family (7.17). The book does not reiterate Amos's words about the devastation of 'the high places of Isaac' and 'the sanctuaries (וּמִקְדְּשֵׁי יִשְׂרָאֵל) of Israel' (יִשְׂרָאֵל וּמְקֹרָא 7.9). Instead the local shrines of both nations are replaced by Bethel as the principal northern sanctuary. Using Amaziah as its mouthpiece, the book states that Bethel is the place of 'the king's sanctuary' (מִקְדַּשׁ־מֶלֶךְ 7.13) and the reason for Amos's banishment from Israel to the land of Judah.

With Amaziah's declaration that the land is not able to bear all the

49. Amos 7.9 and 7.11 are thought to be 'essentially equivalent': Andersen and Freedman, *Amos*, pp. 767-68.

words of Amos (7.10b), a new context is provided for Amos's description of the land. Depictions of locusts devouring the grass (עשׂב הארץ 7.2a) and the land (החלק 7.4b) are used by Amos to refer to the whole earth which God has threatened to destroy and return to chaos. The book, however, uses the noun הארץ, simply to refer to the land of Israel which is unable to endure all the words which, Amos has spoken against it (7.10b). The noun החלק which Amos used as a reference to the portion of the world that is not water is replaced by the book's *pual* form of the verb חלק (7.17a) to refer to Amaziah's property that is to be divided with a measuring cord. Such changes in perspective show that the book uses the language of the visions to give priority to divine judgment on Israel.

The book modifies the original vision of doom for both nations (8.2) by the preemptive account of the fate of Amaziah and his family (7.17). As the narrative develops, the revision drifts away from the dynasty and Jeroboam to the priesthood. Indeed the king is involved only indirectly in the story. Falling into three parts, the narrative contains the priest's report to the king (7.10-11), Amaziah's command to Amos (7.12-13), and Amos's response (7.14-17). The book concentrates on the punishment of Amaziah, turning his own words against him (7.11). Thus Amaziah's own children will die by the sword, his wife will be treated as a city prostitute by the enemy, his land will be confiscated, and he will die in exile (7.17). These consequences of invasion and defeat are related to the book's report of particular casualties of war in the city (5.3; 6.8-11): The book presents war as having a terrible particularity for Amaziah in the city of Bethel as it had for other cities in Israel (5.3) and Judah (6.8-11), but it does not mark the terrible and final end of a whole people that is visualized by Amos.

The book's story anticipates Amos's fourth vision. That Yahweh compels Amos to prophesy to his people Israel (7.15b) is a prolepsis of the climax of Amos's vision: 'the end has come upon my people Israel' (8.2b). The editor interprets 'my people Israel' to include both Israel and Judah, as suggested by the original pairs, Israel–Isaac (7.16; cf. 7.9a), but preempts Amos's text by changing Yahweh's proclamation of 'the end' to his announcement of Israel's exile (7.17b). Thus the Amaziah episode shows the editor at work summarizing parts of Amos's text that are crucial for the argument of the book. In the book, then, Amos confirms the priest's prediction, 'Israel shall surely go into exile away from his land' (7.11b; 7.17b). The book, by having Amos repeat the words of Amaziah, recapitulates the prophet's original message: he first compares the deportation of Samaria's inhabitants to driven cattle (4.2-3) and then announces,

'Gilgal shall surely go into exile' (5.5b). The book summarizes what Amos said in his earlier poems but ignores his prediction about the deportation of Judah's leaders (6.7a) so as to emphasize his prophecy about the exile of Israel.

The reviser homogenizes the text by rounding off Amos's 'house of Jeroboam' (7.9b) with 'house of Isaac' (7.16b). Just as the house of Jeroboam refers to the dynasty of the North, the house of Isaac has something to do with the dynasty of the South. Since the reviser is not interested in saying that the monarchy has come to an end, the threat against the dynasty of Judah is limited to Amos's synopsis of Amaziah's orders, 'Do not preach against the house of Isaac' (7.16b). The house of Isaac points backwards to Amos's text (7.9) but also forwards to the restoration of the house of Isaac by the raising up of the booth of David (9.11).

The editor imitates the rounded development that Amos gave his composition from beginning to end. Inserted towards the end of Amos's text, the intrusive story is composed to fit the immediate context of Amos's visions and to correspond with his introductory diatribe against the nations.[50] So the attack on King Jeroboam (ירבעם מלך ישראל 7.10-11a) and the announcement of Israel's exile (וישׂראל גלה יגלה 7.11b, 17b) correspond to what Amos said about God's judgment of foreign rulers (e.g. והלך מלכם בגולה 'and their king shall go into exile', 1.15) and the exile of other peoples (e.g. וגלו עם־ארם 'the people of Aram shall go into exile' 1.5b). The book retrieves Amos's motif of flight (2.13-16) to make a thematic connection between the beginning and the end of Amos's text. Using the noun מנוס (2.14a) and the verb נוס (2.16b), Amos tells us twice that the cream of Israel's army takes flight. The reviser, not interested in reiterating the image of total defeat, applies the imperative ברח to describe Amos's flight from Bethel to Judah (7.12a). The book expands on Amos's identification of himself as a shepherd or herder (נקד 1.1a) by having him report how God took him, 'a herdsman' (בוקר), from his flock and compelled him to prophesy (7.14-15).

The editor's story also gives the book a rounded development from beginning to end. So the reviser has Amaziah address Amos as 'a seer', חזה (7.12a), thereby cross-referencing other parts of the book where the words of Amos are presented as something 'which he saw (חזה) concerning Israel' (1.1b), and where the visions are linked from the outset

---

50. The placement of the Bethel story in the sequence of visions is 'deliberate and intentional': see David Noel Freedman, 'Confrontations in the Book of Amos', *Princeton Seminary Bulletin* 11 (1990), pp. 240-52.

with the words spoken by the prophet (דברי עמוס 1.1a; הדבר הזה 3.1; 4.1; 5.1). Just as important is the fact that the reviser introduces the book with a preemptive correction of the viewpoint expressed in Amos's visions. While the visions record what Amos saw and foretold concerning the destiny of Judah, the commentator changes their perspective to what Amos saw and foretold concerning the fall of Israel.

Amos's title (1.1a) is also expanded by the book (1.1b) to anticipate the conflict between prophet and king (7.10-11) and to situate Amos in the reign of Jeroboam II. The book's heading distinguishes the Northern from the Southern Kingdom by referring to the king of Judah and the king of Israel (1.1b). The distinction anticipates the priest's dispute with Amos over Israel or Judah as the land for his prophecies (7.12a), just as Amaziah's order that Amos should prophesy in the land of Judah is pre-pared by the proclamation against Judah to match the one against Israel (2.4-5, 6-8) and by the motto designating Zion and Jerusalem as the origin of the divine impulse for Amos's words (1.2; 1.1a). The book insists that Amos prophesied in advance of the fall of Samaria but concedes from the outset that his prophecy was relevant to Judah.

The story of the role of the prophet connects the beginning and the end of the book. Early on in the commentary the editor anticipates Amos's encounter with Amaziah by setting up a contrast between God's appoint-ment of the prophets (2.11; 3.7-8) and Israel's rejection of them (2.12a). Just as the sons of Israel scorn the prophets by prohibiting them from speaking (2.12a; 3.7-8), so Amaziah spurns Amos by silencing him at Bethel (7.13, 16). However, in accordance with the theory of the over-whelming compulsion of the divine word upon the prophet (3.8), Yahweh overturns Amaziah's prohibition and orders Amos to prophesy (7.15). The book's theory that Yahweh does nothing without first revealing it to his servants the prophets (3.7) is confirmed by the story of Amos, who predicts of the fall of Israel and the removal of its priesthood (7.10-17).

Part 8 (8.1-14)

The eighth part of the book includes the fourth vision (8.1-3) and the concluding summary of the original prophecy (8.4-6, 9-10). The reviser uses Amos's language but gives it new significance by combining it with topics peculiar to the book. Editorial comments are added piecemeal and alter the meaning of Amos's final vision about the day of Yahweh.

The first passage of the commentary (8.3b) is marked as an editorial comment because it appears directly after the refrain 'says the Lord Yahweh', a formula used repeatedly by Amos to close off a unit of text. The insertion at 8.3b contradicts Amos's vision of the complete end of Yahweh's people (8.1-3a) by limiting the death toll to many bodies. The verb שלך (hiphil, 4.3b) that was used by Amos to describe the deportation of the women of Samaria is now retrieved by the editor to describe the disposal of many corpses (4.2-3; 8.3bB). The reference to the corpses being cast out in every place in silence has nothing to do with its actual context but is related to the book's story about corpses being brought out of a house under the warning of 'silence' (8.3b; 6.9-10; cf. 5.13).[51] Both the story and the editorial comment at 8.3b confirm the severity of God's judgment upon his people but imply that survivors go around quietly removing the bodies of their dead.

The second passage of the book (8.7-8) is attached to Amos's summary of injustices (8.4-6) by the deictic connective כל־מעשׂיהם 'all their deeds' (8.7b), a phrase which refers generally to Amos's text but disrupts its context. The book's statement, 'Yahweh has sworn by the pride of Jacob' (6.7), is a formal cross-reference to 6.8 where the book combines a quotation from its source (נשׁבע יהוה 4.2) with the idea of Jacob's pride (גאון יעקב). The rhetorical question, 'Shall not the land tremble...and everyone mourn' (8.8), pertains to the book's argument (4.13; 5.8-9) and is added as a preemptive comment on Amos's day of Yahweh (8.9-10).

Amos described Yahweh's day as an abnormal day when the sun sets at noon and when the whole earth is darkened by an eclipse of the sun (8.9a). These physical changes in the cosmos are anticipated by the book's report about disturbances in the earth. The land trembles, is heaved about, and its inhabitants mourn (8.8a). But the book downplays these abnormalities by likening the upheaval of the land, its rise and fall, to the regular seasonal swelling and subsiding of the Nile (8.8b). If tremors in the earth are normal cyclic occurrences, then solar eclipses too are normal, natural events in the cyclic order of things. For Amos defeat was the bitter end of a whole nation and was marked by the sun's disappearance. For the book defeat is not the end of Yahweh's people but occurs on an unlucky day in accordance with cosmic design.

The third passage of the commentary (8.11-14) is connected to Amos's summary of the day of Yahweh by means of the deictic phrase הנה ימים באים 'look, the days are coming'. With the addition of 8.11-14, the revi-

---

51. Cf. Gary V. Smith, 'Amos 5.13—The Deadly Silence of the Prosperous', *JBL* 107 (1988), pp. 289-91.

sion now encloses the Amos text and submerges its views about the day (8.9-10). Although the editorial passages are separate from one another, they are not isolated fragments but part of the cumulative revision of the original version.[52] So 8.13-14 is connected to 8.11-12 by צמה (8.11, 13) and develops the idea of 'thirst' for God's word. Again, 8.13-14 continues the book's argument by explaining the point of 8.7-8. Yahweh's oath (נשבע יהוה) 'by the pride of Jacob' (8.7) points back to 6.8 but leads to the fall of those who swear (הנשבעים) by Ashimah of Samaria or other gods (8.14). The earth's heaving up and down is compared with the rising and falling of the Nile (8.7-8). The report of those who shall fall (נפל) and never rise (קום 8.14b) continues the comparison with the Nile. The analogy here, unlike that used by Amos (5.2), does not mean the end of the nation but restricts destruction to worshippers of pagan gods. Young idolaters search for God's word from sea to sea, and from north to east (8.12), and this allusion to the whole country is completed by the statement that foreign gods are worshipped everywhere between Dan and Beersheba (8.14).[53]

The commentary in 8.11-14 continues to interpret Amos's day of Yahweh. In its original context 'the coming days' (4.2-3) referred to the deportation of Samaria's citizens. The book, however, moves away from imagery of war and applies 'the coming days' to its argument on prophecy by the editorial process of repetition and cross-reference. So the reviser copies the words from the oath (8.11a = 4.2a), imitates Amos's summons to hear the word of Yahweh (8.11b = 3.1; 4.1; 5.1), repeats his exhortation to seek Yahweh, substituting בקש for Amos's דרש (8.12b = 5.4, 6) and alludes to the dirge addressed to the young woman Israel (8.13a, 14b = 5.1-2). Quotations develop a contradictory argument: the coming days will not result in total deportation (4.2-3) or the end of a whole people (8.1-3a) but the end of prophecy itself (8.11b). Amos lamented the death of the woman Israel fallen in battle, never to rise (5.1-2), but the book tells us that only certain people from Israel and Judah have fallen, never to rise again (8.13-14; cf. 4.10). The positive note in Amos's message of doom is his appeal to 'seek Yahweh and live' (5.4, 6). But for the book, 'seeking Yahweh' means death by unquenchable hunger and thirst for his word

52. Cf. the usual view that Amos 8.4-14 is composed of distinct oracles: Andersen and Freedman (*Amos*, pp. 802-803, 817-23).

53. Pilgrimage is a theme in Amos and the book: Saul M. Olyan, 'The Oaths of Amos 8.14', in Gary A. Anderson and Saul M. Olyan (eds.), *Priesthood and Cult in Ancient Israel* (JSOTSup, 125; Sheffield: Sheffield Academic Press, 1991), pp. 121-49.

(8.12, 13, 14b). Amos stressed that God's word must be heard (3.1; 4.1; 5.1), but the people listen to non-words (6.13). The book conveys the opposite idea of the withdrawal of Yahweh's words (8.11b) and the terrible longing for those very words (8.12, 13).

The book resumes Amos's discussion of places of worship by pairing Dan and Bethel and repeating his reference to Beersheba (8.14; 5.5). The phrase וחי דרך באר־שבע 'and the way/road of Beersheba lives' (8.14) is an allusion to the treks made by the house of Israel to Beersheba (5.5a). Amos condemned these treks to Bethel and Gilgal, to Beersheba and Jerusalem, because worshippers ignored justice (5.5, 7; 6.1b, 21-24; 6.12b). The book rejects these shrines because they existed as centres of pagan worship. Amos envisaged the end of worship and feasts on the day of Yahweh (8.10a), but the book claims that there will be no more worship of foreign deities (8.14).

The editor smoothes in the additions by quoting and interpreting parts of Amos's text to agree with the continuous argument of the book. The addition at 8.11-14 is a cross-reference because it elaborates on earlier parts of the book. So the imagery of famine and drought reappears with its key words 'bread' and 'water' (8.11ab; 8.13b = 4.6, 8). In associating famine with Yahweh's word (8.11), the book recalls the disasters that the prophet announced in advance (4.6-12). The problem is the people's rejection of the prophet's warning to repent (4.6-13). Continuing this point in 8.11-14, the reviser explains that the grave consequence for not returning to Yahweh (4.6b, 8b, 9b, 10b) is the cessation of prophecy, and its end coincides with his days of judgment. The book also develops its earlier report that two or three cities wandered (ונעו) to another city in quest of water by stating that they wandered (ונעו) not in thirst for water but in thirst for the word of Yahweh (4.8a; 8.11b, 12a).

The book also uses cross-references to make the end of Part 8 correspond to the end of previous parts. Just as the conflict between prophet and priest (7.10-17) is added to the conclusion of the first three visions, so remarks about prophecy are appended to the conclusion of the fourth vision (8.11-14). The first text tells a story about a priest who refused to 'hear the word of Yahweh' (7.16), and the second text reports that 'the word of Yahweh' was withheld from those who rejected it (8.11b, 12b). The elimination of the Bethel priesthood is the punishment for its denial of the prophetic authority of Amos. The report that Amaziah's children shall 'fall' by the sword (כפל 7.17) cross-references and anticipates the report that girls and boys who worship foreign gods shall 'fall' and not rise (כפל

8.13-14). The theme of idolatry closes Part 8 (8.14a), and it concludes Parts 4 and 5 (5.8, 26). Just as the worship of astral gods is cited as the reason for the fall of the house of Israel (5.8; 5.26), so the fall of youth from Dan to Beersheba is attributed to the worship of alien gods (8.13-14). Pagan worship extending from the northern boundary of Israel to the southern boundary of Judah corresponds to an adversary overrunning the nation of Israel from its northern boundary in Hamat to its southern boundary in Arabah (8.14; 6.14).

The reviser continues to round off the end of the second edition by linking comments and interpretations in Part 8 with those in Part 1. When Yahweh utters his oath the land trembles and everyone mourns (אבל 8.8). Similarly, when Yahweh speaks from Zion, pasture lands mourn (ואבלו) and vegetation withers (1.2). The book's motto expresses the idea, appropriate to its contents, that devastation of the land is not an unusual event but typical of natural disasters that occur from time to time. The flooding of the Nile is cited as an example, and the inclusion of Egypt links the comment to the initial reference to Egypt (8.8b; 2.10; 3.1b). Particularly noteworthy is the topic of prophecy that connects the beginning and the end of the book. The book's comment that the people will be denied access to God's word is explained by their rejection of his prophets (8.11; 2.11).

The reviser makes the additions at the close of Part 8 look like the original text so as to obscure the meaning of Amos's visions and to leave the impression that his prophecy continues into 8.11-14.[54] So Amos's words are used to recapitulate the argument of the book. The use of his familiar language combined with the book's cross-references changes the climax of Amos's visions by redirecting attention to yet another vision (9.1-4) and to a new conclusion of his prophecy. Thus Part 8 functions as a transition to Parts 9 and 10 of the book: the Nile's rising and sinking anticipates God's sovereign power over the universe (8.8; 9.5). Images of people running from one place to another correspond to those of people running away and escaping (8.12; 9.1). Worship at various shrines leads into the fifth vision about the altar (8.14; 9.1-4). The search for God's word in four directions (8.12) anticipates the search that Yahweh makes to the farthest reaches of the universe (9.2-3). The wandering from sea to sea (8.12a) is a proleptic reference to the hiding place at the bottom of the sea

---

54. The reviser imitates Amos's corresponding patterns and rhetorical surprise: see Robert H. O'Connell, 'Telescoping N+1 Patterns in the Book of Amos', *VT* 46 (1996), pp. 56-73.

(9.3b). The idea of people hunting for God (8.12-13) anticipates the reference to the people being hunted down by Yahweh to the depths and heights (9.2-3).

Part 9 (9.1-6)

Part 9 (9.1-6) begins with a vision (9.1-4) that replaces Amos's last vision (8.1-3a).[55] The book breaks away from the structure of Amos's visions by having the prophet report what he saw (ראתי את־אדני 9.1) and not what was shown to him by Yahweh (הראני אדני 7.1, 4, 7), by substituting Yahweh's command to Amos for the dialogue between them (9.1aB),[56] by confining the visual element to the statement that Amos saw Yahweh standing beside the altar (9.1aA), and by moving immediately to God's word which becomes the substance of the vision (9.1aB-4). These structural differences are intended to be obvious and signal the fifth vision as the climactic point of the series.

The commentator has the fifth vision resemble parts of the Amos text in order to make it the last vision of the prophet. Amos's declaration, 'I saw the Lord standing beside the altar' (ראתי את־אדני נצב על־המזבח 9.1), is modelled after the third vision in which Amos reports, 'the Lord was standing beside a wall' (אדני נצב על־חומת 7.7a).[57] The words that are retrieved from the end of Amos's fourth vision (ועל־כל־ראש 'on every head' 8.10aB = בראש כלם 'on the head of every one of them' 9.1a; ואחריתם 'and the last of them' 9.1a = ואחריתה 'and the last of it' 8.10b) are used in his earlier poems (ואחריתכם 'and the last of you' 4.2b; בראש 'on the head' 2.7a; בראש גלים 'at the head of the exiles' 6.7a; cf. ראשית 'the first of the nations' 6.1b and 'the first ointments' וראשית שמנים 6.6a). The book also takes up the language of flight and escape (ינוס נס,

55. Ernst-Joachim Waschke, 'Die fünfte Vision des Amosbuches (9,1-4)—Eine Nachinterpretation', *ZAW* 106 (1994), pp. 434-45. For discussions of the visions, see Paul R. Noble, 'Amos and Amaziah in Context: Synchronic and Diachronic Approaches to Amos 7–8', *CBQ* 60 (1998), pp. 423-29; James R. Linville, 'Visions and Voices: Amos 7–9', *Bib* 89 (1999), pp. 22-42.

56. Against the traditional view supported by a few commentators that Yahweh addresses a member of his court (Driver, *Joel and Amos*, p. 216; Harper, *Amos*, p. 188; Martin-Achard, 'End of the People of God', p. 62; Andersen and Freedman, *Amos*, p. 835). But Amos has already been identified as the addressee in the previous visions (see Eslinger, 'Education of Amos', p. 54 n. 42).

57. So also Eberhard Ruprecht, 'Das Zepter Jahwes in den Berufungsvisionen von Jeremia und Amos', *ZAW* 108 (1996), pp. 55-69.

ימלט 9.1b) that Amos used to describe the day of Israel's overwhelming defeat in war (ינוס, ימלט 2.14-15).[58] The statement that Yahweh commands 'the serpent and it will bite them' (את־הנחש ונשכם 9.3b) is a quotation from Amos's tale of the man who fled into his house only to have a snake bite him (ונשכו הנחש 5.19b). All the familiar language that is borrowed by the book leaves the impression that Amos wrote the fifth vision, but his words are given a new context and meaning.

The same language conceals the fact that the fifth vision alters the meaning of the fourth vision. Amos's last vision reports the end of the whole people without discrimination (8.1-3a). However, by adding the fifth vision (9.1-4), the book leaves room for hope by shifting the focus from the complete bitter end that Amos envisaged to God's judgment on Israel and to the specific destruction of the Bethel altar: Yahweh commands the prophet to shake and shatter the columns of the Bethel temple until they come crashing down upon the heads of 'all of them' who worship there (9.1a). The word אחריתם (9.1a) does not mean that a remnant is slain with the sword, nor does it point to total annihilation or loss.[59] The term אחריתם 'last of them' recalls אחריתכן 'last of you' (4.2b), a term Amos used to describe the women of Samaria who are at the end of the column of deportees. The comparison is between the leading women of Samaria who are deported last and Judah's leaders who are deported first (בראש 6.7a). The book alludes to Amos's text by linking בראש with אחריתם (9.1a),[60] but the context is the death of all the worshippers in the Bethel temple, not exile or deportation. The implication is that Yahweh will kill the last of those who worshipped in the temple just as Amos's activity in striking and shaking the capitals has presumably killed the first of them.[61]

The fifth vision is couched in Amos's war imagery of flight and escape (9.1), but the book goes beyond the battle context by contrasting worshippers who cannot escape (9.1b) with those who flee to the underworld of the dead or to the heavens (9.2b), who hide themselves on the highest mountains (9.3), who cower at the bottom of the sea (9.3b) or go into

---

58. Paul (*Amos*, p. 276 n. 33) recognizes the pairing of the two verbs at the beginning and the end of the book.

59. Cf. Wolff, *Amos*, p. 340; Andersen and Freedman, Amos, pp. 836-37.

60. Paul (*Amos*, p. 276) sees the catchword principle at work in the pairing of the terms and in the repetition of the words 'head' and 'Caphtor' (9.1, 3, 7).

61. NJPSV connects בראש with אחריתם to give the reading 'the first of them...the last of them': see also Andersen and Freedman, p. 835.

captivity to a foreign land (9.4a). The thrust of God's speech (9.1aB-4) is that there is no place where people are beyond his reach because of his sovereign power over the entire universe. While Amos spoke of a man who is doomed to die by a snake-bite (5.19), the book turns the snake into a mythic serpent or sea–monster who at God's command bites those who hide in the depths (9.3).

The fifth vision repeats elements of Amos's text but also contains numerous cross-references to the continuous argument of the book. That the altar (9.1aA) is the temple at Bethel is evident from the book's proleptic reference to Yahweh's destruction of Bethel altars (3.14a).[62] The insistence that God will kill (אהרג...והרגתם 9.1b, 4) Bethel worshippers with the sword (9.1b, 4) is anticipated by his killing of Israel's young men with the sword (הרגתי 4.10b). The sword is the weapon of war that the book uses to portray the fall of Israel's dynasty and priesthood (7.11, 17). Earlier in the book God enjoins the house of Israel to 'seek good and not evil', or 'hate evil and love good' (5.14, 15). This distinction between good and evil prepares the way for God's decision to set his eyes upon them 'for evil and not for good' (9.4b). Yahweh's oath of judgment causes destruction upon the earth that is comparable to the flooding and sub-sidence of the Nile (ועלתה כאר כלה ונגרשה ונשקה כיאור מצרים 8.8). The hymnic comment on the fifth vision repeats the same point (ועלתה כיאר כלה ושקעה כיאר מצרים) but adds that God touches the earth to make it melt (9.5-6).

The end of Part 9 (9.5-6) contains cross-references to the ends of the preceding parts and the beginning of the book. So the end of the fifth vision (9.5-6) reaffirms the name of God (יהוה שמו 'Yahweh is his name' 9.6b = 4.13b; 5.8b), his lordship over celestial bodies (יהוה הצבאות 9.5a = 3.13b; 4.13b; 5.27b; 6.14) and repeats verbatim what the book has already said about Yahweh summoning sea-waters to pour out upon the earth (9.6b = 5.8b). The motifs of sword (1.11; 9.1, 4) and Carmel (ראש הכרמל 'top of Carmel' 1.2; 9.3) are artificial connectives binding the beginning and end of the book, just as the words הרעש/רעש link the earthquake and the shaking of the Bethel temple (1.1b; 9.1).[63]

---

62. This identification is commonly accepted by scholars (see Paul, *Amos*, p. 274).

63. On the basis of the connection between הרעש and רעש (1.1b; 9.1), it has been argued that Amos predicts the earthquake and his editor validates the prophecy: David Noel Freedman and Andrew Welch, 'Amos's Earthquake and Israelite Prophecy', in Michael D. Coogan, J. Cheryl Exum and Lawrence E. Stager (eds.), *Scripture and Other Artifacts: Essays on the Bible and Archaeology in Honor of Philip J. King*

The passages in Part 9 logically follow on from one another and are part of the continuous argument of the commentary. After reporting how the people in the temple are going to be killed (9.1a), the book insists on the futility of their flight (9.1b). Then it explains why worshippers will not escape and declares that Yahweh's power extends to every region of the world (9.2-4). The hymnic commentary (9.5-6) completes the prose section (9.1-4) by affirming God's dominance over all the earth. Certain key words and themes link verses in Part 9. After ordering the prophet to smite the capitals (9.1), God announces that he will command the serpent and the sword to become his agents of destruction (אצוה 9.1, 3-4). Balancing Amos's words, 'I saw the Lord' (ראיתי 9.1a), is God's promise, 'I will set my eyes' (עיני) upon worshippers 'who hide from my eyes (עיני מנגד) at the bottom of the sea' (9.3b, 4b). The final verses (9.5-6) repeat the language of the vision (9.1-4) and develop its ideas. So the reference to אדני 'the Lord' (9.1a) is matched by two references to Yahweh (9.5a, 6b). The sea motif (9.3b, 6b) links the vision and hymnic commentary. The emphasis on כל marks off the beginning (כלם 'all of them' 9.1) and the end of Part 9 (כל־יושבי בה 'all who dwell in it' and כלה 'all of it' 9.5). Heaven as a hiding place (השמים 9.2b) anticipates the naming of אדני (9.1a, 5a) as Yahweh of Hosts (9.5a) and the report about his upper chambers in the heavens (בשמים 9.6a).

The title 'Yahweh God of Hosts' is introduced at 3.13b, and its use in the context of the Bethel altars (3.14b) becomes clear in Part 9. After describing the destruction of the Bethel temple and its worshippers (9.1a, 1b-4), the book adds the new idea that Yahweh does not dwell in any human sanctuary but has built his residence in the heavens (9.6a). All the passages which affirm Yahweh's transcendent omnipotence (4.13; 5.8-9, 14-15, 16-17, 26-27; 6.14; 8.7-8) are added piecemeal to the end of Amos's poems in anticipation of the book's great summary which stresses the universal dominion of Yahweh God of Hosts. Since Yahweh has sovereign authority over the entire universe, he is not bound to a certain place or to the sanctuary at Bethel. Indeed destruction of the Bethel temple is only the beginning of the unrelenting divine pursuit that leads to the ends of the earth (9.1b-4).

(Louisville, KY: Westminster/John Knox Press, 1994), pp. 188-97. Shaking of the temple does not necessarily refer to earthquake tremors; רעש is used without the sense of earthquake (e.g. Ezek. 26.10): Jean Ouellette, 'The Shaking of the Thresholds in Amos 9,1', *HUCA* 43 (1972), pp. 23-27.

Part 10 (9.7-15)

Part 10 (9.7-15)[64] develops language and ideas found in Part 9. Yahweh's sovereignty over all realms of the cosmos (9.1-4, 5-6) is proleptic of his dominion over all the nations of the world (9.7). The comment on the Nile of Egypt (9.5b) anticipates the historical recollection of Yahweh's saving action in bringing up Israel from the land of Egypt (9.7b). Yahweh is determined to kill the worshippers in the Bethel temple, but he also sets his eyes upon the Northern Kingdom, whose sinfulness (9.8) is symbolized by the destruction of Bethel and all its worshippers (9.1-4).[65]

The ideas of the book are developed with reference to its ongoing argument. The revision has insisted from the beginning that Yahweh's punishment is not total and allows for the preservation of a remnant (3.12, 14-15; 4.11a; 5.3, 15b; 6.9-10; 9.1-4). The book also stresses the collapse of the Bethel sanctuary (3.14-15; 9.1), its priests and Jeroboam's dynasty (7.10-17). Accordingly, the Northern Kingdom will be destroyed, and the Southern Kingdom or 'house of Jacob' will be spared (9.8).[66] The book's distinction between the end of the sinful kingdom of Israel and the survival of the kingdom of Judah is anticipated by the book's separation of those who dwell in Samaria (3.12) from those who dwell in 'the house of Jacob' (3.13a). The Ashdodians and the Egyptians are summoned to testify against the house of Jacob (3.13a; cf. 3.9a), but Yahweh specifically punishes Bethel, smashing the horns of the altars to the ground. Parts 9 and 10 make explicit what is implied in Part 2: that the house of Jacob/Judah survives the destruction that befalls the sinful Northern Kingdom.

All the passages in the ninth and tenth parts are woven together with images and ideas to produce a wholly consistent argument. So the book builds on the distinction between the destruction of the sinful kingdom and the survival (9.8a, 8b) of the other kingdom by limiting divine judgment to

64. Scholars treat 9.7-15 as a collection of discrete and disconnected parts: Andersen and Freedman, *Amos*, p. 894.

65. Cf. those who think that the restriction of destruction to the sinful kingdom (9.8a) and to 'all the sinners of my people' (9.10a) contradicts the description of total destruction (9.1-4): see Wolff, Amos, pp. 340, 346; Martin-Achard, 'End of the People of God', p. 65.

66. As Andersen and Freedman (*Amos*, pp. 867-70, 900, 908) point out, 'if the house of Jacob is the same as the sinful kingdom the statements are contradictory'. However, they argue that the difference is not that Israel will be destroyed and Judah will be spared: 'That would be reading too much history into the material'.

all the sinners of Yahweh's people (9.10a), whether they be Israelites or Judaeans who stayed in the land or went into captivity. Worshippers in the Bethel temple and those who go into exile are representative of all the sinners who will die by the sword (9.10a). The book anticipates the restoration of the kingdom of Judah (9.11) by focusing on the fall of Israel (9.8a) and by limiting the extent of Judah's destruction (9.8b). By restricting judgment to all sinners of Israel and Judah (9.10a), the book suggests the survival of a faithful innocent remnant from both kingdoms as the restored community (9.11-15).[67]

Throughout the book the commentator develops a contradictory line of argument to repudiate Amos's view that divine judgment is indiscriminate.[68] The editor's final message of hope beyond destruction is prepared for by the idea of a remnant (3.12; 4.11a; 5.3, 15; 6.9-10). Amos juxtaposed the Northern and Southern Kingdoms (6.1-3) to make the point that the fall of Joseph/Israel (6.6) will be matched by the fall of Judah and the exile of its leaders (6.1, 7). But the book juxtaposes Israel and Judah to confirm both their defeat in war (6.8, 14) and their survival as a small nucleus. A remnant of Joseph escape destruction (5.15b), and the few who are left in Judah stay alive by not uttering the name of God (6.9-10). What Amos said about Israel became the paradigm for his prophecy to Judah. Without rejecting Amos's prophecy to Judah, the book stresses that Amos was a prophet to Israel, and that he condemned Bethel, its priesthood and its dynasty (3.14; 7.10-17; 9.1-4). Such ideas anticipate the conclusion of the book, which contrasts Israel with Judah and stresses the preservation of an innocent remnant.

The book's idea of the survival of a remnant from both nations con-

---

67. See also Wolff, *Amos*, pp. 349-50; Andersen and Freedman, *Amos*, pp. 871-82.

68. Amos's day of Yahweh is a day of battle which does not discriminate between rich and poor, oppressor and oppressed (e.g. 1.13; 2.13-16). The book acknowledges the realities of war (7.17) but contrasts the sinners who die with the innocent who survive (9.10). Cf. the recent views of Judith Sanderson, 'Amos', in Carol A. Newsom and Sharon H. Ringe (eds.), *The Women's Bible Commentary* (London: SPCK, 1992), pp. 205-209; R. Mark Daniel Carroll, *Contexts for Amos: Prophetic Poetics in Latin American Perspective* (JSOTSup, 132; Sheffield: Sheffield Academic Press, 1992), pp. 185-233; David J.A. Clines, 'Metacommentating Amos', in Heather A. McKay and David J.A. Clines (eds.), *Of Prophets' Visions and the Wisdom of Sages: Essays in Honour of R. Norman Whybray on his Seventieth Birthday* (JSOTSup, 162; Sheffield: Sheffield Academic Press, 1993), pp. 142-60 (143, 157-59); Paul R. Noble, 'Amos' Absolute 'No'', *VT* 47 (1997), pp. 329-40.

tradicts the message of Amos.[69] Amos used the phrase עַמִּי יִשְׂרָאֵל 'my people Israel' (8.2a; 7.8b) to announce Yahweh's indiscriminate destruction of Israel and Judah. The reviser repeats עַמִּי 'my people', but has Yahweh declare 'all the sinners of my people (כֹּל חַטָּאֵי עַמִּי) shall die' (9.10a). The book has said all along that there will be survivors and that a few of them will come from Samaria (3.12; 5.15b). Amos enumerated Israel's sins (חַטֹּאות 5.12), but the book uses sin (חטא 9.8a, 10a) as a concept for making distinctions between people. Now for the first time in Part 10 the book distinguishes the sinful from the innocent and limits God's judgment to all the sinners of his people' whether they come from the North or the South.

The reviser uses Amos's vocabulary to contradict his description of the day of Yahweh. Amos employed בַּיּום הַהוּא 'on that day' (8.3a, 9a) to announce the destruction of a whole people. The book repeats בַּיּום הַהוּא to convey the opposite idea of the restoration of the Davidic kingdom (9.11a). It cross-references its own text (8.11a) and quotes Amos: הִנֵּה יָמִים בָּאִים 'Behold, the days are coming' (9.13a; 4.2). Amos described the imminent days to refer to the deportation of Samaria's citizens in contrast to the book's idyllic vision of the return from exile of a faithful remnant (4.2a; 9.13-15).

The book describes the reconstruction of the kingdom of Judah with language that formerly painted a picture of total defeat and destruction. Amos used נפל and קום to describe Israel who has fallen, with no one to raise her up (5.2), but in the commentary, the verbs refer to idolaters who perish (8.14). The reviser argues that Yahweh raises up the fallen booth of David (אָקִים אֶת־סֻכַּת דָּוִיד הַנֹּפֶלֶת), a reference to the restored dynasty or kingdom of David (9.11). The suffixes in וַהֲרִסֹתָיו אָקִים 'I will raise up his ruins' and וּבְנִיתִיהָ 'I will rebuild it' agree with the context: the masculine singular suffix וַהֲרִסֹתָיו refers back to David, and the feminine singular suffix וּבְנִיתִיהָ refers back to the booth (9.11).

The book visualizes some future reconstruction of the North that corresponds to the expected restoration of the South. The third person feminine plural suffix in וְגָדַרְתִּי אֶת־פִּרְצֵיהֶן 'I will fence up their breaches' does not fit the context (9.11bA). The plural noun פְּרָצִים is retrieved from Amos's portrayal of the fall of Samaria and deportation of its citizens (4.2-3). The

---

69. Some scholars think that Amos himself talked about a remnant: e.g. Bernard A. Asen, 'No, Yes, and Perhaps in Amos and the Yahwist', *VT* 43 (1993), pp. 433-41; Michael E.W. Thompson, 'Amos—A Prophet of Hope?', *ExpTim* 104 (1992–93), pp. 71-76.

quotation פִּרְצֵיהֶן 'their breaches' (9.11bA) is an artificial reference to women captives who, according to Amos, exit in a straight line through breaches (וּפְרָצִים תֵּצֶאנָה 4.3a) in the walls of the ruined city.[70] The quotation appears in a context that speaks about the destruction and restoration of the Davidic kingdom. Just as God promises to raise up David's ruins and rebuild his booth, so he will repair the walls of Samaria. The book's future reconstruction of the South and the North (9.11) is consistent with the idea of innocent survivors from the whole people (9.10).

The solution to the problem of different suffixes (9.11) means that the unnamed subject 'they'[71] in יִירְשׁוּ (9.12a) can be identified as the remnant of Israel and Judah who will dispossess the remnant of Edom and all the nations.[72] Reference to the remnant of Edom is a thematic reminder that the book is speaking about the remnant from both the North and the South. The reference to 'all the nations' (9.12) is a reiteration of the universal theme which marks the beginning of the tenth part (9.7).

The book dismisses Amos's argument that Yahweh has known only the children of Israel out of all the families of the earth (9.7 = 3.1a, 2).[73] It contradicts special status for the children of Israel by imitating Amos's rhetorical questioning: 'Are you not like the Cushites to me, O children of Israel?... Did I [Yahweh] not bring up Israel from the land of Egypt, and the Philistines from Caphtor and the Syrians from Kir?' In contrast to Amos, whose rhetorical series produced a negative response (3.3-6; 6.12-

---

70. Most scholars follow LXX in harmonizing the suffixes in 9.11. The different MT suffixes are basic to a correct understanding of 9.11, however, and should be understood in light of the immediate and larger context: see also James Nogalski, 'The Problematic Suffixes of Amos IX 11', *VT* 43 (1993), pp. 411-17.

71. Cf. Andersen and Freedman (*Amos*, pp. 917-18) who argue that 'all the nations' will dispossess the remnant of the Edomites (9.12). The origin of this reading is found in the LXX. The problem in identifying וְכָל־הַגּוֹיִם as the subject is the presence of the conjunction ו which indicates that 'all the nations' are part of the direct object.

72. The absence of the direct object marker אֵת in וְכָל־הַגּוֹיִם (9.12) makes it ambiguous whether the phrase should be translated as a second direct object, 'and all the nations' (e.g. Mays, Amos, p. 163) or as a second genitive alongside אֱדוֹם dependent on שְׁאֵרִית 'all of (the remnant of) the nations' (Wolff, *Amos*, pp. 350-51, n. e-e); cf. Jer. 14.9.

73. For harmonization of 9.7 and 3.2, see Theodorus C. Vriezen, 'Erwägungen zu Amos 3, 2', *Archäologie und Altes Testament* (Festschrift Kurt Galling; ed. A. Kuschke and E. Kutsch; Tübingen: J.C.B. Mohr [Paul Siebeck, 1970]), pp. 255-58; Walter Vogels, 'Invitation à Revenir à l'Alliance et universalisme en Amos IX 7', *VT* 22 (1972), pp. 223-39; Bruce Vawter, *The Conscience of the Prophets* (New York: Sheed & Ward, 1961), p. 96.

13), the book's questions evoke a positive answer: Yahweh is God of the whole world and treats all the nations as equals.[74] It reduces the significance of the Exodus by noting that Yahweh has been involved in the movements of other peoples from their places of origin: he has graciously acted not only on behalf of 'the children of Israel' but also in the interest of other nations.

Just as 9.7 corrects Amos's 3.1a-2a,[75] the revision at 9.8 continues to modify his argument: Yahweh will not punish all the children of Israel for their iniquities (3.2) but will destroy only the sinful kingdom of the North (9.8a). The book applies this idea of limited divine punishment to the sinners of Yahweh's people (9.10). That he spares the house of Jacob (9.8b) and an innocent remnant from the North and the South (9.10a) is compatible with his deliverance of Israel out of Egypt (9.7). His equal interest in other nations does not diminish his concern for the destiny of his people.

The restoration of the land is described with language (בנה 'to build'; ישב 'to dwell'; נטע 'to plant'; כרמים 'vineyards'; שתה to 'drink'; יין 'wine' 9.13-14) that was originally used to depict its destruction. Amos spoke about divine judgment in terms of building houses but not dwelling in them, or planting vineyards but not drinking their wine (5.11). But the book contradicts Amos by declaring that the people of Israel will plant vineyards and drink their wine (9.14b). And the book replaces Amos's reference to individual houses (5.11) with a reference to cities that will be rebuilt and reinhabited (9.14a).[76]

The book's concern to rebuild ruined cities is consistent with its interest in the destiny of cities (4.6-8; 5.3, 9b; 6.8). Conversely a restoration without houses is consistent with the book's argument that houses must be destroyed because somehow they contribute to the overall problem that

74. So also Norman K. Gottwald, *All the Kingdoms of the Earth: Israelite Prophecy and International Relations in the Ancient Near East* (New York: Harper & Row, 1964), p. 112.

75. The rejection of the special status of Yahweh's people in the world (9.7) makes it possible to comprehend and accept their downfall (9.8): Harmut Gese, 'Das Problem von Amos 9,7', in Antonius H.J. Gunneweg and Otto Kaiser (eds.), *Textgemäß: Aufsätze und Beiträge zur Hermeneutik des Alten Testaments: Festschrift für Ernst Würthwein zum 70. Geburtstag* (Göttingen: Vandenhoeck & Ruprecht, 1979), pp. 33-38.

76. M.D. Terblanche (' "Rosen und Lavendel nach Blut und Eisen": Intertextuality in the Book of Amos', *Old Testament Essays* 10 [1997], pp. 312-21) observes that intertextual relations exist between 9.11-15 and preceding announcements of doom.

necessitates divine judgment. So Yahweh's promise to demolish buildings includes extravagant winter and summer houses, houses of ivory (3.15) and the great house with the little house (6.11). Even the sole survivor in a single house must keep quiet unless God unleashes further destruction against it (6.9-10). What is rebuilt is a humble booth or hut (9.11) which contrasts with the opulent structures that have been destroyed (3.15; 6.11).

The vision of restoration combines quotations and cross-references. The book cross-references its own text with the motif of gardens and their cultivation. The future recreation of gardens (ועשו גנות 'and they shall make gardens', 9.14) is just the opposite of divine havoc on gardens and vineyards (4.9a). God once sent a swarm of locusts to devour (יאכל) fig trees and olive trees (4.9), but in the future his people will eat (ואכלו) the fruit from their gardens (9.14b). The book of Amos closes with the theme of planting which is used metaphorically to describe the permanent re-establishment of Yahweh's people in the land: 'I will plant them upon their land; they shall never again be plucked up out of the land which I have given them' (9.15). The motif of planting is used for the purpose of proclaiming the return of God's people to their land where they will live in prosperity, enjoying the fruits of their labour, and from where they will never again be uprooted.

The reviser rounds off the book by repeating content and language from the beginning of Amos's text.[77] The book recalls Amos's initial setting of Israel among the nations with specific reference to the pairing of Syria and Philistia (9.7b = 1.3-5, 6-8). What sets off 9.7b as a quotation is the reversed order of Philistia and Syria. There is no evidence that the Syrians came from Kir, but the book recalls their exile to Kir (1.5b).[78] The book's idea that 'the remnant of Edom' (שארית אדום) will be dispossessed (9.12a) balances Amos's claim that 'the remnant of the Philistines' (שארית פלשתים) will perish (1.8b). Amos envisaged the day as the time of universal battle and defeat (1.14b; 2.13-16), but the book narrows the perspective by making the day the time of Judah's restoration (9.11). Amos characterized the drinking of wine as an oppressive act against the underprivileged (2.8). But the book borrows the wine motif for its idyllic vision of a productive land whose grapes are so abundant that mountain

77. A series of *inclusios* fashion Amos 1.1–9.6: see Erich Bosshard, 'Beobachtungen zum Zwölfprophetenbuch', *BN* 40 (1987), pp. 30-62 (33).

78. The concern is not to fix the place of origin but to show that the same God was behind the exodus of Syrians and that of Israelites: see Martin-Achard, 'End of the People of God', p. 64.

and hilltop vineyards flow with fresh wine (9.13, 14a). The book binds the beginning and end of the tenth part with נאם־יהוה 'says Yahweh' (9.7a, 8b) and אמר יהוה אלהיך 'says the Lord your God' (9.15b): It imitates Amos's procedure of using the repeated refrain in order to divide the units of his first poem, and it creates a chiastic pattern by reversing Amos's order of אמר and נאם.

Towards the end of Part 10 the book retrieves שוב from Amos's speech against the nations. The positive message in the clause ושבתי 'I will restore' (9.14a) reverses the prophet's לא אשׁיבנו 'I will not cause it to turn back' (chs. 1–2). Amos used שוב in the hiphil to describe the day of war which Yahweh says he will not turn back, but the book employs שוב in its qal form to describe the coming days of restoration in which Yahweh will act to revive the fortunes of his people.

The reviser adds cross-references to make the end of the book correspond to its beginning. All the cross-references contribute to the homogenization of the commentary, but some cross-references advance the developing argument. The motif of Yahweh bringing Israel up from Egypt (2.10) is repeated with a change of meaning (9.7). The verbs שמד and ירשׁ appear only at the beginning and end of the book. Just as Yahweh destroyed (השמדתי 2.9a) the Amorites, so he will destroy the sinful kingdom of Israel (והשמדתי 9.8a). These initial references (2.9) are balanced by the book's final distinction between Israel, which will be destroyed (9.8a), and Judah, which will survive the destruction (9.8b). The book reports that Yahweh led the children of Israel to possess (לרשׁת) the land of the Amorite (2.10), an introductory motif which corresponds to the closing statement that the remnant of Israel and Judah will dispossess (ייר שׁו) the remnant of Edom and the nations (9.12).[79] The negative reference to Edom (9.12a) is linked with the proclamation of war against Edom (1.11-12). The specific reference to the remnant of Edom is confirmation of Edom's destruction. The book compares the destruction of the fruit of the Amorite (פריו 'his fruit' 2.9a) with the abundance of the fruit of Yahweh's people (פריהם 'their fruit' 9.14b). The drinking of wine is associated with the people's rejection of the Nazirites (2.12a), but at the end of the commentary, the drinking of wine symbolizes Yahweh's reversal of the fortunes of his people (9.13-15).

---

79. Paul (*Amos*, p. 292) observes that 9.12 is 'analogous to the beginning of the book' and forms 'an overarching inclusio'.

Summary

Most editorial material is added as footnotes at the end of Amos's poems (3.12-15; 4.6-13; 5.8-9, 25-27; 6.8-14; 7.10-17; 8.11-14). The footnotes revise Amos's text and develop the continuous argument of the book. Only a few interior additions do not fall under the category of footnote commentary. The majority of internal insertions are found at the beginning of the book (1.1b, 1.2, 9-10, 11-12; 2.4-5, 9-12; 3.1b) and these additions introduce themes that are mainly taken up in later parts of the book. The other interior comments (5.3, 13-17; 8.3b, 7-8) contain the theology of remnant which links one part with another, is developed throughout the footnote commentary (3.12-15; 4.11; 5.8-9; 8.13-14) and is recapitulated in the reviser's final argument (9.8-10).

There are two very different types of addition. Some are visible (1.9-10, 11-12; 2.4-5, 9-12; 4.6-13; 5.8-9, 13, 25-27; 6.8-11, 14; 8.3b, 7-8) and some are invisible (1.1b-2; 3.1b, 7-8, 12-15; 5.3, 14-17; 7.10-17; 8.11–9.1-4). Visible insertions stand out from their context as digressions and have little or nothing to do with the immediate context. They are formally attached to the context, are generally marked by deictic elements[80] but refer to a distant context. They continue to anticipate or develop the secondary argument of the book and are characterized by cross-references. By contrast invisible insertions are blended into the original by borrowing the language of Amos's prophetic text, either from the immediate or from the distant context. Invisible insertions alter the meaning of the original version and are especially characterized by quotations.

The two types of addition reflect what scholars have always noticed about the book of Amos. On the one hand, there is the common perception that the prophet's words are mixed with secondary material. On the other hand, there is the completely opposite perception that many additions look as if they are original. What has been clearly seen is that some passages interrupt original thought patterns while others seem to flow as a single unified text. The jagged and uneven way in which visible insertions are

---

80. To summarize, ואנכי (2.9a) points back to לא אשׁיבנו 'I will not cause it to turn back'; וגם־אני (4.6a) and וגם אנכי (4.7a) point back to the original context with its recurring references to Yahweh (4.1-5). The proper noun 'Yahweh' (5.8b) points back to his name in 5.4a, 6a. The adverb לכן 'therefore' connects the comment in 5.13 with the preceding text. The second person plural pronominal suffixes in the verbs of 5.25-27 point back to 5.21-24 where God speaks in the first person and directly addresses the Israelites.

added makes clear to the reader that the book of Amos combines original text with commentary. Obvious insertions signal the intrusion of commentary and interpretation. Conversely, the smooth and even way in which invisible insertions are added is the means by which the book creates the impression that the additions are original. Inconspicuous insertions are supposed to look as though the passages were written by Amos.

Editorial additions should not be understood as a later repudiation of the Amos text or disrespect for the prophet's message.[81] The high regard for Amos's writing is apparent in the reviser's decision to preserve it. Far from ignoring or suppressing the original version, the editor uses the prophet's words as the authority on which to base new possiblities of interpretation. The reviser's task is not only to transmit Amos's written text but also to transmit the new meaning or interpretation it has acquired.

The purpose of the book of Amos is to update or give contemporary relevance to the prophet's text by supplementing and correcting it. The result of this activity is the completion, enhancement and enrichment of the original content. In adding useful information and new ideas, the author of the book supplies what is lacking or makes explicit what is only implied in the original argumentation. The additions strengthen Amos's prophecy by making it a complete whole. The book indicates that material is added by its repetition of the immediate or distant context. Quotations from Amos often turn the prophet's words into their opposite, but the reviser obviously appreciates and values the prophet's writing. Otherwise there is no reason for preserving his words and passing them on. Often the reviser wants us to think that Amos himself added the contradictory passages. Or, to put it another way, the book is not contradictory at all but for the reviser is an authentic expression of what the prophet actually said or meant to say. Esteem for the prophet's work is conveyed by this insistence that the book is the actual text of Amos.

The overall effect of the reviser's cumulative quotations and cross-referencing is that the book of Amos seems to be a single homogenized text with a unified argument. The reviser is an author who has rewritten what Amos has expressed about the past and future in the light of present realities and future expectations. The author of the book deals with all the elements of Amos's argument but gives the original version a different meaning to fit a new historical era with its own concerns and interests.

---

81. Contrast Andersen and Freedman (*Amos*, p. 863), who argue that the contrary message (9.11-15) means that the editor had a low estimate of the authority of the prophet's own words.

Chapter 3

PROPHECY AS A PERFORMING ART
AND THE EMERGENCE OF BOOK CULTURE

The literary distinction between Amos's poetry and its prophetic update is matched by a difference in the form of the two works.[1] Amos composed a song cycle he could perform before a live audience, but his editor changed it into an historical and biographical piece of archival interest.

The Comic Structure of the Book

Northrop Frye's critical theory identifies 'narrative categories of literature broader than, or logically prior to, ordinary literary genres'.[2] Two such categories are the tragic and the comic. The book of Amos contains laments, riddles, messenger speech, exhortations, hymns, biography, myths of creation and flood, to mention only a few genres.[3] But we must stand back from all these individual literary forms to see that comedy is the organizing design of the entire book. Comedy does not seem to be a fitting classification for a book full of gloom and catastrophe. Since we tend to classify a piece of literature by its predominating mood, 'comic' has come to mean funny and 'tragic' sad. But tragedy and comedy are also names of a structure: the book of Amos contains a parody of the tragic form (7.10-17), and it has the structure of a comedy.[4]

Comedy has a U-shaped plot, with the action sinking into a series of

1. J. Rilett Wood, 'Tragic and Comic Forms in Amos', *BibInt* 6 (1998), pp. 20-48.

2. Northrop Frye, *Anatomy of Criticism: Four Essays* (Princeton: Princeton University Press, 1957), p. 162; see also pp. 94, 140.

3. Claus Westermann, *Basic Forms of Prophetic Speech* (trans. Hugh Clayton White; Philadelphia: Westminster Press, 1977), esp. pp. 90-128, 199-209.

4. Northrop Frye, *A Natural Perspective: The Development of Shakespearean Comedy and Romance* (New York: Columbia University Press, 1965), pp. 49-50.

misfortunes and then turning upward to an unexpected happy ending.[5] The book of Amos works this way, with a series of declines and ending with a rise in the action. Technically a comedy by virtue of its happy ending, it ends with a vision of renewal, restoration and prosperity: God promises to re-establish the fallen kingdom of Judah, to create a new society in which a remnant from both the North and the South will return to the land with all its imaginable abundance to rebuild the ruined cities (9.11-15).

Comedy's rising movement is apparent both in the overall structure of the book and in its individual parts. Each part ends with a comic piece that lifts the falling action. Each part moves in the direction of the idealized perfect world described in the book's conclusion. So the historical summary of God's beneficence (2.9-11) relieves the dramatic tension of Israel's defeat in war (2.13-16) and foreshadows the apocalyptic vision of restoration (9.11-15). The action of Part 2 (3.1-15) sinks to a low point with fallen Israel and its capital city (3.9-11). But the concluding segment sends the action upwards by using rescue to express destruction (3.12) and by depicting the fall of Samaria in restrictive terms. So Part 2 ends with a plot segment whose narrow focus is the fallen altars of Bethel and the ruin of lavish northern houses (3.13-15).

The mythical basis of comedy is a movement towards the rebirth of nature.[6] What causes the rising action at the end of Parts 3, 4, 5 and 9 (4.13; 5.8-9; 5:25-27; 9.5-6) are the recurrences in nature—the regular return of dawn out of dark, day out of night, the sinking and rising of the Nile. The book's movement towards the restoration of the human community is symbolized by nature's power of renewal and by the belief that the whole natural order, including wind and stars, mountains and sea, is under God's control. The predictable movement from death to rebirth makes it possible to contemplate a world in which God creates a new society out of defeat.

The action of Part 6 (6.1-14) plunges downwards with the report of Israel's tragic fall and the inevitable fall of Judah (6.6-7). But a rising movement occurs when a story is told about a man who survived the destruction of a house and the death of its occupants, and the story represents the survival of Israel and Judah as a remnant (6.9-11, 14). Similarly, in Part 7 (7.1-17) a vision of God overthrowing the dynasty and destroying

5. Northrop Frye, *Fables of Identity: Studies in Poetic Mythology* (New York: Harcourt, Brace & World, 1963), p. 15; *The Great Code: The Bible and Literature* (Toronto: Academic Press, 1982), p. 169.

6. Frye, *Natural Perspective*, pp. 119-23.

northern and southern sanctuaries causes the plot to turn downwards (7.7-9). But the action turns upwards as God's message drifts away from the impending doom of God's people to target an individual priest in Israel (7.10-17). Again, the action in Part 8 (8.1-14) begins on a gloomy note with a vision of the end of a people (8.2-3a). This sense of fatality is heightened by the description of the horrible day (8.9-10). The turning around of the plot from total doom occurs as the action comes to rest on the death of idolaters in Israel and Judah (8.13-14).

The tenth part (9.7-15) begins on a low point with the destruction of the sinful Northern Kingdom (9.8a). But immediately the rising movement begins to occur when total destruction is ruled out and allowance is made for the preservation of a remnant (9.8b). The action rises further with God's proclamation that only the sinners of his people will die (9.10). This survival theme anticipates the book's impossible but desirable dream of a whole people living forever in the land God has given them (9.11-15).

All the comic structures and themes in the book advance towards the new society of the final vision. The world we find there is a world whose reality is created out of human desire.[7] The new society is based on the old but is completely transformed to fit our dreams and aspirations. The idyllic society emerging at the end of the book is what a fallen people recognized as the desirable solution to their situation. The book's resolution is a reflection of the people's yearning for future renewal in response to the destruction of Jerusalem, to the collapse of nationhood and loss of land. Its comic vision was achieved in an era when nothing was left: it was satisfying and relevant to look beyond defeat and exile to future renewal and restoration.

The Tragic Poetry of Amos

Embedded in the book of Amos is a cycle of poetry with the shape of a tragedy.[8] Tragedy works in the opposite way to comedy. The nature of comedy is to rise, and the nature of tragedy is to fall. Tragedy has an inverted U, the action rising in crisis to a point of 'peripety' or reversal

---

7. Frye, *Natural Perspective*, pp. 75, 115.
8. Norman K. Gottwald ('Ideology and Ideologies in Israelite Prophecy', in Reid [ed.], *Prophets and Paradigms*, pp. 136-49, esp. 139) recognizes that the first stage of Amos ends on a tragic note 8.9-10; see also N.K. Gottwald, 'Tragedy and Comedy in the Latter Prophets', Semeia 32 (1984), pp. 83-96.

and plunging downwards to catastrophe.[9] Each poem is set off as a separate entity, yet the individual poems are interrelated and share a unity since a whole story is developed from one poem to another. The best modern analogy is the German Lied and can be illustrated in Robert Schumann's *Frauenliebe und -leben*, a popular song cycle of eight poems which tells the story of a woman's awakening love, her courtship, engagement, wedding, maternity and bereavement. The action steadily rises until it reaches its highest point, the woman's delight in motherhood, but her mood of joy is abruptly broken with her song of sorrow over her beloved's sudden death.[10] Amos's tragic cycle of poetry works in this way: the action rises to reversal and turns down to an unexpected grievous ending. The cycle's rising and falling movement is evident in the overall structure of the cycle and in the individual poems.

Aristotle, the first literary critic, emphasized 'Reversal of Intention' as the emotional power in tragedy.[11] Reversal in tragedy is not the change of fortune from good to bad but arises from the internal structure of the plot.[12] So, as Amos's cycle of poetry shows, reversal refers to a situation that first develops in one direction but suddenly develops in an opposite direction. His first poem (chs. 1–2*) begins with a diatribe against the nations for their war crimes. The escalation of the declamatory speech against one nation and another disguises the real purpose of the poem. The audience condemns the nations, but now Israel's crimes are held up for condemnation, and the audience cannot withhold assent. It is lured to the logical conclusion that Israel deserves punishment. The abrupt reversal of direction is followed by the downwards movement of the action to Israel's defeat in battle.

A paradoxical statement opens the second poem (3.1a, 2-6, 9-11). This taking back what is said is a clue that things are not what they seem. The paradox introduces a popular riddle which leads to the ominous question, 'Does evil befall a city unless Yahweh has done it?' The climactic

---

9.   Frye, *Great Code*, p. 176; *Fables of Identity*, p. 25.

10.   Robert Schumann (1810–1856) set to music the intimate domestic poetry of the German Romanticist, Adalbert von Chamisso (1781–1838), but omitted the comforting verses of the ninth poem so that his songs of innocence would end with tragic experience: Eric Sams, *The Songs of Robert Schumann* (London: Ernst Eulenburg, 2nd edn, 1975), pp. 128-38.

11.   For a translation of Aristotle, *De Poetica* (*Poetics*), see Richard McKeon (ed.), *The Basic Works of Aristotle* (New York: Random House, 1941), pp. 1453-87.

12.   Aristotle, *Poetics* 1452a15-20.

moment has been reached, and the action falls as Samaria is cited as the object of destruction. The action of the third poem (4.1-5) does not veer around to its opposite but ends with a reversal of what is expected. It concludes with the startling statement that though the people faithfully offer up their sacrifices at Bethel and Gilgal, they come to sin.

The fourth poem (5.1-7) is best described as 'a recognition scene'. Reversal and recognition belong together as complementary parts of the tragic plot. Aristotle defined reversal as a change of a situation into its opposite, while recognition is a change from ignorance to knowledge.[13] Poem four starts at the bottom with the death of the woman Israel. The melancholy and despair of the opening lifts with the repeated summons to seek Yahweh and live. But this respite is short-lived as the action plunges downwards. What emerges from the reversal is the disquieting recognition that the fire rages at Bethel with no one to quench it and that it reaches beyond the kingdom of Israel (5.6). Poem 4 gives the first clue that the poet's 'you' (5.1, 7) embraces more than the North. The fifth poem (5.10-12, 18-24) ends with unexpected catastrophe: Yahweh's day will be an exact reversal of people's hopes and desires; there will be no light or brightness in it, only gloom and darkness (5.18-20). The shocking verdict is that doom could fall on any feast day when the people deliver up their offerings to God (5.21-24).

In the sixth poem (6.1-7, 12-13) the plot begins to unravel. The poem is ostensibly an attack on the complacency and indolence of the rich classes in Zion and Samaria. But the scene breaks off with the surprising condemnation of Judah's leaders for failing to grieve over the ruin of Israel. This unexpected shift from the North to the South is the change upon which the tragic plot pivots. In this moment of discovery lies the crisis of the whole cycle. The plot defeats expectations as it comes to focus on Judah. What follows reversal and recognition is a sinking of the action to the exile of Judah's rulers (6.7).

The cycle's seventh and last poem (7–8*) consists of four visions. The visions of locusts overrunning the land and fire destroying the sea are horrors revoked by God on the grounds of Judah's size and vulnerability (7.1-6). This pattern of doom and reprieve raises expectations that Judah will survive after all. But the third vision of the plumb line creates suspense because it is left standing as a threat of destruction (7.7-9). Out of the positive image of the summer fruit (8.1-2a), the unexpected erupts

---

13. *Poetics* 1452a30-b10, 1454b16-1455a20.

with an announcement of doom. Downward movement towards catastrophe is expressed by the terrible day of Yahweh which brings the end of the cycle into line with its beginning. God's words, 'I will not take it back', push forward to the tragic day which marks the end of his people (8.3a, 4b, 9-10).

The act which undoes the tragic hero is, according to Aristotle, some flaw or error. It could be a moral flaw or an intellectual mistake, but the calamity proceeds from within. Heroes and heroines are not arbitrarily struck down but cause their own doom. The cycle is a social tragedy because it relates the fall of a nation. It focuses on upper-class figures who are not evil or worthless people[14] but observant worshippers who believe they are righteous. Ancient tragic heroes are usually famous or prosperous and have an extraordinary destiny within their grasp until they lose it.[15] So the cycle portrays Israel as no ordinary people. At the outset it tells us that God has chosen them 'out of all the families of the earth' (3.2a).

A tragic plot is designed to provoke our emotions. Aristotle's standard formula is pity and fear.[16] Such emotions are best produced when events come on us by surprise, and Amos's reversals and recognitions produce strong emotional effects. At the outset of the cycle audience sympathy is aroused for fallen Israel. Though the nation is portrayed as deserving defeat, brave and noble warriors die pitiful deaths (2.13-16), and the dirge over the body of the girl Israel intensifies the pathos (5.1-2). Pity turns into fear at the cycle's mid-point where reversal is coupled with recognition. Terror is occasioned by uncertainty, by the expectation of disaster, and it becomes the key emotional response to the awareness of an even greater disaster lurking on the horizon.

The Greek Analogy

When we have, as we do here, a series of poems with a tragic structure that strives to evoke an emotional response from an audience, then we must learn to hear and see the poetry as a performing art. The song cycle is the creative work of a tragic poet who composed a dramatic monologue both for entertainment and to effect a change in his audience. The analogy for the idea comes from archaic Greek poetry of the seventh and sixth centuries, and it can be classified into three main types: solo or lyric monody

---

14. Frye, *Anatomy of Criticism*, p. 65.
15. Aristotle, *Poetics* 1453a1-17.
16. *Poetics* 1453b14-1454a15.

sung to the accompaniment of the lyre (*kithara*); elegy sung to the double flute (*aulos*) or recited without musical accompaniment; and choral lyric sung by groups of young men and women, accompanied instrumentally and reinforced by the power of the dance. Performance poetry from Homer onwards was intended for contexts of social feasting, the public religious festival for choral lyric, and the aristocratic drinking party called the symposium for monodic poetry.[17]

The symposium is the Greek equivalent of the *marzeaḥ*, a social institution which spans nearly two thousand years, from the thirteenth century BCE to the sixth century of the present era, with textual and visual evidence from Phoenicia, Syria and Palestine.[18] The term *marzeaḥ* is found in two biblical texts (Amos 6.7; Jer. 16.5), and among the prophets, Amos provides the most comprehensive description of a Judaean symposium.[19] His poetry is particularly relevant for a comparison of the eastern *marzeaḥ* and its Greek counterpart because it reproduces all the characteristics which define the symposium in the ancient world.[20] an organization owning a *marzeaḥ*-house with fields and vineyards, a banquet

17. Richmond Lattimore (trans.), *Greek Lyrics* (Chicago: University of Chicago Press, 2nd edn, 1960), pp. iv-vi, 24, 47; Herington, *Poetry into Drama*, pp. 5-39, 49-57, 112-26; Oswyn Murray, 'Forms of Sociality', in Jean-Pierre Vernant (ed.), *The Greeks* (trans. Charles Lambert and Teresa Lavender Fagan; Chicago: University of Chicago Press, 1995), pp. 218-53; Ezio Pellizer, 'Outlines of a Morphology of Sympotic Entertainment', in Oswyn Murray (ed.), *Sympotica: A Symposium on the Symposion* (Oxford: Clarendon Press, 1990), pp. 177-84.

18. Jonas C. Greenfield, 'The *Marzeaḥ* as a Social Institution', in J. Harmatta and G. Komoroczy (eds.), *Wirtschaft und Gesellschaft im Alten Vorderasien* (Budapest: Akadémiai Kliado, 1976), pp. 451-55; Bezalel Porten, *Archives from Elephantine: The Life of an Ancient Jewish Military Colony* (Berkeley: University of California Press, 1968), pp. 179-86; Brian Peckham, 'Phoenicia and the Religion of Israel: The Epigraphic Evidence', in Patrick D. Miller, Jr, Paul D. Hanson and S. Dean McBride (eds.), *Ancient Israelite Religion: Essays in Honor of Frank Moore Cross* (Philadelphia: Fortress Press, 1987), pp. 79-99; Philip J. King, 'The *Marzeaḥ*: Textual and Archaeological Evidence', *Eretz Israel* 20 (1989), pp. 98*-106*.

19. For a discussion of the *marzeaḥ* in the prophets, see Susan Ackerman, 'A *Marzeaḥ* in Ezekiel 8.7-13?', *HTR* 82 (1989), pp. 267-81.

20. Jane B. Carter, 'Thiasos and *Marzeaḥ*: Ancestor Cult in the Age of Homer', in Susan Langdon (ed.), *New Light on a Dark Age: Exploring the Culture of Geometric Greece* (Columbia, MO: University of Missouri Press, 1997), pp. 72-112 (78-79); Philip J. King, *Amos, Hosea, Micah–An Archaeological Commentary* (Philadelphia: Westminster Press, 1988), pp. 137-61 *idem*, 'The *Marzeaḥ* Amos Denounces', BARev 15.4 (1988), pp. 34-44.

held in honour of a patron God, with eating and drinking wine from cups or bowls while reclining together amorously on beds or couches, singing and listening to music, slaughtering animals for feasting or sacrifice, cultic anointing with oils or perfume,[21] and mourning the dead with memorial rites.

Ancient Near Eastern reliefs establish banquets as places of performance by depicting musicians entertaining the upper classes, and some of the evidence points to a possible *marzeaḥ*.[22] What is missing from most of

21. Amos talks about participants at the *marzeaḥ* anointing themselves with oil (6.6a). Archilochus and Alcaeus bear witness to the practice of anointing the breast and head with perfume: see Archilochus, fr. 30, in J.M. Edmonds (ed. and trans.), *Greek Elegy and Iambus*, II (LCL; Cambridge, MA: Harvard University Press, 1931), pp. 112-13; Alcaeus, fr. 50, in David A. Campbell (ed. and trans.), *Greek Lyric*, I (LCL; Cambridge, MA: Harvard University Press, 1982), pp. 262-63.

22. Several Phoenician bronze and silver bowls dating from the late eighth to early seventh centuries combine military activity with banquet scenes of male and female participants, both seated and reclining, and in the company of musicians: Eleanor Ferris Beach, 'The Samaria Ivories, *Marzeaḥ* and Biblical Texts', *BA* 55 (1992), pp. 130-39 (134). One Phoenician bowl from Salamis in Cyprus, dated between 675 and 625 BCE, portrays a possible *marzeaḥ* with its bowls of wine, naked men and women engaging in explicit sexual activity, and a nude male and female playing the lyre and tambourine: Glenn Markoe, *Phoenician Bronze and Silver Bowls from Cyprus and the Mediterranean* (Classical Studies, 26; Berkeley, CA: University of California Press, 1985), pp. 174-75; V. Karageorghis, 'Erotica from Salamis', *Rivista di Studi Fenici 21 Supplement* (1993), Plate I, pp. 7-13. An early eighth-century shrine at Kuntillet 'Ajrud in northern Sinai might be a *marzeaḥ*-house, a rectangular building with benches for sitting, containing large stone mixing bowls and wine jars, and among the discovered drawings on storage jars are the figures of a lyre player and worshippers with forearms raised: Z. Meshel, *Kuntillet 'Ajrud: A Religious Center from the Time of the Judean Monarchy on the Border of Sinai* (Israel Museum Catalog No. 175; Jerusalem: Israel Museum, 1978); King, '*Marzeaḥ: Textual and Archaeological Evidence*', pp. 101*-102*. Similarly, in the Greek world, the sanctuary provided for ritual dining in both rectangular and circular buildings, with the former being the norm: Frederick Cooper and Sarah Morris, 'Dining in Round Buildings', in Murray (ed.), *Sympotica*, pp. 66-85. A twelfth-century ivory plaque from Megiddo depicts a king raising a cup in celebration of some victory in war; he appears with a female musician playing a lyre and with two servants standing beside a large mixing bowl of wine: King, *Amos, Hosea, Micah*, pp. 142-43. A late seventh-century relief from Nineveh depicts Ashurbanipal reclining on an ornate couch at a garden feast with musicians providing entertainment while the king and queen drink from bowls. This banquet scene has been designated as a *marzeaḥ*: Richard D. Barnett, 'Assurbanipal's Feast', *Eretz Israel* 18 (1985), pp. 1*-6*; King, *Amos, Hosea, Micah*, pp. 148-49.

the eastern evidence is the poetry itself or the songs that were sung to musical accompaniment.[23] Recent studies, however, show that a large part of extant archaic Greek poetry was composed for singing before a symposium audience. By the late eighth century sympotic poetry was already created and performed by group members, as attested by a poem inscribed on Nestor's cup which playfully associates drinking with sexual desire.[24] The seventh-century poets Archilochus, Callinus and Tyrtaeus talk about symposium themes and thus offer many points of contact with the contemporary poetry of Amos. Greek poetry of both the seventh and sixth centuries is the proximate and explicit analogy for understanding that early prophetic poetry is performance poetry and that poetic recitation was an important aspect of the ancient symposium.

Inferences from the actual poems themselves indicate the circumstances or occasions on which they were performed. Greek poets are frequently found in their poetry drinking wine. In one such elegy, Archilochus summons soldiers to become drunk on the watch, a song evoking guard duty without actually emulating an actual situation and containing allusions to

---

23. A notable exception is thirteenth-century Ugaritic poetry, which has all the elements that are familiar to participants in a *marzeah*: gods and heroes depicted in banquet and war scenes, recurring themes of eating and drinking, drinking cups and bowls, slaughter of animals, singers and musical instruments (the lyre, drum and cymbals), reclining couches and pleasures of the bed, death and mourning rituals, concern for justice at the city gate, and laws regulating the relations between citizens. Ugaritic poetry was composed to be recited, as indicated by the repeated formulae and the reciter's name in the Baal cycle. The literary evidence points to the *marzeah* as one important context of performance. References to the *marzeah* and its features occur in both Akkadian and alphabetic texts from Ras Shamra, and one text concerns El's drunken stupor at a drinking feast or *marzeah*: Marvin H. Pope, 'A Divine Banquet at Ugarit', in J.M. Efird (ed.), *The Use of the Old Testament in the New and Other Essays: Studies in Honor of W.F. Stinespring* (Durham, NC: Duke University Press, 1972); John L. McLaughlin, 'The *marzeah* at Ugarit', *UF* 23 (1991), pp. 265-81. A handy translation of Ugaritic poetry is Michael David Coogan (ed.), *Stories from Ancient Canaan* (Philadelphia: Westminster Press, 1978). Eighth-century Hebrew inscriptions found at Kuntillet 'Ajrud are in the form of poetry and refer to the patron God (Graham I. Davies, *Ancient Hebrew Inscriptions: Corpus and Concordance* [Cambridge: Cambridge University Press, 1991], pp. 78-82). One poetic fragment (No. 8.023, p. 82) describes a divine theophany which causes the mountains to melt (cf. Mic. 1.4), and to judge from the broken text, the addressee is summoned to bless Baal and the name of El on the day of battle.

24. Oswyn Murray, 'Nestor's Cup and the Origins of the Greek Symposion', *Annali di Archeologia e Storia Antica* NS 1 (1994), pp. 47-54.

the sympotic activity of a warrior group.[25] As for Archilochus's song in praise of the military life in which he boasts that bread and wine are won by his spear on which he reclines when he drinks, the references are to the practice of feasting and sprawling on a symposium couch.[26] Callinus summons young men of Ephesus to rise and fight for their country, but his rhetorical questions, 'How long will you lie idle? Have you no shame of your sloth?', indicate that his martial elegy is directed to warriors reclining at a symposium and enjoying pleasant relaxation.[27] In his political poems, Alcaeus exhorts his companions at symposia to drink wine and forget their sorrows, the military setbacks and hardships of exile.[28] All the texts cited here illustrate that archaic poetry typically mixes contemporary imagery of the fighting man with that of the private drinking party.

Similar combinations of banquet and war scenes are found throughout Amos's poetry, and he, like his Greek counterparts, communicates the fact that the world of his audience is dominated by banquet and war. Representations of the symposium are used to structure his monody and its arguments. So the first poem introduces a symposium in Samaria which is attached to a particular sanctuary: it features citizens drinking wine and lying down together in a group context for pleasures of sex and sleeping, but members of the all-night drinking group are condemned for financing their association with money they have taken from the poor by extortion (2.6-8). So sympotic leisure gives way to war in which divine punishment involves the whole northern kingdom of Israel, both the wrongdoers and their victims (2.13-16).

The next allusion to the drinking party is found in the third poem which, in common with Greek poetry, contains short pieces of exhortation. Amos's elegy is replete with the familiar vocatives in direct address, either to individuals or to an entire group (Amos 3.1; 5.1; 8.4), that typify contemporary Greek lyric and elegy. Archilochus, for example, says 'O

25. Archilochus, fr. 4, in Edmonds, *Greek Elegy*, II, pp. 98-99; Ewen L. Bowie, 'Early Greek Elegy, Symposium and Public Festival', *JHS* 106 (1986), pp. 13-25 (16).

26. Archilochus, fr. 2, in Edmonds, *Greek Elegy, II*, pp. 98-99; Bowie, '*Early Greek Elegy*', p. 18.

27. Callinus, fr. 1, in J.M. Edmonds (ed. and trans.), *Greek Elegy and Iambus, I* (LCL; Cambridge, MA: Harvard University Press, 1931), pp. 44-47; Bowie, '*Early Greek Elegy*', pp. 15-16.

28. Alcaeus, frs. 70, 73, 129, 332, 335, in Campbell, *Greek Lyric, I*, pp. 274-78, 296-99, 372-73, 378-81.

Glaucus', 'O Pericles';[29] Amos addresses the women of Samaria, 'you cows of Bashan' (4.1). While Alcaeus adopts for himself the persona of an imbiber by appealing to a companion, 'Drink, and get drunk, Melanipus, with me',[30] Amos depicts the women of Samaria as dramatic personae who order their husbands, 'Bring, let us drink' (4.1). Women drink with men at a symposium held at Bethel, as suggested by the pun, 'house of their God' (2.8).

Just as Greek poems mention the symposium's cultivation of the vine and the drinking customs connected with it,[31] so Amos's fifth poem contains references to the planting of vineyards, the drinking of wine (5.10b) and the delights of the feast-days which are celebrated in honour of Yahweh the patron God (5.21-24; 4.4-5). The imagery of light and darkness in the poem is characteristic of Amos's poetry and that of his Greek counterparts. Alcman's choral work *Partheneion* contains references to the night, sun and dawn, and was probably performed at a festival shortly before daybreak in celebration of the movement from darkness to light.[32] Alcaeus describes an all-night drinking party whose celebrants wait for daylight to be over so they can light the lamps and take down the large decorated cups.[33] Analogously, Amos depicts an all-night symposium whose participants wait for dawn to break but meet instead a day of darkness and death (5.18-20; 8.9-10).

Amos's sixth poem describes typical symposia in Samaria and Jerusalem, and the individual elements of the symposium are scattered throughout the cycle. The rich recline upon ivory-panelled beds and couches, a practice which is well adapted to the pleasures of love already hinted at in the opening poem. Alcman, in the late seventh century, provides the earliest literary evidence for a reclining symposium in Greece and its typical food, tables laden with poppy cakes, linseed, sesame and honey cakes.[34] At an earlier point in the same century, Amos itemizes the food for a reclining

29. Archilochus, frs. 9-13, 14, in Edmonds, *Greek Elegy*, II, pp. 102-105; On Archilochus, see Barron and Easterling, 'Elegy and Iambus', in Easterling and Knox (eds.), *Early Greek Poetry*, pp. 76-87.

30. Alcaeus, fr. 38A, in Campbell, *Greek Lyric, I*, pp. 250-53.

31. Alcaeus, frs. 119, 342, in Campbell, *Greek Lyric, I*, pp. 292-93, 376-77.

32. Alcman, fr. 1, in David A. Campbell (ed. and trans.), *Greek Lyric, II* (LCL; Cambridge, MA: Harvard University Press, 1988), pp. 360-69; Segal, Archaic Choral Lyric', in Easterling and Knox (eds.), *Early Greek Poetry*, pp. 129-38.

33. Alcaeus, fr. 346, in Campbell, *Greek Lyric, I*, pp. 378-81.

34. Alcman, fr. 19, in Campbell, *Greek Lyric, II*, pp. 410-11; Murray, 'Forms of Sociality', p. 224; *idem*, 'Nestor's Cup', p. 48.

symposium which may be connected to a Passover feast,[35] where members eat prohibited leavened bread as well as unspecified cereal food (4.5a; 5.22) along with lambs and calves (6.4b) in keeping with reclining banquets of bread and meat represented on Greek archaic vases.[36]

The poetry of the early prophets and their Greek contemporaries was composed to be sung to musical accompaniment. Because their audiences could see the instruments and hear the songs, there was no need for explicit statement. However, the poetry of Amos and Archilochus, Isaiah and Alcaeus makes it clear that music is the vehicle of their messages. Isaiah sings his love lyrics at a drinking party, and mentions the timbrel and flute and two different types of lyre (Isa. 5). Alcaeus also says that the lyre plays a merry part in the symposium banquet, and elsewhere mentions the lyre and singing in the context of wine and love.[37] In his elegies, Archilochus mentions the flute, talks about a female who drank to its melody, sings the tune of Dionysus and asserts the power of song to soothe.[38] Amos situates his elegy within the context of a great *marzeah* feast whose participants idle away their time by singing noisy songs and empty words to the tune of the lyre (6.5; 5.23).[39]

In Amos's elaborate banquet scene symposia members drink wine from bowls (6.6). References to drinking cups and bowls are found also in Greek poetry[40] and on pottery finds. This ancient custom of drinking from capacious vessels called mixing bowls[41] is not a sign of inordinate

35. Peckham, 'Phoenicia and the Religion of Israel', p. 95 n. 58.

36. Pauline Schmitt-Pantel, 'Sacrificial Meal and Symposion: Two Models of Civic Institutions in the Archaic City?', in Murray (ed.), *Sympotica*, pp. 14-33 (18, 27-30).

37. Alcaeus, frs. 38B, 41, 58, 70, in Campbell, *Greek Lyric, I*, pp. ix-x, 252-53, 254-57, 264-65, 274-75.

38. Archilochus, frs. 32, 76, 77, 98A, in Edmonds, *Greek Elegy*, II, pp. 114-15, 136-37, 152-53. On musical writings from Archilochus to the late sixth century, see Andrew Barker (ed.), *Greek Musical Writings. I. The Musician and his Art* (Cambridge: Cambridge University Press, 1984), pp. 47-53.

39. The translation 'lyre' for נבל seems preferable to 'harp': King, *Amos, Hosea, Micah*, pp. 154-55.

40. Alcaeus refers to mixing bowls, frs. 206, 367, in Campbell, *Greek Lyric, I*, pp. 320-21, 396-97.

41. Cf. Homer, *Iliad* I.470; III.269-370. A broad shallow drinking bowl cast in bronze has survived in perfect condition from the Persian period. The Phoenician inscription written on the edge of the bowl shows that was it was clearly destined for a *marzeah* in celebration of the god Shamash: 'Bowls we offered two to *marzeah* of Shamash': cf. N. Avigad and J.C Greenfield, 'A Bronze *phialē* with a Phoenician Dedicatory Inscription', IEJ 32 (1982), pp. 118-28.

drinking but concerns the obligatory mixing of wine with water, normally diluting it by half.[42] Alcaeus's description of the wild drinking habits of barbarians, who take their wine neat, stands in contrast to Alcaeus's drinking companions who are asked to mix one part of water to two of wine, pour it in brimful and forget their sorrows.[43] The ritualization of alcohol consumption shows that symposia were not intended to be times of excessive drinking. The mental world of the Greek archaic age is most clearly shown in the poetry composed for performance at the symposium and in the great decorative works of art, such as the drinking bowl, that were created for the ritual there.[44]

Archaic poets, such as Archilochus and Amos, are sympotic legislators, and through their poetry they portray what is proper or improper behaviour in the symposium.[45] For example, Archilochus berates an individual for coming to a banquet uninvited, becoming drunk on neat wine, and perverting his mind and wits with shameful behaviour.[46] Having the poetic freedom to assume different personae, Archilochus presents himself as a rogue and a drunkard and thus represents negative morality.[47] Amos, however, neither drinks in his poetry nor complains about the insobriety of the *marzeaḥ*. Members practise sympotic restraint by drinking mingled wine, but Amos condemns their *marzeaḥ* because it fails in its appropriate purpose of grieving over the ruin of Joseph (6.6).[48] The occasion for an ancient symposium could be joyful or sorrowful. Weeping does not heal

42. Cf. King, '*Marzeaḥ*: Textual and Archaeological Evidence', pp. 104*-105*; *idem*, Amos, Hosea, Micah, pp. 157-59; Oswyn Murray, '*Sympotic History*', in Murray (ed.), *Sympotica*, pp. 1-13.

43. Alcaeus, frs. 72, 346, in Campbell, *Greek Lyric, I*, pp. 276-77, 378-81.

44. Murray, '*Sympotic History*', in Murray (ed.), *Sympotica*, p. 6-7.

45. Murray, '*Forms of Sociality*', pp. 231-32.

46. Archilochus, fr. 78, in Edmonds, *Greek Elegy, II*, pp. 136-37. Writing his elegiac poetry in the late sixth or early fifth century, Theognis says that drinking beyond due measure makes a man no longer master of his own tongue or mind, causes loss of judgment, and turns even a wise man into a fool: see Elegiac Poems, Book I, 211-12, 467-510, 837-44, 873-84, 989-90, in Edmonds, *Greek Elegy, I*, pp. 252-53, 284-89, 328-29, 332-35, 344-45. His contemporary, Anacreon, sings a song in which a mixing bowl is filled with five parts wine to ten parts of water. He summons his companions to drink moderately while singing beautiful songs to one another: fr. 356, in Campbell, *Greek Lyric, II*, pp. 54-55.

47. Archilochus, fr. 4, in Edmonds, *Greek Elegy, II*, pp. 98-99; Gregory Nagy, *Poetry as Performance: Homer and Beyond* (Cambridge: Cambridge University Press, 1996), pp. 217-21.

48. Beach, 'Samaria Ivories, *Marzeaḥ*', p. 136.

the wounds, so Archilochus and Alcaeus exclaim, and the best remedy the gods give to fight grief is endurance and wine.[49]Archilochus tells his audience that they can make nothing worse by being merry with wine, but Amos by contrast warns his *marzeaḥ* audience in Jerusalem that their omission of prayers for the dead brings their downfall, and the world of the symposium irrevocably passes away (6.6-7).[50]

The mood of levity is dominant in Greek poetry, but beneath the lightness and play appears the deep moral seriousness which characterizes prophetic poetry. Poetry sung or recited, either for solo or choral performance, was for the early Greeks the prime medium for the dissemination of values, political and moral, public and private. The poetry of Amos's seventh-century contemporaries seems to have been composed and received by its audiences as an instrument of civil or military policy. So Callinus exhorts his citizens to rouse themselves to war in face of the Cimmerian invasion; or Tyrtaeus addresses his elegy, the *Eunomia*, to his community as a whole in order to reconcile disagreements between rich and poor.[51]

Amos dramatizes the fall of Samaria, which occurred two generations or more before his own time (5.2), by addressing its citizens in the present (3.1-6, 9; 4.1, 3-5; 5.1, 4-7, 21-24) and portraying the city's impending doom as an object lesson for his audience in Jerusalem (2.13-16; 3.11; 4.2-3; 5.18-20).[52] So too Greek poets evoke events or situations familiar to

49. Archilochus, frs. 9-13, 13, 38, 66, in Edmonds, *Greek Elegy*, II, pp. 102-105, 116-17, 130-31; Alcaeus, frs. 38A, 332, 335, 346, in Campbell, *Greek Lyric, I*, pp. 250-53, 372-73, 378-81.

50. According to one recent study, the connection of *marzeaḥ* with mourning rites (6.6) is not original but the result of redactional work in Jer. 16: Christl Maier and Ernst Michael Dörrfuss, ' "Um mit ihnen zu sitzen, zu essen und zu trinken" Am 6,7; Jer 16,5 und die Bedeutung von *marzeaḥ*', *ZAW* 111 (1999), pp. 45-57. Underlying this conclusion is the thesis that the primary meaning of *marzeaḥ* centres around drinking and that its association with funerary customs arose as the result of abundant alcohol consumed by mourners to console themselves: T.J. Lewis, *Cults of the Dead in Ancient Israel and Ugarit* (HSM, 39; Atlanta: Scholars Press, 1989), pp. 88-93; cf. McLaughlin, '*marzeaḥ* at Ugarit', pp. 272-75, 280-81.

51. Callinus, fr. 3, Tyrtaeus, frs. 1-4, in Edmonds, *Greek Elegy, I*, pp. 48-49, 58-65; Aristotle, *Politics*, 5.1306b, 1307b; Herington, *Poetry into Drama*, pp. 3, 32-33; Barron and Easterling, 'Elegy and Iambus', in Easterling and Knox (eds.), *Early Greek Poetry*, pp. 87-92.

52. Amos also mentions foreign cities that had already fallen by his time: Syrian cities, Calneh and Hamath, were conquered by Tiglath-Pileser III in 738 BCE. Gath, the Philistine city, was conquered earlier by King Uzziah of Judah, but came under

their audiences and describe as present what in fact was past.[53] Archilochus composed elegiac poems about calamities that struck his city in war and at sea,[54] but in some fragments, he recreates the terrors which await him and other individuals.[55] Tyrtaeus, in his elegies about war at Sparta, graphically describes soldiers after a defeat, and when he instructs warriors to bite their lips and shake the crests of their helmets, he addresses warriors in his audience or stock characters in an entertainment.[56] Alcaeus assures his audience that 'warlike men are a city's tower', but he speaks of the enemy assailing the city walls, shifting back and forth from the present moment to the recent past.[57] He addresses companions on a storm-tossed ship or uses seafaring as an allegory to describe a civil war, but he sings his lyrics after the danger is over to those who have shared the experience or have knowledge of it.[58] Mimnermus's *Smyrneis* and Simonides' *Salamis* are large-scale elegies narrating local historical events, and in Mimnermus' case, his historical elegy has a moral for the present.[59] Long before Aeschylus created a dramatic illusion of an imminent future out of disasters at Salamis and Plataea (*Persae*), the Greek and Hebrew poets are found developing a tension between past and future in the present moment of the performance.[60]

The Greek poets, like the Hebrew prophets, were committed to expressing views about events that would influence an audience. They did not consider their poetry as a mere pastime but thought of themselves as speaking at the urging of the gods or Muses.[61] Amos was a poet of his

Assyrian rule in 734 and was destroyed by Sargon II about 712. He also destroyed Hamath in 720: King, '*Marzeaḥ*: Textual and Archaeological Evidence', p. 99*.

53. Bowie, '*Early Greek Elegy*', pp. 13-35.

54. Archilochus, frs. 9-13, 22, 97A, in Edmonds, *Greek Elegy, II*, pp. 102-103, 108-109, 150-51.

55. Archilochus, frs. 54, 66, 70, 114, in Edmonds, *Greek Elegy, II*, pp. 124-25, 130-33, 166-67.

56. Tyrtaeus, frs. 1-14, in Edmonds, *Greek Elegy, I*, pp. 59-79; Lattimore, *Greek Lyrics*, pp. 13-16.

57. Alcaeus, frs. 70, 112, 298, in Campbell, *Greek Lyric, I*, pp. 274-75, 284-85, 338-39.

58. Alcaeus, frs. 6, 208, in Campbell, *Greek Lyric, I*, pp. 211, 238-41, 320-23.

59. Bowie, '*Early Greek Elegy*', pp. 27-30.

60. Aeschylus, *The Persians*, in David Grene and Richmond Lattimore (eds.), *The Complete Greek Tragedies: Aeschylus II* (trans. Seth G. Benardete; Chicago: University of Chicago Press, 1956), pp. 43-86.

61. Archilochus, fr. 1, in Edmonds, *Greek Elegy, II*, pp. 98-99. On the Muses in

times, insisting that the words he sang or chanted came from outside himself at the urging of Yahweh. Just as Amos presents Yahweh as demanding righteousness (5.24), so Archilochus appeals to Apollo to destroy the guilty, or describes Zeus as the overseer of human deeds, taking count of right and wrong actions.[62] Archilochus refers to sin and retribution, but when he speaks of justice, he refers to an outrage committed against himself, or to a state of equity which the gods constantly restore.[63] Archilochus paves the way for Solon who, like Amos, does not express his indignation at wrongs done to himself, but diagnoses the behaviour of society as a whole.[64]

Solon and Amos address their elegies to a symposium, combining monologue with brief speeches put into the mouth of other individuals or groups. Both poets warn their audiences about the evils that afflict the city. Amos talks about the outbreaks of violence, robbery and extortion in Samaria and Jerusalem, and the oppression of the destitute and weak by the rich and powerful. Solon declares that the leaders of Athens become rich by unrighteous deeds, plundering the city's wealth, disregarding justice, and forcing the poor into servitude.[65] The poor break into Solon's

Homer, see *Iliad* I:1, 603-604, 2.594-600, 14.508, 16.101-23. On Hesiod's Muses, see *The Theogony* I.1-115; Herington, Poetry into Drama, pp. 58-59; C.M. Bowra, Landmarks in Greek Literature (Cleveland, OH: The World Publishing Company, 1969), pp. 15-16, 61, 106-107, 113-14.

　62. Archilochus, frs. 27, 88, in Edmonds, *Greek Elegy, II*, pp. 112-13, 142-45.

　63. Archilochus, frs. 56, 65, 73, 109, in Edmonds, *Greek Elegy, II*, pp. 126-27, 130-31, 134-35, 158-59; Bruno Snell, *The Discovery of the Mind: The Greek Origins of European Thought* (trans. T.G. Rosenmeyer; New York: Harper & Row, 1960), pp. 64, 175.

　64. Otto Kaiser ('Gerechtigkeit und Heil: bei den israelitischen Propheten und griechischen Denkern des 8.-6 Jahrhunderts', in Otto Kaiser, *Der Mensch unter dem Schicksal: Studien zur Geschichte, Theologie und Gegenwartsbedeutung der Weisheit* [festschrift für Rudolf Bultmann] [BZAW, 161; Berlin: Walter de Gruyter, 1985], pp. 24-40) discusses 'the divine norm of justice' in the prophets and the classical Greek thinkers from the eighth to the sixth centuries. He concludes that Amos, Isaiah and Micah correspond to Hesiod and Solon. Recent German scholarship shows a renewed interest in exploring the idea of justice among the early Greeks and the Israelite prophets as well as the relations between the ancient Orient and the Greek world: see Klaus Seybold and Jürgen von Ungern-Sternberg, 'Amos und Hesiod: Aspekte eines Vergleichs', in Kurt Raaflaub (ed.), *Anfänge politischen Denkens in der Antike: Die nahöstlichen Kulturen und die Griechen* (Schriften des Historischen Kollegs, 24; Munich: R. Oldenbourg, 1993), pp. 215-39.

　65. Solon, fr. 4, in Edmonds, *Greek Elegy, I*, pp. 116-21.

speech to address the rich and counsel moderation; the poor assert that they will endure, and the rich talk to the poor about the decrease of their possessions.[66] Amos also interrupts his speech to represent the merchants, who confess that they rob the poor by using false weights (8.5-6).[67] Solon, like Amos, refers explicitly to jovial feasting and to gatherings, presumably the symposia associations or clubs, where the unrighteous leaders, in their greed, destroy the city. Just as Zeus punishes injustice, so Yahweh punishes evil with evil, and no person, rich or poor, can escape the consequences of bad leadership. Nevertheless the two poets predict different futures: Yahweh will destroy Jerusalem, but Athens will never perish by the destiny of Zeus. Athena will guard the city, and through her all is made wise and perfect.[68]

The symposia of the archaic period, then, were times of great creative writing and thinking, occasions for which poetic texts of different genres were composed, memorized and performed. As the poems themselves show, the symposia members met over their drinking cups, and inspired by wine, love and song, they discussed and debated political and social issues, and through confrontation in performance, participants challenged each other's views and exhibited their intellectual and artistic abilities.[69] Symposia were occasions of entertainment, both light and serious, times in which both Greek and Hebrew poets became prophets, reflecting on the past, present and future, while reciting or singing the predictions of Yahweh or Zeus.[70]

66. Solon, fr. 28 a, c, b, in Edmonds, *Greek Elegy, I*, pp. 142-43.

67. The 'notables' of Israel and Judah are merchants involved in 'international trade and the royal economy': see Peckham, 'Phoenicia and the Religion of Israel', pp. 94-95.

68. Solon, fr. 4, with fr. 28 a, c, b; fr. 13, 32, 33, 33A, in Edmonds, *Greek Elegy, I*, pp. 116-21, 126-33, 146-47. The introduction of two speakers is already a technique used by Archilochus: see Bowie, 'Early Greek Elegy', pp. 19-21; Easterling and Knox (eds.), *Early Greek Poetry*, pp. 83-85, 105-111; Snell, *Discovery of the Mind*, pp. 175-76.

69. Snell, *Discovery of the Mind*, pp. 68-69; Pellizer, 'Sympotic Entertainment', pp. 178-79, 182-83; E.L. Bowie, 'Thinking with Drinking: Wine and the Symposium in Aristophanes', *JHS* 117 (1997), pp. 1-21.

70. Just as Amos represents Yahweh as a prophet who predicts the fall of Israel and Judah (e.g. 2.13-16; 8.1-2a), so Archilochus presents Zeus as 'the surest prophet among the Gods', who determines the future and its fulfilment (Edmonds, *Greek Elegy*, II, pp. 156-57).

The Performance Text

The view of Amos's poetry as a performance text is corroborated by comparative data, but the prophetic text itself is our primary evidence for claiming its original use as a script for performance. A major piece of evidence of a live performance is Amos's well constructed tragic plot with artistically constructed incidents that turn upon surprises known as reversals and recognitions. The plot has a beginning, middle and end, and the performance must have been determined by time constraints. The running time of the cycle is about twenty minutes; analogously, performances of Greek poetry were brief, lasting up to a quarter of an hour.[71]

Another indication of a live performance is the evidence of an audience in the cycle, and throughout there is a constant address to a double audience,—the ostensible audience and the actual audience who listens to the performance. This phenomenon of double audience is a commonplace feature of Greek poetry, in which we often find the poet addressing individuals or gods his audience knew. In Amos's cycle the implied audience is Israel, as is clear from his address to 'you cows of Bashan' (4.1), 'you, O house of Israel' (5.1) and the like. At the cycle's mid-point, the audience perspective suddenly shifts to the actual audience in Judah.

The evidence of an active performer is a further indication of the cycle's live presentation. Amos identifies himself as the speaker of his monody (1.1a). Right from the beginning he focuses the tragic mood in his role as messenger of doom, first to his implied audience, Israel, and then to his real audience, Judah. The analogy for this dramatization of the poet himself in his own work is the clear evidence of Greek poets who use dramatic personae—Solon plays the role of a herald, Archilochus a professional soldier, Alcaeus an intercessor, and Alcman a choral director.[72]

The cycle's final poem marks a departure in Amos's performing role: he plays the role of intercessor as he pleads in private conversation with God to spare Judah (7.1-6). As intercessor, Amos discloses to his Jerusalem

71. Herington, *Poetry into Drama*, p. 32.

72. Archilochus, fr. 66, in Edmonds, *Greek Elegy, II*, pp. 166-67; Solon, fr. 1, in Campbell, *Greek Elegy, I*, pp. 114-15; Alcaeus, fr. 129, in Campbell, Greek Lyric, II, pp. 296-99; Alcman, fr. 1, in Campbell, *Greek Lyric, II*, pp. 360-69; Aristotle, *Rhetoric* 1418b24-34; Barron and Easterling, 'Elegy and Iambus', in Easterling and Knox (eds.), *Early Greek Poetry*, pp. 77, 80, 106; Segal, 'Archaic Choral Lyric', in Easterling and Knox (eds.), *Early Greek Poetry*, pp. 129-38; Herington, *Poetry into Drama*, pp. 20-24.

audience that he is on their side, he motivates them to listen and act on what he says. The audience is asked to become involved in the dramatic action by making a decision about its future. And this decision is made off-stage, so to speak, after the performance is over.

We think of tragedy as something gloomy or depressing, and the cycle's only glimmer of hope is the phrase 'Seek Yahweh and live' (5.4, 6).[73] But this positive note appears exactly at the cycle's mid-point, where reversal gives way to recognition: the Jerusalem audience suddenly realize that their lives are being held in the balance and that Israel's doom inevitably will overtake them. His exhortation to seek Yahweh and live represents the choice Israel was once given but turned down, but which still stands as the choice offered to Judah. The cycle ends with death and destruction, a common tragic ending, but the dramatic action strives to achieve some sort of affirmation in the audience. So tragedy in its best sense celebrates the greatness of human nature and expresses tremendous optimism, belief in the capacity of human beings to change.[74]

Amos, like his contemporary Archilochus, recited or sang his tragic poetry[75] in the seventh century, some time during the reign of King Manasseh of Judah, a confident and peaceful age in which people could afford the luxury of listening to tragic poetry, even deriving pleasure and satisfaction from it. But when Judah fell a century later the cycle lost its former appeal, and interest in the performance of tragedy came to an end.

Prophecy in Book Culture

When the author of the book incorporated the poetic cycle every attempt was made to remove traces of live performance. The book recognized the unity of the tragic plot but broke it up with sections of comic relief at the end of each poem and by interweaving commentary at crucial stages in the cycle. The book removes the suspense and surprises of the reversals and recognitions by giving away the whole plot at the beginning: Judah was

---

73. A. Vanlier Hunter, *Seek the Lord! A Study of the Meaning and Function of the Exhortation in Amos, Hosea, Isaiah, Micah, and Zephaniah* (Baltimore, MD: St Mary's Seminary and University Press, 1982), pp. 56-105.

74. Sylvan Barnet, Morton Berman and William Burto (eds.), *Eight Great Tragedies* (New York: Mentor Books, 1985), pp. 8, 12, 434.

75. According to Plutarch, Archilochus is credited with the device of reciting some lines of poetry to music and singing the others, a device later employed by the tragic poets of Greek theatre: see Edmonds, *Greek Elegy, II*, pp. 88-89.

added to the list of nations, thus making it known from the outset that
Amos predicted its collapse. But the book also turns Israel, the implied
audience, into the actual audience by presenting Amos as a prophet who
predicted the fall of the North. The book, as early as the title (1.1b),
stresses that Amos's words were in the form of a vision about Israel.
Accordingly, the book makes an audience out of both Israel and Judah by
adding addresses to both kingdoms.

Amos's biographer identifies him as a prophet or נביא (7.14-15), but
Amos introduces himself as a shepherd from Tekoa (1.1a). It was common
in antiquity for poets to play the role of shepherd, a convention used to
introduce a poem and to justify the voice of the singer or reciter. So the
persona of shepherd or peasant poet dominates the work of Hesiod, and his
figure as rustic bard was subsequently turned into brief biographies that
were regarded, even in antiquity, as containing mythic elements.[76] Likewise the figure of Amos as shepherd was elaborated by the creative imagination of his biographer. The book used the conventional shepherd motif
to turn Amos into a historical shepherd and a farmer whom Yahweh
selected to prophesy.[77] The biographer recognized that Amos was a
performer but played down this historical fact. While Amos implied his
own promotion from shepherd to poet, his biographer stresses his promotion from shepherd to prophet. The biographer makes Amos a larger-than-
life figure with incredible powers of prediction, an eighth-century prophet
who saw the imminent doom of Israel as well as the fall of Judah.

The book fits Amos into the orthodox history of prophecy, in which a
prophet is described as God's servant (3.7) and typically tells people to
repent (2 Kgs 17). Amos presupposed that citizens of Judah would listen
to his dramatic monologue and would be motivated by it to save themselves from disaster. However, the author of the book argues that prophecy
means that prophets are opposed by their hearers (2.12). Written roughly

---

76. Robert Lamberton, *Hesiod* (New Haven: Yale University Press, 1988), pp. 3-4,
38.

77. Thus scholars have taken literally the idea that Amos once earned his living as
a 'shepherd' or 'herdsman' (נקד 1.1a; בוקר 7.14) before he was called to prophesy: see
e.g. Ronald E. Clements, *Prophecy and Covenant* (SBT, 43; London: SCM Press,
1965), pp. 27-44 (38); Peter C. Craigie, 'Amos the *noqed* in the light of Ugaritic', *SR*
11 (1982), pp. 29-32; Yehoshua Gitay, 'Amos', in Mircea Eliade and Charles J. Adams
(eds.), *The Encyclopedia of Religion*, I (New York: MacMillan Publishing Co., 1987),
pp. 240-43; Stuart, *Hosea–Jonah*, p. 290; Rosenbaum, *Amos of Israel*, pp. 44-47; Paul,
Amos, p. 248.

fifty years after the fall of Jerusalem, the book of Amos marked the end of any interest in the tragic poetry which was eventually forgotten, left buried within a book deposited in the Jerusalem archives or library under the classification of comedy, valued for the hope and renewal it offered in an age of pain and despair. With the transition from song culture to book culture, attention became focused on written texts rather than on their performance. The scholarly community from the exile onwards brought together the great literary texts that were once performed, and disposed them into editions. The function of a prophetic book was to be read aloud, and all thought of solo or choral performance of the prophets' written texts, to the accompaniment of musical instruments before an audience, became a thing of the past.

Structure of the Cycle and the Book

We can now turn our attention to the larger structure that binds and separates the seven individual poems, and to the larger structure that sets out all the material, both old and new, into ten parts. Amos's poetic cycle is composed of chants and recitations, but its dramatic development, its tragic genre, its shifting locations and perspectives, make it possible to conceive of 'acts' and 'scenes' as the overall organizing principle.

The poet fashions four acts, of which each is divided into two or three scenes. The technique of joining together through separation establishes the coherence of the cycle while simultaneously distinguishing acts and scenes from one another. Each act and scene has an analogous structure, but each has its own distinctive movement.[78] The book adopted the poet's technique by creating a new structure that is both unified and differentiated in its parts. The reviser recognized the acts and scenes, their independence and interdependence, but converted them into corresponding distinct parts.

a. Structure of Acts and Scenes
1. *Act 1*. It consists of three distinct scenes. Damascus and Philistia form the first scene and are paired by the phrase 'I will cut off the inhabitants from X and him that holds the scepter from X' (1.5, 8). Ammon and Moab are set off as the second scene. Variation in the standard formula, 'kindle a

---

78. David A. Dorsey ('Literary Architecture and Aural Structural Techniques in Amos', *Bib* 73 [1992], pp. 305-30) identifies the many aural structuring techniques (i.e. rhetorical devices; repetitive formulae; new addressees; abrupt transitions and genre shifts) that aid the listener to recognize the beginnings and ends of major units.

fire', is the clue that Ammon marks a new scene. The day for Ammon and Moab is marked by war cries (בתרועה 1.14b; 2.2b) and the death or exile of king and princes (1.15; 2.3).

The topic of the third scene is the nation Israel. The poet sustains the pairing effect of the previous scenes by expanding on Israel's crimes and punishment and by making each theme approximately the length of the preceding paired nations. The reviser saw the pairing of Damascus–Philistia and Ammon–Moab, and added three more pairs, Tyre–Edom, Judah–Israel, and Amorite–Israel. Tyre and Edom are linked by the words 'brotherhood' (אחים 1.9bB) and 'his brother' (אחיו 1.11aA). Judah and Israel are joined in advance by the title synchronizing Uzziah of Judah with Jeroboam of Israel (1.1bA); they are also verbally connected by 'their fathers' (אבותם 2.4bB) and 'his father' (אביו 2.7bA). Amos makes the final pair (2.6-8, 13-16) look different from the previous pairs by eliminating any verbal connection between the crimes and the punishment. The book follows the same formal procedure in its concluding pair, Amorite–Israel (2.9-12, 13-16). The theme of destruction links the Amorite and Israel, but neither שמד nor a verbal marker is used to relate the two.

The three scenes can be separated from another, but they belong to the same act, having the same introduction and conclusion ('Thus says Yahweh'/'says Yahweh') and the same formula-like sentences ('For three crimes of X and for four…', 'I will send fire on X…'.). Scenes 1 and 2 are linked by a crime against Gilead (1.3b, 13b). Scenes 2 and 3 are tied by the word 'day' (1.14; 2.16) and battle imagery (1.14; 2.2, 13-16). Each scene has two segments which lead to war and build to a climactic threat against Israel (1.4-5, 7-8, 14-15; 2.2-3, 13-16).

The reviser recognized the cycle's main division into 'acts' and also its smaller units or scenes. The two segments on Tyre–Edom were added to the end of Scene 1, the segment on Judah became the conclusion of Scene 2, and an extended commentary (2.9-12) was inserted towards the end of Scene 3. The new endings are related by covenant and law (1.9-12; 2.4-5), and prophecy links the beginning and end of the commentary (1.2; 2.9-12). The movement of the cycle is towards future divine action, but the new endings direct attention to the past and, as a result, Amos's day of war is made subordinate to the ideas of law, covenant, history and prophecy.

2. *Act 2*. It consists of three scenes, and each scene combines two segments of text: (1) 3.1-6, 9-11; (2) 4.1-3, 4-5; (3) 5.1-2, 4-7. Each scene begins, 'Hear this word' (3.1; 4.1; 5.1), and the second segment begins

with a command (3.9; 4.4; 5.4) followed by a series of imperatives. The reviser recognized the scenes and segments. Each scene is treated separately, with text added piecemeal to a segment and an appendix added at the end of a scene. The additions to each scene develop the topics of interest to the book. The appendices at the end of a scene often repeat what Amos said in a corresponding scene. So the book adds a comment to Scene 1 at the beginning (3.1b) and end of the first segment (3.7-8). The second segment (3.9-11) receives a new ending (3.12), and Scene 1 ends with an appendix (3.13-15). The footnote commentary ends where Scene 1 began, 'Hear this word'/'Hear and testify' (3.1, 13), and imitates Amos's repetitive pattern of imperatives.

The book adds nothing to the beginning of Scene 2 (4.1-5) but ends it with an appendix (4.6-13). 'Says Yahweh' marks the close of each segment in Scene 2 (4.3b, 5bB). The reviser imitates Amos by concluding sections of the commentary with 'says Yahweh' (4.6, 7-8, 9, 10, 11). The appendix ends the way Amos began: 'The mountains' (הרים 4.13) is a verbal link with 'in the mountain' (בהר 4.1), and the divine oath first reported by Amos (4.2) is uttered by God himself (4.12). God's address to Israel begins in the masculine singular, shifts to the feminine singular and switches back to the masculine singular (4.12). This gender change reflects the masculine and feminine forms of Amos's address to the men and women of Samaria (4.2).

The book makes additions to Scene 3 (5.1-2, 4-7) at both the beginning and the end. Added to the first segment (5.1-2) is the defeated city (5.3), and this new ending refers back to the revised ending of the previous scene (4.6-8, 11). The addition at the end of the scene (5.8-9) cross-references the book's earlier ending (4.13).

3. *Act 3*. It consists of two scenes. The first scene has three segments, 5.10-12, 18-20, 21-24, and the second scene has two segments, 6.1-7, 12-13. Scene 1 opens with 'they hate' (שנאו 5.10), the second segment begins 'woe' (הוי 5.18), and the third segment ends with 'I hate' (שנאתי 5.21).[79] Scene 2 resumes with 'woe' (הוי 6.1), and ends with participles (6.13) consistent with its participial series.

Each of the two scenes has its own distinct structure, but they belong together. Amos mentions the righteous at the opening of Scene 1 (צדק 5.12) and ends with the theme of righteousness (וצדקה 5.24). The endings

79. Andersen and Freedman (*Amos*, p. 470) observe that the confrontation between divine and human 'haters' is dramatic.

of both scenes are marked by the same concern for justice and righteousness (צדקה...משפט 5.24; 6.12). The feast-days bring the first scene to a
close (5.21-24), a topic detailed in the second scene (6.4-7). In Scene 1
animal offerings are mentioned generally as 'the peace offerings of your
fatted beasts' (שלם מריאיכם 5.22), but are specified as lambs and calves in
Scene 2 (עגלים...כרים 6.4b). Both scenes mention festal music, particularly songs accompanied by the lyre (נבליך...שריך 5.23; שיר...הנבל 6.5).

The reviser observed the scenes and segments and changed their
structure. The book's addition (5.13-17) to Scene 1 separates the first
(5.10-12) and second segments (5.18-20). A new ending (5.13-17) is
attached to the first segment by repeating 'in the gate' (בשער 5.10a, 12b,
15a). The book's ending anticipates Amos's day of Yahweh (5.18-20) and
preempts it with a different interpretation (5.13-17).

The book's footnote (5.25-27) refers to the end of Scene 1 (5.21-24), as
indicated by the repetition of 'offerings' (ומנחתיכם 5.22a; ומנחה 5.25a).
With its astral imagery and interest in the name of Yahweh (5.27), the
footnote also cross-references the book's annotation at the end of the
previous two scenes (5.8; 4.13).

The reviser attached comments (6.8-11) to the first segment (6.1-7) of
Scene 2 and a postscript (6.14) to the second segment (6.12-13). The
postscript returns to the beginning of the scene: 'first of the nations'
(ראשית הגוים 6.1) and 'Great Hamath' (חמת רבה 6.2) are completed by
references to the enemy nation (גוי 6.14a) and the borders from Hamath to
Arabah (הערבה...חמת 6.14b [i.e. hē, 'ayin, rêš, bêt, hē]).

4. *Act 4*. It consists of three scenes, and each scene has two segments: (1)
7.1-3, 4-6; (2) 7.7-9; 8.1-3a; (3) 8.4-6, 9-10. The four visions (7.1-3; 7.4-6;
7.7-9; 8.1-3a) belong together because they have the same basic pattern:
'Thus Yahweh showed me' (7.1aA, 4aA, 7aA*; 8.1a), the report of what
was seen, and a dialogue between God and Amos. The visions have a
common structure, but like the oracles (chs. 1–2), are organized into
separate pairs and distinct scenes.

The first pair falls into Scene 1 (7.1-3, 4-6): the paired visions are linked
by the petition of Amos (7.2aB, 5a), by the reference to Jacob (7.2b, 5b),
and by God's repentance (7.3, 6). The second pair (7.7-9; 8.1-3a) is
structured differently, with a terse vision report and a statement of the
action that God will take against his people Israel. The second pair of
visions are formally connected by 'I will never again pass by him' (7.8bB;

8.2bB)and 'my people Israel' (7.8bA; 8.2bA), and have the sanctuary as a common theme (7.9a; 8.3a).

The reviser, noting the developing movement in the scenes from repentance to disaster and the end of a people, breaks up the sequence of the second pair of visions with a narrative (7.10-17) which is a commentary on the second scene: proper names and specific terms, namely, 'Jeroboam' (7.7b, 10a), 'Isaac' (7.9aA, 16bB), 'my people Israel' (7.8bA, 15bB), 'sanctuary' (7.9aB, 13bA), 'house' (7.9b, 10ab) and 'sword' (7.9b, 11aB, 17abA) are key elements in Amos's second scene that are taken up by the book and given a new context and structural arrangement.

The third scene has two paired segments (8.4-6, 9-10). The first refers to 'the new moon' (8.5aA) or the first day of the month. This implicit reference to some festival occasion is thematically completed by the explicit reference to 'your feasts' in the second segment (8.10aA). From the outset of Scene 3 (8.4-6, 9-10), it becomes obvious that the cycle is drawing to a close. The third scene returns to the corresponding scene in Act 1 (2.6-8, 13-16) which starts the action and sets the tone of the cycle: the third scene of Act 1 introduces the characters (2.6-8) and gives us a preview of what lies ahead (2.13-16) or a prelude to everything that follows, and its corresponding scene in the final act is a summary of the plot. The postlude rounds off the cycle by recalling the familiar words of the opening act, 'you who trampled upon the needy, and brought the afflicted of the land to an end' (8.4a; 2.7a), 'we buy the poor for silver and the needy for a pair of sandals' (8.6; 2.6b). A flow of tragic recitative follows (8.9-10), and Amos ends the cycle, as he began it, with the ominous image of God's day (8.9aA*,10bB; 2.16).

The reviser recognized that the day marks the close of the last two scenes in Act 4. So a comment (8.3b) was added to the end of the second scene, and an appendix (8.11-14) was added to the end of the third scene. The book's appendix (8.11-12, 13-14) interprets the day of Yahweh, using Amos's language in a climactic scene (8.11-14 = 5.1, 2, 4-7: 'hear' שמע; 'seek' בקש; 'fall' נפל; 'rise' קום; the young women הבתולת versus the young woman בתולת) and cross-referencing its own subtext or footnote commentary (8.11, 13; 4.6-7; 7.16; 2.12b).

b. *Structure of the Whole*
1. *Mutual Relation of the Acts in Amos*. Act 1 includes all the elements necessary for the progression of the action. Amos mentions the people, the capital city, the kingdom and the king, and these topics are taken up in

subsequent scenes. Act 1 mentions the nations' towns and capital cities (Damascus, Rabbah, Kerioth) but not Israel's capital city. In the opening scene of Act 2 (3.1–5.7*), Amos offers a portrait of Samaria under siege (3.6, 9-11) which corresponds to the picture of war in foreign cities (1.5, 6-8, 14; 2.2). The second scene shifts attention to the people of the city of Samaria, and they are analogous to the people of Syria (1.5b) who are destined to be deported or exiled (4.2-3). The third scene opens with another shift to the kingdom of Israel, referred to as the 'house of Israel' (5.1) or the 'house of Joseph' (5.6). Its demise projects us back to images of destruction of foreign kingdoms (1.3– 2.3*) and to the defeat of Israel (2.13-16).

In Act 3 we witness a movement away from the Northern Kingdom to the Southern Kingdom and to its capital city and people. The kingdom of Judah is identified obliquely in the citation, 'first of the nations' (ראשית הגוים 6.1b), and together with the kingdom of Israel is compared with foreign cities (הממלכות האלה 6.2b). The comparison comes to focus on the size of their respective territories (אם־רב גבולם מגבלכם 6.2b), a theme which recalls Ammon's border war into Gileadite territory to expand its own territory (גבולם 1.13b). The second act alludes to the Southern Kingdom under the umbrella term 'the children of Israel' (ישראל בני 3.1a; 4.5b), but in the third act, the city of Zion (בציון 6.1aA) is mentioned for the first time, and even takes priority over the city of Samaria (שמרון 6.1aB). Zion is associated with David (6.5b), and these references to the royal city and its king and founder recall the initial statements about the royal city of Damascus and Benhadad, its king and founder (1.4-5). The activities of Zion's nobility are described (6.4-6), and their destination in exile unites them with foreign kings and princes (1.15).

Kingship is the predominant topic in Act 4 (7.1–8.10*) and is associated with key themes of the cycle. The act begins with a general but explicit reference to 'the king' (המלך 7.1b), a term that was formerly used to speak of foreign rulers (מלכם 1.15a; מלך־אדום 2.1b). The first scene depicts the king as involved in the land's destruction because he reaped for himself the first spring crop, while the locusts devoured the second crop of the season (7.1-2). A fire eats up a portion or tract of land (החלק 7.4bB). Its destruction is symbolic of what happens to the whole world when fire strikes the great deep (תהום רבה 7.4bA; cf. 1.4a, 7, 14; 2.2a, 5a; 5.5). The apportioned property refers either to the territory of Judah (cf. 'an adversary shall surround the land', i.e. the territory of Samaria, 3.11aB) or to the share of land belonging to the king (7.4). In any case, the king is implicated in the natural disaster, since by virtue of his title, he was held responsible for ensuring the prosperity and security of the community. The references to David (6.5b) and Judah's leaders (6.1) anticipate the references to 'the king' (7.1b) and Jacob (7.2, 5). David is associated with Jacob, Jacob is personified as the kingdom of Judah, and the unidentified king, by implication, is the Davidic monarch.

The second scene develops the ideology of kingship by turning to the socio-religious spheres. In the third vision Yahweh is stationed beside a wall (נצב על־חומת 7.7) with a plumb line in his hand. The allusion is to the walls of a city, which corresponds to God's initial promise to send a fire upon the walls of Gaza (בחומת עזה 1.7a) and Rabbah (בחומת רבה 1.14bA). Since the city of Samaria has already fallen, the walls to be demolished are the walls of the royal city of Zion (cf. 6.1). The locust swarm is indirectly attributed to the king (7.1-2), but in the second scene, the monarchy is directly implicated in the impending doom. Devastation falls on the royal dynasty of Jeroboam (בת ירבעם 7.9bB) just as it falls on the royal dynasty of Hazael (בבית חזאל 1.4a), and the insinuation is that it will fall on the dynasty of David. So Jeroboam, the founder of Israel's dynasty, becomes linked with David (6.5b), Judah's first king and founder of the dynasty.

The plumb line for destruction that is going to be used against the people Israel (7.8b) will take its toll on both the Southern state cult, identified as 'the high places of Isaac' (7.9aB), and its rival state cult in the North, identified as 'the sanctuaries of Israel' (7.9aB). Included in the devastation are the royal shrines, made explicit by the reference to the royal temple (8.3a). The term היכל designates both the temple of the Davidic king and the dynastic palace, and their mutual destruction symbolizes the end of the monarchy. 'The end has come upon my whole people Israel' (עמי ישראל 8.2a) corresponds to divine judgment against the people of Syria (עם־ארם 1.5b) and is inclusive of citizens and their kings (1.5).

The audience is told repeatedly that death and exile come to foreign peoples and their rulers alike (1.5, 8, 15; 2.3), and so Act 4 closes appropriately with a mourning ritual that can be viewed as both a dirge for the loss of an only child and a lament sung on the occasion of the death of an only heir to the Davidic throne (8.10b). In the light of this interpretation, the term הקץ has a *double entendre*, pointing to the end of both God's people and the dynasty. Act 4, in common with Act 1, mentions all the topics of the cycle, and they are brought together into a final statement about the destiny of the nation or the kingdom of Judah, its capital city and people, its king and dynasty.[80]

2. *Mutual Relation of the Acts in the Book.* Amos connected the poems dramatically. The book, however, ruins or even changes the dramatic action by adding historical or rational argument, and then reconnects the poems artificially either by repeating Amos's words or by adding secondary verbal links to the ends and beginnings of the poems. So by adding the phrase: 'children of Israel' (בני ישראל 2.11b) to the first poem, the reviser establishes a verbatim parallel with Amos's words in the second poem (בני ישראל 3.1a). Again, the reviser relates Acts 1 and 2 by prolepsis and resumption, a common form of repetition. So 'prophets' (נביאים) and 'to prophesy' (נבא) are added at the end of Act 1 (2.12b) in anticipation of the book's resumptive reference to the same two terms (3.7-8) at the beginning of Act 2. Likewise the book's opening statement about 'Egypt' (2.10) is proleptic of its resumptive statement about 'Egypt' (3.1b).

The book obscures the dramatic connection between the second and third acts by the preemptive comment 'He keeps turning darkness into morning, and darkened (החשיך) the day into night' (5.8-9), to correct Amos's day of darkness (חשך) and not light (5.18, 20). The reviser also makes verbal connections between the end of Act 3 and the beginning of Act 4. At the end of Act 3, the commentary repeats 'house' several times (6.9-11), thus linking Amos's text and the book: the references to 'house' anticipate Amos's 'house of Jeroboam' (7.9b) and are also proleptically connected to the book's narrative about Bethel (בית־אל 7.10aA) and the 'house of Israel' (בית ישראל 7.10bA).

3. *The Relation of the Parts in the Book.* The book uses the same system to connect the different parts of the new version that it used to reconnect the acts of Amos's poetic cycle. The ten parts of the book are joined by

---

80. Given that Act 4 stresses the ideology of kingship, it would be tempting to suggest that אנך has not just the literal meaning of 'plumb line' but is also a wordplay on the Greek words for 'king' (ἀναξ) and 'necessity' or 'fate' (ἀναγκη). The consonants קץ stand for both 'harvest' and 'end', and so the term אנך also has more than one meaning. Cf. the comparative use of Egyptian sources to demonstrate the double meaning of 'plumb bob' and 'justice' in Amos's third vision: see James K. Hoffmeier, 'Once Again the 'Plumb Line' Vision of Amos 7.7-9: An Interpretive Clue from Egypt?', in Meir Lubetski, Claire Gottlieb and Sharon Keller (eds.), *Boundaries of the Ancient Near Eastern World: A Tribute to Cyrus H. Gordon* (JSOTSup, 273; Sheffield: Sheffield Academic Press, 1998), pp. 304-19.

establishing a relationship between beginnings and ends. The parts are reconnected by adding a quotation to Amos's text or by adding cross-references to the book. So the phrase 'the altars of Bethel' (בית־אל על־מזבחות 3.14bA) is added at the end of Part 2 in anticipation of Amos's injunction, 'Come to Bethel' (באו בית־אל 4.4aA), at the beginning of Part 3. The vocative 'O Israel' is added to the end of Part 3 (4.12) as a verbal link to Amos's references to 'Israel' (5.1-4); and the end of Part 4 is hinged to the end of Part 3 by the cross-references to עשׂה (4.13aB; 5.8aA) and the name of Yahweh (4.13b; 5.8bB).

These and other examples show that the reviser is not only familiar with the structure of Amos's cycle but is interested in replacing it with another interpretation requiring a totally different organization. As Amos's dramatic structure marks a movement of his text, so the book's constant quotation and cross-referencing of the edited text mark the pause and reflection of the new interpretation. Amos composed a continuous dramatic text, while the book is an insistent, repetitive historical updating and a continuous theological exhortation.

Linguistic Evidence for Dramatic Composition

The constant fluctuation in person is the linguistic evidence for Amos's dramatic composition. Shift in person allows for the identification of different speakers, addressees and characters. Speakers can refer to themselves in the first or the third person, and characters can be spoken about in the third person or addressed in the second person. Amos's text can be understood as a monologue recited or chanted by a solo performer who quoted the words of other speakers. Such a monologue of different 'voices' must have involved a wide range of intonation and gesture. Whether performed by one person or by several, the text is dramatic and requires an explanation for its frequent shifts in person.

a. Act 1 (1.1–2.16*)
Act 1 is one long speech of a MESSENGER, a role assumed by Amos as he reports God's words. Yahweh speaks in the first person and talks about foreign nations, their cities, peoples and kings:

> **I** will not turn it back because **they** have...
> **I** will send a fire on **X**...
> it shall consume **her** fortresses
> **I** will cut off the **inhabitants** [or **the ruler**]...
> **people** of X [or **their king**] shall go into exile (1.3–2.1-3).

In his role as ACCUSER, Yahweh states the crime, and in his role as JUDGE, announces the punishment.

Third–person report style, both singular and plural, is also used in God's first-person speech. His accusations against Israel are formulated in the third person plural (2.6-8), and the third person singular is adopted to describe the terrible punishment or destiny of the individual warrior (2.14-16):

> **I** will not turn it back
> **they** sold the righteous for silver…
> **they** trampled…
> **they** stretched themselves out upon garments…
> **they** drank the wine…(2.6-8).

> **the warrior** shall not save his life
> **he** who draws the bow shall not stand
> **he** who is swift of foot shall not escape
> **he** who rides the horse shall not save his life (2.14-16).

The only time the third–person narrative pattern is broken in Act 1 is towards the end of the oracle against Israel when Yahweh briefly addresses Israel in the second person plural to announce his decree of judgment:

> I am pressing [**you**] down in **your** place (2.13)

Israel stands out as the only nation whom God directly confronts and threatens to destroy. The whole of Act 1 consists of divine words in the first person, and reporting style prevails throughout, with the exception of this abrupt shift from third person plural (2.6-8) to second person plural address (2.13) and back again to third person singular (2.14-16). The dramatic intention of the divine address is to disturb the audience, to startle it out of complacency and to alert it to the significance of the fall of Israel.[81]

b. Act 2 (3.1–5.7*)

The title of the dramatic text is 'the words of Amos' (1.1a), but we must wait until Act 2 to come to the words of Amos. In Act 1 he speaks on behalf of Yahweh, but in Act 2, Amos emerges as a principal speaker in his own right. Amos's words dominate the first scene (3.1-6, 9-11), but the

---

81. Andersen and Freedman (*Amos*, p. 209) observe that the placing of Judah or Israel at the end of the list reflects a dramatic interest on the part of the speaker or author.

remaining two scenes (4.1-5; 5.1-2, 4-7) evenly distribute the words of Amos and Yahweh.

Act 2 opens with Amos's imperative voice and speaking as HERALD, he summons the people to hear God's words.

> **Hear**…Yahweh has spoken against **you** (3.1a).

The HERALD speaks about Yahweh, directly addresses the people in the second person plural and introduces Yahweh's first person address in the second person plural:

> Only **you** have I known…
> I will punish **you** for all **your** iniquities (3.2).

Amos and Yahweh are talking not just to Israel but to the whole family of Israel. So Amos is calling on his audience to listen, and Yahweh includes them in his judgment.

Amos takes up his new role as NARRATOR. He propounds a parable or riddle consisting of a series of questions, formulated first in the third person plural and then in the third person singular:

> Do two walk together unless **they** are agreed?
> Does a lion roar…without having prey? (3.3-6).

The shift to second person plural address occurs with the resumption of Amos's function as HERALD (3.9). The content and grammar suggest that Amos issues a summons to the MESSENGERS of the nations, authorizing them to carry news about Samaria to the palaces or strongholds of Ashdod. Amos speaks directly, in the second person plural, to the MESSENGERS, commanding them to summon the leaders of Ashdod and report to them the situation in Samaria, the capital city, now conceived as a woman:

> **Proclaim** to the strongholds in Ashdod and **say**,
> '**Gather yourselves** upon the mountains…
> **see** the great disorder within **her**
> **see** the oppressions in **her** midst' (3.9).

The Messengers command prominent people from Ashdod to come and witness destruction and injustice within Samaria, and their speech is formulated as a second person plural address.[82]

Suddenly, without introduction, Yahweh speaks about the inhabitants of Samaria, and taking up the role of PLAINTIFF, accuses them of crimes:

82. Andersen and Freedman (*Amos*, pp. 199-200) mention the dramatic role of those who summon the Philistines to observe the Israelites (3.9-10).

> '**They** do not know how to do right', says Yahweh,
> '**those** who have been storing up violence...
> in **their** fortresses' (3.10).

The shift from the speech of the MESSENGERS (3.9b) to God's speech
(3.10) is unmarked. The phrase נאם־יהוה 'says Yahweh' appears at the
mid-point of the speech and marks it as God's quoted speech.

Amos speaks again as MESSENGER and introduces the words of Yahweh
who, after speaking about the enemy in the third person, addresses Samaria
in the second person feminine singular and announces the punishment.

> Therefore thus says the Lord Yahweh:
> 'An enemy, now round about the land
> soon [he] will bring down **your** strength from **you**
> **your** fortresses will be plundered' (3.11).

At the beginning of the second scene, Amos assumes once again the voice
of HERALD, and in the masculine plural imperative, he summons the
people to listen to 'this word' (4.1aA). His address is in the feminine
plural (4.1aAb), and he quotes and impersonates what the women of
Samaria say to their husbands,

> 'Bring [**m.s.**] and let **us drink**!' (4.1bB).

Each woman addresses her husband and tells him to bring the wine. Then
the women speak together in the first person plural and call on their husbands to drink.[83] Amos reciprocates with an address to their husbands in
the second person masculine plural:

> The Lord Yahweh has sworn by **his** holiness
> the days are coming upon **you**
> **he** shall take **you** away with hooks (4.2abA).

Amos talks about God the JUDGE and in his role as PROSECUTOR, Amos
announces God's punishment upon the men of Samaria.

Suddenly Amos shifts to the feminine second person plural address, and
finishes off his summation with the announcement to the women of
Samaria whom Yahweh will deport:

> even the last of **you** with fish-hooks (4.2bB).

---

83. The masculine plural construct אדניהם 'their lords' is compatible with the
singular imperative הביאה 'Bring'. One expects the participial clause, 'those who say
to their lords' to introduce a speech where all the women together address the males.
What happens instead is that each woman addresses her male counterpart.

The women of Samaria are first addressed by Amos in his roles as
HERALD (4.1) and PROSECUTOR (4.2bB), but Yahweh breaks in as JUDGE
with his own speech to the women. He addresses them in the feminine
plural, speaks about them in the feminine singular, and returns to the
feminine plural address. God's words to them are marked at the end by
כה־אמר יהוה:

> '**You** shall go out...**each woman** straight before **her**;
> **you** shall be cast out'...says Yahweh (4.3).

Yahweh continues to speak, and as PLAINTIFF, he extends a
mocking invitation to come and rebel:

> Come to Bethel and commit crimes...
> bring **your** sacrifices...**your** tithes...
> because thus **you**...love to do (4.4-5).

The divine invitation is a series of imperatives in the masculine plural, and
the audience, at first, draws the logical conclusion that Yahweh is addressing the husbands and wives of Samaria. The vocative, 'children of Israel',
comes as a surprise because it tells us that the address is directed not only
to the people of Samaria but also to the Judaean audience who makes up
the wider Israel. As the second scene progresses, the audience learns that
the initial masculine imperative plural address, 'Hear this word' (4.1),
includes both the words of Amos and of God, and that the addressees are
the citizens of Israel and Judah.

The third scene begins with the words of Amos (5.1), but for the first
time, the proclamation is made by Amos in the first person singular, and
speaking once again as HERALD, he opens with a call to attention in the
second person imperative plural:

> Hear this word, which **I** take up over **you** as a lament....(5.1).

The new addressee is the house of Israel whom Amos summons to hear
the dirge[84] which he sings over woman Israel:

> Fallen, no more to rise is the girl Israel
> Abandoned on **her** land, with no one to raise **her** up. (5.2).

The nation Israel is spoken about and personified as a woman, and her
pathetic figure recalls the women of Samaria who used to make merry
over their drinking cups.

---

84. Mays (**Amos**, p. 85) describes the dirge as a dramatic expression of the
prophet's own grief.

As MESSENGER, Amos introduces the divine words. Yahweh speaks, refers to himself in the first person and addresses the house of Israel in the second person plural:

> For thus says Yahweh to the house of Israel:
> '**Seek me** and live; but do not **seek** Bethel…' (5.4-5a).

This second–person divine appeal is followed up by God's words in the third person singular, expressing the destiny of Gilgal and Bethel in a judgment:

> **Gilgal** shall surely go into **Golah**
> **the House of El** shall become **a house** of idols (5.5b).

Urgently Amos takes up the divine threat, speaks about Yahweh and partially repeats his words. There is a quick shift from Yahweh to a fire, then to an indefinite personal subject represented by the masculine singular participle:

> **Seek Yahweh** and live,
> lest **he** break out on the house of Joseph
> like a fire, and **it** consume,
> there is **no one** to extinguish it
> for Bethel….(5.6).

Amos's second person plural address is directed to those who are destined to be devoured by the flames that spread out from the house of Joseph and Bethel. At the turning point in the dramatic action Amos, who has been the PROSECUTOR against Israel, now becomes the ADVOCATE for Judah (5.6). But abruptly at the end of Act 2, Amos resumes his role as PROSECUTOR (5.7). From the impersonal description of a devouring fire that spreads from the North, he returns to the imperative in vocative style and accuses the Judaean audience directly of perverting justice (5.7):

> **you** who overturned justice to wormwood
> **you** who cast righteousness to the earth…(5.7).

c. Act 3 (5.10-6.13)

In Scene 1 (5.10-12, 18-24) Amos continues speaking in his role as ACCUSER, and refers to himself in the third person singular as the REPROVER at the gate.[85] Speaking either to the audience or to himself, he soliloquizes about the people in the third person plural and reports their hostility against him for standing up for justice:

---

85. So also Andersen and Freedman, **Amos**, p. 48.

> **They** hate **him** who rebukes in the gate,
> **they** abhorred **him** whoever spoke the truth (5.10).

Abruptly he turns to the people he has spoken about (5.10), and taking up his role as PROSECUTOR, accuses them in the second person plural and suggests guidelines for the punishment:

> Therefore, because
> **you** trampled upon the poor...
> **you** took from him exactions of grain,
> **you** built houses...but
> **you** shall not live in them;
> **you** planted splendid vineyards, but
> **you** shall not drink their wine (5.11).

In the first person, without any transition or introduction, Amos cites himself as REPROVER or PROSECUTOR and reformulates the charge in the second person plural:

> For **I** know how numerous are **your** crimes...
> **you** who afflict the righteous
> **you** who take a bribe
> **you** who turn aside the needy...(5.12).

All the characters at the gate are represented in this first-person address. The PROSECUTOR is Amos, the accused are those with houses and property, and the poor are the victims. Yahweh is the PLAINTIFF, JUDGE AND VINDICATOR: Amos takes up Yahweh's words in Act 1 (2.6-7), rephrases them, and turns God's speech about the people into a direct accusation against them in the second person plural.

Amos continues his speech (5.18-20) by speaking about the defendants at the gate:

> Woe to **those** who long for
> the day of Yahweh (5.18a).

Assuming the roles of NARRATOR and PROFESSIONAL MOURNER, Amos describes the day of Yahweh and talks about God (5.18-20).

Amos interrupts the opening words of his dirge with a question addressed ostensibly to the defendants who do not admit their guilt. He answers it himself, and his single-sentence thesis is illustrated with a parable:

> What is this day of Yahweh to **you?**
> It is darkness, and not light;
> as if **a man** fled from a lion
> but a bear met **him**;

or **he** went into the house
and leaned **his** hand against the wall
and a serpent bit **him** (5.18b-19).

Amos restates his thesis by a rhetorical question which is an aside or an indirect address to the audience:

Is not the day of Yahweh darkness and not light? (5.20).

Yahweh suddenly interjects in the first person singular and as PLAINTIFF speaks to the defendants in the second person plural:

I hate, **I** despise **your** feasts
I do not delight in **your** solemn assemblies.
Surely if **you** offer **me your** burnt offerings…
I will not accept them…(5.21-22).

Yahweh continues speaking but this time uses second person singular address:

Remove from **me** the sound of your songs;
to the music of **your** lutes I will not listen (5.23).

Yahweh's speech (5.21-24) is not introduced or marked anywhere by the formula נאם־יהוה 'says Yahweh'. It begins abruptly, and we gather from the content that God is the speaker. Amos said that there will be no day or light, only night and darkness (5.18-20). Yahweh breaks in to answer Amos's question, 'What is this day of Yahweh to you?': God replies that the day of sacrifice and song is not his day and that he will have nothing to do with their feasts (5.21-24).

The singular masculine imperative, 'remove', and the singular suffixes, 'your songs' and 'your lutes', indicate a new addressee.[86] God's message is at first addressed to the people, but the singular address is directed to the individual singer and musician, who, like Amos, took part in the performances at the symposia. The text is set off from other speeches of Yahweh and Amos as the only one in which there is direct singular address. The singers, songs and occasion are described in the subsequent scene (6.1-7).

At the end of his speech, God shifts from his complaint directed to the people to an exhortation in the third person:

86. Andersen and Freedman (**Amos**, pp. 59, 527-28) observe that 'the unusual shift' from the second person masculine plural to the second person masculine singular in 5.23 'may be a deliberate element in the switch from the group to the individual'. They link 5.23 and 6.5, arguing that the individual is the king who is responsible for justice.

> But let justice roll along like waters… (5.24)

The second scene (6.1-7, 12-13) begins with Amos resuming the dirge (5.18-20; 5.1-2) or an impersonal song about the people in the third person plural:

> Woe to **those**…in Zion,
> and to **those**…on the mountain of Samaria (6.1).

Immediately Amos resumes his role as HERALD by summoning the leaders of Samaria and Zion to look at individual foreign cities (6.2abA). Then he switches abruptly from indirect third person plural to direct address in the second person plural (6.2bB-3), drawing a comparison between foreign cities and the kingdoms of Israel and Judah:

> Cross over to Calneh and see
> Go from there to great Hamath
> Go down to Gath of the Philistines (6.2abA).

> Are **they** better than **these** kingdoms?
> Is **their** territory better than **your** territory,
> **you** who ward off the evil day…? (6.2B-3).

The question is addressed to the leaders of Samaria and Zion but is not immediately answered. Amos comes back to his role as NARRATOR, reporting the happy times of the people at their feasts and the sad consequences of their activities:

> **Those** who are reclining upon beds of ivory
> **Those** who are sprawling upon **their** couches…
> **Those** who are improvising at the sound of the lute
> **They** invent for **themselves** instruments of music
> **Those** who drink wine in bowls…
> **They** are not grieved over the ruin of Joseph
> **They** shall go into exile at the head of exiles
> a symposium of the supine shall be suppressed (6.4-7).

At the end of the narration, Amos gives a negative answer to the question he posed earlier (6.2bB-3). Foreign cities who are no better or larger have disappeared, and so too Israel and Judah have the same fate (6.6-7). Amos gives his third-person description a subtle ironic twist by implying that there will be no memorial or song of mourning for those in Zion who have shown no remorse over the death of Joseph.

Still in the role of narrator, Amos sets forth another riddle (6.12; cf. 3.3-6) by way of rhetorical questions, and they are directed to the people, whom Amos accuses in the second person plural:

> Do horses run on rock?
> Or is it ploughed with oxen?
> But **you** turned justice into poison… (6.12).

The context establishes that the addressee is the people in Zion (6.1-7), and Amos continues to reprove them, using vocative style, and quotes their own words, which are uttered in the first person plural (6.13):

> **you** who rejoiced in a non-word,
> **you** who said:
> 'Is it not by **our** strength **we** acquired horns?' (6.13).

The distinguishing feature of Act 3 is that all the speeches, with the exception of one (5.21-24), come from Amos. The preponderance of God's words in Act 1 is counterbalanced by the preponderance of the words of Amos in Act 3. For variety in dramatic speech, the second and fourth acts are a mixture of the words of Amos and Yahweh.

d. Act 4 (7.1–8.9)

The act opens with Amos's first-person soliloquy, reporting what he saw and speaking about God and the king:

> Thus the Lord Yahweh showed **me**;
> **he** was forming locusts…;
> it was…after the **king's** reaping (7.1).

The soliloquy is followed by a dialogue initiated by Amos who addresses Yahweh, speaks about Jacob, reports God's response and quotes his words:

> When they finished eating the grass… **I said**:
> 'O Lord Yahweh, pardon, **I** pray!
> How can **Jacob** stand?
> **He** is so small!'
> Yahweh repented concerning this:
> 'It shall not be', **said Yahweh** (7.2-3).

The second vision (7.4-6) is formulated on exactly the same pattern of first-person soliloquy and dialogue between Amos and God but in stronger language. Amos begins the conversation, assumes the role of INTER-CESSOR,[87] and pleads with God to 'stop' the fire he has started. Yahweh revokes the destruction with the decree: 'This also shall not be'.

The third and fourth visions are constructed with the same elements of

---

87. Andersen and Freedman (**Amos**, pp. 615, 625, 731) describe the first two visions as 'a dramatic literary interlude'.

soliloquy and dialogue, but Amos no longer appears in his role as INTER-CESSOR and has much less to say. The third vision begins with Amos's first-person monologue in which he speaks about Yahweh. In contrast to the earlier dialogues, God initiates the conversation and speaks in the first person. He addresses Amos, speaks about the people Israel in the third person masculine singular, and refers to Israel and Isaac as individuals:

> He showed **me**:
> the Lord was standing…a plumb line in **his** hand.
> And Yahweh said to **me**: 'Amos, what do **you** see?'
> And **I** said, 'A plumb line'.
> Then Yahweh said:
> 'I am going to set a plumb line in the midst of **my** people…
> I will never again pass by **him**;
> the high places of **Isaac** shall become desolate,
> the sanctuaries of **Israel** shall be devastated
> I will rise against the house of Jeroboam…' (7.7-9).

Amos is assigned the same small role in the fourth vision. His soliloquy becomes even shorter and God starts the dialogue and has the most to say. Both Yahweh and Amos speak in the first person: God addresses Amos, Amos responds, and God refers to the people of Israel in the third person singular:

> Thus the Lord God showed **me**…summer fruit
> And **he** said,
> 'Amos, what do **you** see?'
> And **I** said, 'a basket of late summer fruit'.
> Then Yahweh said to **me**,
> 'The end has come upon **my** people Israel;
> I will never again pass by **him**' (8.1-2).

Amos ends the visions by reporting God's words:

> 'The songs of the palace shall become wailings…' (8.3a).

Amos continues to speak but resumes his role of HERALD by summoning the people to listen, in the second person imperative plural. Employing vocative style, he acts as a REPROVER and sums up his accusation against the people, and quotes their own words against them. They speak in the first person plural and condemn themselves in a lengthy speech:

> Hear this, **you** who trampled…saying,
> 'When will the new moon be over

that **we** may sell grain?
And the sabbath that **we** may sell wheat
that **we** may make the ephah small...
that **we** may buy the poor for silver...?' (8.4-6).

The extended quotation or speech of the people is followed by Yahweh's first-person speech, which is marked as quoted speech by נאם אדני יהוה. At first Yahweh talks about the day in the third person; he then turns to address the people in the second person plural, tells them specifically what will happen to their feast days, and reverts to his third-person reporting style about the day ahead:

'And on that day', says the Lord God,
'I will make the sun set at noon....
I will turn **your** feasts into mourning
and turn **your** songs into lamentation;
I will put sackcloth upon **all** loins,
and bring baldness on **every** head;
I will make **it** (= your lamentation)
like the mourning for an only child
and make the end of **it** like a bitter day'.[88] (8.8-9).

Change of person is the basis of Amos's dramatic text. God is the sole speaker in Act 1, and Amos is the chief speaker in Act 3. There is a regular alternation of the speeches of Amos and Yahweh in the other two acts. Their speeches are carefully interwoven in terms of content and meaning, but Amos and God do not actually talk to one another until the final act. The principal speakers address other people or talk about them in various numbers and genders. The addressees are Israel, the children of Israel, the messengers of Ashdod, the city of Samaria, the people of Samaria, the women of Samaria, the house of Israel, the defendants at the city gate, the singer or musician, the leaders of Samaria and Zion, and the people of Israel. There are other characters who appear in the monody but are not addressed, and these include the men of Samaria, the woman Israel, and the individual males, Jacob and Isaac. Along with the principal speakers

88. The third person feminine singular pronominal suffixes, 'I will make it...and the end of it', point back to the lamentation (קינה) that will occur on the day of Yahweh: Driver, *Joel and Amos*, p. 213. A contrasting view is that feminine singular suffixes 'are used neutrally and refer to the sequence of activity depicted in 8.10a as a whole' (GKC, no.135 p, pp. 440-41; Wolff, *Amos*, n. n p. 322). 'It' has been explained as referring to 'the earth' (Amos 8.9; *NJPSV*), the occasion itself, or 'the day of Yahweh' (see Paul, *Amos*, n. 19 p. 263).

are the voices of women in Samaria and of the people of Zion and Israel.

Principal speakers assume a variety of roles. Yahweh's role is primarily that of JUDGE, but he is also the PLAINTIFF who accuses the people and announces the judgment. Amos plays the parts of MESSENGER, HERALD, NARRATOR, PROSECUTOR, MOURNER, ADVOCATE, and INTERCESSOR. As the plot develops, he becomes the ACCUSER alongside God. Amos's text has the appropriate title 'words of Amos'. Amos puts himself into his poetry, creates a dramatic character for himself, speaks in a variety of roles, and becomes a dominant voice in communicating the words of Yahweh. God is JUDGE and PLAINTIFF, Amos is his PROSECUTOR and ADVOCATE for the people. They are involved in worship and war, and Amos is the poet who invents songs and dirges to mimic their activities. The book, for which all issues had been settled in the fall of both kingdoms, omits the people, emphasizing the role of Amos as true prophet of the True God.

Evidence for Historical Writing

a. Change of Person
The reviser blends in more messenger speeches, more abrupt Yahweh speeches and more third person narration so as to be consistent with the style of the original composition. What is striking about the book are the number of God's first-person speeches: 1.9-12; 2.9-12; 3.1b, 13-14; 4.6-12; 5.16-17, 25-27; 6.8, 14; 8.7-8, 11-14; 9.1-4, 7-15. The book emphasizes Yahweh's words and gives Amos's words a subordinate place. Yahweh is the dominant speaker, and his voice can be heard in all parts of the commentary.

b. Time, Action and Place
The action is what counts in the poetic cycle, and the action is seen from many changing perspectives, from the vantage point of the present, past and future. The reviser, however, is not interested in particular action, but shows a strong impulse to generalize and to typify all action.[89] Amos has particular interest in the future tense because it contributes to the suspense and fear of the action. Drama implies past actions or a present situation,

---

89. Herodotus and Thucydides exploit the personages of their histories for their typicality by presenting events as manifestations of a cyclical rhythm that inevitably repeats itself, or yields the particularity of events to the structure of a story: see Charles Rowan Beye, *Ancient Greek Literature and Society* (Ithaca, NY, and London: Cornell University Press, 2nd rev. edn, 1975), pp. 198-222.

but it is always directed towards the future with an ominous forward movement.[90] The book of Amos, by contrast, may be called a history because it creates an awareness about past events. The dramatic action, with its future orientation, is transformed into a rehearsal of events that compose a past. The reviser is writing history and so describes a variety of past times. History is not seen as a sequence of unique events but of repetitions of model or pattern situations.

A dramatic plot differs from a history, which is a narrative or story of an event or series of events. A plot is much more restricted and selects events out of the wider history. Incidents of history are time-bound and are usually told in chronological order, but incidents of a plot are not time-bound, and inversions of chronological order are common.[91] These considerations point to the structural differences between Amos's text and the book.

The dramatic cycle spans the action from the point of time just prior to the defeat of Israel to the antiphonal dirge over the fallen nation through to the present and the prediction of Judah's demise. The book, by contrast, presents a whole history of a people, arranging a sequence of events in a time-scheme suggestive of a rough chronology. The history leads from the time of the nation's origins (2.9-12) to the fall and exile of Israel (3.13–5.27*) through to the fall of Judah and Jerusalem (6.8, 9-10, 14; 8.11-14). Particular incidents stand out in the history: the destruction of Bethel's altars and Amos's encounter with the priest at Bethel (3.13-14; 7.10-17). Amos does not arrange his scenes in a chronological time-scheme; he gives a forward glance to Israel's defeat (2.13-16) before it has occurred (5.1-2), and glances backwards to the visions that have already occurred (7.1–8.1-3a*). The commonest example of chronological inversions is the flashback, and Amos makes frequent use of this dramatic technique.

The cycle begins: 'The words of Amos, who was among the shepherds of Tekoa… Thus says Yahweh' (1.1a, 3aA). Amos introduces himself in present time as the person who used to be a shepherd but is now transformed from shepherd to poet. The book turns the present dramatic moment into a narrative about Amos in past time: his words are a report of what he *saw* and *said* in the time of King Jeroboam II.

---

90. Susan K. Langer, *Feeling and Form: A Theory of Art Developed from Philosophy in a New Key* (New York: Charles Scribner's Sons, 1953), pp. 306-25.

91. On the distinctions between a dramatic plot and a story, see Elder Olson, *Tragedy and the Theory of Drama* (Detroit: Wayne State University Press, 1961), pp. 33-36; Edwin Wilson, *The Theater Experience* (New York: McGraw–Hill, 4th edn, 1976), pp. 141-43.

In Act 1 (1.1–2.16*), the poet moves from what the nations did wrong in the past to what Yahweh will do to them in the future. The book fits in Tyre–Edom–Judah by following Amos's past–future sequence (1.9-12; 2.4-5), but the focus is on past time. The announcement of future punishment is reduced to the basic formula, but the description of past guilt is elaborated. The reviser ends Part 1 (1.1–2.16) by focusing exclusively on past time and explaining divine action in the time of origins or the remote past (2.9-12). The book is not dealing with contemporary events but with legendary events in the distant past when God destroyed the aboriginals of Canaan.

In Act 1 the messenger announces in present time the future collapse of Israel. Suspense is achieved by a foreshadowing glimpse of Israel's imminent defeat (2.13-16). The book interrupts the dramatic movement from present reality (2.6-8) to impending future (2.13-16) with an excursus into Israel's relationship with Yahweh. The historical summary (2.9-12) slows down the speed of the action and is essentially undramatic and static. The book deals with events belonging to exemplary time or with foundational events as a model for divine future action.

The first two scenes in Act 2 (3.1–5.7*) have the poet talking in present time about events in the future. God's words 'I am going to kill you' (3.2) are a threat. A threat is inevitably dramatic because it focuses audience attention on the future, which becomes pregnant with possibilities. Amos conveys a sensation of time passing by shifting attention from the world stage (1.1–2.16) to the rural locale or the open countryside (3.3-5) and suddenly to the sight of the city of Samaria under siege (3.9-11). The perspective shifts again to another location, to a religious banquet at Bethel where men and women eat and drink, but this peaceful scene of celebration is disrupted by further threatening images of war (4.1-5).

The reviser softens the dramatic impact of Yahweh's threat of destruction (3.2) by emphasizing that he once acted to deliver them from the land of Egypt (3.1b). Amos seems to talk generally about evil befalling a city (3.6), but then talks about real time and concrete action against the city of Samaria (3.9-11). The book, however, moves from particular concrete action to the general and abstract idea. Employing generic past time, the reviser argues that God has always spoken to his servants the prophets before taking action (3.7-8). The fall of Samaria has not unfolded, but the book breaks the developing tension between past and future by interjecting comments about rescue (3.12) and by narrowing the scope of the action to the destruction of Bethel's altars (3.13-14).

The dramatic situation develops, and the action builds from one crisis to another. There are three different movements in the final scene of Act 2. Amos begins to talk in present time about the fall of Israel as a tragic event already played out and past (5.1-2).[92] The fall of Israel, previously seen to be imminent, is now a completed reality. The audience receives a flash-back to a time before the fall of Israel when God uttered his appeal and threat to the house of Israel (5.4-5). At the end of Act 2, Amos looks into the future and foresees the impending destruction of Judah (5.6). The action of the cycle leads to the fall of Israel only to move to a future beyond it and to a final and more significant climax (8.1-3a).

The book, in agreement with Amos, talks about the fall of Israel as a past event but offers a different interpretation. Unlike Amos, the reviser does not perceive the event to be unique but imposes a pattern or typology upon it. The catalogue of natural and military disasters shows the book's explicit concern with the past (4.6-12). Its commentary is a report of typical disasters experienced by Israel, and it talks in general and in abstract terms about Northern cities that have suffered defeat (5.3). The fall of Israel is viewed from the perspective of the great events of mythic time, in the absolute beginning, when God created the world, the mountains and wind, and separated daylight from the darkness of the night (4.13; 5.8-9).

The poet places enormous demands of imagination upon his audience as the narrative races from vignette to vignette and lurches through time. Act 3 (5.10–6.14*) opens in a new location, and the setting of the first scene is the court at the city gate (5.10-12). The shift to yet another location is indicated at the end of the first scene (5.21-24), and the new place is the banquet at Zion where the leaders of the nation celebrate over food and drink, as once did the privileged people of Samaria (6.1-6).[93] The poet talks about the people's past misdeeds (5.10-11, 12b) and their present activities (5.12a; 6.1-6), and the action moves inexorably forward to the foreboding future, to the inevitable day of Yahweh (5.18-20), to Judah's doom (6.7).

The book gives a sense of endless time in the hymnic sections (4.13; 5.8-9), and this perspective preempts the poet's vision of Yahweh's day as the end of the physical day, of festival time, and time as such (5.18-20; 8.1-3a, 8-9). However, the book offers the reassurance that at the end of the night we shall return to the world of day and consciousness, light and

92. Andersen and Freedman, *Amos*, p. 471.
93. See also Andersen and Freedman (*Amos*, p. 545), who show that the rhetorical series in 6.1-7 'embodies the classical dramatic elements of time, place and action'.

stability. The stars will continue to lighten the dark night, and this tranquil image replaces the poet's fearful image of uninviting darkness and gloom.

The poet's day of Yahweh (5.18-24) creates a mood of apprehension about the future. But the mood of tense anticipation is broken with the book's postscript (5.25-27). The cycle loses impetus and slows down into a static interpretation of past events. The retrospective historical sketch recalls the remote wilderness sojourn when the house of Israel sacrificed to other gods and ends with Israel's exile beyond Damascus. The commentary's tone is reminiscence, not immediacy. The cycle moves towards Judah's future exile (6.7), but the book circumscribes the dramatic action by focusing attention on the exile of Israel.

The visions are the substance of Act 4 (7.1–8.1-3a*), and the poet narrates a series of events that have already occurred. As flashbacks to recent divine action, the visions are directed towards divine action in the immediate future. The poet gives a panoramic view of agricultural life presented season by season. He begins with the last growth in spring or the time of ingathering, goes through the dry period of the hot summer and ends with the autumn harvest. Time is telescoped, and through the use of this dramatic technique, the audience is made to feel the progress of destruction through all the changing seasons.[94] The agricultural year is a preview of the unlucky days of Yahweh that lie ahead: the last vision is of the first fruit of the autumn season, but suddenly the agricultural cycle is broken, the lucky days of harvest are over, and there is no more passing from spring to summer or summer to autumn.

The book's biography about Amos breaks the dramatic continuity between divine past and future action (7.10-17). It imitates the poet's interest in the past, but the wide scope of space and time in Amos's visions contrasts with the narrower focus of the biographical sketch about Amos's dispute with a Bethel priest. The book minimizes the dramatic effect of the original by putting Amos in the distant past as a prophet against Israel and Jeroboam II. It replaces the end of a people with Israel's exile, the death of a priest and his family.

The cycle reaches its ultimate climax when the poet prophesies the end for God's people (8.1-3a). It ends at the point at which action is about to take place and with a glance forward in time to the inevitable day when the whole land will be filled with lamentation (8.9-10). The poet's tragic vision of the impending end of time is replaced by the reviser's comic

---

94. Mays (*Amos*, p. 128) notes the compression of time in the vision reports and its dramatic effect.

vision of cyclical recurrence. The book gives a static vision of the future days beyond the destruction and exile of the nation (9.1-15), presenting events as manifestations of a recurring rhythm in nature. The vision of restoration is a symbol of endless renewal, like the constant rising and sinking of the Nile (9.5-6; 8.8). Nothing changes, and so the future days of Yahweh are a time of new beginnings, an eternal beginning again on the land, a virtual image of harmony in the world.

Chapter 4

PROPHETIC TRADITION AND CULTURAL CONTEXT

Amos's choice of tragedy as a literary form was innovative,[1] but it arose out of the conflict between historical theory and prophetic vision. The Yahwist epic and its sequel (Dtr 1) theorized how God should relate to his people by holding out a future of prosperity for Judah and security for Jerusalem. But Isaiah was critical of the epic's confidence in God's covenant and reversed this historical view with his prediction of the fall of Judah.[2]

Amos challenges the assumptions and expectations of his audience that were preserved in contemporary history writing, and using Isaiah as his model for the future, introduces tragedy as a literary genre into Hebrew tradition. A modern reader, who wants to understand audience reaction to Amos's performance, has to appreciate that when he appeared on the scene there was little antecedent Judaean literature, and that it was all available and easy to remember. Quotation from or allusion to the literature, or criticism of beliefs and assumptions, would not be missed by the audience. An attempt to reconstruct these presuppositions or expectations must be made if we want to find our way into Amos's poetry at a deeper level and come to know the ideas that commanded an audience response.

Dialogue with History and Prophecy

a. *1.1–2.16**

Amos's opening diatribe against the nations must have provoked an enthusiastic response from his Jerusalem listeners who assumed that God was

---

1.   Katharine J. Dell ('The Misuse of Forms in Amos', *VT* 45 [(1995], pp. 45-61) argues that Amos borrowed and subverted traditional forms for the purpose of shocking his audience and producing a distinctive message.

2.   The literary traditions before Amos included the Yahwist epic, the epic sequel or the first edition of the Deuteronomistic history (= Dtr 1) and Isaiah. The particular texts that are cited from these works depend on the literary analysis of Peckham, *History and Prophecy*, pp. 29-132, 135-58, 207-22.

on their side, assuring them of victory over their enemies. According to the epic, God made a covenant or treaty with Moses and Israel to drive out the peoples in the land (Exod. 34.10-12, 14, 19, 24, 27-28abA). The attitudes of Amos's audience were shaped by the nationalistic sentiments of the epic, which saw Israel as a people dwelling alone among the nations (Num. 23.9). So Yahweh sets Abraham apart from the peoples of the world (Gen. 11.1, 4-7, 8b, 9b) by promising to make of him a great nation, by blessing those who bless him and cursing those who curse him (Gen. 12.1, 2a, 3a). Israel as a people is founded on a treaty blessing, and at the end of the epic, Balaam blesses the people and declares that Yahweh will be with them when they defeat the nations (Num. 22–24).[3]

Amos identifies traditional enemies which appear in Dtr 1's narration of the history of Israel from Moses to Hezekiah. The audience is invited to recall different episodes in their past and look forward to a future day when Yahweh will destroy the enemy nations. The effect of Amos's diatribe is that it reinforces audience confidence that God will continue to fight on their behalf. The idea was basic to the epic covenant and was stressed by Dtr 1's version of the covenant, according to which Jerusalem's security was guaranteed as long as the people trusted in Yahweh.

With respect to Amos's oracle against Damascus and the dynasty of Hazael (1.3-5), the image communicated to the audience and transposed from Dtr 1's pre-exilic history is Hazael's invasion of Ramoth-gilead (2 Kgs 8.28-29). Amos connects the Syrian invasion of Gilead in the ninth century with the eighth-century Assyrian conquest of Damascus. By including a literal quotation from the Dtr 1 history about the exile of the Syrians to Kir (קירה גלה 2 Kgs 16.9 = Amos 1.5b), Amos makes his audience recall a whole sequence of events, beginning with the formation of the Aramean–Israelite league and ending with the fall of Damascus and Tiglath-pileser's deportation of its people (732 BCE; 2 Kgs 16.2a, 5, 7-9).[4]

The audience would have welcomed Amos's oracle against the Philistines (1.6-8), especially since they were remembered in the Dtr 1 history as longstanding enemies who fought against Saul and David (e.g. 1 Sam.

---

3.   Peckham (*History and Prophecy*, Fig. 2, p. 33) identifies the episodes in 'The Yahwist Epic', including the story of Balaam (Num. 22–24).

4.   Henri Cazelles ('La Guerre Syro-Ephraïmite dans le Contexte de la Politique Internationale', in Garrone and Israel [eds.], *Storia e Tradizioni di Israele*, pp. 31-48 [32-33, 46-47] argues that the initial tableau depicting the punishment of Israel, Damascus and other nations (Amos 1.3–2.16) partially concerns the campaigns of Tiglath-pileser III (2 Kgs 15.29).

17; 31).[5] Amos links the proclamation against Philistia with the previous one against Aram by suggesting, in agreement with the sequel, that Hazael's subjugation of Gilead was followed by his conquest of Gath (2 Kgs 12.17).[6]

Citing Ammon's crime of killing women in Gilead (Amos 1.13), Amos has his audience reflect on the Dtr 1 history of the Ammonite invasion of Gilead during the reign of Saul (1 Sam. 11.1-5, 7, 9-11, 12aAg). Especially appropriate is the reference to the fire in the wall of Rabbah (Amos 1.14) because it recalls Dtr 1's account of David's victory over the Ammonites in the battle of Rabbah (2 Sam. 11.1, 14-19) and the slaying of Uriah at the city wall (2 Sam. 11.20, 21b-24).

The audience would have understood Amos's oracle against Moab[7] in light of the Yahwist story of Balaam.[8] But the surprise in Amos's rhetoric is that he turns this traditional story on its head. The king of Moab summons Balaam to utter a curse upon Israel, but he replies, 'I received a command to bless; he [i.e. God] has blessed, and I cannot revoke it' (ולא אשיבנה Num. 23.20). Amos reiterates that God cannot reverse his war against the nations, and when God's words לא אשיבנו 'I cannot revoke it', are used against the Moabites, the audience sees that Moab receives God's curse that its king intended for Israel.

The poet Amos has a sense of history and thus his appeal to the past is the means by which he prepares his audience for his vision of the future. Amos summons his audience to remember events from the days of the early monarchy down to the last days of the kingdom of Israel. Amos used the Assyrian campaigns into Aram,[9] Philistia, the Transjordan and Israel

5.   Brian Peckham, 'The Deuteronomistic History of Saul and David', *ZAW* 97 (1985), pp. 190- 209.

6.   Amos accuses Gaza of deporting a whole people to Edom (1.6), a crime for which there is no independent historical source. As for the judgment on Gaza (Amos 1.7), the exilic Deuteronomistic historian notes that Hezekiah defeated the Philistines as far as Gaza (2 Kgs 18.8). Amos excludes Gath from future destruction because the city has already fallen (6.2), and the surviving cities are the remnant of the Philistine pentapolis (1.8).

7.   Amos condemns Moab for burning the bones of the Edomite king. The crime is original to Amos and has no precedents or antecedents in biblical history. The exilic Deuteronomistic historian presents Moab as a traditional enemy: e.g. Judg. 3.29-30; 1 Sam. 14.47; 2 Sam. 8.2; 2 Kgs 3.4-27; 13.20; 24.2.

8.   Num. 22.4b-6, 7b-21aAb, 36-41; 23.1-30; 24.1-6, 8-13, 25: see Peckham, *History and Prophecy*, pp. 33, 860.

9.   Wayne T. Pitard, *Ancient Damascus: A Historical Study of the Syrian City-*

as the prime model for his prophecy of a coming day of Yahweh when the nations of the world would be destroyed.[10]

The inclusion of Israel among the defeated peoples would not have shocked the audience. It was anticipated when Amos threw the spotlight upon Syria, Philistia, Ammon and Moab. It was anticipated by Amos's reference to Tiglath-pileser's policy of uprooting mass populations from their homelands and exiling them to remote parts of the Assyrian empire (1.5b = 2 Kgs 16.9).[11] What the audience least expected to hear, especially in light of God's curse on Moab, was the startling announcement that the fall of Israel is the evidence for the undoing of God's blessing on his people. Amos uses Balaam's words 'I cannot revoke it' in an opposite sense to refer to Israel's defeat in war and withdrawal of divine assistance. Accordingly, God cancels his former covenant blessing on Israel, the promise to be with his people and to protect them from their enemies (Amos 2.6; Num. 23.20-24; 24.1-9).

Isaiah denounced the citizens of Jerusalem who erroneously believed they could escape the Assyrian threat by taking refuge in the covenant. He ridiculed the covenant as a pact with death and Sheol, predicting that a scourge would soon come through, beat them down, and wipe away their covenant (Isa. 28.14-15, 18-19). The alternative to the covenant is the laying of a cornerstone in Zion, a cornerstone built with a sure foundation having justice as the line and righteousness as the plummet (Isa. 28.16-17).

State from Earliest Times until its Fall to the Assyrians in 732 BCE (Winona Lake: Eisenbrauns, 1987), pp. 145-189.

10. Volkmar Fritz ('Amosbuch, Amos-Schule und historischer Amos', in Fritz, Pohlmann and Schmitt [eds.], *Prophet und Prophetenbuch* pp. 29-43) argues that Amos 1.3-5, 6-8, 13-15 and 2.1-3 reflect events of the period of Assyrian expansion under Tiglath-pileser III (744–727 BCE). Fritz ascribes the oracles to redactors of the 'Amos school' working after the fall of Samaria. Cf. other scholars who argue that the oracles reflect the historical circumstances of the first half of the eighth century: Gerhard Pfeifer, 'Die Fremdvölkerspruch des Amos—später vaticinia ex eventu?', *VT* 38 (1988), pp. 230-33; Dieter Vieweger, 'Zur Herkunft der Völkerworte im Amosbuch unter besonderer Berücksichtigung des Aramäerspruch (Am 1, 3-5)', in Peter Mommer and Winfried Thiel (eds.), *Altes Testament und Wirkung: Festschrift für Henning Graf Reventlow* (Frankfurt am Main: Peter Lang, 1994), pp. 103-19.

11. According to the exilic Deuteronomistic history, Tiglath-pileser struck Israel with full force, deporting portions of the population from Gilead, Galilee and Hazor (2 Kgs 15.29). In his annals, Tiglath-pileser reports that he received tribute from Menahem of Samaria: see *ANET*, p. 283.

Isaiah's insistence on justice is taken up by Amos, who cites specific injustices that are detailed in the later Elohist law code.[12] When Amos compares God's judgment upon Israel to the effect of an overloaded cart (Amos 2.13), he has his audience remember Isaiah's image of the people in Jerusalem drawing sin with cart ropes (Isa. 5.18). Upon hearing the punishment for Israel's crimes (Amos 2.13-16), Amos's Jerusalem audience is given an opportunity to recall Isaiah's prediction of the coming siege of Zion (Isa. 1.8 = Isa. 30.17), his description of its people speeding away upon swift horses or fleeing away on foot from their swift pursuers (Isa. 30.15-17). On the one hand, the pattern of Aram–Philistia–Ammon–Moab allows the audience to remember the Assyrian invasion and the fall of Israel. On the other hand, the allusions to Isaiah allow the audience to anticipate the application to Zion and Jerusalem.

b. *3.1–5.7**

'Hear this word' (3.1; 4.1; 5.1) recalls Moses' address to all Israel concerning the covenant at Horeb and its stipulations (Deut. 1.1a; 5.1aA, 2; 6.4). The emphasis of the epic history and its sequel is on the covenant words (Exod. 34.27) and on Israel hearing all that Yahweh speaks (Deut. 5.4, 27). The terms פָּקַד 'to punish' and עָוֹן 'iniquity' refer to the epic covenant, according to which Yahweh forgives iniquity, transgression and sin, but punishes the iniquity of the fathers upon their children to the third and the fourth generation (Exod. 34.6-7). Amos begins his text with the covenant word פֶּשַׁע 'transgression' (1.3a, 6a, 13a; 2.1a, 6a; 4.4a; 5.12). As he proceeds he adds the other standard covenant words (3.2; 5.12), and his use of covenant theology is confirmed when Yahweh promises to 'punish' his people for their 'iniquities' (3.2).

The audience had no trouble believing Amos when he said that God selected the family of Israel out of all the families of the earth (3.2b). But he totally reverses expectations when he makes election the reason for

12. Selling the righteous (Amos 2.6b) refers to corrupt judges or officials who decide cases against the innocent in return for bribes or profit (Exod. 23.7-8). Trampling the poor is used in legal contexts describing the perversion of justice (Exod. 23.2, 6). Sexual relations of a father and son with the same female (Amos 2.7b) are cited in a law prohibiting a man from having sex with a female servant whom he has designated for his son (Exod. 21.9). Associated with this sexual misconduct in the temple is the taking of garments in pledge (Amos 2.8), a practice that is regulated by a law requiring that a man's outer garment be returned before sundown for his own use during the night (Exod. 22.26-27).

their punishment. Amos follows the sequence of the epic by moving from a reference to God's punishment of the crimes of the guilty (Amos 3.1 = Exod. 34.7) to his future deeds (Amos 3.6b = Exod. 34.10-12). The Yahwist epic stressed the wonderful works that God promised to do as part of his covenant (Exod. 34.10). But Amos overturns this covenant promise when he announces that God will do evil in the city (עשה Exod. 34.10; Amos 3.6).

Divine punishment of Samaria was an idea already available to the audience from the Dtr 1 history. Ending with the Assyrian siege of Samaria (2 Kgs 18.9aAb, 10aBbB, 11), the history explains that Israel fell because it did not observe the covenant and commandment of Moses (2 Kgs 18.12). Amos subtly invites his audience to compare the crimes of Samaria with those of Jerusalem observed by Isaiah. Isaiah said that the people of Jerusalem resisted hearing what is right (נכחות Isa. 30.10) and that their trust 'in oppression' (בעשק Isa. 30.12) was 'the iniquity' (העון Isa 30.13 = Amos 3.2) that would bring about their ruin. Amos echoes Isaiah's words when he mentions the oppressions (ועשוקים Amos 3.9b) in Samaria and declares that its people did not know how to do right (נכחה Amos 3.10a).

Amos's description of the defeat of Samaria shows a marked resemblance to Isaiah's description of the Assyrian campaign against Jerusalem: the enemy invades and overruns the land, lays siege to the city, and plunders its fortifications or property (Amos 3.11b; Isa. 10.6b). Amos never mentions Assyria by name, but alludes to Isaiah's account of Sennacherib's invasion and siege of Jerusalem (Isa. 10.5-7, 13-14; cf. Isa. 5.26-29; Amos 3.4, 12). Through allusions to past events, the audience begins to comprehend Amos's ominous vision of the future.

The references to ritual activity (Amos 4.1-5) are unambiguous for an audience familiar with the standard of behaviour set out in the Dtr 1 law of centralization. It assumed that the festivals would be celebrated at the central sanctuary where the people would freely eat, drink wine and party (Deut. 12.17-18aAb, 20, 26; 14.25-26). In light of the sequel's objection to worship at places other than the central sanctuary, Amos's summons to Bethel would have been interpreted as an ironic invitation (4.1aA) and a direct contradiction to what the Dtr 1 historian said about the required journey to the central sanctuary (Deut. 12.26).

Amos argues that worshippers once transgressed at Bethel (4.1a), and through historical allusion his audience is allowed to perceive that even contemporary worship at the central sanctuary in Jerusalem is associated with sin (4.4b-5). His exhortation to bring sacrifices every morning (4.4b) recalls the law on Passover sacrifice, according to which the animal from the flock or the herd would be brought to the central sanctuary to be boiled and eaten at night before the worshippers returned home in the morning (Deut. 16.1-2, 7). The topic of leavened bread comes up in the Dtr 1 legislation and there the Passover sacrifice is to be eaten without leavened bread (Deut. 16.3aA). Amos quotes and reverses the Dtr 1 law by representing the Passover sacrifice as being eaten with leavened bread.

Amos's Jerusalem audience are reminded of their own ritual practices. The bringing of 'tithes' every three days (Amos 4.4b) recalls the Dtr 1 prescription to eat the 'tithe' of grain, wine and oil at the place chosen by Yahweh (Deut. 12.17, 18aAb). The audience might also think of the Dtr 1 instruction to tithe all the yield of the annual seed, convert it into money, and go to the central sanctuary where they may buy food and wine to eat and drink (Deut. 14.22, 25-26). Amos refers to the 'freewill offerings' (4.5), which were also to be consumed at the place Yahweh chooses (Deut. 12.17). What starts out as Amos's criticism of Bethel turns into a criticism of the central sanctuary (4.4-5). The drinking party he mentions is accompanied by oppression (4.1), and the audience are alerted to their own acts of injustice when they party at the central sanctuary. The audience has assumed that worship should be conducted at the central sanctuary in Jerusalem; the problem, however, is not their place of worship but the unjust things they do when they come to worship (5.1-7).

c. *5.10–6.13**

Amos describes the feasts in Samaria and Zion (5.21-24; 6.1-7). Allusion to the Dtr 1 history allows the audience to guess that Amos not only criticizes what the people of Samaria once did at Bethel and Gilgal but also what the people of Jerusalem do at the central sanctuary. In the early stages of the Dtr 1 history, the author does not identify the place that Yahweh chooses, but in the closing episode, Hezekiah is credited with removing the high places and centralizing worship in Jerusalem (2 Kgs 18.22). So too Amos discloses, towards the end of his monody, his interest in Zion's feasts and thus with proper worship at the central sanctuary in Jerusalem.

The words Amos puts into God's mouth are intended to be a repudiation of the Dtr 1 law (Amos 5.21-23), according to which burnt offerings (עלות) should be consumed not at any place of worship but at the place which Yahweh chooses (Deut. 12.13-14). Amos's audience is told that they do what the law requires by eating their sacrifices (עלות) at the central sanctuary, but that God rejects their feasts and offerings (Amos 5.22; Deut. 12.17, 18aAb; 14.22, 25-26).

Prosperity was part of the treaty or covenant blessing, and so the Dtr 1 history begins with a report of how God brought his people into the land, giving them cities they did not build, houses they did not fill, and vineyards they did not plant (Deut. 6.10-12). The treaty blessings are reiterated at the end of the Dtr 1 history, but this time by Sennacherib, who tries unsuccessfully through an administrator to conclude a peace-pact with Judah during the Assyrian invasion and siege of Jerusalem. The list of treaty blessings ensures that citizens will live and eat of their own vines and drink water of their own cisterns until they are deported to a land like their own, abundant with grain and vineyards (2 Kgs 18.28-32a). The people of Jerusalem did not answer the Assyrian speech (2 Kgs 18.36), and their silence indicates that they observed the covenant, in contrast to the Israelites of Samaria who disobeyed the covenant (2 Kgs 18.12). The Dtr 1 history ends with covenant theology, thus directing the reader back to the beginning where God's covenant blessing is described.

In accordance with this Dtr 1 historical perspective, Amos's audience believed that the miraculous deliverance of Jerusalem was the result of their reliance on the covenant and on Hezekiah's law of centralization (2 Kgs 18.22).[13] However, Amos has his audience ponder the interpretation the standard history of the day gave of the events and crisis in Jerusalem. To this end he portrays a court scene of a reprover at the city gate which resembles Dtr 1's portrayal of Absalom, who, in standing at the city gate, proclaims that if he were judge in the land, every man could come to him and receive justice (Amos 5.10; 2 Sam. 15.1-6). As much as Amos's audience might have affirmed this ideal form of justice, they are taught indirectly through performance that they too have subverted justice at the gate, and that their very survival depends on their ability to distinguish right from wrong.

Although Amos adopts Dtr 1's treaty language, he turns the covenant blessing into a treaty curse: 'You have built houses, but you shall not dwell in them; you have planted pleasant vineyards, but you shall not drink their wine' (Amos 5.11; cf. Deut. 6.10-11). The treaty curse is directed against those who extort and accept bribes (Amos 5.11-12). Fidelity to the covenant, according to Dtr 1, was shown when the people resisted alliances

13. Brian Peckham, *The Composition of the Deuteronomistic History* (HSM, 35; Atlanta, GA: Scholars Press, 1985), pp. 9, 80 n. 39.

with foreign powers and when they conducted worship at the central sanctuary. Isaiah argued that justice was missing from the covenant and that
the new city of Zion would have justice as its foundation (Isa. 28.16-17).
Amos agrees that the covenant should be replaced with justice, and that
God will even revoke his covenant blessings because of violations against
the poor.

Amos's criticism of the symposia feasts in Samaria and Zion was also
inspired by Isaiah's song of the vineyard (Isa. 5). The first-person singer is
probably Isaiah himself, but it is important to see that 'I-statements' in
archaic poetry in general, and in monody or solo song in particular, may
refer to any personality the composer chooses: so Archilochus represents
Charon the carpenter, or Sappho, in a love song, speaks as Aphrodite, or
Alcaeus impersonates a woman.[14] Similarly, Isaiah adopts the dramatic
persona of a woman who sings in the first person about a vineyard that her
beloved planted and cared for, but the vineyard, instead of yielding sweet
grapes, produced wild grapes (5.1-2).[15] Then Isaiah assumes the role of the
beloved who talks in the first person of his desperation at seeing the sour
grapes (5.4) and his decision to trample down the vineyard (5.5). The
action then shifts from the song to the setting of the song, a typical
symposium feast at which people drink wine and are entertained by songs
sung to the melody of lyres, timbrels and flutes (5.11-12a). The people are
criticized for celebrating their feasts and not recognizing the works of God
(5.12b). Without understanding the criticism directed against them, they
respond by challenging God to speed up his work so that they may see it
(5.18-19). But instead of the anticipated marvels, they receive a vision of
an enemy who advances against them (5.26-29).

14. Archilochus, frs. 19, 122, in Douglas E. Gerber (ed.), *Greek Iambic Poetry*
(LCL; Cambridge, MA: Harvard University Press, 1999), pp. 92-95, 160-63; Sappho,
fr. 1, and Alcaeus, fr. 10b, in Campbell, *Greek Lyric*, I, pp. 52-55, 242-43; Kenneth
James Dover (ed.), *Ancient Greek Literature* (Oxford: Oxford University Press, 1980),
pp. 32-33; Easterling and Knox (eds.), *Early Greek Poetry*, p. 77; Nagy, *Poetry as
Performance*, pp. 97-100.

15. Susan Ackerman ('Isaiah', in Newsom and Ringe [eds.], *Women's Bible
Commentary*, p. 163) argues that the song must come from a woman's mouth because
the beloved is male. If Isaiah is speaking directly about his own personal feelings, then
he is expressing his love for another male. Cf. William L. Holladay (*Isaiah: Scroll of a
Prophetic Heritage* [New York: Pilgrim Press, 1978], p. 62) who observes that the
Hebrew word for 'beloved' is masculine but says that Isaiah 'is talking about a friend'.
When Isaiah's song of the vineyard was revised by II Isaiah, the 'beloved' turns out to
be God (Isa. 5.7; see Peckham, *History and Prophecy*, p. 144).

Amos's monologue, in imitation of Isaiah's solo song, contains the same narrative development. It begins with the vineyard and the drinking of wine (Amos 5.11), moves to the symposium feast and the songs, and then to the same climactic solution of defeat in war (Amos 5.21-24; 6.4-6). Isaiah associated the festivals with iniquity and sin (Isa. 5.19), and Amos develops the connection between the festivals and the unjust things the people do (Amos 5.23-24). Isaiah's audience became aware that the fate of the vineyard would be their own, and Amos's audience, similarly, discover that the tragedy of Joseph will soon overtake Zion (Amos 6.6b).

d. *7.1–8.10**

Amos returns to the beginning of his poetry when he has his audience recall once again the visions and oracles of Balaam. In the epic narrative, Balaam promises to disclose 'whatever Yahweh shows him' (מֶה־יִרְאַנִי Num. 23.3), describing himself as one who both hears the words of God and sees the vision of the Almighty (Num. 24.4). Alluding to the Balaam story, Amos begins each vision with what Yahweh has shown him (הִרְאַנִי כֹּה). But while Balaam is shown a future of prosperity and security for Yahweh's people, Amos receives terrifying visions of the future. Balaam's blessing ensured the defeat of the enemy nations (24.8), but Amos turns the Balaam blessing into a curse by prophesying the defeat and end of God's people (7.9b; 8.9).

In the final moments of his monody, Amos returns to the problem of the festivals. His novel solution is the day of Yahweh which brings to an end the halcyon feast-days associated with covenant observance. Yahweh's day goes beyond the physical destruction of high places and sanctuaries on a given day of battle (7.9). The divine curse, 'I will never again pass by him' (= 'my people Israel': 7.8b; 8.2b) refers to a coming day when God abandons his people and is no longer accessible to them in worship. The monologue concludes on this alarming note: the audience is left to ponder a day without festivals and songs, prayer or sacrifice.

Poetic Dialogue in the Greek World

Amos entered into a dialogue with both history and prophecy. Because he was situated at the beginning of the prophetic tradition, he inspired and captivated all the prophets who came after him. They composed their poetry with reference to him and other prophets, either by direct quotation or allusion.[16] The analogy is the great poetic dialogue that flourished among the archaic poets of the Greek world. Poets conversed with poets who lived close by or far away and also with poets who were long dead. As the repertoire of poetry increased with time, new meanings or ideas were injected into earlier poems in the light of more recent ones and in response to new political, intellectual and emotional experience. A comprehensive survey of this rich poetic dialogue is yet to be compiled.[17] What follows is a selection of a few texts in which poets can be found conversing or commenting on one another and whose subject matter is akin to that of Amos's poetry.

An overt example is Solon's literary dependence upon Mimnermus. Mimnermus had chanted: 'Oh! that the fate of Death would overtake me without disease at three-score years!' The optimistic Solon chants back: 'If you will listen to me so late in the day, erase this couplet, Ligyastades; ...write it as follows: 'May the fate of death overtake me at four-score years'.[18]

With rare exception Greek poetic dialogue is developed by quotation and allusion and not by calling a poet by name. So Semonides instructs a boy: 'The end of all that happens in the world is in the hand of Zeus... We are like cattle, whose life is of the day, so we too live in ignorance, not knowing how the gods shall end it. Hope and trust makes us work for that which does not come...'. Semonides adopts Hesiod's counterplay of flattering hope and ugly reality. But while Hesiod left it ambiguous as to whether hope is the one solace left for human beings in a troubled world, Semonides argues that the ills of human life frustrate all hope for a better future.[19]

The idea that human life is as brief as the leaves of a tree is a variation made by Mimnermus on a Homeric theme: Homer's description of 'insig-

16. J. Rilett Wood, 'Prophecy and Poetic Dialogue', *SR* 24 (1995), pp. 309-22.

17. Herington, *Poetry into Drama*, pp. 61-62.

18. Mimnermus, fr. 11, and Solon, fr. 20, in Edmonds, Greek Elegy, I, pp. 96-98, 134-37. According to ancient historians, Mimnermus was called Ligyastades because his poetry was musical or 'sweet-and-clear' (λιγυς): see pp. 82-83. On Mimnermus and Solon, see Hermann Fränkel, *Early Greek Poetry and Philosophy: A History of Greek Epic, Lyric and Prose to the Middle of the Fifth Century* (trans. Moses Hadas and James Willis; Oxford: Basil Blackwell, 1975), pp. 207-17.

19. Hesiod's *Works and Days* (92-104) in Hugh G. Evelyn-White (trans.), Hesiod: The Homeric Hymns and Homerica (LCL; Cambridge, MA: Harvard University Press, rev. edn, 1936 [1914]), pp. 8-9; Semonides, fr. 1, in Edmonds, Greek Elegy, II, pp. 213-15.

nificant mortals' is offset by his insistence that they win glory in war or are remembered for their exceptional bravery. Mimnermus, by contrast, argues that what gives our brief lives meaning is 'the sunny pleasures of youth'.[20]

Archilochus adapts the words which Homer assigned to Odysseus, 'For the mind in men upon earth is even such as the day which the father of Gods and men brings upon them'. These sentiments of Homer are quoted by Archilochus and made his own: 'The mind of mortals, O Glaucus… becomes just as the day Zeus brings upon them; their thoughts are such as the events they meet'. Yet the day human beings receive from the gods is given a different interpretation. The misery of the beggar hero in the *Odyssey* is only temporary because he is after all a king. No such security underlies the thought of Archilochus who stresses the changeability of human fortune at the hands of the gods.[21]

Using epic language, Archilochus sets forth an outlook on warfare that is fundamentally different from the Homeric warrior who acts according to a heroic code, to fight for honour even at the risk of his own life.[22] Archilochus rejects the idea that it is better to die in the fighting than to take flight. In one poem, he adopts the persona of a soldier, bragging that he hid his shield behind a bush to save his life. Archilochus's attitude is radically new but does owe something to Achilles's brief challenge of the heroic code: 'fate is the same for the man who holds back, the same if he fights hard'. But Homer's Achilles takes up arms and returns to battle, whereas Archilochus's soldier gives up the fighting and leaves his armour behind.[23]

---

20. On the comparison of human life to leaves: *Iliad* 6.145-53; 21.464-64. Bravery in war is discussed in such texts as *Iliad* 4.223-26; 5.252-53, 529; 6.123-24, 208, 441-46; 12.322-28; A.T. Murray (trans.), *Homer The Iliad*, I (LCL; New York: G.P. Putnam's Sons, 1924; A. T. Murray (trans.), Homer The Iliad, II (Loeb Classical Library; Cambridge, MA.: Harvard University Press, 1925); Richmond Lattimore (trans.), *The Iliad of Homer* (Chicago: University of Chicago Press, 1951); Bowra, *Landmarks in Greek Literature*, p. 75; Mimnermus, fr. 2, in Edmonds, *Greek Elegy*, I, pp. 90-91.

21. *Odyssey* 18.136-37; A.T. Murray (trans.), *Homer The Odyssey* (2 vols.; LCL; Cambridge, MA: Harvard University Press, 1919) Richmond Lattimore (trans.), *The Odyssey of Homer* (New York: Harper & Row, 1965); Archilochus, frs. 56, 70, in Edmonds, *Greek Elegy, II*, pp. 126-27, 132-33.

22. *Iliad* 4.349-53; 6.208; 11.782-83; 12.310-28.

23. Archilochus, fr. 6, in Edmonds, *Greek Elegy, II*, pp. 100-101; *Iliad* 9.314-63, 400-20.

Tyrtaeus adapts from Homer the vivid portrait of a young soldier and an old warrior lying dead on the battlefield. There is the same description of beautiful youth contrasted with the old man's hoary head and beard, and the same reference to the uncovered and mutilated private parts. But while Homer mentioned the boy first, Tyrtaeus changes the order and mentions the old man first. Furthermore, for Homer the sight of an old hero fallen in battle was pitiful, but for Tyrtaeus it was shameful. Finally, Tyrtaeus recasts the Homeric lines into a exhortation to young men to risk their lives for old men.[24]

Semonides said that the sea has two natures, one calm and harmless, and one raging and roaring, and in the general ancient outlook the sea was associated with injustice. By contrast Solon uses an analogy to argue that neither sea nor people is unjust: the sea is stirred and tossed only under the influence of grievous winds, but when the sea is left at rest, 'it is the justest of all things'. The sea represents the people, and the winds their leaders. Thus people exhibit their true nature when they are calm and peaceful, and they become violent and unpredictable only in response to unrighteous leaders.[25]

Solon opens an elegy in imitation of Hesiod's opening invocation of the Pierian Muses in his *Works and Days*. Solon echoes Hesiod's distinction between wealth given by the gods in a just fashion and wealth acquired by unjust deeds. While Hesiod thought that evil appears in the form of riches gained by crooked verdicts in lawsuits, Solon finds the root of evil in the unjust desire for wealth. Hesiod believed in Zeus's random punishment of wrongdoing. But Solon describes the casual relationship between specific unjust acts and Zeus's punishment.[26]

Early Greek poetry provides independent corroboration of how writing was created in the ancient world. A rich poetic dialogue developed among the poets of the Greek world. The seventh-and sixth-century poets reacted

---

24. *Iliad* 22.71-76; Tyrtaeus, fr. 10, in Edmonds, *Greek Elegy, I*, pp. 68-71. All the poetry of Tyrtaeus shows close knowledge of the vocabulary of the Homeric epics: see Easterling and Knox (eds.), *Early Greek Poetry*, pp. 89-92.

25. Semonides, fr. 7, in Edmonds, *Greek Elegy*, II, pp. 218-21; Solon, frs. 12, 13, in Edmonds, *Greek Elegy*, I, pp. 125, 127-33; Fränkel, *Early Greek Poetry and Philosophy*, p. 228 n. 11.

26. Hesiod, *Works and Days* (1-5, 212-84, 321-30); Solon, fr. 13, in Edmonds, *Greek Elegy, I*, pp. 126-33. For a discussion of Solon's debt to Hesiod, see Friedrich Solmsen, *Hesiod and Aeschylus* (Ithaca, NY: Cornell University Press, 1949), pp. 107-23.

to one another and responded to epic poetry of the eighth century. Sometimes an earlier image was borrowed for a contemporary setting; sometimes a word or a whole sentence was borrowed to suit a new context; but often the applications contrast strikingly with their originals. Poets added to the literary tradition they inherited, but spoke for themselves as they adapted and updated the subject matter and changed it to fit contemporary experience. The Hebrew prophets, similarly, were inspired by one another and composed their poetry from the same repertory of images, themes and topics. The development of both early Greek and Judaean literature can be seen in this common construction of a tradition out of an ongoing dialogue with poets or writers of the immediate and distant past.

The Day of Yahweh and the Greek Analogy

Amos is the earliest writer and the first prophet to use the phrase 'the day of Yahweh'. It is a major theme in Amos, its elements are dispersed throughout his poetry, and together they form a continuous and coherent picture of God's day. The conception of the day as it unfolds in Amos is not unparalleled in the ancient world. Most of the motifs and images connected with it can be found in eighth-century Homeric epic. If we move through the pages of the *Iliad* and its sequel, we see a continuous development of the idea of the day, and it receives yet further expression in the transition from epic to lyric and elegy. What follows is a comparative study in which literary parallels are drawn between Amos and Homer and other ancient texts without establishing historical connections between them.[27] Analogy rather than genealogy is the goal.[28]

---

27. The assumption that ancient Israel and Greece were unrelated cultures was resisted decades ago by Cyrus H. Gordon, 'Homer and the Bible', *HUCA* 26 (1955), pp. 43-100; *idem*, *The Common Background of Greek and Hebrew Civilizations* (New York: W.W. Norton, 2nd edn, 1965), pp. 5, 9-12, and in recent times by John Van Seters, 'The Primeval Histories of Greece and Israel Compared', *ZAW* 100 (1988), pp. 1-22. For sample discussions of the ancient Near Eastern evidence, see Wilson, *Prophecy and Society in Ancient Israel*, pp. 89-134; Moshe Weinfeld, 'Ancient Near Eastern Patterns in Prophetic Literature', *VT* 27 (1977), pp. 178-95; Abraham Malamat, 'A Forerunner of Biblical Prophecy: The Mari Documents', in Miller, Hanson and McBride (eds.), *Ancient Israelite Religion*, pp. 33-52; A. Bentzen, 'The Ritual Background of Amos i 2–ii 16', *OTS* 8 (1950), pp. 85-99; W.E. Staples, 'Epic Motifs in Amos', *JNES* 25 (1966), pp. 106-12.

28. The importance of comparative study as an analogical or intellectual enterprise is stressed by Jonathan Z. Smith, Drudgery Divine: On the Comparison of Early

a. *The Day of Battle*

Amos describes the defeat of the nations as 'the day of battle' (1.14). But the battle 'on that day' (2.16b) comes to focus on Israel's grievous defeat. So too Homer's *Iliad* narrates four days of the Trojan war, and the fighting occurs 'on that day',[29] 'at daybreak' (3.7), in 'the bloody days' (9.326), on 'the day' (13.98), on the 'day of destruction' (ὀλέθριον ἦμαρ 19.294), 'all day' (11.279; 19.162), 'today' (20.126-27), 'the day before' (21.5). The day becomes identical with the events it brings, and the particular day brings defeat to Greek or to Trojan warriors.

Amos's terse account of the panic and flight of Israel's army (2.13-16) is illuminated by the *Iliad*'s graphic narration of the battle formation and methods of fighting.[30] There is first the strength and bravery of the more heavily armed front-line warriors upon whom the mass of more lightly armed infantry depends for its survival.[31] The second method of warfare is more open fighting, when speed of foot becomes necessary for success or escape. The *Iliad* refers to the victories of fast runners, as indicated by the stock epithets 'the swift foot'/'swift feet' being applied to heroes, and notably to Achilles, who pursues Hector around the walls of Troy until he is killed.[32]

If Amos's battle scene is read with the two fighting situations in mind, we gain a better sense of what the day of battle might have meant to the original hearers. It is a day when front-line soldiers, known for their prowess and valour, lose their fighting strength and their courage (Amos 2.14a, 16a). Even the most capable warrior in weapon drill is unable to defend himself and is forced to run for his life (Amos 2.14b, 16). The foot-soldiers who have gained their reputation for being fast runners lose their speed and mobility; they are not quick enough either to run after their attackers or to run away from them (Amos 2.14a, 15a). 'He who is swift of foot' takes on ironic meaning as the fast foot-soldier is chased to his death. The guerilla or lightly-armed troops who operate in the rear, with slings

Christianities and the Religions of Late Antiquity (Chicago: University of Chicago Press, 1990), esp. pp. 36-53, 85-115.

29. *Iliad* 2.36; 4.543; 8.475; 18.453-54; 23.87.

30. Malcolm M. Willcock, A Companion to the Iliad: Based on the Translation by Richmond Lattimore (Chicago: University of Chicago Press, 1976), pp. 148, 279-280.

31. *Iliad* 4.223-26, 265-67, 349-53; 5.252-53, 529, 680-81; 6.208, 441-46, 522-24; 8.152-54; 11.408-10; 12.310-28; 13.496-527; 15.508-10.

32. *Iliad* 1.21, 84, 364; 5.37-73; 10.110; 13.112-16, 325, 348; 14.520-23; 22.136-374; 23.776.

and arrows, are vulnerable when the front lines collapse, and they cannot even stand upright to shoot their arrows (*Iliad* 13.701-22). Even the rider or charioteer cannot save his life. He is hit as he mounts his chariot or before he has a chance to drive away from the battlefield.[33]

b. *Evil in a City*

According to the Homeric view, the day of defeat is something evil. Following a Trojan victory, Odysseus summons Achilles to save his Achaian comrades from the Trojan onslaught: 'There will be no remedy found to heal the evil thing when it has been done... No, beforehand take thought to beat the evil day (κακὸν ἦμαρ) aside from the Achaians' (*Iliad* 9.247-51).[34] The evil day symbolizes defeat and death in war, and there will be no chance to reverse the situation once destruction is accomplished. Hector expresses similar sentiments when he cries out to Ajax, his Greek opponent: 'This is a day that brings evil (ἡμέρη ἥδε κακὸν φέρει) to all the Argives. You will be killed with the rest of them, if you have daring to stand up against my long spear' (*Iliad* 13.828-32).

For Amos, like Homer, the day that bears evil is a day that brings defeat in battle. The question posed is whether evil occurs in a city unless Yahweh has done it (3.6b). The term 'evil day' is not used here, but the context for the question is a trumpet blast which signals both attack and retreat (3.6a; 2.2b). The day in both Hebrew and Greek thought is characterized by divine activity: Yahweh brings about the fall of the city of Samaria (3.9-11), and the Homeric gods decide to destroy major cities.

The Homeric text that has direct bearing on Yahweh's evil in the city is the scene on Mount Olympus where the gods sit in council and make plans for battle (*Iliad* 4.1-72). Zeus wants to end the war (*Iliad* 4.14-19), but Hera and Athena 'devise evil (κακὰ) for the Trojans', insisting that the city of Troy must be destroyed (*Iliad* 4.20-21; cf. 8.457-58). Hera censures Zeus for rendering fruitless all her efforts in bringing evil (κακὰ) to Priam, the king of Troy, and his children (*Iliad* 4.26-29). Zeus responds, 'What can be all the great evils (τόσσα κακὰ) done to you by Priam...that you

---

33. The rider on a horse may refer to the person on the chariot who drives the horses: Andersen and Freedman, *Amos*, pp. 340-341. Homeric warriors travel to, around and away from the battlefield in chariots but do not fight from chariots. The terms 'horseman'/'rider' refer to those Greeks whose skill is driving chariots (*Iliad* 9.52, 432, 438, 581; 16.20, 33): Willcock, *Companion to the Iliad*, pp. 104, 177, 279.

34. Translations are adapted from Richmond Lattimore, *The Iliad of Homer*, and *The Odyssey of Homer*.

are thus furious forever to bring down the strong-founded city of Ilion?'
(*Iliad* 4.30-33). Dissent over what will happen to Troy does not disturb the
gods' peace (*Iliad* 4.37-39). The compromise is to let Hera destroy the city
of Troy favoured by Zeus (*Iliad* 4.44-47) but on condition that he may,
if he chooses, destroy cities which are favoured by Hera (*Iliad* 4.40-43,
50-54).

There are striking parallels between the Homeric and Hebrew texts. The
people of Ashdod assemble upon the mountains of Samaria, look down on
the capital city, and witness the clamour and commotion of battle (Amos
3.9). So too the Greek gods look down on the city of Troy, watch the
fighting and observe the Greek warrior Menelaus defeat Paris, the Trojan
warrior (*Iliad* 4.9-13).[35] Just as God brings evil on Samaria, so Greek gods
haggle with one another about the destruction of cities and plan evil
against Troy.

The gods on Mount Olympus are ruthless and amoral, bargaining with
one another about the destruction of cities and acting as if it were all a
game.[36] By contrast Yahweh decides to destroy Samaria, not out of any
arbitrary ruling, but because of its wicked deeds. God's evil against the
city stems from the moral principle that oppressors deserve to be punished.
Amos alludes to the proceedings proper to a court of law where people are
asked to witness acts of violence and robbery (3.9). By mixing battle
imagery with ethical and legal language, the poet establishes solid grounds
for God taking action to bring evil upon the city.

c. *The Days of Captivity*

Amos's picture of the day when the city is taken, its ruler and people
deported (1.5b, 15; 3.9-11; 4.2-3), reads like a page out of the *Iliad*.
Hector, in a speech to his wife Andromache, envisages a day when some
bronze-armoured Achaian will lead her off, taking away 'her day of
liberty' (ἐλεύθερον ἦμαρ): 'Some day seeing you shedding tears a man
will say of you, 'This is the wife of Hector, who was ever the bravest
fighter of the Trojans...in the days when they fought about Ilion'... For
you it will be yet a fresh grief, to be widowed of such a man who could
fight off the day of your slavery (δούλιον ἦμαρ). But I may be dead and
the piled earth hide me under before I hear you crying and know by this
that they drag you captive' (*Iliad* 6.455, 459-65).

With superb economy the scenes in Amos and the *Iliad* explore the

---

35. See also *Iliad* 3.340-82, 437-39, 455-57.
36. Willcock, *Companion to the Iliad*, p. 45.

consequences of war on the non-combatants. Hector shouts these words to the wounded Patroclus just before he is is fatally stabbed by a spear: 'You thought perhaps of devastating our city, of stripping from the Trojan women the day of their liberty and dragging them off in ships to the beloved land of your fathers' (*Iliad* 16.830-33). The Homeric descriptions are designed to arouse our pathos for the women and children who are the innocent spoils of war (*Iliad* 6.95, 9.590-94). A similar effect is created by Amos when he speaks about the pregnant women from Gilead who were disembowelled at the hands of their Ammonite conquerers (1.13).[37] This vignette of the innocent wives of warriors anticipates the antitype of the typical tale concerning the capture of a city and its citizens. The women of Samaria are not portrayed as innocent victims, but as the instigators of oppression who deserve exile (4.1-3).

d. *The Day of Choice*

The fall of Samaria is seen by Amos as an inevitable event in a causal sequence that started with miscarriages of justice. Yet Amos argues that the day of Israel's doom could have been prevented if the nation had accepted Yahweh's appeal, 'Seek me and live'. His appeal offers a choice between life with Yahweh or death at Bethel and Gilgal (5.4-6). This cursory treatment of the nation's destiny being governed by two choices finds its rich background in the *Iliad*, from which we gain a better understanding of what the idea must have conveyed to Amos's audience.

Homer's great Trojan and Greek heroes recognize that their fate is governed by a choice that either wards off or leads to the day of their doom. Hector, for example, refuses his wife's tearful plea to put family above country by staying on the rampart (*Iliad* 6.405-39), deciding instead to take up his helmet and go out to the plain of war and danger (*Iliad* 6.440-65). The moment marks Hector's choice, and both parties recognize it as such, with Hector speaking about his future death (*Iliad* 6.462-64) and Andromache initiating mourning rites for her husband (*Iliad* 6.499-502). Hector's choice foreshadows his later death scene in which he makes the fatal decision to stay outside Troy, rejecting all appeals to seek safety inside the city walls (*Iliad* 22.5-361; 6.35-92).

The best example for our understanding of Amos's exhortation, 'Seek Yahweh and live', is the famous choice of Achilles. The *Iliad* is the story of Achilles: his mother informs him that his life will be brief and bitter and

---

37. See also M. Cogan, ' "Ripping open Pregnant Women" in Light of an Assyrian Analogue', *JAOS* 103 (1983), pp. 755-57.

that she bore him to a bad destiny (*Iliad* 2.350, 416-18).[38] But Achilles is only fated to die young if he chooses to fight against the city of Troy. He knows that twofold fates hold his life in the balance: 'I carry the twofold doom of death and destiny (κῆρας...θανάτοιο τέλοσδε); if I stay here and fight beside the city of the Trojans, my return home is gone, but my glory shall be everlasting; but if I return home to the beloved land of my fathers...there will be a long life left for me' (*Iliad* 9.411-16).[39]

The important correspondence between the Greek and Hebrew texts is that Achilles and Israel are represented as receiving knowledge about their own destiny. Since Achilles has a goddess for a mother, he becomes privy to information unavailable to most mortals; similarly, Yahweh warns the house of Israel about what lies ahead. Achilles knows for certain that his fate might go one of two ways, either a short life of honour, or a long life of obscurity. Likewise the choice of the house of Israel is life and justice, or death and ignominy. Homer and Amos preserve the dignity of human beings by letting them make their own choices. Human beings are seen deciding their own fate and are neither victims of destiny nor pawns in the hands of the deity (*Iliad* 1.206-207)

e. *The Inevitable Day of Darkness*

Amos's idea of destiny grows as he moves away from the nation Israel, which fulfilled the fate of its choice, to the nation Judah, which is invited to make a decision about its future. The day of defeat in battle emerges as 'the evil day' (6.3) in which all hopes and aspirations come to nothing. Homer's hero Odysseus criticizes his contemporaries for thinking that they will never suffer evil in future days: 'The gods bring sad days upon human beings against their will'. Odysseus confesses to a life of violence, and his lesson to others is to have a sense of righteousness and accept whatever day the gods bestow (*Odyssey* 18.130-37). Just as Amos insists that the evil day will come as the result of evildoing, so Homer argues that human beings deserve the day they receive.[40]

Homer's *Iliad* clarifies the pairing in Amos's poetry of darkness and

---

38. See also *Iliad* 18.9-11.

39. Cf. *Iliad* 11.793-94.

40. The gods of the *Iliad* take sides in human disputes without regard for the merits of the case. The reference to divine rejection of human wickedness (*Iliad.* 16.386-88) is developed in the *Odyssey*: 'The blessed gods have no love for a pitiless action, but rather they regard justice' (*Odyssey* 14.83-84): Willcock, *Companion to the Iliad*, p. 43.

light, brightness and gloom. With formulaic lines about the goddess of Dawn who rose from her bed to 'carry her light to men', Homer announces the start of a new day of battle (*Iliad* 11.1-4).[41] The Trojans begin at daybreak to attack the Greeks (*Iliad* 3.7), but when night comes the Trojans abandon the fighting (*Iliad* 7.279-82, 90-93). On the second day warriors throw their weapons as long as light continues or until black night puts an end to the fighting. The Trojans regret the sinking of daylight because premature darkness prevents a decisive victory (*Iliad* 8.66-67, 485-88). As daylight increases on the third day the fighting becomes heavy, and Agamemnon proposes that the Trojans give up the battle when night comes (*Iliad* 11.84-85; 14.78-81). In the thick of the fighting the battlefield becomes covered with a gloomy dark mist. As Greek troops are encouraged not to panic, Athena comes to their rescue by removing the mist from their eyes, and the light comes out to them on both sides (*Iliad* 15.665-70; cf. 12.239-40).

Opposed to gloomy mist and darkness is light or bright air, and these opposites become attached to a deity who assists or hinders warriors. The fight is even for a long time, as is shown by Zeus, who favours one side and then the other. Zeus sends shafts of bright light onto the mountainsides so that the Greeks can drive the Trojans away from their ships (*Iliad* 16.297-300), and envelops the battlefield in baneful night so that there will be dire work in fighting over the corpse of a Trojan warrior (*Iliad* 16.565-68). The darkness results in the death of Greek and Trojan warriors alike (*Iliad* 16.569-62). Again Zeus expresses his grief over the death of a Greek warrior by spreading a thick mist that leads to confusion and danger and the deaths of Greek and Trojan leaders (*Iliad* 17.269-70, 274-368). The dark fog covers men and horses and leads Ajax to make his famous prayer to Zeus: 'Father Zeus…in shining daylight destroy us, if to destroy us be now your pleasure' (*Iliad* 17.643-47). So Zeus scatters the dark mist so that the battle is plain before them (*Iliad* 17.649-50). What characterizes the subsequent activity of Athena and Hera is this same alternate sending of light and dark mist to assist the Greeks and hinder the Trojans (*Iliad* 20.94-95, 126-28; 21.5-7).

Homer's imagery of the four-day war is the appropriate context for understanding Amos's day of destiny. For Homer the day of battle does not refer to a period of twenty-four hours but is the time between daybreak and the onset of night. Amos, similarly, describes the day of war as his

---

41. See also *Iliad* 2.48-52; 8.1, 529-30, 565; 9.240; 10.251-52; 19.1.

contemporaries understood it, and they look foward to daytime, or the part of the day when there is light. In the language of Homer and Amos good fortune in battle is 'daylight' and 'brightness', and its opposite is 'night', 'darkness' and 'gloom'.

Light is figurative of deliverance or victory in battle, and darkness is figurative of ruin and calamity,[42] but light and darkness are more than metaphors. Amos and Homer are talking about physical light and physical darkness. Zeus has the power to sweep shafts of light or ghastly night over the battlefield; he can cover the warriors with a dark mist or fog, or he can replace it with bright or clear air. Yahweh, like Zeus, has power over both light and darkness. Amos's contemporaries look forward to a day when God will give them the bright light to kill their enemies. But Amos argues that there will be no daytime as warriors become quickly shrouded in the blackness of night; they will neither see the enemy as they attack, nor see the enemy's counter- attack. Darkness leads to fright and panic, and the warriors who looked forward to a glorious victory on a day of light now meet an inglorious death on the battlefield.

Amos associates the darkness of the day of battle with Yahweh's manifestation in the thunderstorm (1.14b). Likewise Homer's Zeus strikes terror in the Greeks by letting go a lightning flash and a loud thunderbolt (*Iliad* 17.593-95). The aegis which Zeus holds has its origin in a view of the dark underside of the stormcloud (*Iliad* 4.166-67),[43] and the terror it puts in the Greek warriors causes them to flee. Zeus's whirlstorm puts an end to a whole day of fighting. The stormy wind darkens the air, making the warriors lose their courage to stand and fight (*Iliad* 17.597-624).[44] Similarly, the dark storm caused by Yahweh is part of the panic and fear that grips the mighty warriors when they take flight on the day of battle (Amos 2.13-16).

Amos does not speak explicitly about a day of destiny or dark fate, but by using a succession of comparisons (5.11, 19) he does picture a future day on which there is no escape from death and destruction. Whatever attempts are taken to frustrate it, the day cannot be avoided: Yahweh's people are fated to die and the nation state is fated to perish. The day is

---

42. For a discussion of the ancient fear of darkness, see Weston W. Fields, 'The Motif 'Night as Danger' Associated with Three Biblical Destruction Narratives', in Michael Fishbane and E. Tov (eds.), *Sha'arei Talmon: Studies in the Bible, Qumran and the Ancient Near East presented to Shemaryahu Talmon* (Winona Lake: Eisenbrauns, 1992), pp. 17-32.

43. Willcock, Companion to the Iliad, pp. 8, 21, 63, 198.

44. See also *Iliad* 5.864-65; *Odyssey* 14.268-70; 24.41-42.

identified three times as Yahweh's day, and this emphasis should not be missed (5.18, 20). The day is Yahweh's doing, and analogous Homeric warriors die on whatever day Zeus or the other gods choose to accomplish it (*Iliad* 22.365-66). The crucial difference is that Homer establishes a relationship between Zeus and fate (*Iliad* 16.431-61),[45] but Amos never views fate as separate from Yahweh.

Amos's idea that the day is bound up with fate is expressed in Homeric thought by the phrases 'the pitiless day' (νηλεὲς ἦμαρ),[46] 'the day of necessity' (ἦμαρ ἀναγκαῖον *Iliad*. 16.836), 'the day of destiny' (αἴσιμον ἦμαρ *Iliad* 21.100). The idea that fate is imminent receives expression in 'the day of destruction (ἦμαρ ὀλέθριον) is near you' (*Iliad* 19.409) or 'the day of destiny stands near them' (*Odyssey* 16.280). So Hector was destined 'to have only a short life and already the day of doom (μόρσιμον ἦμαρ) was being driven upon him by Pallas Athena through the strength of Achilles' (*Iliad* 15.612-14). Odysseus regrets that his fate was due on a more distant day and that he did not die with his Greek companions in Troy: 'I wish I too had died and met my evil destiny on the day (πότμον …ἤματι) when…Trojans threw…weapons upon me' (*Odyssey* 5.308-10).

Darkness or blackness characterizes the fateful day of death and destruction, as shown by 'dark doom' (κῆρα μέλαιναν *Iliad* 5.22; 11.360; 14.462) and 'hateful fate' (μοῖρα δυσώνυμος *Iliad* 12.116). The 'doom of dark death' (κῆρες μέλανος θανάτοιο) drives warriors on to be killed in battle (*Iliad* 11.332). With a spear thrust a warrior finds 'death and evil destiny' (θάνατον καὶ πότμον *Iliad* 15.495). Odysseus warns the Trojan Sokos: 'I declare that…slaughter and dark doom will come upon you this day' (φόνον καὶ κῆρα μέλαιναν ἤματι τῷδ ἔσσεσθαι *Iliad* 11.443-44).

Amos stresses the inevitability of the day of Yahweh, giving it a sense of fatality or destiny. So he likens the day of darkness to a man who escapes death by entering his house, but is bitten by a snake when he leans against the wall. The simile does not identify the man, but by considering the build-up of war imagery, we get the sense of a warrior who flees to save his life. The warrior may survive the fighting and perilous flight but will not survive the day at home (5.19). The snake is also a symbol of lurking death in Homer and illustrates a warrior's efforts to avoid his death-day (*Iliad* 3.30-37). Amos's poetry reflects Homeric narrative development. So the *Iliad* depicts defeat and death in war and identifies warriors who perish about Troy. The *Odyssey* continues with the story of

45. Willcock, *Companion to the Iliad*, pp. 185-86.
46. *Iliad* 11.484, 588; 13.514; 17.511, 615; *Odyssey* 8.525; 9.17.

warriors who escape the fighting, only to encounter the perils of the homeward journey and of the return home.[47] Particularly pertinent is the tableau on Agamemnon's fate, which is a perfect match for Amos's day of destiny. Agamemnon escapes death in battle and returns home safely but is unexpectedly killed at his own hearth by the treacherous plot of his wife (*Odyssey* 3.232-38).

Amos's idea that no one will escape destruction on the appointed day corresponds to the Homeric view that death befalls a person when the fates have ordained it. Callinus, a seventh century poet, expresses the idea in language that is reminiscent of both Homer and Amos:

> 'Hold your spearpoints in poise as we meet our foe in the battle…for by no means may a man escape and keep black death at a distance…not even he who has God as his sire. Often, it may be, he returns home safe from the conflict of battle and the thud of spears, and the fate of death (μοῖρα… θανάτου) comes upon him there in the house'.[48]

f. *Thrusting Aside the Evil Day*

'Escaping the day of evil' means 'escaping dark death' or 'avoiding black fate', and the Homeric expression sheds light on Amos's speech about those who 'push away the evil day' (6.3). Death on a day of battle often comes so quickly to warriors that it cannot be avoided (*Iliad* 11.451-52). But some fighters are able to evade it, and in such contexts, 'avoiding evil' has the spatial sense of a warrior getting out of the way of a fatal blow (*Iliad* 11.354-63). The Homeric expression has also the temporal sense of delaying the evil day or even preventing its arrival. In such contexts heroes of war are viewed as being able to 'ward off the day of evil' from their people (ἀπαμύνω/ἀλέξω κακὸν ἦμαρ).[49] 'You who push away the evil

---

47. At the outset of the *Odyssey*, the wanderings of its hero Odysseus are placed among the general homecomings of the Greek warriors (*Odyssey* 1.11-12; cf. 3.190-93). 'The day of homecoming' is a recurrent expression in the epic. Sometimes it refers to those who lost their homecoming when they perished in battle, or lost the day of their return when they died on the homeward journey (*Odyssey* 1.9, 166-68, 354-55; 12.419; 17.253). More frequently, it refers to the day when Odysseus might come home, escaping hardships, death and the fates (1.16-17; 2.342-43, 351-52; 5.219-20; 6.310-15; 8.465-66; 16.149; 17.571; 19.369). Of the warriors in his company, Odysseus is the only one who survives both the day of battle and the day of his homecoming.

48. *Callinus, fr. 1, in Edmonds, Greek Elegy*, I, pp. 45-47.

49. Famous heroes, Achilles, Agamemnon and Eurylochus, push away the evil day: *Iliad.* 9.247-51, 596-99; 10.19-20; *Odyssey* 10.266-69. Odysseus staves off his own

day' is how Amos characterizes the activities of the leaders of Samaria and Jerusalem. Just as Greek war heroes think they can rescue their people from the day of evil by making certain plans, so the wine-drinking leaders of Jerusalem think they can prevent the death-day from coming on themselves and their people by means of particular ritual observances.

For Amos the evil day refers to the end of the city of Zion. Neither 'evil' nor 'the evil day' is associated directly with the destruction of the city of Troy or Ilion, but Homer lets it be known that Troy will perish on some future day. The idea is conveyed first in a speech by the Greek attacker Agamemnon, and repeated verbatim by the Trojan defender Hektor: 'For I know this thing well in my heart, and my mind knows it. There will come a day when sacred Ilion shall come to an end' (ὀλώλη *Iliad* 4.163-64; 6.447-48). The imminent doom of the city is a theme in both early Hebrew and Greek literature. A major difference between the two texts is that Homer already knows about the fall of Troy, but Amos prophesies the fall of Zion and models it after the fall of Samaria.

g. *Divine Intervention or Non-Interference of the Deity*

Amos's first two visions reflect the common belief that the gods can intervene in human destiny and delay the day of our death. In Homeric epic the gods frequently step in to forestall fate or postpone the death-day of their protégés. So on the first day of battle Aphrodite stands by Paris and wards off his doom (κῆρας ἀμύνει 3.374-76, 380-82). 'Death and evil' (θάνατον...κακός) come near Hector, but Apollo saves him twice (*Iliad* 11.362-63; 20.443-54).

Amos's third and fourth visions convey the idea that the deity can withdraw protection or support. The god who saves on a particular day of battle can destroy on another day or even on the same day. So Apollo rescues Hector on a day of battle but Hector attributes his coming death on the same day to Zeus and his son Apollo: 'Now evil death (θάνατος κακός) is close to me...there is no way out. So it must long since have been pleasing to Zeus, and Zeus's son who strikes from afar...though before this they defended me gladly. But now fate (μοῖρα) is upon me' (*Iliad* 22.300-303). Amos's visions follow the same sequence of divine protection and withdrawal of support that we find in the *Iliad*. Apollo saves Hector on a day of battle, and Yahweh saves Jacob. At the climactic moment of both texts, protection and rescue give way to death and

death-day and escapes the fate of Agamemnon by entering his own house disguised as a beggar (*Odyssey* 17.336-605).

destruction. Just as Apollo and Zeus abandon Hector and let him die, so Yahweh abandons Judah and lets the fatal end come upon his people.

The exchange between Zeus and Hera (*Iliad* 16.431-61) is a particularly informative text for our understanding of the relationship between deity and fate in Amos's visions. Sarpedon is destined to die, but Zeus wonders whether to release the Trojan warrior from grim death. The situation is that Zeus can cancel what is fated, but in practice does not do so because of Hera's argument that it would upset the balance of the world. Amos describes a similar situation. Judah is destined to fall, and so Yahweh forms locusts and sends a fire to destroy the land. But at the urging of the prophet Yahweh decides to stop the destruction and rescue Judah from imminent death. Yahweh has the power to go against what he has fated. Just as Zeus can overturn fate by bringing Sarpedon back to his house alive (16.445), so Yahweh can change Judah's destiny by making Jacob stand up after he has fallen in battle (Amos 7.2b, 5b).

The question posed by both texts is not whether a deity has the power to save a warrior or a people, but whether a deity should interfere with human destiny at all. Zeus and Yahweh are responsible for all that happens in the world. The day of death and destruction is now due, and the two deities let the inevitable happen. Zeus no longer wards off the fates from his son Sarpedon (*Iliad* 16.462-507), and so Sarpedon dies. Yahweh stops protecting Jacob, and so Judah comes to an end.

That a deity destroys as punishment for wrongdoing is a prominent idea in the Hebrew text, but has no bearing on Zeus's decision to fulfil a warrior's death and destiny.[50] Zeus has only agreed to protect the Trojans until such time as Agamemnon realizes his folly in slighting Achilles (*Iliad* 1.5, 498; 15.61-77). But as a consequence of their injustices (Amos 8.4-6), Judaeans will find themselves in battle facing opponents alone, without Yahweh at their side.

h. *Darkness at Noon*
Darkness at noon (Amos 8.9) is analogous to Homeric descriptions about the sun's disappearance during daylight hours. For Homer the luck of the

50. Only two texts in the *Iliad* talk about the gods' disapproval of the corruption of human beings. Homer's reference to Zeus's vengeance on dead men marks the beginning of a belief in divine retribution for wrongdoing (*Iliad* 3.278-79). In a simile at 16.386-88, the poet speaks about Zeus's anger being directed against mortals who pass decrees that are crooked, and drive out righteousness: Willcock, *Companion to the Iliad*, pp. 43, 45.

battle is sun and daylight, and its opposite is gloomy mist and darkness. As long as the sun is secure in its place in the sky, warriors fight with ease and confidence in the bright air, with the sun's sharp glitter around them. But when darkness prematurely covers the battlefield, fighters are unable to avoid an opponent's deadly attack (*Iliad* 17.366-73). The expectation of Amos's contemporaries is that God will give them the power to kill the enemy from sunrise to sunset. This popular idea is expressed in Homer when Zeus grants the Trojans the glory of killing warriors until the sun goes down and darkness comes over (*Iliad* 11.193-95; 17.453-55). Again, Apollo is reprimanded for disobeying Zeus's orders to stand by the Trojans and defend then until the sun sets and darkens all the ploughland (*Iliad* 21.231-32).

In Greek and Hebrew thought, victory in battle is associated with the noonday sun. As the sun steadily rises to the middle heaven, or when Zeus climbs to his mid-day position, the fighting becomes stronger (8.68; 16.777-79; 18.241-42). The deliverance of Jabesh-gilead comes at noon when the sun is hot, and the expectation is that Saul's warriors will cut down the Ammonites from early morning until the heat of the day (1 Sam. 11.9, 11). The delayed setting of the sun is a Homeric theme,[51] and analogously, Joshua defeats his enemy by making the sun stand still, and it stays in the middle heaven the whole day (Josh. 10.12-14).

Defeat in battle is associated with the sun going down and especially with darkness at noon. The hastened setting of the sun is another stock Homeric theme, as is shown by the decision of the goddess Hera to drive the sun into the ocean in order to stop Trojans from killing more Greeks (*Iliad* 18.239-40). At noon, when the sun has reached mid- heaven (ἦμος δ' Ἥέλιος μέσον οὐρανὸν ἀμφβεβήκει *Iliad* 8.68), Zeus sets two fateful portions of death (κῆρε…θανάτοιο *Iliad* 8.70) for Trojans and Achaians, and his day of destiny (αἴσιμον ἦμαρ *Iliad* 8.72) is a heavy death-day for Greek warriors who are stunned and terrified by thunder and lightning (*Iliad* 8.75-78). Behind Amos's poetry is this same idea of the delayed and hastened setting of the sun, the first bringing success, and the second, defeat in battle. Amos's contemporaries anticipate victory at noon, but Amos prophesies that God will make the sun disappear at midday. Zeus's thunderstorm brings darkness at noon, and the storm is one physical reality in Amos's poetry that darkens the earth at noon (1.14).

An exact parallel to the Amos text (8.9) comes from Archilochus, Amos's

---

51. Willcock, *Companion to the Iliad*, p. 205.

seventh-century contemporary: 'Nothing can be unexpected, nothing can be disbelieved, nothing wondered at since Zeus, our father in the heaven above, brought us midnight out of midday; took the sunlight clean away. Everyone was filled with terror; all who saw it blanched with fear'.[52] There is no other single passage that captures so well the spirit and mood of Amos's final words. The fragment breaks off before the context is established, but the poet tells his audience that the future day, its events and circumstances, can be the opposite of what we anticipate, that the gods can surprise us, and that we should expect anything.

i. *The Day of Yahweh*

To sum up, Amos's day of Yahweh is a day of war (1.14; 2.13-16) associated with disaster in a city (3.6-11) and the deportation of God's people (4.2-3). It has to do with the nation's choice (5.5-6) and is thus a day of inevitable darkness (5.18-20), an evil day of destiny which cannot be thrust aside (6.3), a time when divine intervention is over (7.7-9; 8.1-2a) and when God's people come to an end (8.2a).

Amos's day of Yahweh is eschatological in the sense that it incorporates the notions of futurity and end, necessity or destiny. The day refers to a future time determined by God. The going down of the sun at noon marks the end of the physical day and thus the end of time for God's people. The day of Yahweh does not refer to a final eschatological time associated with ideas of the end of the world. Amos does not consider the day as pointing beyond the existing relationship between God and his people. Excluding natural and cosmic catastrophe (7.1-6), Amos gives the day of Yahweh a limited view of finality–the death of a particular people, the destruction of a city, and the end of Judah. The day of destiny in Homeric epic is also limited to the death of certain people, the destruction of a city, and the end of Ilion's people.[53]

Amos proclaims that on Yahweh's day the seasonal festivals or feast-days are now a thing of the past. The joyful songs of the temple cease and turn into songs of mourning (8.3a, 10). This idea of God's day as marking the end of ritual observance finds its correspondence, not in the Greek world, but in Near Eastern lament literature,[54] specifically in Sumerian

52. Archilochus, fr. 74, in Edmonds, *Greek Elegy, II*, pp. 134-35.

53. *Iliad* 4.163-70; 6.57-60, 447-48; 9.48-49; 11.439-44; 14.507; 19.162-63. See Willcock, *Companion to the Iliad*, pp. 185-86.

54. Several scholars argue that the direction of cultural influence in the Near East was from east to west: Walter Burkert, *The Orientalizing Revolution: Near Eastern*

literary compositions, in which the poet, like Amos, sings a song of lament over the destruction of a city and its temple, the overturning of its rites or festivals, and associates the enemy onslaught with the sudden darkening of a bright sunny day.[55] What finally makes God's day a day of destiny and doom is the realization that all hope of divine intervention is gone (8.10).

Comparison of Amos's poetry with other ancient literature allows us to appreciate the richness of imagery and ideas associated with the day of Yahweh. The Greek analogy tells us how Amos's battle formation might be conceived. It highlights the narrative development in Amos or explains the narrative flow from one poem to another. It interprets the dictum 'seek Yahweh and live'. It redescribes the inevitable day of Yahweh as a day of dark or black destiny. It sets 'the evil day' in the context of inescapable death and destruction. It establishes the day of Yahweh as a physical day, and it provides the category of divine intervention by which we can explain the ordering of the visions. The day is a common idea in both early Greek and Hebrew poetry. The literary parallels have been analysed systematically so as to inform us of the striking similarities but also the important differences in the development of the idea.

Influence on Greek Culture in the Early Archaic Age (Cambridge, MA: Harvard University Press, 1992); John H. Corbett, 'Thither Came Phoenicians: The Greeks and the Phoenicians from Homer to Alexander', *Scripta Mediterranea 3* (1982) 72-92; Peter C. Craigie, *Ugarit and the Old Testament* (Grand Rapids: William B. Eerdmans, 1983), pp. 86-88; Charles Penglase, *Greek Myths and Mesopotamia: Parallels and Influence in the Homeric Hymns and Hesiod* (London: Routledge, 1994).

55. Margaret W. Green, 'The Eridu Lament', JCS 30 (1978), pp. 127-67 (1.5-27); Samuel Noel Kramer, *Lamentation over the Destruction of Ur* (Chicago: University of Chicago Press, 1940), pp. 17-71 (2.90-99; 3.115-18; 4.135-43; 5.185-204; 6.208-16; 8.355-60; 9.390-96; 10.405-409); *idem*, 'Lamentation over the Destruction of Nippur', *Acta Sumerologica* 13 (1991), pp. 1-26 (1.10-14; 2.53-60; 3.95-101; 4.118); Piotr Michalowski, *The Lamentation over the Destruction of Sumer and Ur* (Winona Lake, IN: Eisenbrauns, 1989), pp. 37-69 (1.5, 28-56, 79-84; 2.115-22, 162-71, 214-15; 3.305, 315, 324, 380-88, 441-48). For a recent discussion of the city lament genre in Amos and the other prophets, see F.W. Dobbs-Allsopp, *Weep, O Daughter of Zion: A Study of the City-Lament Genre in the Hebrew Bible* (BibOr, 44; Rome: Editrice Pontificio Istituto Biblico Daughter of Zion: A Study of the City-Lament Genre in the Hebrew Bible (BibOr, 44), pp. 97-153.

Chapter 5

FROM SONG CULTURE TO BOOK CULTURE

Amos recited his elegy before a Jerusalem audience and summoned it to listen and act. Theatre is an event, a live relationship between performer and audience, and the latter's role is to observe and respond. Amos challenges his fellow citizens to think about the fall of Samaria, to recall Israel's sins, acknowledge their own, and take action before it is too late. His recital ends on a note of foreboding, the certain doom of Judah. At this moment of crisis the action is stopped to provoke a decision from the audience.

The prophets who followed Amos were performers and orators, but all knew his text and felt compelled to react to it. Hosea agreed with Amos and went beyond him. Micah and Jeremiah challenged his vision of the future and reversed it. Obadiah gave it a practical reference. Zephaniah modelled his speech on Amos's prophecy and quoted parts of it verbatim. Nahum and Habakkuk illustrated his day of Yahweh, composed psalms and ballads to accompany it, and blended it into the prophetic tradition. All these prophets knew the text of Amos in its actual sequential order, recognized its dramatic movement, its climax and denouement. Every prophet was different from all the others. Each one appreciated Amos's distinctive message, each responded to it in his own way, and the result was a plurality of viewpoints. Eventually Amos's dramatic monody was converted into a book by an editor whose rewriting and updating met the needs of a people for whom the original prophecy had come true.[1]

---

1. There is a common repertoire of ideas and images in the prophetic tradition, but each prophet is distinct from the others. The diversity of theologies within prophetic literature was the significant claim of Gerhard von Rad, *Old Testament Theology*. II. *The Theology of Israel's Prophetic Traditions* (trans. D.M.G. Stalker; Edinburgh: Oliver and Boyd, 1965). The uniqueness of each prophet and book has been recently stressed by Ehud ben Zvi, 'Twelve Prophetic Books or "The Twelve": A Few Preliminary Considerations', in Watts and House (eds.), *Forming Prophetic Literature:*

Performers and Dialogue

a. Hosea

Hosea, like Amos, presented his written prophecy in a dramatic setting.[2] He begins with a story of God's marriage with the land, the birth of their children, the divorce, the reconciliation and joyful reunion with the children (chs. 1–2).[3] Then Hosea comes back and talks about the bad times of the divorce when God abandoned the land and obliterated the Northern Kingdom and its people. In the third part of his text (chs. 7–10), Hosea refers to Amos, and explains what the day of Yahweh meant for Amos and for his generation.

Hosea composed a formal dialogue (9.1-17) whose dramatic quality is shown by the constant change in speaker from God to Hosea and back again,[4] by different addressees[5] and frequent shift in person,[6] by rapid

pp. 124-56 (155-56). Cf. Paul R. House, *The Unity of the Twelve* (JSOTSup, 97; Sheffield: Almond Press, 1990).

2. Brian Peckham, 'The Composition of Hosea', *HAR* 11 (1987), pp. 331-53; *History and Prophecy*, pp. 183-206.

3. The diachronic approach of fragmenting the text into independent units has made it difficult to see the movement of the story: Hans Walter Wolff, *Hosea: A Commentary on the Book of the Prophet Hosea* (Hermeneia; Philadelphia: Fortress Press, 1974), pp. xxix, 11, 12, 19, 25, 31-33, 47-48, 59; L. Ruppert, 'Erwägungen zur Kompositions und Redaktionsgeschichte von Hosea 1–3', *BZ* 26 (1982), pp. 208-33; Bernard Renaud, 'Le Livret d'Osée 1–3', *RSR* 56 (1982), pp. 159-78; ' "Osée 1–3": Analyse Diachronique et Lecture Synchronique', *RSR* 57 (1983), pp. 249-60. The synchronic approach focuses on the overall structure and story of Hos. 1–3: see Umberto Cassuto, 'The Second Chapter of the Book of Hosea' (1927), in Umberto Cassuto (ed.), *Biblical and Oriental Studies* (trans. Israel Abrahams; Publications of the Perry Foundation for Biblical Research in the Hebrew University of Jerusalem; Jerusalem: Magnes Press, Hebrew University, 1973), I, pp. 101-40; E.M. Good, 'The Composition of Hosea', *SEÅ* 21 (1966), pp. 21-63; Henryk Krszyna, 'Literarische Struktur von Os 2,4-17', *BZ* 13 (1969), pp. 41-59; Walter Vogels, ' "Oseé-Gomer" car et comme "Yahweh-Israel": Os 1–3', *NRT* 103 (1981), pp. 711-27; Francis I. Andersen and David Noel Freedman, *Hosea: A New Translation with Introduction and Commentary* (AB; Garden City, NY: Doubleday, 1980), pp. 58, 161.

4. God addresses Israel (9.1), Hosea speaks (9.2-4), and God continues his address (9.5). Hosea resumes his speech (9.6), and God announces bad days for Israel (9.7a). The alternating pattern is briefly broken (9.7bA-8) by the people, who interrupt Hosea to speak about him (9.7bA). Hosea finds fault with the people (9.7bB), identifies the role of the prophet (8.8a), and the people interrupt him again (8.8b). God talks about Israel whom he addresses (9.10a), then about Ephraim (9.11-13). Hosea responds to

movements back and forth in time,[7] and by varied viewpoints.[8] Verbal references to Amos are confined to the first scene (9.1-8), but the whole dialogue is a reflection on Amos.

The alternating speeches of God and Hosea represent separate lines of action that diverge or run parallel in the first scene (9.1-8) but converge in the second scene (9.10-17). In a dramatic plot, divergence is common at the beginning of the action because it permits complication, and convergence is common at the end of the action because it achieves resolution. The two speeches develop independently, with God and Hosea speaking at cross-purposes but not addressing each other. The parallel lines are continuous and intersect at the point at which Hosea refers directly to God's speech (9.14). The person who plays God takes on the guise of a messenger, and Hosea becomes involved in God's message.

There is a straight line of development in God's speech which moves from his accusation that Israel abandoned him by playing the harlot (9.1) to his questions about the future day (9.5) and to his answer that the days of punishment have arrived (9.7a). In the second scene, God describes

God with a question and answer (9.14). God talks about Ephraim (9.16), and Hosea interprets God's speech (9.17).

    5.   Israel is addressed in the singular as a group (9.1, 7bB) and in the plural as individuals (9.5, 10aB).

    6.   The first scene (9.1-8) contains frequent shifts from second to third person: God's second person singular address (9.1); Hosea's speech in the third person plural (9.2-4); God's plural direct address (9.5); Hosea's third person plural report about Israel (9.6) and God's singular report (9.7a). The people interrupt Hosea with a speech in the third person singular (9.7bA); there is an abrupt move to Hosea's direct singular address (9.7bB) and the people answer back in third person singular reporting style (9.8). The second scene is set off from the first because the addressees are dropped. God's brief address to Israel in the plural (9.10aB) is replaced by his speech about Ephraim in the singular (9.11, 13, 16aA) and plural (9.12, 16aBb). Hosea questions God directly (9.14aB), speaks about him (9.17aB), and speaks about Ephraim in the third person plural (9.14aAb, 17). Ample variety in person is evident from the first-person speeches of God (9.10a, 12-13a, 16b) and Hosea (9.17aA).

    7.   Among the adjustments in a performance accepted by an audience are changes in perspective. The dialogue between God and Hosea contains abrupt movements from the past to the future and back again. Past references include 9.1, 6aA, 7aA, 10a, 13aA, 16aA, 17aB. Future references include 9.2-5, 6aBb, 11-13, 16aBb-17aAbA. There is also the occasional shift to the present (9.7b-8, 14).

    8.   So God discusses 'the day' (9.5, 7a) or Hosea, the prophet's role (9.8, 14). Or Hosea talks about the infertile land (9.2-4) and God about infertile Ephraim (9.10a, 11-13, 16).

Israel's fate from the perspective of the future (9.11-13, 16aB) and the past (9.16aA) and refers to himself as the slayer of Ephraim's children (9.16b).

Individual elements of Hosea's speech are also linked. In the first scene Hosea announces that the land will become infertile, no longer yielding the grain and wine essential for Israel's rituals, with nothing to offer in the house of God. As a consequence the people will lose their land and become exiles in Egypt or Assyria (9.2-4). The argument is developed in Hosea's narrative about the people who will die in Egypt or be buried in Memphis (9.6). Hosea addresses Israel, claiming that iniquity and hatred (9.7bB) are the causes of the land's destitution and the people's deportation (9.2-4, 6). His speech is the reversal of God's speech because he begins with the punishment (9.2-4, 6 = 9.5, 7a) and ends with an accusation (9.7bB = 9.1).

At the end of the first scene the alternation between the two speakers is broken by the people's speech. This alternating pattern, the habitual problem of talking at cross-purposes, is now broken and resolved. When the people interrupt, the characters begin to talk to one another. God has just spoken (9.7a), it is Hosea's turn to speak, but before he has a chance to talk, the people cry out against him (9.2-4, 6): 'The prophet is a fool, the man of the spirit is mad' (9.7bA). Hosea defends the prophet's role as the watchman of Ephraim who cares for or looks after God's people (9.8a). The people answer back that the prophet traps Ephraim with snares (9.8bA); they dismiss Hosea who accuses them of showing hatred (מַשְׂטֵמָה 9.7bB) by counter-charging that the prophet himself acts with hatred in the house of Ephraim's God (מַשְׂטֵמָה 9.8bB).

The essential ingredients for the development of a dramatic plot are action and conflict.[9] The action moves from God's report that Israel has rejected him to the people's outcry of opposition to the prophet (9.1, 7bA, 8b). The first scene builds to a crisis and ends with the unresolved dispute between the people and the prophet. The people's speech marks the turning point of the plot and leads to the convergence of the separate lines of action in the second scene. When the people reject the prophet, Hosea rejects his role as their watchman and takes the side of God against them. Hosea no longer intercedes for the people but petitions God to give them no more children (9.14) in fulfilment of the divine promise (9.11). The

9.   Cf. Kirsten Nielsen ('Is 6.1–8.18* as Dramatic Writing', *ST* 40 [1986], pp. 1-16) who argues that the structure of Isa. 6–8 resembles that of classical Greek drama, which delineates the conflicts between dramatic personae. However, this does not mean that Isa. 6–8 is a drama; rather it is 'a dramatic composition' (p. 9).

second scene resolves the issues of the plot: Hosea accepts God's argument that Ephraim should be abandoned (9.17).

The speech Hosea assigns to God contains explicit quotations from Amos.[10] Amos associated the day of Yahweh with feasting (Amos 5.18-20, 21-24) and quoted God's address to the people, 'I hate, I despise your feasts' (שנאתי מאסתי חגיכם Amos 5.21a). Now God asks Israel, 'What will you do...on the day of the feast of Yahweh?' (ליום הג־יהיה Hos. 9.5). God replies that the day has arrived, but instead of the expected festival, Israel 'shall know' (ידעו) or experience 'the days of punishment' (ימי הפקדה Hos. 9.7a).[11] God's words are a reworking of his earlier speech in Amos: 'You have I known (ידעתי); therefore, I will punish you (אפקד Amos 3.2)...the days are coming against you' (ימים באים 4.2aB).

In the second scene Hosea alludes to the end of Amos's text where God announces a day of mourning for an only child (Amos 8.10b). This idea of children dying is developed when God declares that he will kill Ephraim's beloved children (Hos. 9.16b). The question God asks is now answered. What the people will do on God's feast-day is lead their children to the slayer (Hos. 9.5, 13b).[12]

The speech Hosea assigns to himself contains allusions to Amos's text. Hosea, like Amos, relates the coming days of deportation to Israel's ritual practices (Hos. 9.2-4, 6 = Amos 4.2-3). He repeats what Amos said about

10. Cf. Jörg Jeremias, 'The Interrelationship between Amos and Hosea', in Watts and House (eds.), *Forming Prophetic Literature*, pp. 171-86.

11. 'Israel may cry' (יריע) is generally substituted for 'Israel knows' (ידעו) because the phrase is treated as introducing the words of the prophet's opponents: Wolff, *Hosea*, n. p, pp. 150, 156. If the MT is replaced, we miss the reference to Amos. The protest of the people does not require an introduction. In a performance, the change in speaker takes place without needing to be indicated.

12. The practice of child sacrifice alluded to by Amos and described by Hosea was eventually repudiated in later writings as a reprehensible practice of worshipping a god (מלד) of the nations (Lev. 18.21; 20.1-5; Num. 3.11-13, 40-43; Deut. 12.29-31; 18.9-14; Jer. 32.35; Ezek. 20.25-26). For discussions of child sacrifice among the Israelites and their neighbours, see George C. Heider, *The Cult of Molek: A Reassessment* (JSOTSup, 43; Sheffield: JSOT Press, 1985); J. Day, Molech: A God of Human Sacrifice in the Old Testament (University of Cambridge Oriental Publications, p. 41; Cambridge: Cambridge University Press, 1989); Peckham, 'Phoenicia and the Religion of Israel', pp. 79-99 (79-80, 90, n. 20); Frank Moore Cross, 'A Phoenician Inscription from Idalion: Some Old and New Texts Relating to Child Sacrifice', in Michael D. Coogan, J. Cheryl Exum and Lawrence E. Stager (eds.), *Scripture and Other Artifacts: Essays on the Bible and Archaeology in Honor of Philip J. King* (Louisville, KY: Westminster/John Knox Press, 1994), pp. 93-107.

God's displeasure with Israel's sacrifices (Hos. 9.4a = Amos 5.21-22). He agrees with Amos that God will put an end to their feast-days (Amos 8.1-3a, 10) but explains it as the land's failure to provide produce for the rituals (Hos. 9.2, 4).

The conversation between Hosea and the people refers to Amos himself.[13] When the people cry out against 'the prophet' (הנביא Hos. 9.8bA), they do not criticize Hosea directly but denounce Amos's words, which Hosea has just paraphrased. Hosea repeats to them what Amos said about their iniquity (עונך Hos. 9.7bB = עונתיכם Amos 3.2bB). The people answer that a fowler's snare is on all Amos's ways and that he utters hatred in the house of his God. Their speech consists of allusions to Amos's text (פח 'snare' Hos. 9.8bA = Amos 3.5aA; בבית אלהיו 'house of his God' Hos. 9.8bB = בית־אל 'house of God'/Bethel, Amos 4.4aA; 5.4aA).

Amos was elusive about the day when the rituals would cease, but Hosea concentrates on the end of the feast-days. Each speaker reworks the end of Amos's prophecy (8.10), clarifies it and elaborates on it. So Hosea speaks about the rituals and the bread of mourning, and God talks about the death of the children. The bread has something to do with the children who have already died, and God's killing of the children has something to do with the festivals. The criss-cross structure of the two speeches should not be missed and it is significant for our understanding of Amos's text. Amos said there would be no more rituals, but Hosea explains why the rituals will not take place. So he describes the day of Yahweh as a time when the land fails to produce crops, when the people bear no more children, and when they mourn for the children whom he has killed. The only thing left to offer at the rituals is the mourners' bread, but it is not allowed to be brought into the house of God.[14]

Hosea gave Amos's prophecy a new dramatic setting, and different elements of the day of Yahweh are distributed among three speakers. The speeches of God and Hosea are intended to be complementary, each explaining some aspect of the day of Yahweh not mentioned by the other. The third speaker is the people, who publicly scorn Amos, resist his message, and even use his own words against him. In a dramatic presen-

---

13. Hosea picks up on Amos's wordplay אשדוד and שד (Amos 3.9aA, 10b). Hosea combines שד with foreign places: 'They have gone from destruction (הלכו משד), Egypt shall gather them, Memphis shall bury them' (Hos. 9.6a). Hence those who survive destruction shall die (cf. Amos 5.19).

14. The law prohibits Israel from eating the tithe of their produce during a mourning period (Deut. 26.14).

tation before an audience, Hosea shows us the impact Amos had on his generation or on the generation that came after him. Hosea restates Amos's prophecy and insists that it should be accepted as God's word. The people, however, dismiss Amos as a fool and a madman who spoke hateful things about them in their worship. Hosea's dispute with the people represents typical contemporary responses to Amos's text. The people refuse to listen to Hosea and reject his reliance on written prophecy.

b. *Micah*

Micah's drama is the sequel to Amos's monody. Amos' audience is called upon to respond, and its decision for life or death is taken offstage after the performance is over. Micah, by contrast, dares to act out the response of his audience to the prophecy of Judah's downfall. His text is a dramatic conversation or debate between himself and the people of Jerusalem, and the actors perform their respective parts before a Jerusalem audience.[15]

In imitation of Amos's narrative order, Micah soliloquizes the ruin of Samaria (1.6-7). He responds to Amos's dirge (5.1-2) with his own lament (Mic. 1.8-9) over the impending doom of Judaean cities (Mic. 1.10-16). He confirms that Amos's terminology, 'Jacob' and 'the house of Israel', refers to Judah and Israel (Mic. 1.5; 3.1). He agrees with Amos that Samaria and Zion are partners in sin (Mic. 1.5, 13), their leaders mutually blameworthy for greed, exploiting the poor and perverting justice (Mic. 2.2, 3.1-3, 9). Micah recalls the evil that befalls Samaria (Mic. 1.1a, 2-16; 1.9, 12 = Amos 3.6-11) and declares that God's evil has reached the gate of Jerusalem (1.12b), thus making explicit what Amos said about the fate of the city.

Micah's debate is filled with sudden shifts in person and speaker, and these shifts are characteristic of dramatic performance.[16] Micah speaks to the audience about the wrongdoing in Jerusalem (2.1-2), introduces God's words to him (2.3aB) and to the people (2.3b). Micah announces God's sarcastic song of lament[17] in which he mocks and mimics the citizens'

---

15. For a discussion of Micah's drama within the context of Near Eastern lament literature and Greek drama, see J. Rilett Wood, 'Speech and Action in Micah's Prophecy', *CBQ* 62 (2000), pp. 645-62.

16. Scholars have argued that Mic. 2.1-11 is unintelligible: Delbert R. Hillers, *Micah: A Commentary on the Book of the Prophet Micah* (Hermeneia; Philadelphia: Fortress Press, 1984), pp. 31-33. But the way to understand the abrupt shifts in person is to recognize that Mic. 2.1-11 is a dramatic text.

17. It has become customary to emend the third person in ישא עליכם משל to plural

mournful cries, impersonating them in the first person plural and singular (2.4). Micah talks to the people about God's lament (2.5), they order him to be silent (2.6), and Micah answers back with a series of questions (2.7). The people use his own words against him (2.8-10), and Micah comments on their speech (2.11).[18]

Micah's direct discourse shows his familiarity with Amos's text. Amos referred to the whole family of Jacob's twelve sons by relating 'children of Israel' (3.1a) to 'all families of the earth' (מכל משפחות האדמה 3.2 Amos). In Micah Yahweh says he is devising evil against the whole family (על־המשפחה הזאת Mic. 2.3aB).[19] Amos's God complained about citizens who cause devastation in Samaria (שׁד 3.10), but Micah's God parodies the people of Jerusalem: 'we are utterly ruined' (Mic. 2.4 שׁדוד נשׁדנו). Micah's address, 'You heads (ראשׁי) of Jacob and rulers of the house of Israel' (3.1), is modelled after Amos's address to the confident and secure leaders of 'the first (ראשׁית) of the nations' and 'the house of Israel' (6.1). Amos criticized the leaders, but Micah also attacks the prophets and priests (3.5-7, 11-12).

Micah's monologue shows the influence of Amos's day of Yahweh. The future day (2.4aA) is introduced as a cliché, but Micah develops the idea by impersonating the false prophets who cry 'peace' when they are fed but

(RSV), or interpret it as impersonal or indefinite singular (GKC n.144 d [a], p. 460; e.g. NJPSV: 'One shall recite a poem about you', Mic. 2.4a). It is conceivable that God is the speaker since he has already spoken against his people (2.3). Only three speakers appear in Mic. 2.1-11: Micah, Yahweh, and the people. So in 2.4 Micah introduces God, and God impersonates the people and laughs at what they will say one day: 'he [Yahweh] will take up a taunt song against you; he will wail a wailing wail, and say, "We have been completely ruined; he [Yahweh] changes the portion of my people; there is not anyone who *removes* (ימישׁ) it for me! To our captor he has apportioned our fields."' God quotes an individual who calls the people 'my people', a phrase normally used by God himself, thus providing a touch of humour. The hiphil ימישׁ (2.4b) refers to what God has already said to the people: 'I am planning evil...from which you will not be able to *remove* (תמישׁו) your necks' (2.3b). The allusion is to the yoke around a person's neck (Hos. 11.4; Jer. 2.20; 5.5). God replies to his own words by impersonating an individual who says that no one can free his neck from servitude.

18. Ehud ben Zvi ('Wrongdoers, Wrongdoing and Righting Wrongs in Micah 2', BibInt 7.1 [1999], pp. 87-100) argues that the scene in Mic. 2 does not contain the actual words of the historical Micah or the people of Jerusalem but is a constructed dialogue of characters in a literary work.

19. Amos's editor adds the phrase 'against the whole family which I brought up out of the land of Egypt' (3.1b), and quotes Micah's following words, 'for it will be an evil time' (Mic. 2.3b = Amos 5.13).

declare war when they are hungry (3.5). Rebuking them for their evil deeds, Micah predicts an imminent day when God will not speak to the prophets (3.4, 6-7). God's silence (Mic. 3.4, 7) is expressed metaphorically as a night filled with darkness when prophets receive no more visions and lose their powers to foretell the future (Mic. 3.6a).[20] Amos contemplated the turning of daylight into darkness (5.18-20) or the disappearance of the sun at noon (8.9). Micah follows the sequence of Amos's poetry by mentioning the darkness (Mic. 3.6a חשכה לכם = הוא־חשך Amos 5.18) and the setting of the sun on the prophets (Mic. 3.6b ובאה השמש על־הנביאים = והבאתי השמש בצהרים Amos 8.9a). Amos described the physical phenomena of a day of war and its consequences for the people as a whole. Micah, however, speaks figuratively about the day that becomes dark and limits its consequences to prophets who declare war against their own people (3.5b).

Micah turns Amos's criticism of ritual activity (Amos 5.21-24) into a dialogue between himself and the people (Mic. 6.6-8). In Amos's poetry, the people believe they can prevent the evil day by offering their animal offerings of lambs and calves, but God rejects their sacrifices (Amos 5.22; 6.4). But in Micah's poetry, the people show concern for proper worship of Yahweh: 'Shall I come before him with burnt offerings, with calves a year old?' (Mic. 6.6-7). Micah, unlike Amos, lets the people ponder their ritual responsibilities and consider whether God would be pleased with their sacrifices.

Micah, in imitation of Amos, links worship and social justice (Mic. 6.7-8).[21] Amos portrayed God as addressing the people and insisting that justice is their fundamental obligation (5.24). Micah, like Amos, represents himself as a spokesperson for justice and reiterates what God requires (Mic. 6.8 = Amos 5.7). In Micah's dramatic representation, God addresses Jerusalem, accuses the city of having 'treasuries of wickedness' (אצרות רשע Mic. 6.10a) and reports that her rich men are 'full of violence' (עשיריה

---

20. On the inclusion of Micah in the fate of the prophets, see Robert P. Carroll, 'Night without Vision: Micah and the Prophets', in F. Garcia Martinez, A. Hilhorst and C.J. Labuschagne (eds.), *The Scriptures and the Scrolls: Studies in Honour of A.S. van der Woude on the Occasion of his 65th Birthday* (Leiden: E. J. Brill, 1992), pp. 74-84.

21. For a discussion of the relationship between worship and ethics in Amos, Hosea and Isaiah, see Rick R. Marrs, 'Micah and a Theological Critique of Worship', in M. Patrick Graham, Rick R. Marrs and Steven L. McKenzie (eds.), *Worship and the Hebrew Bible: Essays in Honour of John T. Willis* (JSOTSup, 284; Sheffield: Sheffield Academic Press, 1999), pp. 184-203.

מלאו חמס Mic. 6.12a). His accusations recall God's criticism of those who acquire wealth by storing up violence and destruction (האוצרים חמס ושד Amos 3.10). Amos quoted the oppressors of the poor: 'we may make the ephah small (להקטין איפה)...and be crooked with deceptive balances' (ולעות מאזני מרמה Amos 8.5b). Micah represents God, who questions the people about the unjust grain measure, 'the scant ephah' (איפת רזון Mic. 6.10b), the unfair use of 'wicked scales' (מאזני רשע) and 'deceitful stones' as false weights (אבני מרמה Mic. 6.11).

The city's monologue, with its frequent change in person, is the basis of dramatic performance. A female character,[22] a spokesperson for Jerusalem, speaks in the first person and laments the city's dire predicament (Mic. 7.1).[23] The city addresses the audience and speaks about the people both as individuals and as a group (7.2-6). Specific individuals—prince, judge and important person—are blamed for corruption (7.3). Jerusalem warns her audience to trust no one, speaks about herself in the first person, soliloquizes her trust in Yahweh and her reliance on him for her salvation (7.7). Finally she confesses her sins to 'the enemy' (7.8aA), and looks beyond her punishment to divine intervention and pardon (7.8-9).

Micah creates the mood for the city's expression of grief by recalling Amos's vision of the harvest fruit which marks the end of summer and the end of a people: 'Woe is me! I have become as when the summer fruit (קיץ) has been gathered' (Mic. 7.1 = Amos 8.2). The city likens herself to the land when the harvest produce has been gathered and nothing is left to eat. Her speech supposes a situation of impending doom upon Jerusalem.

Micah, like Amos, associates the image of the summer fruit with the day of Yahweh. Jerusalem's address, 'The day of your watchmen, of your punishment, has come' (7.4bA)[24] is a conflation of Amos and Hosea. Amos proclaimed the day of Yahweh, and Hosea calls the prophet a watchman (צפה Hos. 9.8a). Amos addressed the family of Israel: 'I will

---

22. Analogously, Greek poets use female characters who speak in the first person. One poem of Alcaeus begins with a woman speaking about her misery and shameful destiny: fr. 10B, in Campbell, *Greek Lyric*, I, pp. 242-43; cf. Alcman, frs. 1 and 3, in Campbell, *Greek Lyric*, II, pp. 360-69, 378-81; Segal, 'Archaic Choral Lyric', pp. 129-38.

23. Micah's text opens with a summons to woman Zion to commence funeral rituals (1.16) and closes with her song of lament (7.1-9): see also Lamontte M. Luker, 'Beyond Form Criticism: The Relation of Doom and Hope Oracles in Micah 2–6', *HAR* 11 (1987), pp. 285-301.

24. The quotation is missed by Hillers (*Micah*, p. 84 n. O) who omits the suffixes: 'The day of punishment has come'.

punish you' (Amos 3.2b), but Micah expresses the idea in terms familiar from Hosea (Mic. 7.4bA = 'the days of punishment have come', Hos 9.7a). Micah, unlike Amos and Hosea, argues that Yahweh's day of punishment targets particular groups—rulers, priests, prophets—and not the people as a whole.

Micah quotes Amos's lament over the woman of Israel who 'has fallen, no more to rise' (נפלה לא־תוסיף קום Amos 5.2) but gives it a new context and an opposite meaning. The dirge is now spoken by Jerusalem: 'when I fall I shall rise' (כי נפלתי קמתי Mic. 7.8a). Micah pictures a contrite city sitting in darkness because Yahweh has abandoned her. She waits for him to bring her light and deliverance, a metaphorical reworking of Amos's physical day of light and darkness (Mic. 7.8-9 = Amos 5.18-20; 8.9). Micah ends his poem, as did Amos, with a day of mourning. But the city enveloped in darkness marks neither the end of God's people nor the end of their feast-days, but is the means for their survival (Mic. 7.1-9 = Amos 8.1-3a, 9-10).

It is evident that Amos's poetic text was available to Micah; he follows its narrative development and refers to the poems in their literal order. Relying on Amos 3, 5 and 8 as key texts, Micah moves from God causing evil to a city or family (Mic. 1.10-16; 2.3-5 = Amos 3) to a description of Yahweh's day (Mic. 3.5-7 = Amos 5.18-20), then to an association of worship with social justice (Mic. 6.6-12 = Amos 5.21-24), and finally to the image of summer fruit and the day of lamentation (Mic. 7.1-9 = Amos 8.1-3a, 9-10).

Micah knows the flow and sequence of Amos's text, connects its different parts, and recognizes it as a developing composition whose full meaning is grasped when the poems are viewed in the light of one another. Notable examples of Micah's combining Amos's poems are the images of the day of darkness and the setting of the sun (Mic. 3.6 = Amos 5.18, 20, 8.9), of those who profiteer using violence or false weights (Mic. 6.9-12 = Amos 3.10; 8.5-6), of the nation's defeat and Jerusalem's lamentation (Mic. 7.1, 8-9 = Amos 5.2; 8.1-3a). Micah adopts all the language Amos used to describe the day of Yahweh, knows what Amos meant by the idea, but gives it his own distinctive interpretation.

Essential to tragic performance is the idea that human beings are capable of great mistakes and great accomplishments. Micah shares Amos's moral outrage, grasps the two sides of the tragic equation, but lets his audience see not only their flaws but also their potential for human greatness. So Micah involves his audience in a positive response to the summons 'seek

Yahweh and live' (Amos 5.6). The city of Jerusalem confesses her sins and looks forward to a new relationship with God. Micah cancels Amos's prophecy of doom, replacing the tragic end of a people with the hopeful outcome of their deliverance.

c. *Jeremiah*

Jeremiah struggled with Amos's tragic vision of Judah's fall, and his positive response was influenced by Hosea's image of reconciliation and Micah's prophecy of Jerusalem's repentance. Jeremiah redramatized the lamentation of Zion but went beyond Micah to represent the salvation of the North and the reunion of Israel and Judah. So the conclusion of Jeremiah's prophecy (chs. 30–31)[25] takes us through the lamentations and resolves the problem of the day of Yahweh with clear references to Amos: Jeremiah comes to a final decision about all the issues raised in his drama and negates the tragic vision affirmed by Amos.[26]

Jeremiah's poetic text closes with a series of dramatic speeches. Yahweh is the principal speaker. The other speakers or characters are the people, Jacob, the male Israel, the woman Zion, the enemy, the young woman Israel, the city crier, Rachel and Ephraim. The five speeches (30.5-7, 10-11; 30.12-17; 31.2-6; 31.7-9; 31.15-22) are introduced in the same way by כה אמר יהוה , and each speech carries the action forward.[27]

The action moves along by a series of shifting dramatic impressions in a related sequence. The different times of the drama coincide as the audi-

---

25. Scholars argue that most, if not all, of the poetry in chs. 30–31, is authentic to Jeremiah: William L. Holladay, 'Jeremiah the Prophet', *IDBSup* (1976), p. 471; Norbert Lohfink, 'Der junge Jeremia als Propagandist und Poet. Zum Grundstock von Jer. 30-31', in P.-M. Bogaert (ed.), *Le livre de Jérémie: Le prophète et son milieu, les oracles et leur transmission* (BETL, 64; Louvain: Peeters, 1981), pp. 350-68; U. Schröter, 'Jeremias Botschaft für das Nordreich. Zu N. Lohfinks Überlegungen zum Grundbestand von Jeremia 30–31', *VT* 35 (1985), pp. 312-29; Marvin Sweeney, 'Jeremiah 30–31 and King Josiah's Program of National Restoration and Religious Reform', *ZAW* 108 (1996), pp. 569-83.

26. The last act of the prophet's drama is Jer. 30–31: see Peckham, *History and Prophecy*, pp. 325-27, 337-38, 392-94.

27. The tendency to homogenize voices has been resisted by scholars who recognize the dramatic quality of Jeremiah's poetry: William L. Holladay, *Jeremiah I. A Commentary on the Book of the Prophet Jeremiah*, Chapters 1–25 (Hermeneia: Philadelphia: Fortress Press, 1986), pp. 137-38; Mark E. Biddle, *Polyphony and Symphony in Prophetic Literature* (Macon, GA: Mercer University Press, 1996), pp. 1-13, 17, 28, 31, 115-17.

ence sees the action from the perspective of the past, present and future, or contemplates the act or event which springs from the past, but is projected into the future. The changing times of the drama are matched by changing locations, and the reader removed from the immediacy of the performed text must look to internal clues, notably the shift in person,[28] for distinctions of voice and gender.[29]

The first speech (30.5-7, 10-11) begins with people voicing their fears about the cries of terror they have heard. Yahweh questions the people about Jacob, likens his agonized cries to a woman's labour in childbirth, and says he will be saved. Yahweh addresses Jacob to alleviate his fears, tells the male Israel that Jacob will repent and become quiet.[30] God tells Israel that he will receive punishment, but promises to save him and bring him back from the land where he has been taken captive (30.10aB, 11).

In the second speech (30.12-17a), God speaks to a woman who cries out in pain, and the enemy identifies the suffering female as 'Zion'. Just as Yahweh asked questions about Jacob's cries of distress, so he now says to Zion, 'Why do you cry over your injury?'. God tells her that her guilt is great, that he has dealt her a cruel punishment, and suddenly promises to heal her wounds.[31] But the enemy exclaims: 'It is Zion whom no one seeks out'.

---

28. There are speeches in the first person plural (30.5b; 31.6b) and singular (30.10aB-11, 15b, 17; 31.3-4, 18-20), addresses in the second person plural (30.6-7; 31.6b), addresses in the masculine singular (30.10a, 11; 31.7bB, 18) or feminine singular (30.12-17bA; 31.3b-4, 16-17, 21-22), and third person report style, singular and plural (30.10b, 17bB; 31.2, 5b-6a, 8-9, 15, 16bB, 20).

29. Distinguishing the roles of shifting speakers in prophetic books is a crucial task and is taken up by Paul R. House, *Zephaniah: A Prophetic Drama* (JSOTSup, 69; Sheffield: Almond Press, 1988); *idem*, 'Dramatic Coherence in Nahum, Habbakuk, and Zephaniah', in Watts and House (eds.), *Forming Prophetic Literature*, pp. 195-208. House shows that 'dramatic principles' (e.g. dialogue, character development, plot movement) can be found in prophetic literature and suggests that Greek drama was known in ancient Israel, though this does not mean that Israelites produced plays ('Dramatic Coherence', p. 207). Cf. Adele Berlin (*Zephaniah* [AB, 25A; Garden City NY: Doubleday, 1994], p. 12), who observes, 'It is questionable...if we can speak of drama in ancient Israel, there being no evidence that this genre was known'.

30. Jeremiah uses שוב in two ways. It refers to Israel's return from exile (Jer. 31.16-17) and Judah's repentance (Jer. 30.10b). Jeremiah quotes Isaiah, who spoke about Jerusalem's repentance and quietness (Isa. 30.15).

31. Deliberate rhetorical shifts are made in Jeremiah's poetry to mark changes in a speaker's attitude: Walter Brueggemann, 'The "Uncared For" Now Cared For (Jer 30.12-17): A Methodological Consideration', *JBL* 104 (1985), pp. 419-28.

The third speech (31.2-6) opens with God's narration about a people who escaped the sword in the wilderness. When he mentions Israel's return to his resting-place (31.2), a female begins to speak (31.3). Yahweh enters into conversation with her (31.4-5) and calls her 'O girl Israel' (31.4aB). Yahweh told the man Israel that he would be saved from afar (30.10aB), and now the female Israel announces that Yahweh appeared to her from afar, proclaiming his everlasting love and faithfulness (31.3). He details her imminent restoration, reassures her that she will once again take up timbrels, join the merrymakers in dance, and plant vineyards on the hills of Samaria (31.4-5). A chorus of men, in company with the dancing troupe, casts itself in the role of crier, as it recites on Ephraim's heights, 'Let's go up to Zion' (31.6).

In the fourth speech (31.7-9) Yahweh calls on the people to rejoice in the good fortune of Jacob (31.7a), and they plead with him, 'Save your people, Yahweh, the remnant of Israel' (31.7bB). In reply he promises to bring back his people from the north country (31.8-9).

In the fifth speech (31.15-22) Yahweh reports that Rachel is weeping for her children (31.15).[32] He consoles her with a hopeful message, explaining that her children will return to their own land (31.16-17). Yahweh says that he has heard Ephraim's wails (31.18aA). Ephraim tells his father Yahweh that he has deserved punishment, but has repented, and now requests pardon and restoration (31.18aB-19). In a series of rhetorical questions, Yahweh soliloquizes and expresses mercy for his son (31.20). Once again Yahweh addresses the woman Israel, calls her 'his faithless daughter', and summons her to return to the land (31.21). In telling the woman Israel to set up signposts for herself (צִיֻּנִים 31.21), Yahweh suggests, through a wordplay, that she returns to Zion. He urges her to act decisively in response to his new created order (31.22).

Each speech contributes to the dramatic movement of the plot. Jacob is first to be saved (30.5-7) and then Israel (30.10-11). Yahweh enters into a new relationship with Zion (30.12-17), making it possible for the people of Samaria to return to Zion (31.6). Jacob and Israel are reconciled (31.7). A remnant of Israel returns from exile (31.8-9) and the survivors are called Rachel's children (31.15-17). Yahweh is reunited with his northern son Ephraim (31.18-20), and the woman Israel is summoned to worship Yahweh in Zion (31.21). 'A female surrounds a male' (31.22bB) sums up

---

32. The fifth speech has been identified as a poetic unit and 'a drama of voices': see Phyllis Trible, 'The Gift of a Poem: A Rhetorical Study of Jeremiah 31.15-22', *ANQ* 17 (1977), pp. 271-80.

the dramatic speeches by implying that the woman Zion (31.22a) protects Jacob and welcomes back Israel.

At every major turning point in the development of the plot there are quotations from or allusions to Amos's text and his day of Yahweh. The image of Jacob suffering the distress or pangs of childbirth is how Jeremiah introduces his description of the day of Yahweh (30.6-7). In agreement with Amos, Jeremiah predicts bad times ahead for Jacob, but reverses Amos's day of Yahweh by describing it as a time when Jacob will be saved (Jer. 30.7bB; Amos 7.1-3, 4-6; 8.1-2a).

In the sequel (Jer. 30.10-11) Jeremiah develops his ideas about the day of salvation, claiming that Jacob will repent and be at ease. The participle 'those who are at ease' (השאננים Amos 6.1aA) was used by Amos to criticize the carefree arrogance of Zion's ruling classes, but Jeremiah uses the verb 'to be at ease' (שאן Jer. 30.10b) to express Jacob's freedom from trouble or anxiety. Amos's prophecy of a complete end of Yahweh's people is contradicted by Jeremiah, who says that Israel will be punished in just measure but not completely destroyed (Jer. 30.11). Jeremiah does not use Amos's word קץ 'end' (Amos 8.2b) but expresses the idea of incomplete destruction when God says to Israel 'of you I will not make a full end' (אתך לא־אעשה כלה Jer. 30.11bA).

In the second speech (30.12-17) Yahweh says to the woman Zion, 'Your iniquity is great, your sins are numerous' (רב עונך and חטאתיך עצמו Jer. 30.14bB, 15bA). Jeremiah combines terms which Amos used of Yahweh's people as a whole (כל־עונתיכם Amos 3.1-2; חטאתיכם עצמים Amos 5.12aB). But Jeremiah has Yahweh directly accuse Zion for her behaviour, thus making explicit what is implied by Amos: Israel and Judah are equally guilty and deserve punishment.

In the third speech (31.2-6) Jeremiah acknowledges the truth of Amos's words when he said that the people would not live in houses they built or drink wine from vineyards they planted (Amos 5.11). But now Jeremiah converts Amos's words of punishment into Yahweh's words of salvation: God speaks directly to the young woman Israel (בתולת ישראל Jer. 31.4aB = Amos 5.2aB) about his decision to rebuild her and about the vineyards she will plant upon the mountains of Samaria (Jer. 31.4-5a). The people's pilgrimage from Samaria to Zion (Jer. 31.6b) to worship Yahweh recalls the journey of the house of Israel to Zion for the purpose of attending its feasts (Amos 6.1, 4-6). The practice was criticized by Amos, but Jeremiah looks forward to a future day when Israel will resume worship in Zion.

The fourth speech (31.7-9) combines the beginning and end of Amos's sixth poem by associating Jacob with exile. Amos identified Judah as the first of the nations (רֵאשִׁית הַגּוֹיִם Amos 6.1) and prophesied that its leaders would be at the head of the exiles (בְּרֹאשׁ גֹּלִים Amos 6.7a). Jeremiah identifies Jacob as the head of the nations (בְּרֹאשׁ הַגּוֹיִם Jer. 31.7a), confirms that the name Jacob stands for Judah, but turns Amos's prophecy of doom for Jacob into a prophecy of survival (Jer. 30.10aA; 31.7a). Amos talked about Israel's exile (4.2-3), but Jeremiah details a day of salvation when Israel returns from exile (Jer. 31.8-9).

The fifth speech (31.15-22) develops the theme of a future day when Israel will go up to Zion. Amos described the false worship at shrines in Israel and Judah (2.8; 4.4-5; 5.21-24; 6.1-7), but for Jeremiah the problem of false worship will be resolved when Israel returns to Zion (31.21-22). Jeremiah rehearses and reverses the whole dramatic action of Amos's day of Yahweh: in Amos's text the woman Israel meets her doom and Jacob is destined to die, but in Jeremiah's redramatization, Jacob repents and survives, and his reform leads to the restoration of the woman Israel.

Jeremiah's drama is a resolution of Amos's tragic day. Proper to tragedy are the painful emotions which involve grief and distress. Jeremiah begins with the sadness, dramatizes the emotions Amos aimed to evoke from his audience, but works through the lamentation and goes beyond it. The characters of the drama—Jacob, Zion, Rachel and Ephraim—undergo an emotional cleansing or catharsis, and Yahweh, the protagonist and chief agent of the action, reponds to all their weeping by reversing Amos's terrible day into a great day of joy and reconciliation.

Orators and Dialogue

Jeremiah marks the end of performance in the prophetic tradition. After him oratory emerges as the new vehicle of the prophet's message. The early performing prophets have an indirect relation to their audiences. They include themselves among the actors in their dramatic poetry, or sometimes absent themselves, having other characters do the speaking (Mic. 7.1-9; Jer. 30–31), and they engage their audiences with different voices and viewpoints. The orators, however, are solo speakers who address their listeners directly, speak for them in fact, and demand unity of response.[33] The prophets after Jeremiah are orators: they compose

---

33. Frye, *Anatomy of Criticism*, pp. 246-51; *idem, Words with Power: Being a Second Study of the Bible and Literature* (New York: Viking Penguin, 1990), pp. 17, 66-68.

speeches to be heard or read; they repudiate Jeremiah's resolution of the day of Yahweh, and affirm the truth of Amos's insights for their own time.

a. *Nahum*

The first orator was Nahum,[34] and his speech contains quotations from and allusions to Amos and Jeremiah. Nahum uses the language of Amos and Jeremiah to depict Yahweh's day. In a hymn (Nah. 1.1b-8) God is praised as a refuge 'in the day of trouble' (ביום צרה Nah. 1.7aB). Jeremiah described the day as 'a time of trouble' (עת־צרה Jer. 30.7bA), and Nahum says that the trouble occurs on a day when God vanquishes his enemies. Nahum retrieves from Amos images of storm (סופה Nah. 1.3bA = Amos 1.14bB) and darkness (חשך Nah. 1.8bB = Amos 5.18, 20), with no one standing on the day of defeat (קום Nah. 1.6aB = Amos 7.2aB, 5bB). Nahum reapplies Amos's vision of 'the end' but quotes in reverse order Jeremiah's prediction that God will make a full end of his enemies (כלה עשה Nah. 1.8-9a = אעשה כלה Jer. 30.11b).

Nahum narrates the siege and defeat of Nineveh (Nah. 2.2, 4-5, 6abA, 6bB-8a, 8b-9bA, 9bB-10, 11): he describes the advance of troops and likens their chariots to a flaming fire 'on the day of his preparation' (Nah. 2.4aB). The allusion is to Yahweh, who pursues his enemies the Assyrians and has come up against Nineveh (Nah. 1.8; 2.2).

Nahum's oratory is a declamation about 'the bloody city' and a vision of its ruin (Nah. 3.1-4, 8-11). Listeners expect that God will protect Judah against their enemies. But the idea of Yahweh as Judah's refuge in the day of trouble (Nah. 1.7a) is suddenly repudiated when Nahum says that his hearers must seek refuge from the enemy (Nah. 3.11b), from Yahweh himself who is about to destroy Zion, and the speech ends on this alarming note. The movement of the text, with its quotations and allusions, discloses the city's identity. Nahum imitates the great reversal of the day in Amos, a day which begins with the defeat of foreign cities and closes with the defeat of Zion.

b. *Habakkuk*

Habakkuk sees the Chaldeans advancing against Judah (Hab. 1.5-6, 8-10)

---

34. Duane L. Christensen ('The Book of Nahum as a Liturgical Composition: A Prosodic Analysis', *JETS* 32 [1989], pp. 159-69) argues that Nahum was a musical composition performed within an Israelite liturgical setting. He traces the scholarly interpretation of the book in 'The Book of Nahum: A History of Interpretation', in Watts and House (eds.), *Forming Prophetic Literature*, pp. 187-94.

and interprets his vision with reference to Amos. The vision of plenty in Amos leads abruptly to God's pronouncement, 'the end has come upon my people' (בא הקץ Amos 8.2b). Habakkuk's God declares: 'the vision hastens to the end (לקץ)...it will certainly come' (כי־בא יבא Hab. 2.3). Habakkuk complains about 'the destruction and violence' God made him see (ושד וחמס Hab. 1.3b). Amos used the word pair to designate the crimes that were once committed in Samaria (חמס ושד Amos 3.10b). Jeremiah reapplied the phrase to describe existent wickedness within Jerusalem (Jer. 6.7b). Quoting the words in reverse order, Habakkuk refers to 'the destruction and violence' the Chaldeans will perpetrate against Judah.

Habakkuk prepares for God's answer (Hab. 2.1-3) to his cry for help (Hab. 1.2-3a, 12a-13a) by standing upon a watch-tower (Hab. 2.1). The symbolic gesture builds on the idea of prophet as watchman: 'I will stand upon my watch...and I will watch (ואצפה) to see what he will say to me' (Hab. 2.1). Hosea regarded Amos as the watchman of Ephraim (צפה Hos. 9.8a). Micah suggested that the watchmen were Amos and Hosea (Mic. 7.4bA), and Jeremiah dramatized a day of battle with watchmen announcing 'the sound of the trumpet' (Jer. 6.17 = Amos 2.2bB; 3.6aA). Habakkuk contributes to the growing prophetic tradition about Amos by becoming a watchman who awaits God's answer to his prayer.

Yahweh's response to Habakkuk contains allusions to Isaiah, Amos and Hosea (Hab. 2.1-3). God tells Habakkuk to write down the vision (Hab. 2.2a), a quotation from Isaiah where God instructs the prophet to write down his vision (Isa. 30.8a). Isaiah said that his vision would occur on a future day (Isa. 30.8bA), and Habakkuk, almost a century later, predicts that it will occur in his time, in the way Amos and Hosea predicted: 'the vision is yet for an appointed time' and 'it races to the end' (Hab. 2.3a = Hos. 9.5a; Amos 8.2b).

Habakkuk composed his prophecy as a psalm of lamentation,[35] but the answer to his petition contradicts the usual solution of divine forgiveness. God does not answer Habakkuk's prayer with reassuring words but argues that Amos's day of doom is unavoidable. Habakkuk responds with the same hopeful anticipation that typifies a lament. The first step forward out of the lament is his rehearsal of the battles fought by God for his people (Hab. 3.2, 3-12, 13a, 15). Habakkuk is resigned to wait for 'the day of distress' (ליום צרה) to come upon invaders (Hab. 3.16b). Jeremiah talked

---

35. Brian Peckham, 'The Vision of Habakkuk', CBQ 48 (1986), pp. 617-36; James W. Watts, 'Psalmody in Prophecy: Habakkuk 3 in Context', in Watts and House (eds.), *Forming Prophetic Literature*, pp. 209-23.

about the day of distress (Jer. 30.7bA) that would lead to Jacob's salvation (Jer. 30.7bB). Nahum disagreed, arguing that on such a day Zion would seek refuge in Yahweh (Nah. 1.7a; 3.11b). Habakkuk sees trouble for Judah (Hab. 1.5-6, 8-10) but reverses Nahum's narrative order by concluding with a time of distress for Judah's enemies (Hab. 3.16b). A lament moves from petition out of trouble to joyful praise of Yahweh (Hab. 3.18-19).[36]

c. *Zephaniah*

Zephaniah delivered his oration in a time of crisis when it had become increasingly apparent that the life of the nation was quickly drawing to a close. In a desperate attempt to reverse the fate of Judah, Zephaniah confronts his listeners with the full weight of the terrifying day of Yahweh in prophetic tradition. He restores the whole prophecy of Amos, says that its fulfilment is imminent, and insists that the other prophets understood the day of Yahweh as Amos expressed it. Nothing is left to the imagination or to chance. All the images of the dreaded day of Yahweh are brought together in one grand synthesis (Zeph. 1.14-18), and the accumulated imagery, in all its horror, sums up the urgency of the situation, impressing on its hearers the need for immediate and effective action.

Zephaniah's quotations from Amos include the day of darkness and gloom (Zeph. 1.15b יום חשך ואפלה = Amos 5.20), and in reverse order, the trumpet blast and shouting (Zeph. 1.16 יום שופר ותרועה = בתרועה בקול Amos 1.14b; 2.2b). Amos talked about warriors (גבור...בגבורם Amos 2.14-16) and spoke about the bitter day ahead (כיום מר Amos 8.9b). Zephaniah combines the beginning and end of Amos by associating the bitter day with warrior cries (קול יום יהוה מר צרח שם גבור Zeph. 1.14b). Just as Amos enumerated the crimes of the nations (2.6-8; 5.12aA) and stressed the magnitude of Israel's sins (ועצמים חטאתיכם Amos 5.12aB), so Zephaniah explains that all human beings have sinned against Yahweh (כי ליהוה חטאו Zeph. 1.17aB).

Zephaniah emphasizes that the great day of Yahweh is near, and that it speedily approaches (Zeph. 1.14), in accord with Isaiah, who predicted that a nation would speedily attack in response to Yahweh's whistle (Isa. 5.26). Zephaniah's proclamation of 'a day of wrath' against all the earth (Zeph. 1.15, 18) was suggested by Habakkuk, who presents Yahweh as directing his wrath against the rivers and sea (Hab. 3.8). Amos referred to the day of the whirlwind (Amos 1.14b), Nahum associated the day with

36. Claus Westermann, *Praise and Lament in the Psalms* (Atlanta: John Knox, 1981), pp. 64-81.

clouds (Nah 1.3b), and Zephaniah predicts 'a day of clouds and thick darkness' (Zeph. 1.15). The anguish he describes recalls Jeremiah and Nahum (Jer. 30.7; Nah. 1.7-8), but on the approaching day, Yahweh brings distress on all human beings (Zeph. 1.17aA, 18) and, in accord with Amos, brings about 'a full sudden end' (Zeph. 1.18). 'A day of waste and desolation' is a phrase that is coined by Zephaniah to fit Amos's prophecy of the end.

Zephaniah presents the day of Yahweh as the speedy destruction of the whole world (Zeph. 1.2-3aAb, 18b). Amos saw a cosmic fire consuming the land and devouring the sea, but when he begged Yahweh to cease, he relented, and cosmic upheaval was stopped (7.4-6). Jeremiah too had seen the world fallen apart but heard the assurance that Yahweh would not make a full end (Jer. 4.23-28). Zephaniah reaffirms Amos's vision of the end, but sees it as a cosmic destruction that is the literal undoing and reversal of the Priestly account of creation, and substitutes war for flood as the means of cosmic destruction.[37]

Despite Zephaniah's insistence that the whole earth is coming to an end, he urgently appeals to the nation to change its ways before fate takes its course and disaster strikes (Zeph. 2.1-3). Amos asked his Jerusalem audience to participate in his performance by making a decision about its future. Zephaniah takes up Amos's cause by exhorting his listeners to seek Yahweh (Zeph. 2.3a; Amos 5.4, 6; Hos. 5.6, 15) and righteousness (Zeph. 2.3b בקשׁו־צדק = Amos 5.7, 24; 6.12) if they want to be hidden from his day of wrath.

The defeat of the Philistines is the motivation for the appeal to seek Yahweh. Zephaniah lists the same Philistine cities mentioned by Amos (Amos 1.6-8) but, as is typical of quoted material, reverses the order of Ashdod and Ashkelon (Zeph. 2.3-4). Amos predicted that the end of Yahweh's people would come at midday, and Zephaniah prophesies, in imitation of Amos, that Ashdod's people shall be driven out at noon (בצהרים Zeph. 2.4 = Amos 8.9; 1.8).

Zephaniah develops Amos's contrasting images of light and darkness. The absence of light at noon signals the end of the physical day (Zeph. 2.4). During the night Jerusalem's judges, prophets and priests commit unscrupulous and violent acts (Zeph. 3.1-4), the citizens rise early to do corrupt things (Zeph. 3.7), but Yahweh shows forth his justice every

---

37. Zeph. 1.3aAb = Gen. 1.20, 24, 26; Gen. 6.13, 17; 7.6, 11; 8.13a; 9.11, 15: Michael DeRoche, '*Zephaniah* I 2-3: The "Sweeping" of Creation', *VT* 30 (1980), pp. 104-109.

morning at dawn (Zeph. 3.7). The unrelenting light of day and the unfailing justice of God lead into the image of Yahweh as judge of all the nations, consuming the whole earth with the fire of his wrath, and bringing time itself to a complete end (Zeph. 3.8). Zephaniah was the last prophet to speak before Judah fell to the Babylonians. Other prophets thought that Amos was wrong about the end or that there was some way to circumvent it, but Zephaniah insisted that the end predicted by Amos is at hand.

d. *Ezekiel*

History proved that Zephaniah was right about the imminent arrival of the day of Yahweh. Ezekiel accepted Zephaniah's interpretation, affirmed Amos's prophecy, and spoke repeatedly about the day that had come upon them (Ezek. 7.1-9). Five times Ezekiel refers to Amos and his prophecy about the coming end (Ezek. 7.2-3, 5-6). He sums up the message of Amos in a single word: קֵץ (Ezek. 7.2aB), and quotes Amos: 'the end has come' (Ezek. 7.2b בָּא הקֵץ = Amos 8.2b). In agreement with Zephaniah, Ezekiel applies the concept of the end to the four corners of the whole world. The expression 'the end has come' is repeated twice more, first with reversed word order (קֵץ בָּא), then in its original order (Ezek. 7.6a), and Ezekiel follows up the sequence with a reformulation: 'it [the end] is for you; lo, it has come' (הקֵץ אֵלֶיךָ הנֵה בָּאה).

The fateful day is described with traditional prophetic ideas or expressions. Four times בָּא or בָּאה is employed, in combination with Amos's קֵץ, twice with reference to the coming evil (Ezek. 7.5b) or the coming time (בָּא העֵת Ezek. 7.7b) taken from Micah (Mic. 2.3; 3.11) and Jeremiah (Jer. 4.6), and once to describe the doom that has come upon them (Ezek. 7.7a).[38] Associated with doom is the idea that the time has come, and that 'the day of tumult is near' (קָרוב היום מהומה Ezek. 7.7b). Ezekiel borrows from Zephaniah the phraseology about the nearness of the day of Yahweh (קָרוב יום־יהוה Zeph. 1.14a) and combines it with an allusion to Amos, who called on Ashdod to see 'the great tumults' (מהומת רבות Amos 3.9) or the fighting within the city of Samaria. Ezekiel's linkage of different elements in Amos's text, namely 'day' (Amos 5.18-20) with 'end' (Amos 8.9) and with 'tumults' (Amos 3.9), shows that Ezekiel understands the whole text of Amos as a description of the day of Yahweh.

---

38. This conventional translation (BDB, p. 862) is a guess based on the context where בָּאה הצפירה אֵלֶיךָ is associated with time and day of reckoning: see Moshe Greenberg, *Ezekiel 1–20: A New Translation with Introduction and Commentary* (Anchor Bible, 22; Garden City, NY: Doubleday, 1983), p. 148.

e. *Joel*

It is perfectly evident that Joel knew Amos and the prophets who followed him.[39] Joel calls the day of Yahweh a day of darkness and gloom (ואפלה
יום חשך Joel 2.2a = Amos 5.20; Zeph. 1.15bB), a day of clouds and thick darkness (יום ענן וערפל Joel 2.2a = Nah. 1.3b; Zeph. 1.15bB) and proclaims its nearness (Joel 1.15bA כי קרוב יום יהוה = Zeph. 1.14a). Joel, like Zephaniah, sees the trumpet blast in Amos as signalling the coming of Yahweh's day (תקעו שופר בציון Joel 2.1 = Zeph. 1.16a). Amos spoke about a trumpet sounding in Samaria (3.6a), but Joel identifies the place as Zion. Amos's devouring fire (1.3–2.3; 5.6; 7.4) is recognized by Joel as an important physical aspect of the day (Joel 2.3; cf. 1.19; 2.5). He takes up Amos's vision of the locusts who eat and destroy (Joel 1.4 = Amos 7.1-2) but mixes natural disaster with war imagery, moving freely from viewing the Babylonian invasion as a locust plague (Joel 1.4-7; 2.25) to describing the anguish of the people as they face the warriors who scale the city walls (Joel 2.4-9).

The most significant observation to be made about Joel is that he knows the whole movement of Amos's text from destruction to lamentation but completes the circle to include God's promise of restoration. Amos associated the locust plague with Yahweh's day, but excluded natural calamity from his version of the fatal end. At Amos's insistence, Yahweh intervenes to save Judah, and the locusts stop destroying the crops (7.1-3). In contrast to Amos, who saw the end in terms of defeat in war, Joel describes a locust plague and an invading nation ruining the crops of the land (Joel 1.4-7; 2.25). Amos depicted the day of Yahweh as a day of mourning when worship is over: the songs of the temple become wailings (Amos 8.3a, 10a) because there is no more harvest and there is nothing to offer Yahweh (Amos 8.1-2). The same idea is taken up by Joel when he summons the priests, elders and inhabitants of the land to lament because the grain is destroyed, the fruit trees are withered, and food is withheld from the house of God (Joel 1.2-3, 8-10, 13). But Joel goes full circle when he goes beyond Amos's day of mourning and the end of ritual observance to envisage a time when God will restore what he has destroyed, overflowing the threshing floors with grain and the vats with wine and oil, and giving back the people their temple rituals (Joel 2.18-27). Restoration does not pose a problem for Joel because, in direct antithesis to Amos and

---

39. The book of Joel is appropriately described as a blend or mixture of prophetic statements: see Johannes Lindblom, *Prophecy in Ancient Israel* (Oxford: Basil Blackwell, 1962), pp. 276-77.

the other prophets, the day of Yahweh is a natural disaster unassociated with guilt or sin. Joel moves confidently beyond the experience of the fall of Judah to God's promise of perpetual prosperity and satisfaction.[40]

f. *Obadiah*

Obadiah's prophecy concerns Edom, which receives a divine edict of war for its involvement in the Babylonian invasion of Judah and the capture of Jerusalem. Edom, identified as Esau (Obad. 6), is accused of violence against his brother Jacob (Obad. 10, 12a) on a particular day in the past when Edom joined forces with the Babylonians against Judah. The day when Jerusalem fell is mentioned repeatedly in various ways. Obadiah coins the phrase 'day of your brother' (Obad. 12aA), and in deference to prophetic tradition, he refers to Judah's fall as 'a day of distress' (ביום צרה Obad. 12b, 14b = Jer. 30.7; Nah. 1.7; Hab. 3.16; Zeph. 1.15). When Amos wrote, the day was seen as entirely Yahweh's doing. In Obadiah's time it is singled out as something done by enemy nations and by Edom fighting as an ally of the Babylonians. Amos suggested (1.3–2.3) and Zephaniah confirmed (Zeph. 1.14-18) that the day of Yahweh would affect every nation.[41] On their authority, Obadiah proclaims that Yahweh's day will come upon Edom (Obad. 15). The ruin of Edom and Esau will be matched by the restoration of a remnant of Israel and Judah (Obad. 20).[42]

History and Biography

Roughly fifty years after the fall of Jerusalem, the reviser of the book of Amos wrote a scholarly edition of the prophetic text for readers and drew heavily upon the Deuteronomistic historian (Dtr) who had written the standard history of the age.[43] References to the exilic Dtr can be shown

40. Cf. James D. Nogalski ('Intertextuality in the Twelve', in Watts and House [eds.], *Forming Prophetic Literature*, pp. 102-24), who explains the quotations and allusions in Joel and the twelve not in terms of distinct books, but in terms of a 'united' corpus of literature.

41. Robert Gordis, 'Amos, Edom and Israel—An Unrecognized Source for Edomite History', in Abraham I. Katsch and Leon Nemoy (eds.), *Essays on the Occasion of the Seventieth Anniversary of the Dropsie University* (Philadelphia: Dropsie University, 1979), pp. 109-32.

42. On correspondences between Amos and Obadiah, see Bert Dicou, *Edom, Israel's Brother and Antagonist: The Role of Edom in Biblical Prophecy and Story* (JSOTSup, 169; Sheffield: Sheffield Academic Press, 1994), pp. 36-42.

43. My analysis is based on the insight that Dtr was not just an editor but an author

throughout the editor's work, and three main texts from the history, 1 Kings 13, 1 Kings 8 and 2 Kings 17, provide the overall structure for the book's argument.[44] The whole book is dotted with allusions to the prophets, which, in combination with quotations from Dtr, disclose the reviser's comprehensive knowledge of contemporary history writing and the prophetic tradition. The question yet to be established is the extent to which the reviser confirms or denies Dtr's historical perspective.[45]

After the Babylonian invasion and the fall of Jerusalem, when the prophets were dead and all their terrible predictions had come to pass, stories grew up around them. While prophecy was still a living issue, it made a difference what a prophet said. But in later times the concentration was on the prophets rather than their prophecies. With this shift in focus from the poetry to the prophets as persons, prophecy was transformed into biography and history. The prophetic texts themselves became the principal vehicles for developing the lives of the prophets: their words and actions, their character and achievements, their cultural context and significance, were largely based on claims or suggestions they made in their own literary works.

The analogy is the ancient biographies of Greek poets, whose lives were primarily derived from their own poetry on the premise that poem and poet are synonymous.[46] So Archilochus spoke about love and sexual

---

of a history: see Martin Noth, *Überlieferungsgeschichtliche Studien. I. Die sammeln-denund bearbeitenden Geschichtswerke im Alten Testament* (Tübingen: Max Niemeyer Verlag, 2nd edn., 1957 [1943]), pp. 11-18, 89-100; ET *The Deuteronomistic History* (trans. Jane Doull, John Barton, Michael D. Rutter and D.R. Ap-Thomas; JSOTSup, 15; Sheffield: JSOT Press, 1981), pp. 4-18, 76, 79, 89-99. The analogue to the Deuteronomistic historian in the Greek world is Herodotus: see John Van Seters, *In Search of History: Historiography in the Ancient World and the Origins of Biblical History* (New Haven: Yale University Press, 1983), pp. 8-54.

44. Cf. Nogalski (*Literary Precursors to the Book of the Twelve*, pp. 77-82), who assigns editing in Amos to redactors in Deuteronomistic circles, arguing that a Dtr redaction in Amos 'should not be described merely in terms of occasional unconnected glosses'.

45. Scholars argue that Dtr redaction is evident in Amos 1.9-12; 2.4-5, 10-12; 3.1b, 7; 5.25-26, 8.11-12; 9.11-15: Wolff, *Amos*, pp. 112-13, 139-40, 169-75, 188, 264-65, 330-31; Schmidt, 'Die deuteronomistische redaktion des Amosbuches', pp. 168-93; Roy F. Melugin, 'Prophetic Books and the Problem of Historical Reconstruction', in Reid (ed.), *Prophets and Paradigms*, pp. 63-78.

46. Mary R. Lefkowitz, 'Fictions in Literary Biography: The New Poem and the Archilochus Legend', *Arethusa* 9 (1976), pp. 181-89; *idem*, *The Lives of the Greek Poets* (London: Duckworth, 1981), pp. 12-66.

encounters,[47] and thus is portrayed in biographical tradition as a lecher and an adulterer.[48] Because he wrote invective,[49] he is depicted as a slanderer whose abusive verses drove individuals to suicide and brought about his own death.[50]Tyrtaeus exhorted his audiences to fight with valour, so his biographers make the poet a military adviser and a general.[51] Alcaeus summoned his companions to drink, and so he is accused of murdering a drinking friend.[52] Solon spoke generally of justice, law and order, but his biographers represent him as a statesman and lawgiver.[53]

In ancient biography sources are interpreted in different ways, so that even quite contradictory characterizations are developed out of the same poetry. One biographer remembers Alcaeus as an incorrigible imbiber who drank in all seasons, and the evidence is the poet's frequent allusions to wine and the time of year. But another biographer, using as a starting point Alcaeus's exhortation 'Mix one part of water to two of wine', takes it as evidence of the poet's temperance, arguing that he drank only one or two cups at a time.[54] Early biographers call Archilochus a coward because he said in a poem that it was better to throw away one's shield than be slain. But subsequent biographical tradition corrects this portrait of Archilochus by citing another poem as evidence of his outstanding love and zeal for his country.[55]

Such were the methods used to develop biographies of the prophets, and they were written by Dtr and by later scholars who revised the prophetic

47. Archilochus, frs. 30, 85, 97B, 103, 114, 179, 184, in Edmonds, *Greek Elegy*, II, pp. 112-13, 140-41, 150-53, 169-71, 200-203.

48. Athenaeus on Archilochus, fr. 145; Critias on Archilochus, frs. 149, 150; Aristophanes on Archilochus, fr. 184, in Edmonds, *Greek Elegy*, II, pp. 188-89, 190-91, 202-03.

49. Archilochus, frs. 27, 65, 67, 68, 78, 94, in Edmonds, *Greek Elegy*, II, pp. 110-13, 130-33, 136-37, 146-47; Easterling and Knox (eds.), *Early Greek Poetry*, pp. 82-86.

50. See life of Archilochus, in Edmonds, *Greek Elegy*, II, pp. 84-87, 92-93, 96-97; frs. 143, 149, pp. 186-87, 190-91.

51. On the life of Tyrtaeus, see Edmonds, *Greek Elegy*, II, pp. 50-51, 53-54, 56-57.

52. Alcaeus frs. 346, 347, 352; testimonia 9 (b), in Campbell, *Greek Lyric*, II, pp. 214-15, 378- 81, 388-89.

53. See the life of Solon, in Edmonds, *Greek Elegy*, I, pp. 104-11.

54. Alcaeus, frs. 335, 338, 346, in Campbell, *Greek Lyric*, I, pp. 372-75, 378-81; Janet A. Fairweather, 'Fiction in the Biographies of Ancient Writers', *Ancient Society* 5 (1974), pp. 231-75 (233-34).

55. On Archilochus, see fr. 6 and citation from Plutarch; fr. 114, in Edmonds, *Greek Elegy, II*, pp. 100-101, 160-73; Lefkowitz, *Lives of the Greek Poets*, pp. 28-29.

texts. Their biographies, like those of the Greek poets, were meant to be representational, depicting types rather than historical individuals.[56] The intention was to express something characteristic about the prophet, and in the case of Amos, the theme of hearing the word of God was used by his biographers for opposite purposes. Once we understand that the prophets' lives are based on their poetry, then it becomes easier to see that they are not 'intentional fictions' or 'complete inventions'.[57] The stories of Isaiah (2 Kgs 18–20 = Isa. 36.1–39.8; Isa. 6–8), Amos (1 Kgs 13; Amos 7.10-17), Hosea (Hos. 3.1-5), Micah (1 Kgs 22), Ezekiel (2 Kgs 1-13) and Jeremiah (e.g. Jer. 1) are authentic, if disrespectful, interpretations of the prophets.[58]

In antiquity credible biographical sketches of poets are often combined with incredible re-creations of their poetry. For example, Archilochus recalls his gift for poetry ('I am skilled in the lovely gift of the Muses'), but a story is told of his meeting with women who appear as Muses to make fun of him and miraculously replace his cow with the lyre.[59] In common with their Greek counterparts, Judaean biographers developed fantastic legendary tales or telltale anachronistic situations based on assertions found in literary works. And ancient readers had no difficulty in recognizing and appreciating the stories as rhetorical exaggerations, without taking them at face value as presentations of actual historical realities.[60]

a. *The Story of 'The Man of God'*
Dtr adopts a traditional folktale about 'a man of God' (1 Kgs 13; 2 Kgs 23.15-20) and adapts it to fit a historical perspective.[61] An anonymous

56. So also Klaus Baltzer, Die Biographie der Propheten (Neukirchen–Vluyn: Neukirchener Verlag, 1975), pp. 20, 22, 113, 194; Lefkowitz, *Lives of the Greek Poets*, pp. vii-xi.

57. For a discussion of Greco-Roman biographies, see David E. Aune, *The New Testament in its Literary Environment* (Philadelphia: Westminster Press, 1987), pp. 29, 57, 64-65.

58. See also Peckham, *History and Prophecy*, pp. 25, 611, 655.

59. Archilochus, fr. 1, in Edmonds, *Greek Elegy, II*, pp. 98-99. The story about how Archilochus became a poet is told on the third century 'Inscription of Mnesiepes': text in Gerber, *Greek Iambic Poetry*, pp. 16-19; see also Lefkowitz, *Lives of the Greek Poets*, pp. 27-28; Easterling and Knox (eds.), *Early Greek Poetry*, p. 77.

60. Carles Miralles and Jaume Portulas, *Archilochus and the Iambic Poetry* (Edizioni dell'Ateneo; Rome: Casella Postale, 1983), p. 131.

61. Baruch Halpern (*The First Historians: The Hebrew Bible and History* [San Francisco: Harper & Row, 1988], pp. 248-54) dates the story to the time of the events

prophet[62] journeys from Judah to Israel to proclaim God's word against the altar at Bethel. The man of God predicts that King Josiah will pull down the altar, burn the bones of men upon it, and kill all the priests of the high places (1 Kgs 13.1-5). Jeroboam I invites the man of God to take refreshment, but the prophet refuses, declaring that God has prohibited him from eating bread or drinking water in Bethel (1 Kgs 13.6-9). But shortly thereafter the man of God accepts an old prophet's invitation to eat bread with him (1 Kgs 13.11-24). The man of God disobeys Yahweh, and for this he receives God's word that his body will not be buried in his ancestors' grave (1 Kgs 13.20-22). The old prophet's prediction is fulfilled immediately, just as the man of God's prophecy against Bethel is fulfilled in Josiah's time (2 Kgs 23.15-20). The man of God rides back to Judah on a donkey and is killed by a lion on the road. Next to the body is found the donkey and 'a genuine folktale lion', who neither eats the prophet nor kills his donkey.[63]

Ancient readers knew that stories of the prophets were based on prophetic poetry, so they could easily guess that the anonymous man of God was Amos, and that major elements of his biography were taken from his poetry: his criticism of Bethel (4.4-5; 5.4-6) and the house of Jeroboam (7.9), his reference to the burning of bones (2.1), his command to offer leavened bread as a sacrifice (4.5), his riddle about the lion and his prey (3.4), and especially his insistence on hearing Yahweh's word (3.1; 4.1; 5.1; 8.4).[64] The real point of Dtr's biography of Amos, despite its

it describes, arguing that the pre-exilic Josianic historian (i.e. Dtr 1) invented the story using Amos 7.10-17 as his model.

62. The story suggests its folktale character by leaving the hero and the old prophet at Bethel without names: Hermann Gunkel, *The Folktale in the Old Testament* (trans. Michael D. Rutter; Sheffield: Sheffield Academic Press, 1987), p. 170. The tendency of commentators to downplay the importance of anonymous characters is rightly resisted by Adele Reinhartz, *'Why Ask My Name?': Anonymity and Identity in Biblical Narrative* (New York: Oxford University Press, 1998), pp. 3-15, 149-53, 187-91.

63. Gunkel, *Folktale in the Old Testament*, p. 53.

64. Long ago Julius Wellhausen observed that 1 Kgs 13 is a legend in midrashic style and that the man of God bears a remarkable resemblance to Amos. His views are recorded in the introduction of Friedrich Bleek, *Einleitung in das alte Testament* (ed. Julius Wellhausen; Berlin: Reimer, 5th edn, 1886). Scholars have proposed that 1 Kgs 13 represents 'folk tradition' about the prophet Amos: see Otto Eissfeldt, 'Amos und Jona in volkstümlicher Überlieferung', in Rudolf Seeheim and Fritz Maass (eds.), *Kleine Schriften*, IV (Tübingen: J.C.B. Mohr, 1969), pp. 137-42; Antonius H.J. Gunneweg, 'Die Prophetenlegende I Reg 13: Missdeutung, Umdeutung, Bedeutung',

legendary embellishment, could hardly have been missed by its readers: Amos commanded the people to listen to Yahweh, but he himself was incapable of obeying his word.

Eventually two biographies of Amos existed side by side. The identification of the man of God as Amos is made by his editor, who retells the legendary story and, agreeing with Dtr, presents Amos as a prophet of Judah who speaks out against Bethel. Thus Amos, like Homer, emerges in biographical tradition as an itinerant, and the poets' travels are derived from their poetry.[65] What Amos said about Samaria in a dramatic context is taken literally, and so the two biographies explain that his journey to Samaria actually occurred. Both biographers represent Amos's contempt for the Bethel altar and its priests (Amos 3.14; 7.10-17; 9.1), talk about a king called Jeroboam (1 Kgs 13.4-6; Amos 7.10-11), associate Amos with eating bread (Amos 7.12) and take up his theme about the burning of the bones of the dead (Amos 2.1; 6.10). However striking these similarities in storyline, Amos's biographers offer different portraits of the prophet.

The first biographer reduces the significance of Amos by limiting his prophecy to Josiah's destruction of Bethel and his rites of purification. The second biographer, by contrast, affirms that Amos predicted the fall of Judah (Amos 2.4-5) but exaggerates his significance by making him foretell the fall of Israel (Amos 1.1b; 7.11b). In the first biography, Amos demonstrates miraculous powers of withering and restoring Jeroboam's hand (1 Kgs 13.3-6), but in the second biography, Amos prophesies the king's death (Amos 7.11). The story of Amos's death is missing from the second biography, and so the eating of bread, a quotation from Dtr, is used in an opposite sense: God's prohibition against eating bread at Bethel

---

in Fritz, Pohlmann and Schmitt (eds.), *Prophet und Prophetenbuch*, pp. 73-81 (78, 81). On the similarities and differences between 1 Kgs 13 and the story of Amos, see James L. Crenshaw, *Prophetic Conflict: Its Effect upon Israelite Religion* (BZAW, 124; Berlin: Walter de Gruyter, 1971), pp. 41-42; Ackroyd, 'Amos 7.9-17', pp. 71-87. It has become customary for scholars to discuss 1 Kings 13 without reference to Amos, or to deny that he is the subject of this text: Werner E. Lemke, 'The Way of Obedience: 1 Kgs 13 and the Structure of the Deuteronomistic History', in Frank Moore Cross, Werner E. Lemke and Patrick D. Miller, Jr (eds.), *Magnalia Dei, The Mighty Acts of God: Essays on the Bible and Archaeology in Memory of G. Ernest Wright* (Garden City, NY: Doubleday, 1976), pp. 301-25 (315-16); Pamela Tamarkin Reis, 'Vindicating God: Another Look at 1 Kings XIII', *VT* 44 (1994), pp. 376-86; D.W. van Winkle, '1 Kings XII 25–XIII 34: Jeroboam's Cultic Innovations and the Man of God from Judah', *VT* 46 (1996), pp. 101-14.

65. Lefkowitz, *Lives of the Greek Poets*, pp. 12, 14-16, 137.

(1 Kgs 13.8-10) is replaced by the priest's injunction to flee and eat bread in Judah (Amos 7.12), thus implying that Amos did not eat bread at the northern shrine.[66] Dtr abolishes Amos's objection to the burning of human bones (2.1) by having him predict and approve of Josiah's action in removing bones from the tombs and burning them on Bethel's altar (1 Kgs 13.2; 2 Kgs 23.16-20). The second biographer supports Amos by referring to the burning of rotten bodies in Samaria and the collection of the bones for burial (Amos 6.9-10; 1 Sam. 31.8-13).[67]

In the second biography, Amos tells the Bethel priest, 'I am no prophet nor a son of a prophet' (Amos 7.14), an allusion to the prophet at Bethel and his sons who are presented by Dtr as being instrumental in bringing Amos to an untimely death (1 Kgs 13.11-19). In claiming to be neither a prophet nor a son of a prophet, Amos, in his reviser's biography, declares himself a worthwhile and honest prophet of God, having no connection with the lying prophets at Bethel or their sons (Amos 7.14-15).[68] The first biographer presents the lion as a beast of prey who does not eat and thus is better able than a prophet to pass God's test of obedience (1 Kgs 13.24-25).[69] In contrast, the second biographer reapplies the lion motif to insist on Amos's status as the legitimate prophet of God: (Amos 1.2; 3.8). So, in a nutshell, Dtr ridicules Amos and claims that he did not live up to his role as prophet. But the second biographer corrects this negative portrait by turning Amos into a positive religious hero—an exemplar of what a man of God should be, a prophet who obeyed Yahweh by faithfully proclaiming his word and by taking action to bring it to pass.

Anachronisms abound in ancient biographies, and the goal was often to link together great or well-known individuals. It was common in Greek genealogies to make Homer and Hesiod relatives and contemporaries in

66. Stanley N. Rosenbraun ('Northern Amos Revisited: Two Philological Suggestions', *Hebrew Studies* 18 [1977], pp. 132-48) cites the priest's order to flee as evidence that Amos was a native of Israel, arguing that if he were a Judaean, his prophecy against Israel and King Jeroboam would not be treason.

67. Hayes, *Amos*, pp. 188-90.

68. Cf. Walter Gross, 'Lying Prophet and Disobedient Man of God in 1 Kings 13: Role Analysis as an Instrument of Theological Interpretation of an OT Narrative Text', *Semeia* 15 (1979), pp. 97-129.

69. See also Uriel Simon, '1 Kings 13: A Prophetic Sign—Denial and Persistence', *HUCA* 47 (1976), pp. 81-117 (96); Jerome T. Walsh, 'The Contexts of 1 Kings 13', *VT* 39 (1989), pp. 355-70 (360); James K. Mead, 'Kings and Prophets, Donkeys and Lions: Dramatic Shape and Deuteronomistic Rhetoric in 1 Kings XIII', *VT* 49 (1999), pp. 191-205 (204).

order to accommodate the legend of their competition—a popular legend which, though rejected as anachronistic by some ancient literary historians, starts in the poetry itself.[70] Similar biographies of Amos take him out of the seventh century and project him back into much earlier times. On the basis of Amos's references to Jeroboam I (7.7-9) and Bethel, Dtr dates the prophet to the late tenth century and has him predict Josiah's destruction of Jeroboam's altar at Bethel in the seventh century.[71] Dtr's dating of Amos is rejected as anachronistic by the second biographer, but even the new date is anachronistic, and in common with Dtr, has its own distinctive theological goal. Amos retold the story of Israel's defeat, describing it as both a future and a past event (Amos 2.13-16; 5.2). So his editor stays with the historical fact of the fall of Samaria, puts Amos into the eighth-century reign of Jeroboam II, and presents him as predicting doom for Israel (Amos 1.1b; 7.10-17).

Dtr's legend of Amos's death resembles amazing stories of the death of many Greek poets, and Amos's death, like those of Homer, Hesiod, and Archilochus, fulfils a prophecy.[72] When Hesiod receives an oracle predicting his death, he flees from the place where he thinks he will die, but is killed in another place of the same name. When Amos receives the old prophet's word predicting his death, he sets out for another place, but is killed on the road. The two stories illustrate the inevitability of punishment for wrong-doers: Hesiod is killed by brothers of a girl they claim he has seduced, and Amos is killed for disobeying the word of God. The story of Hesiod is based on the poet's prediction, 'I would not be a just man (δίκαιος)…among evil men, if the more unjust man can have a greater

70. The Greek tradition of the contest of Homer and Hesiod can be traced to the idea of competition in Hesiod's *Works and Days* (25-26) and to the reference to the funeral games and prizes (654-57): see Lamberton, *Hesiod*, pp. 5-6; Fairweather, 'Fiction in the Biographies of Ancient Writers', pp. 256-64.

71. Without the late editing (Amos 1.1b), 'the house of Jeroboam' (Amos 7.9) refers to Jeroboam I, and the linkage between Amos and Jeroboam I continued to be made in later times: see Christoph Levin, 'Amos und Jerobeam I', *VT* 45 (1995), pp. 307-17.

72. See, *Certamen or Contest of Homer and Hesiod*, in Evelyn-White, *Hersiod*, pp. 566-97 (587-91). Martin L. West, 'The Contest of Homer and Hesiod', *ClQ* 17 (1967), pp. 433-50; Mary R. Lefkowitz, 'The Poet as Hero: Fifth Century Autobiography and Subsequent Biographical Fiction', *ClQ* 28 (1978), pp. 459-69 (466-68); *idem*, 'Fictions in Literary Biography', p. 184; Fairweather, 'Fiction in the Biographies of Ancient Writers', pp. 269-72; N.J. Richardson, 'The Contest of Homer and Hesiod and Alcidamas' Mouseion', *ClQ* 31 (1981), pp. 1-10.

justice' (*Works and Days* 270-74). There is no escaping destiny for either Hesiod and Amos, and the futility of all such attempts is a persistent theme in the poetry of Amos (2.13-16; 4.2-3; 5.18-20; 8.1-3a).

The basic plot of Hesiod's and Amos's stories was preserved, but as the biographical traditions developed, new characters and circumstances were added with fresh interpretations. Subsequent biographers vindicated Hesiod's honour by claiming that the girl was seduced by his travelling companion or that she hanged herself. Amos's late biographer vindicated Amos's honour by claiming that he was indeed a genuine prophet of God (3.7; 7.10-17). The evidence of divine favour towards Hesiod is already apparent in the earlier story when the poet's body, after being thrown into the sea, is brought back to land by dolphins three days later and is buried in a tomb built for his bones.[73] Similarly, Dtr lets the reader know that Amos's bones were carried back to Judah and buried in a hero's grave and that Josiah prohibited anyone from disturbing his bones (2 Kgs 23.16-18).[74] Thus different biographical traditions about Greek poets and Hebrew prophets were established and preserved without attempting to reconcile the contradictions among them. The Greek analogy helps us to see that prophecy was rewritten as a biographical record, and that the biographers historicize the prophets, both to criticize them and to praise them.

b. *The Prayer of Solomon*

Another important source for the historian who reworked Amos's text is Dtr's prayer of Solomon (1 Kgs 8).[75] Its key elements are found in Amos 4.6-13 and other parts of the book (5.8-9, 26; 5.16; 6.14; 8.11; 9.5-11). Its setting is the Jerusalem temple where the people gather to dedicate the central sanctuary (1 Kgs 8.1-5, 62-65). Solomon offers up his intercessory

73. Lamberton, *Hesiod*, pp. 9-10; Lefkowitz, *Lives of the Greek Poets*, pp. 3-11.

74. A writer in the first century of the present era supplements and corrects the biography of Amos (7.10-17): Amos was beaten by Amaziah, his son dealt Amos a fatal blow, but before he died, he made it back to his homeland and was buried there. The writer refers to Amos's poetry by citing his place of origin in Tekoa (1.1a): Charles Cutler Torrey, *The Lives of the Prophets: Greek Text and Translation* (Philadelphia: Society of Biblical Literature and Exegesis, 1946), pp. 26, 40.

75. Scholars detect the exilic Dtr in 1 Kgs 8, e.g. in 8.22-53 where it is expected that Yahweh's forgiveness will prompt Judah's return from exile (8.46-50): see J.D. Levinson, 'From Temple to Synagogue: 1 Kings 8', in Baruch Halpern and J.D. Levinson (eds.), *Traditions in Transformation* (Winona Lake: Eisenbrauns, 1981), pp. 143-66. Cf. Halpern, *First Historians*, pp. 168-74.

prayer on their behalf, and so Dtr emphasized that the temple guarantees God's accessibility in times of adversity (1 Kgs 8.30-44). Taking up Amos's criticism of worship at the central sanctuary (Amos 4.4-5), his reviser argues that God is not to be located in any particular place (Amos 4.13; 5.8; 5.27; 6.14; 9.5-6). Because Dtr said God was transcendent and not confined to the central sanctuary (1 Kgs 8.12, 23, 27, 30), Amos's editor depicts a cosmic God who is available to all Israel and peoples of the world (9.7).

The book's catalogue of misfortune is derived from Solomon's prayer, and the disasters typify the fall of Israel (4.6-12). Amos's editor, like Dtr, mentions famine (4.6 = 1 Kgs 8.37), drought (4.7-8 = 1 Kgs 8.35-36), blight, mildew, locusts and pestilence (4.9-10 = 1 Kgs 8.37), and defeat in battle (4.11 = 1 Kgs 8.33), but citations are in a different or reverse order, and the disasters are related to other parts of the book and the Dtr history.

So God's words, 'I will send a famine in the land', are a quotation from Solomon's prayer which presupposes 'famine in the land' (רעב בארץ Amos 8.11 = 1 Kgs 8.37). God's speech, 'I gave you…lack of bread' (וחסר לחם Amos 4.6), is a reversal of his covenant promise of a land in which Israel 'will eat bread' and 'lack nothing' (לא־תחסר Deut. 8.9). 'Hunger and thirst' are covenant curses (ברעב ובצמא Deut. 28.48), but in the book of Amos God says that there will be neither 'hunger for bread' nor 'thirst for water' (לא־רעב ללחם ולא־צמא למים Amos 8.11b, 13b) but a thirst for God's word. Dtr's prayer presupposes that a future famine will precipitate prayer (1 Kgs 8.38), but from the perspective of the book of Amos, the famine has already occurred and did not provoke a return to God (Amos 4.6b).

The book's second disaster is drought (Amos 4.7-8), and according to Solomon's prayer, a drought will provoke the people to repentance (1 Kgs 8.35-36). Dtr anticipates a great drought to come in Ahab's time (1 Kgs 17.1, 7, 14; 18.1, 41, 44, 45) and repeatedly states that such disasters are the result of sin (1 Kgs 8.31-36, 46-50). Amos's editor agrees, and sin is presupposed in the book's overall argument and in the immediate context (9.10; 4.6-11). Dtr argues that if the people pray towards the temple at Jerusalem and 'turn again' to Yahweh, then he will forgive their sin (ושבו 1 Kgs 8.33-34). The book of Amos describes drought as a catastrophe already past, and argues, in contrast to Dtr, that Israel 'did not return' to Yahweh (ולא־שבתם 4.8b). Readers of the Dtr history would have associated drought (1 Kgs 8.35-36) with Elijah's prophecy to King Ahab (1 Kgs 17.1), but readers of the book of Amos would have associated drought with the prophet's warning that Israel should repent (Amos 4.7). Because the book argues that Israel did not return to God (4.8b), it omits Dtr's reference to the central sanctuary and the anticipated prayer of the people.

The third disaster of the book of Amos is blight, mildew and locusts (Amos 4.9; 1 Kgs 8.37a). The description of these natural disasters is elaborated with reference to curses in the Dtr history; God smites with mildew (Deut. 28.22 = Amos 4.9a) or brings locusts (Deut. 28.38, 42 = Amos 4.9b). Dtr is confident that if crop diseases or locusts threaten the land's fertility (1 Kgs 8.37), the people will petition God, and he will forgive them (1 Kgs 8.38-39). Amos's editor omits petition and insists that such disasters have already occurred and that Israel did not repent (4.9b).

The book's fourth disaster is pestilence or plague, but unlike Dtr, who lists it as one of a possible number of natural disasters that might occur (דבר Amos 4.10 = 1 Kgs 8.37), the reviser sets it apart as a separate past event. The book's reference to Solomon's prayer is expanded in light of other Dtr texts.[76] 'I [Yahweh] sent among you a plague after the manner of Egypt' (דבר 4.10a) is an allusion to the covenant curses which result in his affliction of Israel with Egyptian diseases (Deut. 28.27, 60). Pestilence and sword (דבר וחרב) are basic to the covenant curses (Deut. 28.21, 22), and the book combines these traditional punishments (Amos 4.10; Ezek. 5.17).

The book interprets the fall of Israel with reference to Solomon's prayer and other parts of the Dtr history. So the fourth calamity is elaborated with reference to Moses who seeks the permission of the Pharaoh to sacrifice to Yahweh for fear that he will afflict his people 'with pestilence or sword' (Exod. 5.1-3). When the Pharaoh refuses to let the Hebrews go, God brings a 'plague' upon the Egyptians which kills cattle and horses (Exod. 9.1-7). The Exodus story is the model for the book of Amos, and its elements recall the Egyptian plagues, Israel's triumph over the horse and his rider (Exod. 15.1, 21) and the journey from Egypt into the wilderness. The book's term מחניכם 'your camp' (Amos 4.10) is a allusion to Israel's

---

76. Noth's idea of Deuteronomy as a collection of independent traditions with a Dtr framework introducing the history proper (Deut. 1–3 [4]; 31.1-13; 34[*]) 'seems to contradict the theory of a unified Dtr history... On this theory, Dtr should be the author of Deuteronomy': see Brian Peckham, 'The Composition of Deuteronomy 5–11', in Carol L. Meyers and M. O'Connor (eds.), *The Word of the Lord Shall Go Forth: Essays in Honor of David Noel Freedman in Celebration of his Sixtieth Birthday* (Winona Lake: Eisenbrauns, 1983), pp. 217-40 (217-20). Accordingly, Dtr (= Dtr2) is an exilic author and historian who rewrote literary and historical sources (J, Dtr 1, P, E) 'as the history of Israel from creation to the fall of Jerusalem': Peckham, *Composition of the Deuteronomistic History*, p. 1.

wilderness camp (מחנה Exod. 29.14; 32.26-27; 33.11; Num. 1–2). The book has already referred to the deliverance from Egypt and the wilderness sojourn and cited the Exodus as the reason for God's punishment of his people (Amos 2.10; 3.1b). Its historical view is developed: God punished Israel with 'a plague' like those for which Egypt was famous, he killed their young men 'with the sword' together with their captured horses, and made their army camp smell of rotting flesh (Amos 4.11; Exod. 9.3).

The book's fifth calamity is Israel's defeat in war and has its parallel in Solomon's prayer referring to the defeat of the whole people (Amos 4.11; 1 Kgs 8.33-34, 46-51). The verb 'overthrow' הפך (4.11) is a technical term that the book borrows from Dtr texts referring to Sodom and Gomorrah and their fall by fire and brimstone (Gen. 19.21, 24, 29; Deut. 29.22). Amos's editor likens survivors such as Lot to a brand plucked out of the burning.[77]

The book's hymnic passages (Amos 4.13; 5.8-9; 9.5-6) show the influence of Solomon's prayer in their portrayal of Yahweh as a transcendent God. The prayer affirms that there is no God like Yahweh in heaven above or on earth below (1 Kgs 8.23): he neither dwells on the earth, nor can the highest heaven contain him (1 Kgs 8.27). The prayer constantly reiterates that whenever the people make supplication Yahweh will hear them in heaven (1 Kgs 8.30-49). So too the book of Amos constantly associates Yahweh with the heavens, calling him 'God of hosts' יהוה שמו אלהי (צבאות Amos 4.13; 9.5; 3.13; 5.14-16, 27; 6.8, 14).[78]

---

77. Dtr's story of Abraham's intercession for the city of Sodom (Gen. 18.17-33) is the paradigm for the book's report about the overthrow of cities and the survival of a just remnant (Amos 4.11; 5.3). Using numbers that decrease by fives and tens, God agrees to spare Sodom if the city has ten righteous persons, but when they are not found, Sodom is destroyed. Lot and his family are spared and the innocence of Lot is suggested by Dtr in Abraham's question to Yahweh: 'Shall not the judge (השפט) of all the earth do right?' Yahweh agrees to do the right thing when he devises a plan to save the righteous in the city (Gen. 18.25-26). The idea of Lot's righteousness is reinforced when the people of Sodom say, 'This fellow...would play the judge' (וישפט שפוט Gen. 19.9). In a similar vein, the author of the book of Amos uses figures in descending order to represent destruction and survival of a city, arguing that ten per cent escape destruction and a just remnant survives (Amos 5.3). Amos's editor and Dtr have a mutual interest in the question of how the fate of the righteous is related to that of the unrighteous in the corporate community (Amos 5.15; 9.10-14).

78. 'Yahweh of Hosts'/'Yahweh God of Hosts' (יהוה אלהי צבאות or הוה צבארת) is a recurring motif in the Deuteronomistic history (1 Sam. 4.4; 15.2; 17.45; 2 Sam. 5.10; 6.2, 18; 7.8, 26; 1 Kgs 19.10, 14).

This insistence on the name of God is developed differently by Dtr and the author of the book. Dtr claims that Yahweh built a central sanctuary so his name would be there, attached to the Jerusalem temple (1 Kgs 8.16-20, 29, 33, 35, 41-44, 48). The building of a house for the name of Yahweh is anticipated by Dtr's law of centralization, according to which God will choose a place to put his name (Deut. 12.5, 21). Though Yahweh's name dwells in his chosen place (Deut. 12.5b, 11), Dtr declares that God does not dwell in the earth or in the house which Solomon built (1 Kgs 8.27), but dwells in heaven (1 Kgs 8.39, 43) and transcends even the highest heaven (1 Kgs 8.27).

Amos's editor, unlike Dtr, removes Yahweh and his name from the temple. The idea of Yahweh's transcendence and universality was an insight of Dtr, and so the reviser dissociates Yahweh from all shrines, including the central sanctuary, and associates his name exclusively with the heavens. The idea of God's presence in the whole world gives rise to the book's description of him as searching out sinners from Mount Carmel to the depths of the sea (Amos 9.1-4) and performing saving acts on behalf of all peoples (Amos 9.7).

Dtr and the author of the book of Amos share the belief that all peoples of the world have a relationship with God. Solomon's prayer presupposes that a foreigner's prayers will be heard by Yahweh from his dwelling place in heaven, and that he will respond according to all that is asked, 'in order that all the peoples of the earth might come to know his name and fear him' (1 Kgs 8.41-43). The book of Amos specifies the cosmic authority of Yahweh God of hosts (9.5-6), who determines not only the destiny of the people Israel but also the destiny of 'all the nations who are called by the name of Yahweh' (Amos 9.7; 12). However, Dtr and Amos's reviser have quite different perspectives. While Dtr emphasizes Israel's distinctiveness from other peoples on the basis of Yahweh's action in the deliverance from Egypt (1 Kgs 8.51-53; cf. Deut. 4.20, 34, 37), the book of Amos argues that God took action in the exodus of other peoples (9.7).

Dtr interprets the Exodus as proof of the survival of God's people, but Amos's reviser argues that the survival of an innocent remnant from Israel and Judah depends on a new saving act that leads to a repossession of the land and the dispossession of all the nations (Amos 9.11-12). This restoration is not a new Exodus, but by allusion to the prophetic tradition and specifically to Isaiah, it consists in the rebuilding of Zion and the booth of David and in the replanting of Israel (Amos 9.11-15; Isa. 1.8; 5.1-2, 4-5). Showing the influence of Isaiah, Dtr tells of God's promise to

David to plant the people in a place where they will not be disturbed (וּנְטַעְתִּיו 2 Sam. 7.10), and the book's reference to planting the people in the land is a restatement of God's earlier promise (וּנְטַעְתִּים עַל־אַדְמָתָם Amos 9.15a).

c. *Theology of History*

Dtr composed a great theological summary of the history of Israel and Judah (2 Kgs 17).[79] Amos's reviser wrote a version of the history with reference to 2 Kings 17 and related texts from the Dtr history. It is indebted primarily to Dtr, but also includes sporadic quotations from the prophets. Once again the striking points of agreement between Dtr and the book of Amos are offset by different historical interpretations and theological concerns.

1. *Amos 2.4.* The book's diatribe against Judah is connected to the proclamations against Tyre and Edom[80] by a similar interest in the law and covenant.[81] The book's charge that Judah has not kept Yahweh's statutes (2.4) summarizes Dtr's accusation against Judah and Israel (2 Kgs 17.13; 15, 19). 'Keeping Yahweh's statutes' is familiar Dtr terminology (Deut. 4.5-6, 40; 6.17; 7.11). Dtr was preoccupied with the observance of the law (2 Kgs 17.13, 34, 37; Deut. 4.8, 44; 17.18), but the phraseology the book uses, 'they have rejected the law of Yahweh', comes from Jeremiah and Second Isaiah (Amos 2.4bA Jer. 6.19bB; Isa. 5.24).

The book of Amos continues its diatribe against Judah: 'their lies

---

79. On this great epilogue and overview of Dtr's theology of history see Gerhard von Rad, 'The Deuteronomic Theology of History in I and II Kings', in *The Problem of the Hexateuch and Other Essays* (trans. E.W. Trueman Dicken; New York: McGraw–Hill, 1966), pp. 205-21.

80. The book of Amos alludes to the Dtr history which chronicles the peaceful times of treaty-making between Israel and Tyre, when Hiram referred to Solomon as his brother (1 Kgs 5.1-12; 9.13). According to the book of Amos, Tyre violated the treaty of brotherhood with Judah (1.9), and the source used to support this claim is Ezekiel's message of divine punishment on Tyre for not coming to assist Jerusalem during the Babylonian siege (Ezek. 26.2, 9-10, 12). The charge that Edom pursued his brother and cast off all mercy is sign of breaking a treaty (Amos 1.11). The book refers to Obadiah, who talked about Edom (= Esau) abandoning Judah (= Jacob) during the Babylonian siege of Jerusalem (Obad. 10, 12).

81. Some scholars conclude that the final edition of all the oracles in Amos 1–2 is the literary construction of Dtr editors: see Volkmar Fritz, 'Die Fremdvölkersprüche des Amos', *VT* 37 (1987), pp. 26-38.

(כזביהם) have led them astray, after which their fathers went' (2.4bB). The book's statement is unique, but its term 'lies' is found in prophetic texts: Hosea criticizes Ephraim for speaking 'lies' against God or multi-plying 'lies', and Isaiah mocks the rulers of Jerusalem for making 'lies' their refuge (Hos. 7.13; 12.2; Isa. 28.15, 17). Jeremiah talks about the ancestral fathers who went after vanity and became vain (Jer. 2.5). Dtr quotes this text:'they [Judah and Israel] went after vanity, and became vain' (2 Kgs 17.15), thus making it explicit that הבל means going after vain gods or worthless idols (Deut. 32.21; 1 Kgs 16.13, 26).[82] As Amos 2.4b illustrates, the book works out Dtr's ideas with language from the prophets. 'Their lies' (2.4b) refers to religious apostasy or the worship of false gods.[83] Following God is obeying his law and keeping his statutes. The opposite is following lies or going after idols. This criticism of Judah is not a general explanation of wrongdoing but a concrete statement reflecting Dtr's perspective. Dtr said Judah fell because it did not keep God's law but went after false gods or idols (2 Kgs 17.13-19). The book agrees but adds that Amos predicted the fall of Judah for its worship of alien gods (8.14).

2. *Amos 2.9.* The book's reference to the Amorite whom Yahweh destroyed is an allusion to the Dtr history, which discusses the destruction of indigenous peoples (Deut. 7.23; 12.30; 31.4; Josh. 11.14, 20) and refers specifically to the Amorites whom Yahweh drove out before the people of Israel (Amos 2.9a; 1 Kgs 21.26). Dtr regarded the worship of false idols as the religious justification for the expulsion and destruction of the aborigi-nal nations, and so Israel and Judah were destined to a similar fate for adopting the customs of the nations (2 Kgs 17.8, 15, 19; Deut. 12.29-31;

---

82. Going after other gods (Deut. 6.14; 8.19; 11.28; 13.3, 6; 17.3; 28.14; Judg. 2.12; 1 Kgs 11.10; 21.26) is a recurring idea in the law of Deuteronomy and the Dtr history and is contrasted with going after Yahweh (Deut. 13.5; 2 Kgs 23.3). Going after other gods is characterized as turning aside from the way in which their fathers went (Judg. 2.17) or walking in the way of their fathers or in their sins (Judg. 2.19; 1 Kgs 15.3, 26; 22.43, 53; 2 Kgs 21–22). Going after Yahweh is 'keeping his commandments and statutes' (2 Kgs 23.3; Deut. 13.5), 'walking in his statutes' (1 Kgs 8.61) and 'keeping his law' (2 Kgs 10.31).

83. This view was accepted by ancient Greek translators, and is accepted by most scholars, but has been challenged (Hayes, *Amos*, pp. 103-104; Andersen and Freed-man, *Amos*, pp. 301-302). According to a recent proposal, 'their lies' refers to false prophecy and the rejection of prophetic law: Eberhard Bon, 'Das Denotat von כזביהם "ihre Lügen" im Judaspruch Am 2,4-5', *ZAW* 106 (1996), pp. 201-13.

Josh. 23.12-13). A Dtr comparison is made between King Ahab of Israel, who went after idols as the Amorites had done (1 Kgs 21.26), and King Manasseh of Judah, who did more wicked things than all the Amorites who were before him (2 Kgs 21.11). In light of these Dtr passages, the reader can see how the book's reference to the destruction of the Amorites follows on its comment about Judah's apostasy (Amos 2.4b, 9).

The book of Amos says the Amorites were tall as cedars and strong as oaks, but that God destroyed his fruit above and his roots beneath (2.9). It reiterates what Dtr said about the aboriginal peoples being abnormally tall and strong (Deut. 1.28; 9.1-2; cf. Num. 13.28), but also borrows language from the prophetic tradition. It alludes to Ezekiel's allegory about Judah's king who was a shoot from the top of a cedar that became a great vine with strong roots and fresh fruit, but whose roots and fruit withered after it was transplanted (Ezek. 17.1-13abA, 15-18).

3. *Amos 2.11-12.* According to Dtr, God sent prophets to Israel and Judah, but the people did not listen to them (2 Kgs 17.13-14). The reviser reiterates that God appointed prophets but argues that the people silenced the prophets. The book of Amos goes beyond Dtr by envisaging the end of prophecy (2.11a, 12b; 7.10-17; 8.11b).

The book traces the origins of prophecy to God's action in raising up prophets and Nazirites (Amos 2.11). The Nazirites are not mentioned in Dtr's historical summary (2 Kgs 17), but the Dtr history claims that prophets and Nazirites were associated with one another from earliest times. Samson is a Nazirite (Judg. 13.5, 7; 16.17), and Samuel is a prophet and Nazirite (1 Sam. 1.11; 2.20-21). Amos's editor groups prophets and Nazirites together as persons chosen by God as special instruments of his authority (2.11-12). A Nazirite was required to abstain from wine and other strong drink (Num. 6.3-4), but according to the book of Amos, the people of Israel made the Nazirites drink wine (Amos 2.12a). The book insinuates that Amos was both a prophet and a Nazirite. The Deuteronomist is the source of the idea, but it is also based on Amos's criticism of the symposiasts who drank wine at the expense of the poor (2.8; 4.1b; 6.6a). Amos emerges as a Samson-like figure: just as Samson pulled down the pillars of the Dagon-temple upon all the people that were in it (העם־ ועל־כל Judg. 16.30), so Amos is summoned to shake the columns of the Bethel temple until they come crashing down on the heads of all the worshippers there (בראש כלם 9.1).

4. *Amos 3.7-8.* 'His servants the prophets' is a Dtr expression found in the historical summary (2 Kgs 17.13, 23) and other parts of the history (2 Kgs 9.7; 21.10; 24.2). So too Amos's editor claims that God does not act without disclosing his plan to 'his servants the prophets' (3.7). This theory of prophecy reflects Dtr's theological assumptions, according to which God gives his servants the prophets the authority to proclaim his word, interpret events and predict the fall of Israel and Judah (2 Kgs 17.23; 2 Kgs 24.2).

Dtr postulates the institution of a continued line of prophets that can be traced back to Moses (Deut. 18.15-22). Amos's editor indicates a continuous succession of prophets by the term 'servants of Yahweh' and by God's pronouncement, 'I raised up some of your sons for prophets' (ואקים לנביאים Amos 2.11a; 3.7-8). This idea of prophetic succession recalls the law of Deuteronomy concerning the office of prophet founded at Horeb, and the speech of Moses: 'Yahweh your God will raise up for you a prophet like me from among you' (נביא יקים Deut. 18.15, 18; cf. 34.10).[84] The comparison is between Moses and future divinely appointed prophets. Dtr treats Moses as the model prophet (Deut. 18.15, 18), and by quotation and allusion, Amos's editor allows the reader to draw the conclusion that Amos, among the genuine prophets in the history of a people, was comparable to Moses. The author of the book disputes Dtr's characterization of Amos as an untrustworthy prophet (1 Kgs 13.21, 26) by portraying him as the true and worthy prophet of Yahweh (3.7-8; 7.10-17).

Dtr makes it explicit that Israel and Judah were repeatedly warned by God's servants the prophets to *turn* from their evil, specifically their worship of false idols (שוב 2 Kgs 17.13-15). The book of Amos singles out Amos as the servant of God who constantly called on Israel to repent and *turn back* to Yahweh (שוב Amos 4.6-12), and who prophesied the fall of Israel and Judah for their worship of alien gods 'from Dan to Beer-sheba' (Amos 2.14; 8.14; cf. Judg. 20.1; 1 Sam. 3.20; 2 Sam. 3.10; 17.11; 24.2, 15; 1 Kgs 4.25.

5. *Amos 4.13; 5.8, 26-27; 9.5-6.* According to Dtr, the North fell because of a history of sin that began with Jeroboam 1 (2 Kgs 17.21, 23). Jeroboam's sin included his setting up a shrine at Bethel for the worship of golden calves and his appointment of non-Levitical priests at the high

---

84. The singular *a prophet* is a collective form indicating a succession of prophets: cf. Peter C. Craigie, *The Book of Deuteronomy* (NICOT; Grand Rapids: William B. Eerdmans, 1976), p. 262 n. 18.

places (1 Kgs 12.30-33; 13.33-34). The book of Amos, like Dtr, associates Israel's sin with the Bethel altar (Amos 3.14; 7.10-13; 9.1), but attributes the fall of Samaria to Jeroboam II and to the worship of astral gods he promoted in defiance of the worship of Yahweh God of hosts (Amos 4.13; 5.8, 26-27; 6.8, 14; 8.14; 9.5-6). The book of Amos insists, in opposition to Dtr's theory of historical destiny, that Israel fell because Jeroboam II and the people did not heed Amos's warnings (7.10-17; 2.12).

Dtr cites worship of the host of heaven (2 Kgs 17.16b) as evidence of the people's sin and refers to the laws of Deuteronomy warning the people against worshipping the sun, moon, stars and the host of heaven (Deut. 4.19; 17.3). Developing this theological perspective, the reviser of Amos argues that Israel chose to worship star-gods they made as early as the wilderness sojourn (5.25-26) instead of worshipping Yahweh as Lord of the cosmos and Creator of the Pleiades and Orion (5.8).

6. *Amos 6.14; 1.1b*. The book of Amos combines explicit reference to Jeroboam II (1.1b) with historical allusion (6.14). The book's synchronism between Uzziah, king of Judah, and Jeroboam, king of Israel (1.1b), is borrowed from Dtr who relates chronologically the reigns of the kings of Israel and Judah (2 Kgs 14.23; 15.1, 13, 30-34).[85] The book describes the devastation that extends from Hamath in the north to Arabah in the south (Amos 6.14), a quotation from 2 Kgs 14.25, where Dtr credits Jeroboam II with the restoration of the border of Israel from Hamath to Arabah. Amos's historian quotes the text and reverses it, thus implying that God sent invaders to overturn what Jeroboam II had accomplished.

The references in the book of Amos to Dtr's comments on Jeroboam II (Amos 6.14; 2 Kgs 14.23, 25, 27; 15.1) are as revealing for what they omit as for what they include. Given that Dtr wrote only a few verses on Jeroboam (1 Kgs 15.1; 2 Kgs 14.23-29), it is telling that the reviser quotes from Dtr (2 Kgs 14.25) but omits the sentence according to which Jeroboam the son of Joash 'did not depart from all the sins of Jeroboam the son of Nebat, which he made Israel to sin' (2 Kgs 14.24). The book refers to the North as the sinful kingdom (9.8), and Jeroboam is described as sharing in their wrongdoing (7.10-11), but no attempt is made to link Jeroboam II with the founder of Israel by the same name.

---

85. The superscription is typically assigned to Dtr redaction of prophetic writings: Gene M. Tucker, 'Prophetic Superscriptions and the Growth of a Canon', in George W. Coats and Burke O. Long (eds.), *Canon and Authority: Essays in Old Testament Religion and Theology* (Philadelphia: Fortress Press, 1977), pp. 56-70.

7. *Amos 5.26*. Dtr reported Israel's exile from its land to Assyria down to his own time (2 Kgs 17.23b).[86] The historian who revised Amos does not mention Assyria, but simply records the fall of the Northern Kingdom (Amos 4.11; 5.3, 9), its defeat by a foreign power (Amos 6.14) and the exile of its people (Amos 5.27). According to Dtr curses, Yahweh's people will be deported and forced to serve alien gods (Deut. 28.36, 63b-64). Amos's historian adds that the house of Israel carried their star-gods or images into exile (Amos 5.26-27), a comment showing the influence of Hosea, who talks about idols being carried by the people of Samaria into Assyria (Hos. 10.5-6).

8. *Amos 5.15*. The Dtr history said that God removed Israel and none was left but the tribe of Judah (2 Kgs 17.18, 23). So Dtr does not mention a remnant from Israel but describes the chaotic conditions that followed its conquest, when the Assyrians resettled the cities of Samaria with foreign peoples worshipping their own gods (2 Kgs 17.24-41). Of particular interest is the reference to the people of Hamath who dwelt in Samaria and made Ashima' to put in their shrines (אשׁימא 2 Kgs 17.24, 30). Amos's historian agrees that Ashimah was worshipped in Samaria (הנשׁבעים באשׁמת שׁמרון Amos 8.14a), but gives a different interpretation of the past. While the Dtr history describes a religious situation that extends from the time after the fall of Samaria to the time of its author (2 Kgs 17.34), Amos's historian maintains that Samarian youths were swearing by Ashimah before the fall of Samaria (8.14a) and that the practice has continued down to the writer's day (Amos 9.2-4).

The book of Amos, unlike Dtr, insists that a remnant from the North was saved. The fact that Yahweh's punishment was directed against the Bethel temple, its priests and king (Amos 3.14; 7.10-17; 9.1) allows for the preservation of a remnant from Israel. The hymnic texts (4.13; 5.8-9; 9.5-6) function to minimize the destruction of Israel: it is viewed as one event in a long chain of divine acts going back to primordial time. In a complete departure from Dtr theology, the book of Amos affirms that Yahweh 'will be gracious to the remnant of Joseph' (5.15). The sinful kingdom of Israel was destroyed by Yahweh (9.8), but he allows innocent

---

86. On the confluence of history and time in the interpretation of biblical histories, see Brian Peckham, 'History and Time', in Robert Chazan, William W. Hallo and Lawrence H. Schiffman (eds.), *Ki Baruch Hu: Ancient Near Eastern, Biblical and Judaic Studies in Honor of Baruch A. Levine* (Winona Lake, IN: Eisenbrauns, 1999), pp. 295-314.

northerners to return from exile (9.10) and participate in the rebuilding of northern and southern cities (9.11, 14).

9. *Amos 9.8*. Dtr's idea of the tribe of Judah as remnant (2 Kgs 17.18) receives elaboration in a subsequent text: 'for out of Jerusalem shall go forth a remnant, and out of Mount Zion a band of survivors' (2 Kgs 19.30-31). It is linked to Dtr's earlier expression of hope that Yahweh will move the captors to mercy when Judaeans in exile repent (1 Kgs 8.46-50). The historian of Amos shares the view of Dtr that Judah fell because of its sin (Amos 9.10; 2.4-5 = 2 Kgs 17.7, 13-18) and agrees that Yahweh will not completely destroy Judah or the house of Jacob (Amos 9.8b). The reference to the fall of Jerusalem (Amos 2.5) is followed by the report that the few survivors in the city who remain undetected among all the dead bodies must keep silent, daring not to utter even the name of Yahweh (Amos 5.13; 6.8, 9-10). But a day of hope lies ahead when this remnant who stay in Jerusalem will join with the captives who return from exile to rebuild the booth of David and raise up his ruins (Amos 9.11, 14-15).

Dtr's theology of Judah's survival is fleshed out in other parts of the history (2 Kgs 17.18; 19.30-31). The history records the fall of Jerusalem and the temple (2 Kgs 24–25) but ends suddenly with the notice of the release of King Jehoiachin from prison in Babylon (2 Kgs 25.27-30). The abrupt notice about Jehoiachin's release is a sign of the survival of the Davidic dynasty,[87] and this impression is confirmed once we read the end of the history in the light of its beginning. So Moses previews the history of the latter days, and in his role as prophet, he predicts the exile but assures the people that Yahweh is merciful, he will not fail or destroy

87. That Dtr expresses no hope for the future is the view of Martin Noth (*Deuteronomistic History*, pp. 12, 79, 97-99). Scholars agree with him on 2 Kgs 25.27-20, but he is criticized for overlooking Dtr's promise to the house of David: see Frank Moore Cross, 'The Themes of the Book of Kings and the Structure of the Deuteronomistic History', in Frank Moore Cross (ed.), *Canaanite Myth and Hebrew Epic: Essays in the History of the Religion of Israel* (Cambridge, MA: Harvard University Press, 1973), pp. 274-89. Other scholars interpret 2 Kgs 25.27-30 as alluding to the survival of the line of David: Gerhard von Rad, 'The Deuteronomistic Theology of History in the Book of Kings', in Gerhard von Rad (ed.), *Studies in Deuteronomy* (trans. David Stalker; SBT, 9; London: SCM Press, 1953), pp. 74-91 (90-91); *idem, Old Testament Theology*. I. *The Theology of Israel's Historical Traditions* (Edinburgh: Oliver and Boyd, 1962), pp. 334-47 (343); Hans W. Wolff, 'The Kerygma of the Deuteronomistic Historical Work', in Walter Brueggemann and Hans Walter Wolff (eds.), *The Vitality of Old Testament Traditions* (Atlanta: John Knox Press, 1975), pp. 83-100.

them, or forget the covenant promises to their ancestors (Deut. 4.27-31), but will return them from captivity to repossess the land, making them more prosperous and numerous than their fathers (Deut. 30.1-10).

The book of Amos comes to a close with the words of Yahweh: 'I will restore the fortunes of my people Israel' (ושבתי את־שבות עמי ישראל 9.14a), a direct quotation from Deuteronomy which offers hope of restoration to the exiled nation: 'Yahweh your God will restore your fortunes' (ושב יהוה אלהיך את־שבותך Deut. 30.3).[88] Restoring fortunes, for Dtr, means that God will bring his people back from the places to which he scattered them and to the promised land where they will become more prosperous and numerous than their fathers (Deut. 30.3b-5). The historian of Amos argues, in a similar vein, that Yahweh's people will reoccupy the land, become prosperous, and enjoy the fruit of the gardens they plant, and never again be uprooted or exiled from their land (Amos 9.14-15). As Dtr expresses it, God will reinstate scattered exiles in foreign lands and bring back outcasts from the uttermost parts of heaven. The same ideas and language are expressed in the book of Amos, which presupposes the return of some who are in captivity and the regathering of others, who by fleeing to the far reaches of the universe have taken refuge in heaven, Sheol, or the depths of the sea (Amos 9.2-4). The significant difference between the two histories is that Dtr limits God's promise of mercy and renewal to survivors in Judah (Deut. 4.27-31; 30.1-10; 2 Kgs 17.18; 19.30-31), whereas Amos's editor argues that the nucleus of the restored community consists of a faithful remnant from both Israel and Judah (5.15; 6.8-10; 9.8-15).

Summary

The historian who edited Amos's text knew the Dtr history and used it as the primary source. Liberal use is made of different parts of the Dtr history, but the focus is on 'the man of God cycle' (1 Kgs 13; 2 Kgs 23), the prayer of Solomon (1 Kgs 8) and a theological summary of the history (2 Kgs 17). These texts can be traced through the book of Amos, and they are expanded and corrected with reference to related Dtr passages[89] and to prophetic texts.[90]

---

88. Dtr introduced and used the phrase once, but the revisers of the prophetic books employ it often: Jer. 29.14; 30.3, 18; 31.23; 32.44; 33.7, 26; Ezek. 39.25; Hos. 6.11; Joel 4.1; Zeph. 3.20.

89. Other passages in the book of Amos which show the Deuteronomist's influence are Amos 5.26 = 2 Kgs 23.4; Amos 6.11 = 2 Kgs 24.3, 20; 25.9.

90. The author of the book of Amos refers to Isaiah, Hosea, Micah, Jeremiah,

This study of the sources behind the edited version of Amos has shown that the writer is not the same historian who wrote the Dtr history. The author of the book of Amos wrote a distinctive biography of the prophet and fitted it into a new historical interpretation. The text challenged Dtr's portrait of Amos, took issue with the historian's reasons for the fall of Israel and Judah, and counterbalanced Dtr's imaginative picture of the future with an alternative vision of the new age to come.

Contrasted with the Dtr view of Amos as a disobedient and unworthy prophet of Yahweh is the book's vindication of Amos as a genuine and worthy spokesman of Yahweh. On the one hand, Dtr dated Amos in the tenth century, assigning him the limited role of prophesying Bethel's destruction in the era of King Josiah. On the other hand, the book of Amos dates Amos in the eighth century and treats him as a model prophet who foretold the fall of Israel and Judah. Dtr attributed Israel's problems to the sin of Jeroboam I who drove the people to false worship at Bethel. This historical perspective is rejected by Amos's reviser, who censures Jeroboam II for encouraging the worship of astral deities at Bethel and who denounces the priests and people of Samaria for not listening to the words of Amos. Dtr offered a hopeful vision of the future which excluded the North, but the reviser envisages the salvation of a remnant of Israel and Judah, whom Yahweh would restore to their former glory by guaranteeing their reoccupation of the land under the reestablished throne of David. The author of the book of Amos presents the readers with a unique biography of the prophet, and its very different historiography posed a serious challenge to the standard history of the time.

Ezekiel, SECOND Isaiah, Joel and Obadiah. Texts from the book of Amos which allude to the prophets are as follows: Amos 1.2 = Joel 1.10, 20; Amos 1.10 = Ezek. 26.2, 9-10, 12; Amos 1.11-12 = Obad. 9-10, 12; Amos 2.4bA = Jer. 6.19bB; Isa. 5.24; Amos 2.4bB = Hos. 7.13; 12.2; Isa. 28.15, 17; Jer. 2.5; Amos 2.9 = Ezek. 17.1-13abA, 15-18; Amos 4.7, 8b = Jer. 3.1, 3, 22; Amos 4.9 = Joel 1.4, 7, 11, 12; Amos 4.10 = Joel 2.20; Amos 5.13b = Mic. 2.3bB; Amos 5.16-17 = Mic. 1.8; 2.4; Jer. 5.1; 6.26; Hos. 10.5-6; Amos 5.26 = Jer. 7; 44; Amos 6.14a = Jer. 5.15a; Amos 7.16bB, 17aB = Mic. 2.5-6; Amos 9.11 = Isa. 1.8; Amos 9.13-15 = Isa. 5.1-2, 4-5.

CONCLUSION

It is widely assumed that tragedy as a literary form is not to be found within the literary repertory of ancient Israel, and the reasons for this proposition are traced to the fundamental differences in spirit between the Greek and Hebraic traditions. The discovery of a continuous written prophetic text with a tragic form has reopened this issue and has made it necessary to move beyond the well-established questions asked of the text. A new paradigm for understanding prophecy has emerged that permits a fresh inquiry into the roles and contributions of the biblical prophets.

The tragic poetry of Amos corresponds to other biblical texts in which we encounter the sufferings of Jeremiah, the despair of Job, the rejection and suicide of Saul, David's anguish over the death of his rebellious son Absalom, and the broken-hearted figure of the king as a feeble old man. These calamitous situations are present in literary texts which do not have a tragic form but rather a tragic vision.[1]

Since ancient texts were meant to be heard, stories such as these were presented orally.[2] However, Amos's tragedy was not simply read aloud: it was composed to be dramatically performed before an audience. The literary evidence is the recurring direct addresses, the constant shifts in person, the different personae the prophet assumes, the presence of characters who talk to one another, and the instances of invocation. All these elements assimilate the written poetry to the genre of the spoken word and

---

1.   W. Lee Humphreys, *The Tragic Vision and the Hebrew Tradition* (Philadelphia: Fortress Press, 1985); J. Cheryl Exum, *Tragedy and Biblical Narrative* (Cambridge, MA: Harvard University Press, 1992).

2.   Rosalind Thomas (*Oral Tradition and Written Record in Classical Athens* [Cambridge: Cambridge University Press, 1989], pp. 2-64, 93) stresses that Greek society 'heard most of its literature' down to the late fifth and early fourth centuries (p. 3). Similarly, Edgar Conrad ('Heard But Not Seen: The Representation of 'Books' in the Old Testament', *JSOT* 54 [1992], pp. 45-59) observes that the written works of the Bible 'were written to be read aloud', and that they can only be 'remembered' by an audience who hears, for example, the books of Isaiah and Jeremiah, read aloud.

point to some kind of dramatic presentation. Comparison with the early Greek performing artists suggests that Amos recited his elegiac poetry with a certain incantatory quality, declaiming it with some gesture, impersonation and variation in tone, tempo and dynamic. Amos was a tragic poet, but not every prophet was a tragic poet. There are tragic elements in the poetry of Micah and Jeremiah, but these prophets reversed Amos's dramatic form or his prediction of the fall of Judah and Jerusalem by offering alternative dramatizations of deliverance in which the people weep, confess their sins and return to God.

The performing prophets were Isaiah, Amos, Hosea, Micah and Jeremiah. Isaiah was a singer of solo song or lyric monody, and is comparable to Sappho and Alcaeus. Amos composed an elegy with reported conversation that resembles the poetry of Archilochus. Hosea represents the beginning of religious drama in Jerusalem by developing characterization and combining narrative exposition with dialogue and soliloquy. Micah wrote a drama pitting different voices against one another, and he anticipates the development of early Greek drama. Jeremiah composed an intricate text with many rival voices or dramatic parts, including God, the prophet and the people, and his great choral ode is analogous to the choral lyrics of Alcman.

The prophets after Jeremiah were orators: Nahum, Habbakuk, Zephaniah, Ezekiel, Joel and Obadiah. In contrast to the performing poets who reached their public indirectly through dramatic presentation, the orators delivered direct discourses to their audiences and expected unity of response. There are many different genres in prophetic literature, and 'the basis of their distinction appears to be the radical of presentation'.[3] Are they words acted out before an audience, or are they spoken directly to a listener? Are they sung or recited, or are they written for a reader? All these questions must be asked if we hope to uncover the distinctions of acted, spoken and written word in prophetic literature.

Though there is a lack of evidence for the oral transmission of Amos's prophecy, there is evidence for its written transmission. So, for example, Amos's poetic text was clearly available to Micah because he followed its narrative order, called to mind its various scenes, quoted from it and alluded to its themes and images. Micah recognized the cycle's tragic form but gave his own text the dramatic form of a comedy. Similarly, the editor of Amos destroyed the tragic structure of each poem and composed the

---

3. On 'Theory of Genres', see Frye, *Anatomy of Criticism*, pp. 243-337 (246-51).

book on the pattern of a comedy. History confirmed the truth of Amos's prophecy, but his later reviser and historian, in imitation of Micah and Jeremiah, tempered Amos's words with a comic vision of deliverance and restoration.

The old idea that Amos delivered numerous independent oracles over his long career has led to the inevitable conclusion that their different historical settings have been lost in the process of gathering and organizing the oracles into a book.[4] However, the evidence of a single prophetic text has made it possible to reopen the question of the social setting of Amos's prophetic activity. Each poem presents some detail about the *marzeah*, and so by following the progression of the plot, it is possible to reconstruct the specific elements of a typical Judaean symposium. Both the internal and the external evidence leave little room for doubt about the social function of the cycle: Amos composed and recited his poetry as a kind of dramatic parody of the typical symposium or *marzeah* of his day.

Amos argues that a great all-night *marzeah* is the occasion that will mark the arrival of God's day. He presents the dirge and the dreadful news that songs of merriment will be turned into lamentation for the dead. The celebrants' anticipation of the dawn will be frustrated when night does not turn into day, the land becomes dark and the sun sets on the noontide of their expectations. Amos alludes to festal observances or seasonal celebrations—Passover, the sabbath, the new moon, the barley harvest in spring and the first fruits of autumn. The imagery of light and darkness is prominent in Amos's poetry and suggests that the *marzeah* was associated with some great feast concerned with Yahweh's power over light and darkness.

The day of Yahweh sums up the content of the book of Amos. Different aspects of God's day can be traced throughout Amos's text and its recurring imagery combines everything the prophet wanted to say about God's day of festival, battle and lamentation. His editor recognized the synthesis and composed a text that dealt with the festal, martial and lamentation aspects of his prophecy. Amos composed in dirge-form, but the author of the book composed in typical hymnic style. The hymnic elements correspond to the mood of the *marzeah* and the festivals with their praise of Yahweh. But the editor took issue with Amos's day of darkness and doom, stressed that Yahweh controlled the darkness and the light, and insisted, in opposition to the prophet, that God continually turns

---

4. Andersen and Freedman, *Amos*, pp. 10-11; Thomas W. Overholt, 'Prophecy in History: The Social Reality of Intermediation', *JSOT* 48 (1990), pp. 3-29 (7).

night into day and assures his people's survival.

The idea of Amos as a performing poet corresponds to the scholarly belief that prophets made their words more impressive by performing dramatic actions to accompany their oracles. The belief is based on evidence in both the prophetic and the historical books, which speak of prophets performing actions to support and clarify their messages. So Ahijah tears his cloak into twelve pieces, or Isaiah walks around naked, or Jeremiah breaks a pot.[5] While it has become customary for commentators to talk in terms of separate prophetic words and actions, the present study has talked about continuous words and continuous acts. The reviser of Amos, in contrast to the editors of other prophetic books, does not talk about Amos performing strange or distasteful dramatic actions, but does talk about his performance and draws special attention to it by including the reaction of the audience (7.10b). However, the book deliberately converts the immediacy of the performance into biography and history.

No poetic performing texts of women prophets have survived, but the tradition of women prophets can be traced from Huldah to Deborah and especially to Miriam, who sings and performs a dance with timbrels in company with other women. This familiar biblical scene of a female chorus, celebrating some victory with songs and dances and musical instruments, is analogous to the choruses of dancing women who sang the Greek choral poetry of Alcman and Corinna.

The Hebrew prophets claimed that their thoughts and words never came from themselves but that Yahweh their Muse had spoken to them. Similarly, when the Greek poets claimed that the Muses spoke to them or through them, they affirmed the presence of a divine spirit at work in them. In this idea of inspiration there resides an eternal truth, for visionary prophets and poets of all ages are aware that they do not speak in their own name or for their own purposes. The idea of the prophet as an inspired person has led to the naive view that the prophets were mere mouthpieces of Yahweh, proclaiming their revelations in an ecstatic state with very little reflection or thought. This popular perception of prophetic inspiration corresponds to the commonplace view of the inspiration of a creative poet whose ideas, it seems, come like flashes of lightning and who composes poetry in a state of frenzy without conscious consideration, the

---

5. More than forty examples of prophetic actions in the biblical tradition have been examined by David Stacey, *Prophetic Drama in the Old Testament* (London: Epworth Press, 1990).

hand guided by a divine power.[6] Whoever has become acquainted with the process of creativity knows that this image is false. Much practice, much contemplation and much technical ability are necessary to bring a good poem into existence, and similarly, it took much reflection, wisdom, talent and sharp judgment for the prophets of old to challenge what was readily acceptable in their cultural surroundings. Divine inspiration came suddenly upon Hebrew and Greek poets alike, but it fell upon individuals, such as Amos and Solon, who had mastered the technique of poetry, who challenged accepted authority and whose honest social criticism disturbed and shocked their audiences.[7]

The Hebrew prophets were also inspired by one another and by the intellectual, imaginative and emotional life of earlier prophets. They did not sit down with pens and writing boards and write their poetry in a special act of creation *ex nihilo*. They composed poems, in the way human beings always create poetry, in relation to other poems or in imitation of the great themes, images and symbols that were passed on to them by tradition. The prophets conversed with one another, either by direct quotation or by allusion, and they corrected or updated old prophecies in the light of new historical, intellectual and cultural experience. Drawing on the immediate and the relatively distant past, creatively and not slavishly, they conspired to construct a prophetic tradition. The analogy for the development of the prophetic tradition is the vast poetical and musical dialogue that flourished among the archaic poets of the Greek world. The poetic dialogue of the Hebrew prophets was contemporaneous with Greek poetic dialogue, and the two traditions developed into a great heritage of literature that made the same transition from song culture to book culture.

6.   This idea of prophetic and poetic inspiration is detailed by Lindblom, *Prophecy in Ancient Israel*, pp. 1-6.

7.   On the distinction between sacred and secular inspiration, see Gerardus van der Leeuw, *Sacred and Profane Beauty: The Holy in Art* (trans. David E. Green; New York: Holt, Rinehart and Winston, 1963), pp. 145, 149; Frye, *Words with Power*, pp. 53-56; *Anatomy of Criticism*, pp. 95-98.

BIBLIOGRAPHY

Ackerman, Susan, 'A *Marzeaḥ* in Ezekiel 8.7-13', *HTR* 82 (1989), pp. 267-81.

—'Isaiah', in Carol A. Newsom and Sharon H. Ringe (eds.), *The Women's Bible Commentary* (London: SPCK, 1992), pp. 161-68.

Ackroyd, Peter R., 'A Judgment Narrative Between Kings and Chronicles? An Approach to Amos 7.9-17', in George W. Coats and Burke O. Long (eds.), *Canon and Authority: Essays in Old Testament Religion and Theology* (Philadelphia: Fortress Press, 1977), pp. 71-87.

Aeschylus, The Persians, in David Grene and Richmond Lattimore (eds.), *The Complete Greek Tragedies: Aeschylus II* (trans. Seth G. Benardete; Chicago: University of Chicago Press, 1956), pp. 43-86.

Allsopp, F.W., *Weep, O Daughter of Zion: A Study of the City-Lament Genre in the Hebrew Bible* (BibOr, 44; Rome: Editrice Pontificio Istituto Biblico, 1993).

Alster, Bendt, 'Interaction of Oral and Written Poetry in Early Mesopotamian Literature', in Vogelzang and Vanstiphout (eds.), *Mesopotamian Epic Literature* pp. 23-69.

Amsler, Samuel, 'La parole visionnaire des prophètes', *VT* 31 (1981), pp. 359-62.

Andersen, Francis I., and David Noel Freedman, *Hosea: A New Translation with Introduction and Commentary* (AB; Garden City, NY: Doubleday, 1980).

—*Amos: A New Translation with Introduction and Commentary* (AB; Garden City, NY: Doubleday, 1989).

Aristotle, De Poetica (Poetics), in Richard McKeon (ed.), *The Basic Works of Aristotle* (New York: Random House, 1941), pp. 1453-87.

Asen, Bernard A., 'No, Yes and Perhaps in Amos and the Yahwist', *VT* 43 (1993), pp. 433-41.

Auld, A. Graeme, *Amos* (OTG; Sheffield: *JSOT* Press, 1986).

—'Amos and Apocalyptic: Vision, Prophecy, Revelation', in Daniele Garrone and Felice Israel (eds.), *Storia e Tradizioni di Israele: Scritti in onore de J. Alberto Soggin* (Brescia: Paideia, 1991), pp. 1-13.

Aune, David E., *The New Testament in its Literary Environment* (Philadelphia: Westminster Press, 1987).

Avery, Catherine B. (ed.), *The New Century Classical Handbook* (New York: Appleton-Century-Crofts, 1962).

Avigad, N., and J.C. Greenfield, 'A Bronze *phialē* with a Phoenician Dedicatory Inscription', *IEJ* 32 (1982), pp. 118-28.

Baltzer, Klaus, *Die Biographie der Propheten* (Neukirchen–Vluyn: Neukirchener Verlag, 1975).

—'Bild und Wort: Erwägungen zu der Vision des Amos in Am 7.7-9', in Walter Gross, Hubert Irsigler and Theodor Seidl (eds.), *Texte, Methode und Grammatik: Wolfgang Richter zum 65. Geburtstag* (St Ottilien: EOS, 1991), pp. 11-16.

Barker, Andrew (ed.), *Greek Musical Writings*. I. *The Musician and his Art* (Cambridge: Cambridge University Press, 1984).

Barnet, Sylvan, Morton Berman and William Burto (eds.), *Eight Great Tragedies* (New York: Mentor Books, 1985).

Barnett, Richard D., 'Assurbanipal's Feast', *Eretz Israel* 18 (1985), pp. 1*-6*.

Barré, M.L., 'Amos 1.11 Reconsidered', *CBQ* 47 (1985), pp. 420-27.

Barron, J.P. , and P.E. Easterling, 'Elegy and Iambus', in P.E. Easterling and B.M.W. Knox (eds.), *The Cambridge History of Classical Literature*. I/Part 1. *Early Greek Poetry* (Cambridge: Cambridge University Press, 1989), pp. 76-95.

Barstad, Hans M., *The Religious Polemics of Amos: Studies in the Preaching of Am 2,7b-8; 4,1-13; 5,1-27; 6,4-7; 8,14* (Leiden: E.J. Brill, 1984).

Barton, John, *Amos's Oracles against the Nations: A Study of Amos 1.3–2.5* (SOTSMS, 6; Cambridge: Cambridge University Press, 1980).

Beach, Eleanor Ferris, 'The Samaria Ivories, *Marzeaḥ* and Biblical Texts', *BA* 55 (1992), pp. 130-39.

Ben Zvi, Ehud, 'Studying Prophetic Texts against their Original Backgrounds: Pre-Ordained Scripts and Alternative Horizons of Research', in Stephen Breck Reid (ed.), *Prophets and Paradigms: Essays in Honor of Gene M. Tucker* (*JSOT*Sup, 29; Sheffield: Sheffield Academic Press, 1996), pp. 125-35.

—'Twelve Prophetic Books or "The Twelve": A Few Preliminary Considerations', in Watts and House (eds.), *Forming Prophetic Literature* pp. 125-56.

—Wrongdoers, Wrongdoing and Righting Wrongs in Micah 2', *BibInt* 7 (1999), pp. 87-100.

Bentzen, A., 'The Ritual Background of Amos i 2–ii 16', *OTS* 8 (1950), pp. 85-99.

Berlin, Adele, *Zephaniah* (AB, 25A; Garden City, NY: Doubleday, 1994).

Beye, Charles Rowan, *Ancient Greek Literature and Society* (Ithaca, NY, and London: Cornell University Press, 2nd rev. edn, 1975).

Biddle, Mark E., *Polyphony and Symphony in Prophetic Literature* (Macon, GA: Mercer University Press, 1996).

Bleek, Friedrich, *Einleitung in das alte Testament* (ed. Julius Wellhausen; Berlin: Reimer, 5th edn, 1886).

Blenkinsopp, Joseph, 'The Prophetic Reproach', *JBL* 90 (1971), pp. 267-78.

—*A History of Prophecy in Israel* (Philadelphia: Westminster Press, 1983).

Bon, Eberhard, 'Das Denotat von כזביהם 'ihre Lügen' in Judaspruch Am 2,4-5', *ZAW* 106 (1996), pp. 201-13.

Bosshard, Erich, 'Beobachtungen zum Zwölfprophetenbuch', *BN* 40 (1987), pp. 30-62.

Bowie, Ewen L., 'Early Greek Elegy, Symposium and Public Festival', *JHS* 106 (1986), pp. 13-25 (16).

—'Thinking with Drinking: Wine and the Symposium in Aristophanes', *JHS* 117 (1997), pp. 1-21.

Bowra, C.M., *Landmarks in Greek Literature* (Cleveland, OH: The World Publishing Company, 1969).

Boyle, Marjorie O'Rourke, 'The Covenant Lawsuit of the Prophet Amos: III 1–IV 13', *VT* 21 (1971), pp. 338-62.

Bright, John, 'A New View of Amos', *Int* 25 (1971), pp. 355-58.

Brueggemann, Walter, 'Amos IV 4-13 and Israel's Covenant Worship', *VT* 15 (1965), pp. 1-15.

—'Amos' Intercessory Formula', *VT* 19 (1969), pp. 386-99.

—'The "Uncared For" Now Cared For (Jer 30.12-17): A Methodological Consideration', *JBL* 104 (1985), pp. 419-28.

Brunet, Gilbert, 'La vision de l'étain: réinterpretation d'Amos VII 7-9', *VT* 16 (1966), pp. 387-95.

Burkert, Walter, *The Orientalizing Revolution: Near Eastern Influence on Greek Culture in the Early Archaic Age* (Cambridge, MA: Harvard University Press, 1992).

Campbell, David A. (ed. and trans.), *Greek Lyric*, I (Loeb Classical Library; Cambridge, MA.: Harvard University Press, 1982).

—*Greek Lyric*, II (LCL; Cambridge, MA: Harvard University Press, 1988).

Campbell, Edward F., 'Archaeological Reflections on Amos's Targets', in Michael D. Coogan, J. Cheryl Exum and Lawrence E. Stager (eds.), *Scripture and Other Artifacts: Essays on the Bible and Archaeology in Honor of Philip J. King* (Louisville, KY: Westminster/ John Knox Press, 1994), pp. 32-52.

Carroll, R. Mark Daniel, *Contexts for Amos: Prophetic Poetics in Latin American Perspective* (*JSOT*Sup, 132; Sheffield: Sheffield Academic Press, 1992).

Carroll, Robert P. , 'Night without Vision: Micah and the Prophets', in F. Garcia Martinez, A. Hilhorst and C.J. Labuschagne (eds.), *The Scriptures and the Scrolls: Studies in Honour of A.S. van der Woude on the Occasion of his 65th Birthday* (Leiden: E.J. Brill, 1992), pp. 74-84.

Carter, Jane B., 'Thiasos and *Marzeah*: Ancestor Cult in the Age of Homer', in Susan Langdon (ed.), *New Light on a Dark Age: Exploring the Culture of Geometric Greece* (Columbia, MO: University of Missouri Press, 1997), pp. 72-112.

Cassuto, Umberto, 'The Second Chapter of the Book of Hosea' (1927), in Umberto Cassuto (ed.), *Biblical and Oriental Studies*, I (trans. Israel Abrahams; Publications of the Perry Foundation for Biblical Research in the Hebrew University of Jerusalem; Jerusalem: Magnes Press, Hebrew University, 1973), pp. 101-40.

Cazelles, Henri, 'La Guerre Syro-Ephraïmite dans le Contexte de la Politique Internationale', in Garrone and Israel (eds.), *Storia e Tradizioni di Israele*, pp. 31-48.

Christensen, Duane L., *Transformations of the War Oracle in Old Testament Prophecy: Studies in the Oracles against the Nations* (Missoula, MT: Scholars Press, 1975).

—'The Book of Nahum: A History of Interpretation', in Watts and House (eds.), *Forming Prophetic Literature*, pp. 187-94.

—'The Book of Nahum as a Liturgical Composition: A Prosodic Analysis', *JETS* 32 (1989), pp. 159-69.

Clements, Ronald E., Prophecy and Covenant (SBT, 43; London: SCM Press, 1965).

—*A Century of Old Testament Study* (Guildford and London: Lutterworth Press, 1976).

—Amos and the Politics of Israel', in Garrone and Israel (eds.), *Storia e Tradizioni di Israele*, pp. 49-64.

Clifford, R.J., 'The Use of Hôy in the Prophets', *CBQ* 28 (1966), pp. 458-64.

Clines, David J.A., 'Metacommentating Amos', in Heather A. McKay and David J.A. Clines (eds.), *Of Prophets' Visions and the Wisdom of Sages: Essays in Honour of R. Norman Whybray on his Seventieth Birthday* (*JSOT*Sup, 162; Sheffield: Sheffield Academic Press, 1993), pp. 142-60.

Cogan, M. ' "Ripping open Pregnant Women" in Light of an Assyrian Analogue', *JAOS* 103 (1983), pp. 755-57.

Conrad, Edgar, 'Heard But Not Seen: The Representation of "Books" in the Old Testament', *JSOT* 54 (1992), pp. 45-59.

Coogan, Michael David (ed.), *Stories from Ancient Canaan* (Philadelphia: Westminster Press, 1978).

Cooper, Alan, 'The Absurdity of Amos 6.12a', *JBL* 107 (1988), pp. 725-27.

Cooper, Frederick and Sarah Morris, 'Dining in Round Buildings', in Oswyn Murray (ed.), *Sympotica: A Symposium on the Symposion* (Oxford: Clarendon Press, 1990), pp. 65-85.

Coote, Robert B., 'Amos 1.11: RḤMYW', *JBL* 90 (1971), pp. 206-208.

—*Amos Among the Prophets: Composition and Theology* (Philadelphia: Fortress Press, 1981).

Corbett, John H., 'Thither Came Phoenicians: The Greeks and the Phoenicians from Homer to Alexander', *Scripta Mediterranea* 3 (1982), pp. 72-92.

Coulot, Claude, 'Propositions pour une structuration du livre d'Amos au niveau rédactionnel', *RSR* 51 (1977), pp. 169-86.

Craigie, Peter C., *The Book of Deuteronomy* (NICOT; Grand Rapids: William B. Eerdmans, 1976).

—'Amos the noqed in the light of Ugaritic', *SR* 11 (1982), pp. 29-32.

—*Ugarit and the Old Testament* (Grand Rapids: William B. Eerdmans, 1983).

Crenshaw, James L., 'The Influence of the Wise upon Amos: The 'Doxologies of Amos' and Job **5**, 9-16; **9**, 5-10', *ZAW* 79 (1967), pp. 42-52.

—*Prophetic Conflict: Its Effect upon Israelite Religion* (BZAW, 124; Berlin: Walter de Gruyter, 1971).

—*Hymnic Affirmation of Divine Justice: The Doxologies of Amos and Related Texts in the Old Testament* (ed. Howard C. Kee and Douglas A. Knight; SBLDS, 24; Missoula, MT: Scholars Press, 1975).

Cross, Frank Moore, 'The Themes of the Book of Kings and the Structure of the Deuteronomistic History', in Frank Moore Cross (ed.), *Canaanite Myth and Hebrew Epic: Essays in the History of the Religion of Israel* (Cambridge MT: Harvard University Press, 1973), pp. 274-89.

—'A Phoenician Inscription from Idalion: Some Old and New Texts Relating to Child Sacrifice', in Coogan, Exum and Stager (eds.), *Scripture and Other Artifacts*, pp. 93-107.

Dahood, Mitchell, 'To Pawn One's Cloak', *Bib* 42 (1961), pp. 359-66.

Davies, Graham I., *Ancient Hebrew Inscriptions: Corpus and Concordance* (Cambridge: Cambridge University Press, 1991).

Davies, Philip R., 'The Audiences of Prophetic Scrolls: Some Suggestions', in Reid (ed.), *Prophets and Paradigms*, pp. 48-62.

Day, J., *Molech: A God of Human Sacrifice in the Old Testament* (University of Cambridge Oriental Publications, 41; Cambridge: Cambridge University Press, 1989).

Day, Peggy, 'From the Child is Born the Woman: The Story of Jephthah's Daughter', in Peggy Day (ed.), *Gender and Difference in Ancient Israel* (Minneapolis: Fortress Press, 1989), pp. 58-74.

Dell, Katharine J., 'The Misuse of Forms in Amos', *VT* 45 (1995), pp. 45-61.

Dempster, Stephen, 'The Lord is His Name: A Study of the Distribution of the Names and Titles of God in the Book of Amos', *RB* 98 (1991), pp. 170-89.

DeRoche, Michael, 'Zephaniah I 2-3: The "Sweeping" of Creation', *VT* 30 (1980), pp. 104-109.

Dever, William G., 'A Case-Study in Biblical Archaeology: The Earthquake of ca. 760 BCE', *Eretz Israel* 23 (1992), pp. 27-35.

Dicou, Bert, *Edom, Israel's Brother and Antagonist: The Role of Edom in Biblical Prophecy and Story* (JSOTSup, 169; Sheffield: Sheffield Academic Press, 1994).

Dines, Jennifer, 'Reading the Book of Amos', *ScrB* 16 (1986), pp. 26-32.

Dobbs-Allsopp, F.W., *Weep, O Daughter of Zion: A Study of the City-Lament Genre in the Hebrew Bible* (BibOr, 44; Rome: Editrice Pontificio Istituto Biblico, 1993).

Dorsey, David A., 'Literary Architecture and Aural Structuring Techniques in Amos', *Bib* 73 (1992), pp. 305-30.

Dover, Kenneth James (ed.), *Ancient Greek Literature* (Oxford: Oxford University Press, 1980).

Driver, Samuel Rolles, *The Books of Joel and Amos with Introduction and Notes* (Cambridge Bible for Schools and Colleges; Cambridge: Cambridge University Press, 1898).

—*An Introduction to the Literature of the Old Testament* (Edinburgh: T. & T. Clark; 9th edn, 1913) First edition 1891.

Duhm, Bernhard, *Die Zwölf Propheten* (Tübingen: J.C.B. Mohr, 1910).

—'Amos und seine Schrift', in Heinrich Weinel (ed.), *Israels Propheten* (Tübingen: J.C.B. Mohr, 2nd edn, 1922), pp. 89-98.

Easterling, P. E., and B.M.W. Knox (eds.), *The Cambridge History of Classical Literature*. I/Part 1. *Early Greek Poetry* (Cambridge: Cambridge University Press, 1989).

Edmonds, J.M. (ed. and trans.), *Greek Elegy and Iambus*, I (LCL; Cambridge, MA: Harvard University Press, 1931).

—*Greek Elegy and Iambus*, II (LCL; Cambridge, MA: Harvard University Press, 1931).

Eissfeldt, Otto, 'Amos und Jona in volkstümlicher Überlieferung', in Rudolf Seeheim and Fritz Maass (eds.), *Kleine Schriften*, IV (Tübingen: J.C.B. Mohr, 1968), pp. 137-42.

Eslinger, Lyle, 'The Education of Amos', *HAR* 11 (1987), pp. 35-57.

Evelyn-White, Hugh G. (trans.), *Hesiod: The Homeric Hymns and Homerica* (LCL; Cambridge, MA: Harvard University Press, rev. edn, 1936 [1914]).

Exum, J. Cheryl, *Tragedy and Biblical Narrative* (Cambridge, MA: Harvard University Press, 1992).

Fairweather, J.A. 'Fiction in the Biographies of Ancient Writers', *Ancient Society* 5 (1974), pp. 231-75.

Fensham, F.C., 'The Treaty Between the Israelites and Tyrians', VTSup (1969), pp. 71-87.

Fields, Weston W., 'The Motif 'Night as Danger' Associated with Three Biblical Destruction Narratives', in Michael Fishbane and Emanuel Tov (eds.), *Sha'arei Talmon: Studies in the Bible, Qumran, and the Ancient Near East Presented to Shemaryahu Talmon* (Winona Lake, IN: Eisenbrauns, 1992), pp. 17-32.

Fishbane, Michael, 'The Treaty Background of Amos l, ll and Related Matters', *JBL* 89 (1970), pp. 313-18.

—'Additional Remarks on RḤMYW (Amos 1.11)', *JBL* 91 (1972),
pp. 391-93.

—*Biblical Interpretation in Ancient Israel* (Oxford: Clarendon Press, 1985).

Fosbroke, H.E.W., and S. Lovett, 'The Book of Amos: Introduction and Exegesis', IB, VI, pp. 761-853.

Fränkel, Hermann, *Early Greek Poetry and Philosophy: A History of Greek Epic, Lyric and Prose to the Middle of the Fifth Century* (trans. Moses Hadas and James Willis; Oxford: Basil Blackwell, 1975).

Freedman, David Noel, 'Confrontations in the Book of Amos', Princeton Seminary Bulletin 11 (1990), pp. 240-52.

Freedman, David Noel, and Andrew Welch, 'Amos's Earthquake and Israelite Prophecy', in CooganExum and Stager (eds.), *Scripture and Other Artifacts*, pp. 188-97.

Fritz, Volkmar, 'Die Fremdvölkersprüche des Amos', *VT* 37 (1987), pp. 26-38.

—'Amosbuch, Amos-Schule und historischer Amos', in Fritz, Pohlmann and Schmitt (eds.), *Prophet und Prophetenbuch* pp. 29-43.

Fritz, Volkmar, Karl-Friedrich Pohlmann and Hans-Christoph Schmitt (eds.) *Prophet und Prophetenbuch: Festschrift für Otto Kaiser zum 65. Geburtstag* (BZAW, 185; Berlin: Walter de Gruyter, 1989).

Frye, Northrop, *Anatomy of Criticism: Four Essays* (Princeton: Princeton University Press, 1957).

—*Fables of Identity: Studies in Poetic Mythology* (New York: Harcourt, Brace & World, 1963).

—*A Natural Perspective: The Development of Shakespearean Comedy and Romance* (New York: Columbia University Press, 1965).

—*The Great Code: The Bible and Literature* (Toronto: Academic Press, 1982).

—*Words with Power: Being a Second Study of the Bible and Literature* (New York: Viking Penguin, 1990).

Fuhs, Hans F., 'Amos 1,1: Erwägungen zur Tradition und Redaction des Amosbuches', in H.-J. Fabry (ed.), *Bausteine biblischer Theologie (Festgabe G.J. Bötterweck)* (BBB, 50; Bonn: Peter Hanstein, 1977), pp. 271-89.

Gaster, Theodor H., 'An Ancient Hymn in the Prophecies of Amos', *Journal of the Manchester Egyptian and Oriental Society* 19 (1935), pp. 23-26.

Gerber, Douglas E. (ed.), *Greek Iambic Poetry* (LCL; Cambridge, MA: Harvard University Press, 1999).

Gerstenberger, E., 'The Woe Oracles of the Prophets', *JBL* 81 (1962), pp. 249-63.

Gese, Hartmut, 'Kleine Beiträge zum Verständnis des Amosbuches', *VT* 12 (1962), pp. 415-38.

—'Das Problem von Amos 9,7', in Antonius H.J. Gunneweg and Otto Kaiser (eds.), *Textgemäß: Aufsätze und Beiträge zur Hermeneutik des Alten Testaments: Festschrift für Ernst Würthwein zum 70 Geburtstag*; (Göttingen: Vandenhoeck & Ruprecht, 1979), pp. 33-38.

—'Komposition bei Amos', VTSup 32 (1981), pp. 74-95.

—'Amos 8.4-8: Der kosmische Frevel händlerischer Habiger', in Fritz, Pohlmann and Schmitt (eds.), *Prophet und Prophetenbuch*, pp. 59-72.

Gevirtz, Stanley, 'A New Look at an Old Crux: Amos 5, 26', *JBL* 87 (1968), pp. 267-76.

—'"Formative" 'ayin in Biblical Hebrew', *Eretz Israel* 16 (1982), pp. 57*-66*.

Gillingham, Susan, '"Who Makes the Morning Darkness": God and Creation in the Book of Amos', *SJT* 45 (1992), pp. 165-84.

Gitay, Yehoshua, 'A Study of Amos's Art of Speech: A Rhetorical Analysis of Amos 3.1-15', *CBQ* 42 (1980), pp. 293-309.

—'Amos', in Mercia Eliade and Charles J. Adams (eds.), *The Encyclopedia of Religion*, I (New York: MacMillan Publishing Co., 1987), pp. 240-43.

Glanzman, George S., 'Two Notes: Am 3,15 and Os 11, 8-9', *CBQ* 23 (1961), pp. 227-33.

Good, E.M., 'The Composition of Hosea', *SEÅ* 21 (1966), pp. 21-63.

Good, R.M., 'The Just War in Ancient Israel', *JBL* 104 (1985), pp. 385-400.

Gordis, Robert, 'The Composition and Structure of Amos', *HTR* 33 (1940), pp. 239-51.

—'Amos, Edom and Israel—An Unrecognized Source for Edomite History', in Abraham I. Katsch and Leon Nemoy (eds.), *Essays on the Occasion of the Seventieth Anniversary of the Dropsie University* (Philadelphia: Dropsie University, 1979), pp. 109-32.

Gordon, Cyrus H., 'Homer and the Bible', *HUCA* 26 (1955), pp. 43-100.

—*The Common Background of Greek and Hebrew Civilizations* (New York: W.W. Norton, 2nd edn, 1965).

Gottwald, Norman K., *All the Kingdoms of the Earth: Israelite Prophecy and International Relations in the Ancient Near East* (New York: Harper & Row, 1964).

—'Tragedy and Comedy in the Latter Prophets', *Semeia* 32 (1984), pp. 83-96.

—'Ideology and Ideologies in Israelite Prophecy', in Stephen Breck Reid (ed.), *Prophets and Paradigms*, pp. 136-49.

Green, Margaret W., 'The Eridu Lament', *JCS* 30 (1978), pp. 127-67.

Greenberg, Moshe, *Ezekiel 1–20: A New Translation with Introduction and Commentary* (AB, 22; Garden City, NY: Doubleday, 1983).

Greenfield, Jonas C., 'The *Marzeah* as a Social Institution', in J. Harmatta and G. Komoroczy (eds.), *Wirtschaft und Gesellschaft im Alten Vorderasien* (Budapest: Akadémiai Kliado, 1976), pp. 451-55.

Grene, David, and Richmond Lattimore (eds.), *The Complete Greek Tragedies: Aeschylus II* (trans. Seth G. Bernadete; Chicago: University of Chicago Press, 1956).

Gross, Walter, 'Lying Prophet and Disobedient Man of God in 1 Kgs 13: Role Analysis as an Instrument of Theological Interpretation of an Old Testament Narrative Text', *Semeia* 15 (1979), pp. 97-135.

Gunkel, Hermann, 'The Israelite Prophecy from the Time of Amos', in J. Pelikan (ed.), *Twentieth Century Theology in the Making*. I. *Themes of Biblical Theology* (trans. R.A. Wilson; New York: Harper and Row, 1969), pp. 48-75.

—*The Folktale in the Old Testament* (trans. M.D. Rutter; Sheffield: Sheffield Academic Press, 1987).

Gunneweg, Antonius H.J., 'Die Prophetenlegende I Reg 13: Missdeutung, Umdeutung, Bedeutung', in Fritz, Pohlmann and Schmitt (eds.), *Prophet und Prophetenbuch* pp. 73-81.

Halpern, Baruch, *The First Historians: The Hebrew Bible and History* (San Francisco: Harper & Row, 1988).

Halpern, Baruch, and J.D. Levinson (eds.), *Traditions in Transformation* (Winona Lake: Eisenbrauns, 1981).

Hammershaimb, Erling, *The Book of Amos: A Commentary* (Oxford: Basil Blackwell, 1970).

Haran, Menahem, 'The Graded Numerical Sequence and the Phenomenon of 'Automatism' in Biblical Poetry', VTSup 22 (1972), pp. 238-67.

Harper, William Rainey, *A Critical and Exegetical Commentary on Amos and Hosea* (ICC, 18; Edinburgh: T. & T. Clark, 1905).

Hasel, Gerhard F., *Understanding the Book of Amos: Basic Issues in Current Interpretations* (Grand Rapids, MI: Baker Book House, 1991).

Hayes, John H., *Amos The Eighth Century Prophet: His Times and His Preaching* (Nashville: Abingdon Press, 1988).

Heider, George C., *The Cult of Molek: A Reassessment* (*JSOT*Sup, 43; Sheffield: *JSOT* Press, 1985).

Herington, John, *Poetry into Drama: Early Tragedy and the Greek Poetic Tradition* (Sather Classical Lectures, 49; Berkeley: University of California Press, 1985).

Heyns, Dalene, 'Space and Time in Amos 7: Reconsidering the Third Vision', Old Testament Essays (1997), pp. 27-38.

Hillers, Delbert R., *Micah: A Commentary on the Book of the Prophet Micah* (Hermeneia; Philadelphia: Fortress Press, 1984).

Hoffmann, Yair, 'The Day of the Lord as a Concept and a Term in the Prophetic Literature', *ZAW* 93 (1981), pp. 37-50.

Hoffmeier, James K., 'Once Again the "Plumb Line" Vision of Amos 7.7-9: An Interpretive Clue from Egypt?', in Meir Lubetski, Claire Gottlieb and Sharon Keller (eds.), *Boundaries of the Ancient Near Eastern World: A Tribute to Cyrus H. Gordon* (*JSOT*Sup, 273; Sheffield: Sheffield Academic Press, 1998), pp. 304-19.

Holladay, William L., *The Root sûbh in the Old Testament, with Particular Reference to its Usages in Covenantal Contexts* (Leiden: E.J. Brill, 1958).

—*Isaiah: Scroll of a Prophetic Heritage* (New York: Pilgrim Press, 1978)

—'Jeremiah the Prophet', *IDBSup* (1978), pp. 470-72.

—*Jeremiah I. A Commentary on the Book of the Prophet Jeremiah*, Chapters 1–25 (Hermeneia; Philadelphia: Fortress Press, 1986).

—'Amos VI 1bβ: A Suggested Solution', *VT* 22 (1972), pp. 107-10.

House, Paul R., *Zephaniah: A Prophetic Drama* (*JSOT*Sup, 69; Sheffield: Almond Press, 1988).

—*The Unity of the Twelve* (*JSOT*Sup, 97; Sheffield: Almond Press, 1990).

—'Dramatic Coherence in Nahum, Habbakuk, and Zephaniah', in Watts and House (eds.), *Forming Prophetic Literature* pp. 195-208.

Hubbard, David A., *Joel and Amos: An Introduction and Commentary* (Leicester: Inter-Varsity Press, 1989).

Huffmon, Herbert B., 'The Social Role of Amos' Message', in H.B. Huffmon, F.A. Spina and A.R.W. Green (eds.), *The Quest for the Kingdom of God: Studies in Honor of George E. Mendenhall* (Winona Lake, IN: Eisenbrauns, 1983), pp. 109-16.

Humphreys, W. Lee, *The Tragic Vision and the Hebrew Tradition* (Philadelphia: Fortress Press, 1985).

Hunter, A. Vanlier, *Seek the Lord! A Study of the Meaning and Function of the Exhortation in Amos, Hosea, Isaiah, Micah and Zephaniah* (Baltimore: St Mary's Seminary and University Press, 1982).

Isbell, Charles D., 'Another Look at Amos 5.26', *JBL* 97 (1978), pp. 97-99.

Jacob, Edmund, 'Prophètes et Intercesseurs', in M. Carrez, J. Doré and P. Grelot (eds.), *De la Tôrah au Messie: études d'exégèse et d'herméneutique bibliques offertes à Henri Cazelles pour ses 25 années d'enseignement à l'Institut Catholique de Paris, October 1979* (Paris: Desclée, 1981), pp. 205-17.

Jacobs, Paul F., '"Cows of Bashan"—A Note on the Interpretation of Amos 4.1', *JBL* 104 (1985), pp. 109-10.

Jeremias, Jörg, 'Amos 3–6: Beobachtungen zur Entstehungsgeschichte eines Propheten-buches', *ZAW* 100 (1988 Supplement), pp. 123-38; *ET* 'Amos 3–6: From the Oral Word to the Text' (trans. Stuart A. Irvine), in Gene M. Tucker, David L. Peterson and Robert R. Wilson (eds.), *Canon, Theology, and Old Testament Interpretation: Essays in Honor of Brevard S. Childs* (Philadelphia: Fortress Press, 1988), pp. 217-29.

—'Völkersprüche und Visionsberichte im Amosbuch', in Fritz, Pohlmann, and Schmitt (eds.), *Prophet und Prophetenbuch* pp. 82-97.

—'Das unzugängliche Heiligtum', in Rudiger Bartelmus, Thomas Krüger and Helmut Utzschneider (eds.), *Konsequente Traditionsgeschichte: Festschrift für Klaus Baltzer zum 65. Geburtstag* (OBO, 126; Göttingen: Vandenhoeck & Ruprecht, 1993), pp. 155-67.

—'The Interrelationship between Amos and Hosea', in Watts and House (eds.), *Forming Prophetic Literature* pp. 171-86.

—Der Prophet Amos (ATD, 24.2; Göttingen: Vandenhoeck & Ruprecht, 1995); *ET The Book of Amos* (trans. D.W. Stott; OTL; Louisville: Westminster/John Knox Press, 1998).

Kaiser, Otto, 'Gerechtigkeit und Heil: bei den israelitischen Propheten und griechischen Denkern des 8.–6. Jahrhunderts', in Otto Kaiser (ed.), *Der Mensch unter dem Schicksal: Studien zur Geschichte, Theologie und Gegenwartsbedeutung der Weisheit (Festschrift für Rudolf Bultmann)* (BZAW, 161; Berlin: Walter de Gruyter, 1985), pp. 24-40.

Karageorghis, V., 'Erotica from Salamis', *Rivista di Studi Fenici* 21 Supplement (1993), Plate I, pp. 7-13.

Keel, Othmar, and Christoph Uehlinger, *Gods, Goddesses, and Images of God in Ancient Israel* (trans. Thomas H. Trapp; Minneapolis: Fortress Press, 1998).

Keil, Carl Friedrich, *Biblical Commentary on the Old Testament. I. The Twelve Minor Prophets* (trans. James Martin; Grand Rapids, MI: William B. Eerdmans, 1954).

Kennedy, George A (ed.), *The Cambridge History of Classical Literature. I. Classical Criticism* (Cambridge: Cambridge University Press, 1989).

King, Philip J., *Amos, Hosea, Micah—An Archaeological Commentary* (Philadelphia: Westminster Press, 1988).

—'The *Marzeaḥ* Amos Denounces', *BARev* 15.4 (1988), pp. 34-44.

—'The *Marzeaḥ*: Textual and Archaeological Evidence', *Eretz Israel* 20 (1989), pp. 98*-106*.

Knierim, R.P. , '"I Will Not Cause it to Return" in Amos 1 and 2', in George W. Coats and Burke O. Long (eds.), *Canon and Authority: Essays in Old Testament Religion and Theology* (Philadelphia: Fortress Press, 1977), pp. 163-75.

Koch, Klaus, *The Growth of the Biblical Tradition: The Form-Critical Method* (trans. S.M. Cupitt; New York: Charles Scribner's Sons, 1969).

—'Die Rolle der hymnischen Abschnitte in der Komposition des Amos-Buches', *ZAW* 86 (1974), pp. 504-37.

—*Amos: Untersucht mit den Methoden einer Strukturalen Formgeschichte* (3 vols.; AOAT 30; Neukirchen–Vluyn: Neukirchener Verlag, 1976).

Kramer, Samuel Noel, *Lamentation over the Destruction of Ur* (Chicago: University of Chicago Press, 1940).

—'Lamentation over the Destruction of Nippur', *Acta Sumerologica* 13 (1991), pp. 1-26.

Krszyna, Henryk, 'Literarische Struktur von Os 2,4-17', *BZ* 13 (1969), pp. 41-59.

Lamberton, Robert, *Hesiod* (New Haven: Yale University Press, 1988).

Landsberger, B., 'Tin and Lead: The Adventure of Two Vocables', *JNES* 24 (1965), pp. 185-96.

Landy, Francis, 'Vision and Poetic Speech in Amos', *HAR* 11 (1987), pp. 223-46.

Lang, Bernhard, 'Sklaven und Unfreie im Buch Amos (ii 6, viii 6)', *VT* 31 (1981), pp. 482-88.

Langer, Susan K. *Feeling and Form: A Theory of Art Developed from Philosophy in a New Key* (New York: Charles Scribner's Sons, 1953).

Lattimore, Richmond, *The Poetry of Greek Tragedy* (New York: Harper & Row, 1958).

—*The Iliad of Homer* (Chicago: University of Chicago Press, 1951).

—*Greek Lyrics* (Chicago: University of Chicago Press, 2nd edn, 1960).

—*The Odyssey of Homer* (New York: Harper & Row, 1965).

Leeuw, van der, Gerardus, *Sacred and Profane Beauty: The Holy in Art* (trans. David E. Green; New York: Holt, Rinehart and Winston, 1963).

Leeuwen van, C., 'Amos 1.2, épigraphe du livre entier ou introduction aux oracles des chapitres 1—2?', in M. Boertien and Aleida G. van Daalen (eds.), *Verkenningen in een Stroomgebied: Proeven van oudtestamentish Onderzoek (Festschrift M.A. Beck)* (Amsterdam: Theologisch Instituut van de Universiteit van Amsterdam, 1974), pp. 93-101.

Lefkowitz, Mary R., 'Fictions in Literary Biography: The New Poem and the Archilochus Legend', *Arethusa* 9 (1976), pp. 181-89.

—'The Poet as Hero: Fifth Century Autobiography and Subsequent Biographical Fiction', *ClQ* 28 (1978), pp. 459-69.

—*The Lives of the Greek Poets* (London: Duckworth, 1981).

Lemke, Werner E., 'The Way of Obedience: I Kings 13 and the Structure of the Deuteronomistic History', in Frank Moore Cross, Werner E. Lemke and Patrick D. Miller, Jr (eds.), *Magnalia Dei, The Mighty Acts of God: Essays on the Bible and Archaeology in Memory of G. Ernest Wright* (Garden City, NY: Doubleday, 1976), pp. 301-26.

Levin, Christoph, 'Amos und Jerobeam I', *VT* 45 (1995), pp. 307-17.

Levinson, J.D., 'From Temple to Synagogue: 1 Kings 8', in Halpern and Levinson (eds.), *Traditions in Transformation*, pp. 143-66.

Lewis, T.J., *Cults of the Dead in Ancient Israel and Ugarit* (HSM, 39; Atlanta: Scholars Press, 1989).

Limburg, James, 'Amos 7.4: A Judgment with Fire?', *CBQ* 35 (1973), pp. 346-49.

—'Sevenfold Structures in the Book of Amos', *JBL* 106 (1987), pp. 217-22.

—Hosea–Micah (Interpretation: A Bible Commentary for Teaching and Preaching; Atlanta: John Knox Press, 1988).

Lindblom, Johannes, *Prophecy in Ancient Israel* (Oxford: Basil Blackwell, 1962).

Linville, James R., 'Visions and Voices: Amos 7–9', *Bib* 80 (1999), pp. 22-42.

Lohfink, Norbert, 'Der junge Jeremia als Propagandist und Poet. Zum Grundstock von Jer. 30–31', in P. -M. Bogaert (ed.), *Le livre de Jérémie: Le prophète et son milieu, les oracles et leur transmission* (BETL, 64; Louvain: Peeters, 1981), pp. 350-68.

Luker, Lamontte M., 'Beyond Form Criticism: The Relation of Doom and Hope Oracles in Micah 2–6', *HAR* 11 (1987), pp. 285-301.

Lust, J., 'Remarks on the Redaction of Amos V 4-6, 14-15', *OTS* 21 (1981), pp. 129-54.

Maier, Christl, and Ernst Michael Dörrfuss, '"Um mit ihnen zu sitzen, zu essen und zu trinken" Am 6,7; Jer 16,5 und die Bedeutung von *Marzeaḥ*', *ZAW* 111 (1999), pp. 45-57.

Malamat, Abraham, 'A Forerunner of Biblical Prophecy: The Mari Documents', in Patrick D. Miller, Jr, Paul D. Hanson and S. Dean McBride (eds.), *Ancient Israelite Religion: Essays in Honor of Frank Moore Cross* (Philadelphia: Fortress Press, 1987), pp. 33-52.

March, W. Eugene, 'Redaction Criticism and the Formation of Prophetic Books', in Paul J. Achtemeier (ed.), Society of Biblical Literature 1977 Seminar Papers (Missoula, MT: Scholars Press, 1977), pp. 87-101.

Markoe, Glenn, *Phoenician Bronze and Silver Bowls from Cyprus and the Mediterranean* (Classical Studies, 26; Berkeley, CA: University of California Press, 1985).

Marrs, Rick R., 'Micah and a Theological Critique of Worship', in M. Patrick Graham, Rick R. Marrs and Stephen L. McKenzie (eds.), *Worship and the Hebrew Bible: Essays in Honour of John T. Willis* (*JSOT*Sup, 284; Sheffield: Sheffield Academic Press, 1999), pp. 184-203.

Marti, K., *Das Dodekapropheton erklärt* (Tübingen: J.C.B. Mohr [Paul Siebeck], 1904).

Martin-Achard, Robert 'The End of the People of God. A Commentary on the Book of Amos', in *God's People in Crisis* (International Theological Commentary; Grand Rapids: Eerdmans, 1984), pp. 1-71.

Martin-Achard, Robert, and S. Paul Re'emi, *Amos and Lamentations: God's People in Crisis* (International Theological Commentary; Grand Rapids: William B. Eerdmans, 1984).

Mays, James L., *Amos: A Commentary* (OTL; Philadelphia: Westminster Press, 1969).

McKeon, Richard (ed.), *The Basic Works of Aristotle* (New York: Random House, 1941).

McLaughlin, John L., 'The *Marzeah* at Ugarit', *UF* 23 (1991), pp. 265-81.

Mead, James K., 'Kings and Prophets, Donkeys and Lions: Dramatic Shape and Deuterono-mistic Rhetoric in 1 Kings XIII', *VT* 49 (1999), pp. 191-205.

Melugin, Roy F., 'The Formation of Amos: An Analysis of Exegetical Method', in Paul J. Achtemeier (ed.), *Society of Biblical Literature 1978 Seminar Papers*, I (Missoula, MT: Scholars Press, 1978), pp. 369-91.

—'Prophetic Books and the Problem of Historical Reconstruction', in Stephen Breck Reid (ed.), *Prophets and Paradigms*, pp. 63-78.

—'Amos in Recent Research', *CRBS* 6 (1998), pp. 65-101.

Meshel, Z., *Kuntillet 'Ajrud: A Religious Center from the Time of the Judean Monarchy on the Border of Sinai* (Israel Museum Catalog No. 175; Jerusalem: Israel Museum, 1978).

Michalowski, Piotr, *The Lamentation over the Destruction of Sumer and Ur* (Winona Lake, IN: Eisenbrauns, 1989).

Millard, Alan R., 'An Assessment of the Evidence for Writing in Ancient Israel', in International Congress on Biblical Archaeology (1984: Jerusalem) *Biblical Archaeology Today: Proceedings of the International Congress on Biblical Archaeology* ([Jerusalem]: Israel Exploration Society: Israel Academy of Sciences and Humanities in cooperation with the American Schools of Oriental Research, 1985), pp. 301-12.

Miller, Patrick D., Jr, 'Fire in the Mythology of Canaan and Israel', *CBQ* 27 (1965), pp. 256-61.

Miralles, Carles, and Jaume Portulas, *Archilochus and the Iambic Poetry* (Edizioni dell'Ateneo; Rome: Casella Postale, 1983).

Morgenstern, Julian, *Amos Studies: Part I, II, and III* (Cincinnati: Hebrew Union College Press, 1941).

Mowinckel, *Prophecy and Tradition: The Prophetic Books in the Light of the Study of the Growth and History of the Tradition* (Oslo: Jacob Dybwad, 1946), pp. 48-51.

Murray, A.T. (trans.), *Homer The Iliad*, I (LCL; New York: G.P. Putnam's Sons, 1924).

—*Homer The Iliad,* II (LCL; Cambridge, MA: Harvard University Press, 1925).

—*Homer The Odyssey* (2 vols.; LCL; Cambridge, MA.: Harvard University Press, 1919).

Murray, Oswyn, 'Nestor's Cup and the Origins of the Greek Symposion', *Annali di Archeologia e Storia Antica* NS 1 (1994), pp. 47-54.

—'Forms of Sociality', in Jean-Pierre Vernant (ed.), The Greeks (trans. Charles Lambert and Teresa Lavender Fagan; Chicago: University of Chicago Press, 1995), pp. 218-53.

Nagy, Gregory, *Poetry as Performance: Homer and Beyond* (Cambridge: Cambridge University Press, 1996).

Niditch, Susan, *The Symbolic Vision in Biblical Tradition* (Chico, CA: Scholars Press, 1983).

—'The Composition of Isaiah 1', *Bib* 61 (1989), pp. 509-29.

—*Oral World and Written Word: Ancient Israelite Literature* (Library of Ancient Israel; Louisville, KY: Westminster/ John Knox Press, 1996).

Nielsen, Kirsten, 'Is 6.1–8.18* as Dramatic Writing', *ST* 40 (1986), pp. 1-16.

Noble, Paul R., 'Israel among the Nations', *HBT* 15 (1993), pp. 56-82.

—'The Function of *n'm Yhwh* in Amos', *ZAW* 108 (1996), pp. 623-26.

—'Amos' Absolute ' "No"', *VT* 47 (1997), pp. 329-40.

—'Amos and Amaziah in Context: Synchronic and Diachronic Approaches to Amos 7-8', *CBQ* 60 (1998), pp. 423-39.

Nogalski, James D., 'The Problematic Suffixes of Amos IX 11', *VT* 43 (1993), pp. 411-17.

—*Literary Precursors to the Book of the Twelve* (BZAW, 217; Berlin: Walter de Gruyter, 1993).

—'Intertextuality in the Twelve', in Watts and House (eds.), *Forming Prophetic Literature*: pp. 102-24.

Noth, Martin, *Überlieferungsgeschichtliche Studien*. I. *Die sammelnden und bearbeitenden Geschichtswerke im Alten Testament* (Tübingen: Max Niemeyer Verlag, 2nd edn., 1957 [1943]); ET *The Deuteronomistic History* (*JSOT*Sup, 15; Sheffield: University of Sheffield, 1981).

Nowack, Wilhelm, *Die kleinen Propheten übersetzt und erklärt* (Göttingen: Vandenhoeck & Ruprecht, 3rd edn, 1922).

O'Connell, Robert, 'Telescoping N+1 Patterns in the Book of Amos', *VT* 46 (1996), pp. 56-73.

Olyan, Saul M., 'The Oaths of Amos 8.14', in Gary A. Anderson and Saul M. Olyan (eds.), *Priesthood and Cult in Ancient Israel* (*JSOT*Sup, 125; Sheffield: Sheffield Academic Press, 1991), pp. 121-49.

Olson, Elder, *Tragedy and the Theory of Drama* (Detroit: Wayne State University Press, 1961).

Ouellette, Jean, 'The Shaking of the Thresholds in Amos 9,1', *HUCA* 43 (1972), pp. 23-27.

Overholt, Thomas W., 'Prophecy in History: The Social Reality of Intermediation', *JSOT* 48 (1990), pp. 3-29.

Paul, Shalom M., 'Amos 1.3–2.3: A Concatenous Literary Pattern', *JBL* 90 (1971), pp. 397-403.

—'Amos III 15—Winter and Summer Mansions', *VT* 28 (1978), pp. 358-60.

—'A Literary Reinvestigation of the Authenticity of the Oracles against the Nations of Amos', in M. Carrez, J. Doré and P. Grelot (eds.), *De la Tôrah au Messie: Études d'exégèse et d'herméneutique bibliques offertes à Henri Cazelles pour ses 25 Années d'enseignement à l'Institut Catholique de Paris* (Paris: Desclée, 1981), pp. 189-204.

—'Amos 3.3—8: The Irresistible Sequence of Cause and Effect', *HAR* 7 (1983), pp. 203-20.

—*Amos: A Commentary on the Book of Amos* (Hermeneia; Minneapolis: Fortress Press, 1991).

Peckham, Brian, 'The Composition of Deuteronomy 5—11', in Carol L. Meyers and M. O'Connor (eds.), *The Word of the Lord Shall Go Forth: Essays in Honor of David Noel Freedman in Celebration of his Sixtieth Birthday* (Winona Lake: Eisenbrauns, 1983), pp. 217-40.

—The Composition of the Deuteronomistic History (HSM, 35; Atlanta, GA: Scholars Press, 1985).

—'The Deuteronomistic History of Saul and David', *ZAW* 97 (1985), pp. 190-209.

—'The Vision of Habakkuk', *CBQ* 48 (1986), pp. 617-36.

—'The Composition of Hosea', *HAR* 11 (1987), pp. 331-53.

—'Phoenicia and the Religion of Israel: The Epigraphic Evidence', in Miller, Hanson and McBride (eds.), *Ancient Israelite Religion*, pp. 79-99.

—'Literacy and the Creation of the Biblical World', *Scripta Mediterranea* 12–13 (1991–92), pp. 1-36.

—*History and Prophecy: The Development of Late Judean Literary Traditions* (Anchor Bible Reference Library; Garden City, NY: Doubleday, 1993).

—'Writing and Editing', in Astrid B. Beck, Andrew H. Bartelt, Paul R. Raabe and Chris A. Franke (eds.), *Fortunate the Eyes that See: Essays in Honor of David Noel Freedman in Celebration of his Seventieth Birthday* (Grand Rapids: William B. Eerdmans, 1995), pp. 364-83.

—'Tense and Mood in Biblical Hebrew', *ZAH* 10 (1997), pp. 139-68.

—'History and Time', in Robert Chazan, William W. Hallo and Lawrence H. Schiffman (eds.), *Ki Baruch Hu: Ancient Near Eastern, Biblical and Judaic Studies in Honor of Baruch A. Levine* (Winona Lake, IN: Eisenbrauns, 1999), pp. 295-314.

Pellizer, Ezio, 'Outlines of a Morphology of Sympotic Entertainment', in Oswyn Murray (ed.), *Sympotica: A Symposium on the Symposion* (Oxford: Clarendon Press, 1990), pp. 177-84.

Penglase, Charles, *Greek Myths and Mesopotamia: Parallels and Influence in the Homeric Hymns and Hesiod* (London: Routledge, 1994).

Pfeifer, Gerhard, 'Denkformenanalyse als exegetische Methode, erläutert an Amos 1.2–2.16', *ZAW* 88 (1976), pp. 56-71.

—'Unausweichliche Konsequenzen: Denkformenanalyse von Amos III 3-8', *VT* 33 (1983), pp. 341-47.

—'Die Denkform des Propheten Amos (III 9-11)', *VT* 34 (1984), pp. 476-81.

—'"Rettung" als Beweis der Vernichtung (Amos 3,12)', *ZAW* 100 (1988 Supplement), pp. 269-77.

—'Die Fremdvölkerspruch des Amos—später vaticinia ex eventu?', *VT* 38 (1988), pp. 230-33.

Pitard, Wayne T., Ancient Damascus: *A Historical Study of the Syrian City-State from Earliest Times until its Fall to the Assyrians in 732 BCE* (Winona Lake: Eisenbrauns, 1987).

Polley, Max E., *Amos and the Davidic Empire: A Socio-Historical Approach* (New York: Oxford University Press, 1989).

Pope, Marvin H., 'A Divine Banquet at Ugarit', in J.M. Efird (ed.), *The Use of the Old Testament in the New and Other Essays: Studies in Honor of W.F. Stinespring* (Durham, NC: Duke University Press, 1972).

Porten, Bezalel, *Archives from Elephantine: The Life of an Ancient Jewish Military Colony* (Berkeley: University of California Press, 1968).

Rabinowitz, Isaac, 'The Crux at Amos III 12' *VT* 11 (1961) pp. 228-31.

Rad, Gerhard von, 'The Deuteronomistic Theology of History in the Book of Kings', in *Studies in Deuteronomy* (trans. David Stalker; SBT, 9; London: SCM Press, 1953), pp. 74-91.

—'The Origin of the Concept of the Day of Yahweh', *JSS* 4 (1959), pp. 97-108.

—*Old Testament Theology*. I. *The Theology of Israel's Historical Traditions* (trans. D.M.G. Stalker; Edinburgh: Oliver and Boyd, 1962).

—*Old Testament Theology.* II. *The Theology of Israel's Prophetic Traditions*. (trans. D.M.G. Stalker; Edinburgh: Oliver and Boyd, 1965).

—'The Deuteronomic Theology of History in I and II Kings', in *The Problem of the Hexateuch and Other Essays* (trans. E. W. Trueman Dicken; New York: McGraw–Hill, 1966), pp. 205-21.

Ramsey, G.W. 'Amos 4,12—A New Perspective', *JBL* 89 (1970), pp. 187-91.

Reinhartz, Adele, *'Why Ask My Name?': Anonymity and Identity in Biblical Narrative* (New York: Oxford University Press, 1998).

Renaud, Bernard, 'Genèse et Théologie d'Amos 3, 3-8', in A. Caquot and M. Delcor (eds.), *Mélanges bibliques et orientaux en l'honneur de M. Henri Cazelles* (AOAT, 212; Neukirchen–Vluyn: Neukirchener Verlag, 1981), pp. 353-72.

—'Le livret d'Osée 1–3', *RSR* 56 (1982), pp. 159-78.

—'"Osée 1–3": Analyse Diachronique et Lecture Synchronique', *RSR* 57 (1983), pp. 249-60.

Richardson, H. Neil, 'Amos 2.13-16: Its Structure and Function in the Book', in Paul J. Achtemeier (ed.), *Society of Biblical Literature 1978 Seminar Papers*, I (Missoula, MT: Scholars Press, 1978), pp. 361-68.

Richardson, N.J., 'The Contest of Homer and Hesiod and Alcidamas' Mouseion', *ClQ* 31 (1981), pp. 1-10.

Rilett Wood, Joyce, review of *Amos: A Commentary on the Book of Amos* (Hermeneia; Minneapolis: Fortress Press, 1991), by Shalom M. Paul, in *Toronto Journal of Theology* 9 (1993), pp. 253-54.

—'Prophecy and Poetic Dialogue', *SR* (1995), pp. 309-22.

—Tragic and Comic Forms in Amos', *BibInt* 6 (1998), pp. 20-48.

—'Speech and Action in Micah's Prophecy', *CBQ* 62 (2000), pp. 645-62.

Roberts, J.J.M., 'Amos 6.1-7', in James T. Butler, Edgar W. Conrad and Ben C. Ollenburger (eds.), *Understanding the Word: Essays in Honor of Bernhard W. Anderson* (*JSOT*Sup, 37; Sheffield: *JSOT* Press, 1985), pp. 155-66.

Rösel, Hartmut N., 'Kleine Studien zur Entwicklung des Amosbuches', *VT* 43 (1993), pp. 88-101.

Rosenbaum, Stanley N., 'Northern Amos Revisited: Two Philological Suggestions', *Hebrew Studies* 18 (1977), pp. 132-48.

—Amos of Israel: A New Interpretation (Macon, GA: Mercer University Press, 1990).

Roth, W.M.W., 'The Numerical Sequence x/x+1 in the Old Testament', *VT* 12 (1962), pp. 300-11.

Rottzoll, D., *Studien zur Redaktion und Komposition des Amosbuches* (BZAW, 243; Berlin: Walter de Gruyter, 1996).

Rudolph, Wilhelm, Joel–Amos–Obadja–Jonah (KAT, 113.2; Gütersloh: Gerd Mohn, 1971).

Ruppert, L., 'Erwägungen zur Kompositions und Redaktionsgeschichte von Hosea 1–3', *BZ* 26 (1982), pp. 208-33.

Ruprecht, Eberhard, 'Das Zepter Jahwes in den Berufungsvisionen von Jeremia und Amos', *ZAW* 108 (1996), pp. 55-69.

Sams, Eric, *The Songs of Robert Schumann* (London: Ernst Eulenburg, 2nd edn, 1975).

Sanderson, Judith, 'Amos', in Carol A. Newsom and Sharon H. Ringe (eds.), *The Women's Bible Commentary* (London: SPCK, 1992), pp. 205-209.

Schmidt, Hans, Die Schriften des Alten Testaments. II/Part 2. *Die grossen Propheten* (Göttingen: Vandenhoeck and Ruprecht, 1923).

Schmidt, Werner H., 'Die deuteronomistische Redaktion des Amosbuches: Zu den theologischen Unterschieden zwischen dem Prophetenwort und seinem Sammler', *ZAW* 77 (1965), pp. 168-93.

Schmitt, John J., 'The Virgin of Israel: Referent and Use of the Phrase in Amos and Jeremiah', *CBQ* 53 (1991), pp. 365-81.

Schmitt-Pantel, Pauline, 'Sacrificial Meal and Symposion: Two Models of Civic Institutions in the Archaic City?', in Murray (ed.), Sympotica, pp. 14-33.

Schröter, U., 'Jeremias Botschaft für das Nordreich. Zu N. Nohfinks Überlegungen zum Grundbestand von Jeremia 30–31', *VT* 35 (1985), pp. 312-29.

Segal, Charles, 'Archaic Choral Lyric', in Easterling and Knox (eds.), *Early Greek Poetry*, pp. 124-60.

Seybold, Klaus, and Jürgen von Ungern-Sternberg, 'Amos und Hesiod: Aspekte eines Vergleichs', in Kurt Raaflaub (ed.), in collaboration with Elisabeth Müller-Luckner, *Anfänge politischen Denkens in der Antike: Die nahöstlichen Kulturen und die Griechen* (Schriften des Historischen Kollegs, 24; Munich: R. Oldenbourg, 1993), pp. 215-39.

Simon, Uriel, '1 Kings 13: A Prophetic Sign—Denial and Persistence', *HUCA* 47 (1976), pp. 81-117.

Sinclair, Lawrence A., 'The Courtroom Motif in the Book of Amos', *JBL* 85 (1966), pp. 351-53.

Smelik, K.A.D., 'The Meaning of Amos V 18-20', *VT* 36 (1986), pp. 246-48.

Smith, Gary V., 'Amos 5.13—The Deadly Silence of the Prosperous', *JBL* 107 (1988), pp. 289-91.

—*Amos: A Commentary* (Grand Rapids: Zondervan, 1989).

Smith, Jonathan Z., *Drudgery Divine: On the Comparison of Early Christianities and the Religions of Late Antiquity* (Chicago: University of Chicago Press, 1990).

Snell, Bruno, *The Discovery of the Mind: The Greek Origins of European Thought* (trans. T.G. Rosenmeyer; New York: Harper & Row, 1960).

Synder, George, 'The Law and Covenant in Amos', *ResQ* 25 (1982), pp. 158-66.

Soggin, J. Alberto, *Il profeta Amos* (Brescia: Paideia Editrice, 1982); ET *The Prophet Amos: A Translation and Commentary* (trans. John Bowden; London: SCM Press, 1987).

Solmsen, Friedrich, *Hesiod and Aeschylus* (Ithaca, NY: Cornell University Press, 1949).

Speiser, E.A., 'Note on Amos 5.26', *BASOR* 108 (1947), pp. 5-6.

Stacey, David, *Prophetic Drama in the Old Testament* (London: Epworth Press, 1990).

Staples, W.E., 'Epic Motifs in Amos', *JNES* 25 (1966), pp. 106-12.

Steinmann, Andrew E., 'The Order of Amos's Oracles against the Nations', *JBL* 3 (1992), pp. 683-89.

Stuart, Douglas K., Hosea–Jonah (Waco, TX: Word Books, 1987).

Sweeney, Marvin, 'Jeremiah 30—31 and King Josiah's Program of National Restoration and Religious Reform', *ZAW* 108 (1996), pp. 569-83.

Talmon, Shemaryahu, 'Prophetic Rhetoric and Agricultural Metaphora', in Garrone and Israel (eds.), *Storia e Tradizioni di Israele*, pp. 267-79.

Tamarkin Reis, Pamela, 'Vindicating God: Another Look at 1 Kings XIII', *VT* 44 (1994), pp. 376-86.

Terblanche, M.D., ' "Rosen und Lavendel nach Blut und Eisen": Intertextuality in the Book of Amos', *Old Testament Essays* 10 (1997), pp. 312-21.

Thomas, Rosalind, *Oral Tradition and Written Record in Classical Athens* (Cambridge: Cambridge University Press, 1989).

Thompson, Henry O., The Book of Amos: An Annotated Bibliography (American Theological Library Association Bibliographies, 42; Lanham, MD: Scarecrow Press, 1997).

Thompson, Michael E.W., 'Amos—A Prophet of Hope?', *ExpTim* 104 (1992–93), pp. 71-76.

Torrey, Charles Cutler, *The Lives of the Prophets: Greek Text and Translation* (Philadelphia: Society of Biblical Literature and Exegesis, 1946).

Trible, Phyllis, 'The Gift of a Poem: A Rhetorical Study of Jeremiah 31.15-22', ANQ 17 (1977), pp. 271-80.

Tromp, N.J., 'Amos V.1-17: Towards a Stylistic andRhetorical Analysis', *OTS* 23 (1984), pp. 56-84.

Tucker, Gene M., 'Prophetic Authenticity: A Form-Critical Study of Amos 7.10-17', Int 27 (1973), pp. 423-34.

—'Prophetic Superscriptions and the Growth of a Canon', in George W. Coats and Burke O. Long (eds.), *Canon and Authority: Essays in Old Testament Religion and Theology* (Philadelphia: Fortress Press, 1977), pp. 56-70.

Uehlinger, Christoph, 'Der Herr auf der Zinnmauer: Zur dritten Amos-Vision (Am 7.7-8)', *BN* 48 (1989), pp. 89-104.

Van Seters, John, *In Search of History: Historiography in the Ancient World and the Origins of Biblical History* (New Haven: Yale University Press, 1983).

—The Primeval Histories of Greece and Israel Compared', *ZAW* 100 (1988), pp. 1-22.

Vawter, Bruce, *The Conscience of the Prophets* (New York: Sheed & Ward, 1961).

—*Amos, Hosea, Micah, with an Introduction to Classical Prophecy* (Old Testament Message, 7; Wilmington, DE: Michael Glazier, 1981).

Veijola, Timo, 'Die Propheten und das Alter des Sabbatgebots', in Fritz, Pohlmann and Schmitt (eds.), *Prophet und Prophetenbuch*, pp. 246-64.

Vieweger, Dieter, 'Zur Herkunft der Völkerworte im Amos-buch unter besonderer Berücksichtigung des Aramäerspruch (Am 1, 3-5)', in Peter Mommer and Winfried Thiel (eds.), *Altes Testament Forschung und Wirkung: Festschrift für Henning Graf Reventlow* (Frankfurt am Main: Peter Lang, 1994), pp. 103-19.

Vogels, Walter, 'Invitation à revenir à l'alliance et universalisme en Amos IX 7', *VT* 22 (1972), pp. 223-39.

—'"Oseé-Gomer" car et comme "Yahweh-Israel": Os 1—3,' *NRT* 103 (1981), pp. 711-27.

Vogelzang, Marianna E., and Herman L.J. Vanstiphout (eds.), *Mesopotamian Epic Literature: Oral or Aural?* (Lewiston NY: Edwin Mellen Press, 1992).

Vriezen, Theodorus C., 'Erwägungen zu Amos. 3.2', *Archäologie und Altes Testament* (Festschrift Kurt Galling; eds. A. Kuschke and E. Kutsch; Tübingen: J.C.B. Mohr [Paul Siebeck, 1970]), pp. 255-58.

Waard, J. de, 'The Chiastic Structure of Amos V.1-17', *VT* 27 (1977), pp. 170-77.

Wade-Gery, Henry Theodore, *The Poet of the Iliad* (Cambridge: Cambridge University Press, 1952).

Walsh, Jerome T., 'The Contexts of 1 Kings 13', *VT* 39 (1989), pp. 355-70.

Wal van der, Adrian, 'The Structure of Amos', *JSOT* 26 (1983), pp. 107-13.

—*Amos: A Classified Bibliography* (Amsterdam: Free University Press, 3rd edn, 1986).

Ward, James M., *Amos, Hosea* (Knox Preaching Guides; Atlanta: John Knox Press, 1981).

Waschke, Ernst-Joachim, 'Die fünfte Vision des Amosbuches (9,1-4)—Eine Nachinterpretation', *ZAW* 106 (1994), pp. 434-45.

Watts, James W., 'Psalmody in Prophecy: Habbakuk 3 in Context', in Watts and House (eds.), *Forming Prophetic Literature* pp. 209-23.

Watts, James W., and Paul R. House (eds.), *Forming Prophetic Literature: Essays on Isaiah and the Twelve in Honor of John D.W. Watts* (JSOTSup, 235: Sheffield: Sheffield Academic Press, 1996).

Watts, John D.W., 'An Old Hymn Preserved in the Book of Amos', *JNES* 16 (1956), pp. 33-40.

—Vision and Prophecy in *Amos* (Leiden: Brill, 1958).

—Studying the Book of *Amos* (Nashville: Broadman, 1965).

Weinfeld, Moshe, 'Ancient Near Eastern Patterns in Prophetic Literature', *VT* 27 (1977), pp. 178-95.

Wender, Dorothea (trans.), *Hesiod and Theognis* (London: Penguin Books, 1973).

West, Martin L., 'The Contest of Homer and Hesiod', *ClQ* 17 (1967), pp. 433-50.

Westermann, Claus, *Basic Forms of Prophetic Speech* (trans. Hugh Clayton White; Philadelphia: Westminster Press, 1977).

—*Praise and Lament in the Psalms* (Atlanta: John Knox, 1981).

Whallon, William, 'Biblical Poetry and Homeric Epic', in John R. Maier and Vincent L. Tollers (eds.), *The Bible in its Literary Milieu: Contemporary Essays* (Grand Rapids: William B. Eerdmans, 1979), pp. 318-25.

Wicke, Donald W., 'Two Perspectives (Amos 5.1-17),' *CurTM* 13 (1986), pp. 89-96.

Willcock, Malcolm M., *A Companion to the Iliad: Based on the Translation by Richmond Lattimore* (Chicago: University of Chicago Press, 1976).

Williamson, H.G.M., 'The Prophet and the Plumbline: A Redactional-Critical Study of Amos 7', *OTS* 26 (1990), pp. 101-21.

Willi-Plein, Ina, *Vorformen der Schriftexegese innerhalb des Alten Testaments: Üntersuchungen zum literarischen Werden der auf Amos, Hosea und Micha züruckgehenden Bücher im hebräischen Zwölfprophetenbuch* (BZAW, 123; Berlin: Walter de Gruyter, 1971).

Wilson, Edwin, The Theater Experience (New York: McGraw–Hill, 4th edn, 1976).

Wilson, Robert R., *Prophecy and Society in Ancient Israel* (Philadelphia: Fortress Press, 1980).

Winkle van, D.W., '1 Kings XII 25–XIII 34: Jeroboam's Cultic Innovations and the Man of God from Judah,' *VT* 46 (1996), pp. 101-14.

Wolff, Hans Walter, 'The Kerygma of the Deuteronomistic Historical Work', in H.W. Wolff and Walter Brueggemann (eds.), *The Vitality of Old Testament Traditions* (Atlanta: John Knox Press, 1961), pp. 83-100.

—*Hosea: A Commentary on the Book of the Prophet Hosea* (Hermeneia; Philadelphia: Fortress Press, 1974).

—'The Kerygma of the Deuteronomistic Historical Work', in Walter Brueggemann and H.W. Wolff (eds.), *The Vitality of Old Testament Traditions* (Atlanta: John Knox Press, 1975), pp. 83-100.

—*Dodekapropheton 2, Joel und Amos* (BKAT, 14.2; Neukirchen-Vluyn: Neukirchener–Verlag, 1975 [1969]); ET *Joel and Amos* (trans. W. Janzen, S.D. McBride, Jr and Charles A. Muenchow; ed. S.D. McBride, Jr; Hermeneia; Philadelphia: Fortress Press, 2nd edn, 1977).

Wolters, Al, 'Wordplay and Dialect in Amos 8.1-2', *JETS* 31 (1988), pp. 407-10.

Youngblood, Ronald, 'לקראת' in Amos 4.12', *JBL* 90 (1971), p. 98.

Zalcman, Lawrence, 'Astronomical Illusions in Amos', *JBL* 100 (1981), pp. 53-58.

INDEXES

INDEX OF REFERENCES

BIBLE

OTHER

INDEX OF AUTHORS

JOURNAL FOR THE STUDY OF THE OLD TESTAMENT
SUPPLEMENT SERIES